THE BASE BALL PALACE OF THE WORLD:
COMISKEY PARK

EDITED BY GREGORY H. WOLF

ASSOCIATE EDITORS

BILL NOWLIN, KEVIN LARKIN, AND LEN LEVIN

Society for American Baseball Research, Inc.
Phoenix, AZ

The Base Ball Palace of the World: Comiskey Park
Copyright © 2019 Society for American Baseball Research, Inc.

Edited by Gregory H. Wolf
Associate Editors: Bill Nowlin, Kevin Larkin, and Len Levin

Cover Photo:
National Baseball Hall of Fame, Cooperstown, New York

All photos are credited in book; otherwise public domain.

ISBN 978-1-970159-14-1
(Ebook ISBN 978-1-970159-15-8)

Book design: David Peng

Society for American Baseball Research
Cronkite School at ASU
555 N. Central Ave. #416
Phoenix, AZ 85004
Phone: (602) 496-1460
Web: www.sabr.org
Facebook: Society for American Baseball Research
Twitter: @SABR

TABLE OF CONTENTS

1   The Base Ball Palace of the World: Comiskey Park
by Gregory H. Wolf

4   Comiskey Park
by Bob Webster

13   A Ballpark as a Political Football: Florida, Illinois, and a New Home for the White Sox
by John Bauer

19   Negro Baseball at Comiskey Park: The East-West Game (1933 – 1960): An All-Star Legacy
by Alan Cohen

27   July 1, 1910
The "Baseball Palace of the World" Opens
by Bob LeMoine

30   August 4, 1910
An Extra-Inning Scoreless Pitchers' Duel for the Ages: Coombs and Walsh
by Gregory H. Wolf

33   August 27, 1911
Big Ed Walsh Slobberballs His Way To No-Hitter
by Gregory H. Wolf

36   May 31, 1914
Benz Was Humming On All Cylinders
By Gregory H. Wolf

39   August 29, 1915
Jim Scott Tosses Shutout in 68 Minutes: Shortest Game in White Sox History
by Richard Riis

42   October 6, 1917.
Another Comiskey Park First: The World Series Arrives
by John Bauer

46   October 7, 1917
Faber's Pitching, Not Baserunning, Lead to Victory
by Jacob Pomrenke

49   October 13, 1917
"Big Push" Brings Bedlam
by Kevin Larkin

51   September 5, 1918
Babe Ruth Tosses Shutout as Patriotism Prevails in Opening of Fall Classic
by Mike Huber

54   September 6, 1918.
Tyler's Pitching and Batting Tie Series
by Bill Pearch

57   September 7, 1918
Carl Mays Outduels Hippo Vaughn
by Brian M. Frank

THE BASE BALL PALACE OF THE WORLD

60 September 24, 1919
White Sox Clinch AL Pennant on Shoeless Joe Jackson Walk-Off Single
by Jacob Pomrenke

63 October 3, 1919
Rookie Hurler Dickey Kerr Turns Tables on Reds, Gamblers
by Mike Lynch

66 October 4, 1919
Ring's Pitching, Cicotte's Errors Lead Reds Over White Sox
by Mike Lynch

69 October 6, 1919
Hod Eller Scatters Three Hits, Fans 9 to Lead Reds to Victory
by Mike Lynch

72 October 9, 1919
Reds Win First Championship in Franchise History
by Mike Lynch

75 June 22, 1921
Harry Hooper First ChiSox Batter to Homer Twice in Comiskey Park
by Gordon Gattie

79 May 29, 1925
The Line Drive That Changed History
by Matthew M. Clifford

82 May 24, 1929
Lyons Hurls 21-Inning Complete Game; Uhle Goes 20 in Epic Struggle
by Gregory H. Wolf

86 July 6, 1933
A Dream Realized
by Lyle Spatz

89 September 10, 1933
The "Game of Games": The First Negro League All-Star Game
by Bob LeMoine

92 August 26, 1934
The Hottest Show in Town
by Will Osgood

95 August 11, 1935
The Mule Kicks the Maestro
by Frank Amoroso

98 August 31, 1935
Vern Kennedy's No-Hitter KO's Cleveland
by Gregory H. Wolf

101 June 1, 1937.
"Bullfrog" Dietrich Resuscitates Career with a No-Hitter
by Gregory H. Wolf

104 June 22, 1938
Steinbacher's Perfect Six-for Six
by Adam Klinker

107 September 17, 1938
September Call-Up Merv Connors First White Sox to Blast 3 Home Runs in Game at Comiskey
by Gregory H. Wolf

110 August 6, 1939
The East-West All-Star Game Got Their Vote
by Norm King

113 August 14, 1939
Chicago Native Johnny Rigney Pitches White Sox to Historic First Night Game Victory
by Mike Huber

116 April 16, 1940
Bob Feller's Opening Day No-Hitter
by C. Paul Rogers III

119 August 1, 1943
Thrills and Surprises: 51,723 See Satchel Paige and Other Negro League Greats
by Bob Lemoine

122 September 26, 1943
Josh Gibson, Cool Papa Bell, and Buck Leonard Star in the Baseball Palace of the World
by Bob LeMoine

COMISKEY PARK

124 September 9, 1944
Lopat Slings Extra-Inning Gem
by Tom Pardo

127 September 25, 1946
Hilton Smith Goes the Distance as Monarchs Roll
by Richard Cuicchi

130 September 26, 1947
Few Notice as the Negro League World Series Visits Chicago
by Ken Carrano and Richard Cuicchi

133 July 11, 1950
Red Schoendienst's Extra-Inning Homer Gives National League Dramatic Win
by C. Paul Rogers III

137 October 1, 1950.
Gus Zernial's Three Homers Provide Preview of Rest of Decade
by Richard Cuicchi

140 May 1, 1951
Miñoso Homers in First Sox Plate Appearance, but Mantle's First Career Blast Boosts Bombers
by Mark S. Sternman

143 July 12, 1951
Rogovin Goes Seventeen in Losing Effort
by Greg Erion

146 July 3, 1952
Eddie Robinson Knocks in Seven
by Stephen D. Boren

148 August 13, 1954
"16" is Magic Number Again for Jack Harshman in Shutout Duel
by Richard Cuicchi

151 September 18, 1956
The Mick Belts Number 50 as the Bombers Take the Pennant
by Gregory H. Wolf

154 May 8, 1957
The Splendid Splinter Smashes Three in the Windy City
by Gregory H. Wolf

157 June 8, 1957
Sweet Billy's Gem Extends ChiSox Lead
by Tom Pardo

161 August 20, 1957
Keegan Uses New Motion to Toss No-Hitter
by Gregory H. Wolf

164 May 1, 1959
Early Wynn Homers Late, Wins One-Hitter
by Scott Ferkovich

167 October 1, 1959
White Sox Clobber Dodgers in Fall Classic Kickoff
by Russ Lake

171 October 2, 1959
Dodgers Clutch Homers Sink Sox
by Russ Lake

174 October 8, 1959
Dodgers Win Their First World Series as the Los Angeles Dodgers
by Alan Cohen

177 June 26, 1960
Early Wynn Gains 275th Career Victory as ChiSox Erupt for 21 Runs
by Mike Huber

180 August 1, 1962
Monbo Was Unhittable
by Gregory H. Wolf

183 September 21, 1962
Chisox Tally Six in Electrifying Game-Ending Rally
by Richard Riis

186 July 15, 1963
Patient Gary Peters Registers Near-Perfect Game
by Richard Cuicchi

THE BASE BALL PALACE OF THE WORLD

188 September 6, 1964
Pitching Propels White Sox Into First Place
by Richard Riis

191 August 28, 1966
Extra-Inning, Walk-Off Home Runs Times Two
by Alan Cohen

195 September 6, 1967
White Sox Walk-off Creates Four-Way Tie for First Place
by Russ Lake

198 September 10, 1967
Joe Horlen's No-Hitter Rekindles Chisox' Dreams of Pennant
by Gregory H. Wolf

201 May 17, 1968
Joe Horlen Tosses Extra-Inning Shutout
by John Gabcik

204 August 28, 1968
Nyman Shuts Out Yankees in First Career Start – in the Shadows of Convention Turmoil
by Doug Feldmann

207 September 30, 1971
Bill Melton Becomes the First White Sox Player to Lead the League in Homers
by Joe Schuster

210 April 18, 1972
Wilbur Wood Tosses Three-Hit Shutout in First Chicago Night Opener
by Bob Wood

213 May 26, 1973
A Two-Day Marathon
by Joseph Wancho

216 September 4, 1973
Kitty Kaat Mows 'Em Down
by Joe Schuster

220 September 10, 1976
The Ryan Express Fans 18 and Walks 9 in 185-Pitch Effort
by Gregory H. Wolf

223 May 14, 1977
Jim Spencer Knocks in Eight in Chisox Rout
by Don Zminda

226 July 2, 1977
Jim Spencer Drives in Eight Runs for Second Time in Two Months
by Michael Marsh

229 July 12, 1979
Chicago's "Disco Demolition Night" Doubleheader Results in Loss and Forfeit
by Mike Huber

232 July 14, 1979
Irish Night Brings Luck to Claudell Washington, Raining Down Three Homers to Dancing Fans
by Mark Mullane

234 October 4, 1981
White Sox Overcome Seven-Run Deficit in Last Two Innings to Win Season Finale
by Thomas J. Brown Jr.

237 July 7, 1982
Baines Belts Three
by Katie Dickson, with Gregory H. Wolf

240 Atmosphere at the 1983 All-Star Game
by Alan Reifman

242 July 6, 1983
In a Golden All-Star Anniversary, the American League Grand Slams National League Dominance Shut
by Brian Wright

245 September 17, 1983
Three Walks and a Fly Ball — White Sox Clinch Division with Walk-Off
by Mike Huber

248 October 7, 1983
Chisox Routed in First Playoff Game on South Side in 24 Years
by Brian P. Wood

COMISKEY PARK

251 October 8, 1983
White Sox Close Comiskey Postseason History
by Doug Feldmann

254 April 7, 1984
Jack Morris Throws a No-Hitter
by Nathan Bierma

258 May 8-9, 1984
The Longest Game in Major League History
by Ken Carrano

262 May 16, 1984
Carlton Fisk Hits for the Cycle with only Triple of the Season
by Mike Huber

264 July 1, 1985
Baseball's Oldest Diamond Marks Its Diamond Anniversary
by Robert Kimball

267 April 20, 1987.
Brewers Run Perfect Season Streak to 13
by Steven C. Weiner

270 July 22, 1987
Harold Baines Sets White Sox Franchise Home Run Record
by Brandon Lee

273 July 17, 1989
Fisk Records 2,000th Hit
by Paul Hofmann

276 April 9, 1990
White Sox Eke Out a Win in the Final Opening Day at Comiskey
by Nathan Bierma

279 July 1, 1990
Hawkins Tosses No-No and Loses
by Stew Thornley

282 September 30, 1990
"Farewell, old beauty"
by John Bauer

285 Comiskey Parkby the Numbers
by Dan Fields

296 Comiskey Park: A Roster of All-Star Contributors

THE BASE BALL PALACE OF THE WORLD: COMISKEY PARK

By Gregory H. Wolf

Comiskey Park, affectionately known as the "Base Ball Palace of the World," was the home of the Chicago White Sox for parts of nine decades, from 1910 to 1990. Its address was one of baseball's most iconic: located at the intersection of 35th Street and Shields Avenue in the Armour Square neighborhood in the near-southwest side of the Windy City, the ballpark was built on the site of a former dump, which visionary team owner Charles Comiskey had purchased from the daughter of a former Chicago mayor. Known as White Sox Park in its first few years (and later again in the 1960s and part of the 1970s), Comiskey Park was the major leagues' third newly constructed steel-and-concrete ballpark, following Shibe Park in Philadelphia and Forbes Field in Pittsburgh. And it was a palace indeed! Its grand exterior with its arches was modeled after the Roman Coliseum and the ballpark had a seating capacity of in excess of 30,000 when it opened. Chicago has been a two-baseball team city since 1901 — when the American League was elevated to major-league status with the White Sox as a charter member — and few sports topics so divided the city and evoked such passions (and still do) as fan loyalty to the South Side Sox and the North Side Cubs; however, the two teams had a connection: Architect Zachary Taylor Davis designed both Comiskey Park and Wrigley Field, which was known as Weeghman Park when it opened in 1914.

The Base Ball Palace of the World: Comiskey Park is our humble volume which aims to evoke memories of the storied ballpark and introduce others to its exciting history through detailed summaries of more than 80 games played there and several feature essays. From its inaugural game on July 1, 1910, when William Howard Taft was president of the United States, to its last contest on September 30, 1990, Comiskey Park hosted more than 6,000 big-league games, which made our task of choosing just a handful a subjective one. Included are all 13 World Series games played in the Base Ball Palace, the first 10 of which occurred in 1917, 1918, and 1919. That stretch began with skipper Pants Rowland's squad capturing the title against the New York Giants and ended with the infamous Black Sox scandal and loss to the Cincinnati Reds, resulting in the permanent ban of eight White Sox players, catapulting the club into a decades-long period of second-division status. In between those series, the Cubs were given permission to use Comiskey as their home field because of greater seating capacity than Weeghman Park; however, the North Siders fell to the Babe-Ruth-led Boston Red Sox. Also featured are all three games of the 1959 fall classic, when the free-spirited, rough-and-tumble Go-Go Sox, led by Hall of Famers Nellie Fox and Luis Aparicio, came up short against the Los Angeles Dodgers. The White Sox played only two additional postseason games in the venerable park, the final two contests of the 1983 ALCS, and they're included, too.

Some of the games of this volume have historical significance, like the first and last contests at the ballpark, or the inaugural All-Star

THE BASE BALL PALACE OF THE WORLD

Game in 1933, the brainchild of Arch Ward, sports editor of the *Chicago Tribune*, and which took place during the city's World's Fair. Other games recall historically significant or milestone feats, such as the first night game in the ballpark, in 1939; the longest game in major-league history — a 25-inning victory over the Milwaukee Brewers, in 1984; and Carlton Fisk's cycle, which marked the only time in Comiskey Park history that a White Sox player accomplished that feat. We even have the bizarre: Ever heard of Disco Demolition Night?

Throughout its history, Comiskey Park had the reputation as a pitcher's park and *The Base Ball Palace of the World: Comiskey Park* contains some of the greatest mound feats at the park. We've included all nine no-hitters, six of which were by White Sox pitchers. Hard-throwing spitballer Ed Walsh tossed the first; while another Hall of Famer, the Detroit Tigers Jack Morris, tossed the last. Bob Feller of the Cleveland Indians authored the most famous one — on Opening Day in 1940. Other no-nos are from players whose memories and accomplishments this book helps preserve, such as Joe Benz, Vern Kennedy, Bill Dietrich, and Bob Keegan. The weirdest no-hitter occurred on the 80th anniversary of the park, yet is not considered an official no-hitter by MLB and we have it for you: The New York Yankees' Andy Hawkins held the White Sox hitless, yet lost 4-0, and pitched just eight innings. Other twirling highlight included are Ted Lyons's 21-inning complete game and the California Angels' Nolan Ryan's wild 185-pitch, 18-strikeout, 9-walk outing.

As a counter-weight to the pitching exploits, *The Base Ball Palace of the World: Comiskey Park* also features offensive feats, such as Harry Hooper becoming the first White Sox hitter to club two round-trippers in a game at Comiskey, and Merv Connors, who played just 52 big-league games, becoming the first to belt three in a contest, as well as Hall of Famer Harold Baines, who jacked three in 1982, and Jim Spencer, who knocked in eight runs in a game twice in less than two months in 1977. We're not partisan, either. We've included Mickey Mantle's 11th-inning game-winning blast, his 50th of the season, to clinch the pennant for the New York Yankees in 1956; and also a trifecta from the Boston Red Sox' 38-year-old Ted Williams.

Throughout the volume, you'll encounter all of the biggest names in White Sox history: hurlers like Red Faber, Eddie Cicotte, Joe Horlen, and Wilbur Wood, and position players from Eddie Collins, Buck Weaver, Luke Appling, and Al Simmons to Bill Melton, Frank Thomas, Robin Ventura, and Ozzie Guillen. In our quest to present the history of the White Sox through the baseball games played at Comiskey Park, we've not just focused on the stars. We have games featuring the little-known or obscure players like Hank Steinbacher, who played just 203 big-league games, yet tied the White Sox record with six hits in a 1938 game; and Jerry Nyman, who tossed a four-hit shutout in his first start, one of only six big-league victories.

Comiskey park has a rich history and tradition of Negro League baseball. For 28 years, from 1933 to 1960, the ballpark hosted the annual East-West Game, the Negro League All-Star Game. In addition to a must-read, informative essay about the history of those games, we've highlighted five of those contests, including the first three, as well as the 1939 and 1943 contests, the latter of which drew an estimated 52,000 spectators. Those games featured the likes of Cool Papa Bell, Oscar Charleston, Martin Dihigo, Willie Foster, Josh Gibson, Buck Leonard, Mule Suttles, Hilton Smith, Turkey Stearns, and Willie Wells. Comiskey Park also hosted the Negro League World Series, which was sometimes a traveling series with games played in cities not related to the competing teams. Included in our volume are three games featuring six different teams, the Birmingham Black Barons, Cleveland Buckeyes, Homestead Grays, Kansas City Monarchs, New York Cubans, and Newark Eagles, whose rosters were filled with most recognizable names in the Negro Leagues, some of whom became stars in the big leagues, such as Larry Doby, Sam Jethroe, Monte Irvin,

Minnie Miñoso, and Hank Thompson.

The feature essays contextualize the ballpark's history. Included are an in-depth historical sketch of Comiskey itself, and a compelling essay focusing on the White Sox' near move to St. Petersburg, Florida, and subsequent political wrangling that led to the end of Comiskey Park and the construction of its replacement, the "new" Comiskey Park (now known as Guaranteed Rate Field). A reflective piece recalls the pageantry of the park on the 50th anniversary of the inaugural All-Star Game, the third and final midsummer classic the ballpark hosted. For all the trivia buffs, we end with a stat- and factoid-filled piece. Don't forget to take this volume with you when you go out for a drink: you can stump your friends and win a round of drinks.

This book is the result of the tireless work of 50 members of the Society for American Baseball Research. SABR members researched and wrote all of the essays in this volume. These uncompensated volunteers are united by their shared interest in baseball history and a resolute commitment to preserving its history. Without their unwavering dedication, this volume would not have been possible.

I am indebted to the associate editors and extend to them my sincerest appreciation. Bill Nowlin, the second reader; fact-checker Kevin Larkin; and copy editor Len Levin each read every word of all the essays and made numerous corrections to language, style, and content. Their attention to detail has been invaluable. It has been a pleasure to once again work on a book project with such professionals, with whom I corresponded practically every day, and typically more than once. What a team we have!

I thank all of the authors for their contributions, meticulous research, cooperation through the revising and editing process, and finally their patience. It was a long journey from the day the book was launched to its completion, and we've finally reached our destination. We did it! Please refer to the list of contributors at the end of the book for more information.

This book would not have been possible without the generous support of the staff and Board of Directors of SABR, SABR Publications Director Cecilia Tan, and designer David Peng.

We express our thanks and gratitude to Matthew J. Richards, vice president and general manager sales at Getty Images, for arranging the overwhelming majority of photos included in this volume, as well as to Andy Krause, sport product manager at Getty Images, for assisting us with individual images. Special thanks also to John Horne of the National Baseball Hall of Fame for supplying the cover photo.

And finally, I wish to thank my wife, Margaret, and daughter, Gabriela, for their support of and endless patience with my baseball pursuits. They're accustomed to me working on my "SABR-stuff." Thankfully, they are also baseball fans (though, I must admit, Cubs fans).

We invite you to sit back, relax for a few minutes, and enjoy reading about the great games and the exciting history of Comiskey Park.

Gregory H. Wolf
December 1, 2019

COMISKEY PARK

By Bob Webster

In 1890, Charles Comiskey was a member of the Chicago Pirates of the Players' League, a league that only operated for only one season. They played their games at Brotherhood Park on 35th Street between Shields and Wentworth. Comiskey played baseball through the 1894 season, when he retired from playing and bought a Western League team based in Sioux City, Iowa, which he soon moved to St. Paul, Minnesota.

During his playing days, Comiskey knew Bancroft "Ban" Johnson. Johnson was president of the Western League, and they worked together to grow their league into a league that could compete with the National League. Comiskey moved his team from St. Paul to Chicago in 1900 and renamed it the White Stockings, a name discarded by the Chicago National League ball club currently known as the Cubs. A gentleman's agreement with the National League team would keep the White Stockings south of 35th Street. Comiskey searched in the area that he played in 10 years before and found a former cricket grounds on 39th Street between Princeton and Wentworth, just a few blocks from Brotherhood Park.[1]

Fifty years earlier, in 1850, Comiskey would have seen open prairie in that area, broken only by small outposts on the South Branch of the Chicago River. In 1848 the Illinois and Michigan Canal opened and soon after that the area started to grow rapidly.

Between 1870 and 1900, Chicago's population grew from 300,000 to 1.7 million. By the time Comiskey was looking for a place for his team to play baseball, the area he scouted was pretty much filled in. Residential areas ran from the east of where he was looking to Lake Michigan. A combination of residential and industry areas was to the west, but there was a small area between the two that provided enough room for a ballpark.

The American League was formed for the 1901 season and the White Stockings won the pennant that year. In 1906, the White Sox, as they were now known, won the third-ever World Series. Growing attendance demands forced Comiskey to find a location for a new ballpark with more seating capacity.

In December 1908 Comiskey bought a parcel of land from the daughter of Long John Wentworth, a former two-term mayor of Chicago who also served six terms as a member of the US House of Representatives. Wentworth owned 5000 acres of land that included the land that he sold to Comiskey for the ballpark. The parcel was bordered by 35th Street on the south, Wentworth Avenue on the east, 34th Street on the north, and Shields Avenue on the west. The 15-acre site was large enough for a ballpark, which would be placed on the eastern side of the parcel, with a winter amusement park consisting of an indoor skating rink and gymnasium on the western portion. The ballpark would be built of concrete and steel and was expected to hold 30,000 people. The ballpark would be similar to Shibe Park, then being built in Philadelphia, expecting to cost $500,000. Space for stores that would front Wentworth Avenue would be placed under the stands. Charles Comiskey insisted that none of the parcel not used for baseball would be allowed to go to waste.[2]

Ground was broken for the park in May of 1909. William Steele and Sons, the architects of

Charles Comiskey Jr., son of the owner of the Chicago White Sox, flanked by Hall of Famers Pale Hose coach Johnny Evers (on left) and ageless wonder second baseman Eddie Collins. (Photo Reproduction by Transcendental Graphics/Getty Images)

Shibe Park, were hired to design the structure. Comiskey wanted to design his new concrete and steel ballpark after the new parks in Philadelphia (Shibe Park) and Pittsburgh (Forbes Field). The final design, submitted by Zachary T. Davis of William Steele and Sons, called for a grandstand that would hold 15,000. The exterior would be patterned after the Roman Coliseum. Pavilions down each line and outfield bleacher seats could hold another 15,000. The seats would be designed so that "there will be no occasion for the spectators to rise from their seats at any time in order to watch a play."[3]

A steelworkers strike delayed construction for a while but that was overcome and the ballpark was ready by the planned opening date, July 1, 1910.[4] The White Sox played their last game at South Side Ballpark on June 27.[5]

The gates of Comiskey Park opened on July 1, and 32,000 were present to see the St. Louis Browns defeat the White Sox 2-0. Owners and officers of many major-league clubs were in attendance.

Only the bleachers were made of wood. An electric scoreboard measured about 60 to 80 feet long and 25 to 30 feet high. One oddity of the park was that down each foul line, between the outfield bleachers and the field level pavilion seating down each base line, there was iron fencing and gates that allowed access for equipment onto the field. The fences and gates, which were partially in fair territory, were made of one-inch rods with openings of four to five inches. Since fair batted balls could bounce through or roll under these iron gates, the effective fence height in the left and right-field corners was zero. This arrangement had an unintentional but substantial effect as balls that went through the iron gates and fences were considered home runs.

Depending on which newspaper you read, the dimensions of the park were either 362, 363, or 365 feet down the lines and 420 to center. Foul territory was also large, with a distance of 94 feet from the plate to the backstop.

The first remodeling or expansion of Comiskey Park took place in time for the 1927 season. The architect of the expansion was Zachary T. Davis, the 1910 architect. He also designed the park now known as Wrigley Field. The foul-line pavilions and wooden outfield bleachers were removed and replaced by steel and concrete double-deck stands. The construction was not quite completed by Opening Day of 1927; the upper-deck portions of the outfield stands were not finished. The construction was, however, completed by the time Babe Ruth and the New York Yankees came to town for a series beginning May 7. The plan for the expansion called for a seating capacity of 55,000, but the Chicago Fire Department limited the capacity to 52,000. This expansion made Comiskey Park the third-largest major-league park in terms of capacity, behind Yankee Stadium and the New York Giants' Polo Grounds.

The remodeling and expansion changed the dimensions of the field. The left-field and right-field stands were now at a 90-degree angle to the foul lines, resulting in dead center being 455 feet from home plate. The fences now consisted of a four-foot concrete base topped with a six-foot wire screen. The iron gates and fences that allowed the balls to travel through or under were gone.

The White Sox acquired Al Simmons, Mule Haas, and Jimmy Dykes from the Philadelphia Athletics for the 1933 season. After that season, in an attempt to help Simmons, home plate was moved 14 feet toward center field. This also reduced the dimensions in right and left field from 352 to 342 feet. After the 1935 season, Simmons was traded and the plate was moved back 14 feet, returning to the dimensions that were in place after the 1933 season.

The next big change to Comiskey Park was to add lights. Four years after Crosley Field in Cincinnati became the first major-league park to install lights, the first night game was played at Comiskey Park on August 14, 1939. It drew a crowd of 30,000 as the White Sox beat the Browns, 5-2. Comiskey Park was the third American League ballpark to host a night game, all that season; Cleveland's Municipal Stadium had hosted one on June 27 and Philadelphia's Shibe Park hosted a night game on May 16. The players reported that visibility at the White Sox game was nearly perfect.[6]

In 1941 and 1942 the ballpark's capacity was reduced to 46,550 when the original seats were replaced with wider curved-back seats. More of these seats were added in 1947 and some seats were removed in center field to provide a better batter's background, reducing the capacity by another 2,000 seats.

Throughout the lifespan of Comiskey Park, the field dimensions were changed 13 times from the original 1910 dimensions. The distance to the center-field wall varied between 404 and 449 feet and right and left field varied between 349 and 384 feet.

THE NEIGHBORHOOD

After the ballpark was built in 1910 and with the population of Chicago still growing, the surrounding neighborhood evolved once again. Comiskey Park would become surrounded by people from three continents. The neighborhood to the west of the ballpark, called Bridgeport, was started by people with Irish roots, but grew with the addition of people from all over Europe. Douglas, to the east, was Chicago's port of entry for African-Americans. Chinatown, to the north, was the smallest of the three but the most durable over the years with its identity and culture. The ballpark was built in a small neighborhood between those three that was called Armour Square. The combination of the three cultures attending games created a sense of toughness in each of the groups, a toughness that remains at the new ballpark today. The toughness was created by the neighborhoods' inhabitants going after a common dream of making it and succeeding in life. By 1930, the working-class Bridgeport neighborhood was full of well-kept homes. The Irish made up only 6 percent of the neighborhood, now joined by Polish, Lithuanians, Germans, and Italians. Bridgeport supplied the now-legendary string of mayors who ran the city from the early 1930s through 2011, that included Ed Kelly, Martin Kennelly, Richard J. Daley, Michael Bilandic, and Richard M. Daley.

SPECIAL EVENTS AT COMISKEY PARK

Comiskey Park hosted three All-Star Games, one American League Championship Series, and four World Series.

The very first All-Star Game, in 1933, was played at Comiskey Park. It was originally called The Game of the Century instead of the All-Star Game and was expected to be a one-time event to coincide with the Century of Progress Exhibition in Chicago. A coin toss decided between Comiskey Park and Wrigley Field as host for the game.[7] The American League won the game before a sold-out crowd. It was broadcast on WGN radio by Bob Elson and also on NBC and CBS radio, and they raised $46,506 for charity. It was announced immediately after the game that it would become a yearly event.

The All-Star Game returned to Comiskey Park in 1950. The St. Louis Cardinals' Red Schoendienst homered in the 14th inning to win the game for the National League, 4-3. Ted Williams suffered a broken elbow when his arm hit the outfield wall while he caught Ralph Kiner's line drive.[8] Williams had surgery and did not return until September 7. The third and final All-Star Game held at Comiskey Park was the 50th Anniversary Game in 1983. The American League won, 13-3.

The first of four World Series with games at Comiskey Park was played between the New York Giants and Chicago White Sox in 1917. The ballpark's capacity at the time was 32,000, and to accommodate fans who could not obtain seats, the Stockyards Pavilion and Arcadia Hall hired semipro baseball players to re-create the plays as they were telegraphed from Comiskey Park. The White Sox won the series in six games, bringing home the White Sox' second World Series championship.

The Chicago Cubs borrowed Comiskey Park for their home games during the 1918 World Series between the Cubs and the Boston Red Sox. The Cubs' Weeghman Field (now known as Wrigley Field) held only 20,000 at the time while Comiskey Park held 32,000. Due to federal travel restrictions imposed by the World War, the first three games of the Series were to be played in Chicago with the remaining games to be played in Boston.[9] Attendance was disappointing for the Series: The regular season ended on Labor Day and bad weather, the lack of the best players, and general concern for the war resulted in crowds being sparse.

The White Sox returned to the World Series in 1919 against the Cincinnati Reds. The Reds won, five games to three, in the Series that went down in history because of the Black Sox Scandal, in which eight White Sox players plotted to throw games. The players were banned from baseball for life. The 1959 World Series, between the White Sox and Los Angeles Dodgers, was the last one to be played at Comiskey Park. The Dodgers beat the White Sox in six games.

The White Sox advanced to the postseason in 1983, playing the Baltimore Orioles in the American League Championship Series. The teams split the first two games in Baltimore before playing the first ALCS ever at Comiskey Park. The Orioles won Game Three, 11-1 before a crowd of 46,635. Down two games to one, the White Sox had to win the next two to get to the World Series, but they lost Game Four, 3-0, and the Orioles advanced to the World Series.

NEGRO LEAGUE BASEBALL AT COMISKEY PARK

Negro League baseball was played at Comiskey Park as soon as the park opened in 1910. The majority of Rube Foster's American Giants games were played at South Side Park, recently vacated by the White Sox. When the White Sox were out of town, the American Giants played an occasional game at Comiskey Park.

The most notable of Negro League games at Comiskey Park were the East-West All-Star Games, held each year from 1933 to 1960. The game brought African-Americans together from across the country and attracted a who's who of African-American society to Comiskey Park. The ballpark was decorated in red, white, and blue banners and a jazz band played between innings. People like Count Basie, Ella Fitzgerald, and Billie Holiday would always make it a point to be in Chicago at that time and entertain at the jazz clubs at night.[10] It was far more than just a game, as Buck O'Neil proclaimed. He said "(The white major leagues' All-Star Game) was, and is, more or less an exhibition. But for black folks, the East-West Game was a matter of racial pride."[11]

Yankee Stadium hosted the classic in 1961, ending the 28-year tradition of Comiskey Park holding at least one of the annual games. Seven men played in both an East-West Game and a major-league All-Star Game: Jackie Robinson, Larry Doby, Roy Campanella, Satchel Paige, Minnie Miñoso, Ernie Banks, and Jim Gilliam. Twenty-five men enshrined in the Baseball Hall of Fame appeared in an East-West Game.

As the major leagues were signing more black players, the Negro leagues collapsed, bringing to the forefront the Indianapolis Clowns, a barnstorming team with an emphasis on entertainment as much as competition. The Clowns toured the Midwest and made stops at Comiskey Park into the 1970s.

To honor the tradition of the East-West Games at Comiskey Park, on Monday, July 7, 2008, a collaboration between the Negro Leagues Baseball Museum and the Chicago White Sox resulted in the first Double Duty Classic at US Cellular Field, showcasing the finest inner-city high-school talent throughout the Midwest. Part of the day's festivities included a forum on Negro League history.[12]

THE BILL VEECK YEARS

The White Sox' first 19 years were great. Successful teams, large crowds, and a new ballpark. After the 1919 Black Sox scandal, the White Sox headed downhill for a while. Charles Comiskey died in 1931. The White Sox went through a couple of decades of mediocre baseball until, beginning in 1951, they had a winning record for 17 years in a row. In 1959 the White Sox made it to the World Series.

Bill Veeck came onto the scene in 1959. When Comiskey built the park in 1910, it was a state-of-the-art facility. By 1959 it still looked like a turn-of-the-century ballpark. When Comiskey opened for the 1960 season, it had lost some of its early century association: The ballpark was painted white, from its original dark green. It now looked brighter and cleaner.

That was only the beginning. Veeck installed a scoreboard unlike any others. It was eventually known as the Monster. The scoreboard took up the entire center-field backdrop and rose higher than the right- and left-field upper decks. Ten towers rose from the back, surrounding a large clock that was trimmed in lights. When a White Sox player hit a home run, the scoreboard "exploded." Lights around the clock and beneath the scoreboard turned on and off. Fireworks shot up from the top of the scoreboard and from above the right- and left-field upper decks. Lit-up pinwheels spun. The scoreboard caused controversy and resentment. The players hated it. But the technology outlived Veeck and all of the naysayers and proved the critics wrong.

Another unique addition to Comiskey Park was in place in 1960. Part of the left-field wall was replaced by a chain-link fence and behind the fence at ground level was a picnic area. The view of the entire ballpark was obstructed but the view at field level was unique.

Veeck sold the team to Arthur and John Allyn in 1961 and the name of the ballpark was changed to White Sox Park. Despite the 17 straight winning seasons between 1951 and 1967, attendance dwindled. The neighborhood was labeled a "crime-ridden area" that kept fans from the games. Too many seats were behind poles and concessions were inadequate. Allyn wanted to build a new ballpark, but the funding never materialized. In time for the 1969 season, AstroTurf was installed on the infield and the outfield wall was moved in. The White Sox hit more home runs, but so did their opponents. The '70s weren't any nicer to the White Sox and the financially strapped team had to shut off the scoreboard in 1975. The exploding scoreboard was the only constant throughout Allyn's tenure and it looked as though the White Sox were going to move to Seattle.

When Veeck sold the team in 1961 after owning it for just two years, some fans called him an opportunist who just wanted to make a quick buck. When he reacquired the team in 1975, he was looked upon as a savior. Veeck made some immediate changes. The name was changed back to Comiskey Park and the AstroTurf was removed. The ballpark received a new coat of white paint. The center-field fence was removed, creating a 445-foot canyon in front of the center-field bleachers, making the park more conducive to doubles and triples.

The voice of the White Sox, Harry Caray, and organist Nancy Faust helped Veeck bring the fans back to the ballpark. Veeck urged Carey to sing "Take Me Out to the Ball Game" during the seventh-inning stretch with Faust accompanying him on the organ, a tradition he took with him across town to the Cubs in 1982.

Nancy Faust had been with the White Sox for six seasons by the time Veeck purchased the team in 1975. Faust was one of the first female organists at a major-league ballpark. She performed before small crowds in her first few seasons, but that changed in 1977, when the team was called the South Side Hitmen because they could hit for power. Richie Zisk, Oscar Gamble, and Eric Soderholm combined for 86 home runs. In 1970 the White Sox drew 495,000 fans. In the month of July 1977, they drew 480,000.[13]

Nancy Faust became part of the fun and began playing the 1969 song "Na Na Hey Hey Kiss Him Good-Bye" when opposing pitchers were being removed from the game. The song was also played after the last out of a White Sox victory. Both traditions remained as of 2019.

After the last game of the 1977 season, Faust played the song for the last time of the season. Then, nothing happened. No one moved. Everyone stayed where they were. Nobody wanted this to end. The excitement of the season was so overwhelming to the fans that they did not want the season to come to an end. Fifteen minutes went by. Then, 30, 45, 60 minutes went by and everyone was still there. An hour and a half later, the fans started shaking hands and saying goodbye to one another. They were finally ready to say goodbye to this season.

Probably the biggest promotion at Comiskey Park came on July 12, 1979. Local radio disc jockey Steve Dahl was upset that the radio station he worked for changed its format from rock to disco. The White Sox scheduled Disco Demolition night for a doubleheader between the White Sox and the Detroit Tigers. The fans could get into the ballpark for 98 cents and a disco record. Things got out of hand early as the sold-out crowd and the many more who could not get in were supposed to give up their records at the gate, but attendants quit taking them because of the number of people coming in. Some spectators started throwing the records like Frisbees onto the field. Dahl blew up the records in center field between games of the doubleheader. The blast sent pieces of records high into the sky and parts of the field caught fire. About 7,000 fans charged the field, stole the bases, and tore up the field so badly that the White Sox had to forfeit the second game.[14]

For health reasons, Bill Veeck sold the team

to Jerry Reinsdorf and Eddie Einhorn in 1981.[15] It has been said that Veeck owned the White Sox for fewer years than any of the other owners, but his legacy remains long after his death.

INTERESTING FACTS AND RECORDS

- In the first-ever All-Star Game in 1933, Babe Ruth hit a two-run homer to pace the American League to victory.
- Cleveland's Bob Feller threw the major leagues' only Opening Day no-hitter on April 16, 1940.
- Larry Doby, the first African-American in the American League, made his debut with the Cleveland Indians as a pinch-hitter in a game at Comiskey on July 5, 1947.
- In front of more than 51,000 fans, 42-year-old Indians pitcher Satchel Paige threw a shutout on August 13, 1948.
- Red Schoendienst of the Cardinals hit a 14th-inning home run in the 1950 All-Star Game.
- In 1983, Fred Lynn hit the first All-Star Game grand slam.
- Yankee Andy Hawkins threw a no-hitter against the White Sox on July 1, 1990, but lost the game 4-0 on walks and errors.
- On May 8-9, 1984, the White Sox and Milwaukee Brewers played the longest game by time and innings: 25 innings in 8 hours and 6 minutes. Harold Baines hit a solo walk-off home run to win the game for the White Sox.

OTHER SPORTING EVENTS AT COMISKEY PARK

Baseball was not the only sporting event held at Comiskey Park. Notable boxing matches include the 1937 bout between James Braddock and Joe Louis before a crowd of 55,000, in which Louis won the heavyweight championship. In a heavyweight championship fight in 1962, Sonny Liston defeated Floyd Patterson, in their first fight.

Roller Derby, wrestling, and a sport called auto polo were all played in Comiskey Park.

When Soldier Field was scheduled for renovation in 1978, the Chicago Sting, a member of the North American Soccer League, played their home games at Comiskey Park. The Sting played several more games at Comiskey Park until the league disbanded after the 1984 season. In addition to the Sting, the Chicago Mustangs of the United Soccer League played at Comiskey Park in 1967 and 1968.

FOOTBALL AT COMISKEY PARK

In 1920 the Chicago Cardinals became a charter member of the American Professional Football Association (which became the National Football League in 1922) after playing in the Chicago area off and on for 20 years. The team, which is now the Arizona Cardinals, played home games at Comiskey Park from 1922 to 1925 and again from 1929 to 1958. The Cardinals played at Soldier Field and Metropolitan Stadium in Minnesota in 1959 before the team was moved to St. Louis for the 1960 season.[16]

NON-SPORTING EVENTS AND CONCERTS

Two other non-sporting events at Comiskey Park involve Charles Lindbergh in 1927 and the Jehovah's Witnesses in 1955. After Lindbergh returned to the United States from his solo flight across the Atlantic to Paris, he was awarded the Congressional Medal of Honor and then took a victory tour across the country. In Chicago, Lindbergh stopped at Comiskey Park to be awarded a "gold star" by Chicago Police Chief Michael Hughes. On June 22 and 23, 1955, 20,000 Jehovah's Witnesses attended a convention at Comiskey Park.

Rock concerts that were too large for indoor venues started to play in outdoor sports arenas.

On August 20, 1965, the Beatles played afternoon and evening concerts at Comiskey Park. The afternoon concert drew 25,000 fans, and the evening show 37,000. Each show consisted of 10 songs lasting a total of 45 minutes. Ticket prices ranged from $2.50 to $5.50.[17] Apparently, the teenage girls who dominated the audience screamed so much during the two shows that the Beatles were hardly heard.

Bill Veeck wanted to increase the revenue brought in by Comiskey Park, so a number of concerts were held there. Groups including the Police, Journey, Santana, the Beach Boys, Blondie, Aerosmith, AC/DC, Foreigner, Foghat, and South Side Johnny and the Asbury Dukes played concerts or mini-festivals there in front of as many as 70,000 people. A three-night show in October 1984 by Michael Jackson and his brothers drew 40,000 each night.

DEMOLITION OF COMISKEY PARK

In 1990 Chicago had a collection of classic sports arenas. Still in use besides Comiskey Park were Soldier Field (1924), where the Bears played, Chicago Stadium (1929), the home of the Bulls and Blackhawks, and Wrigley Field (1914), the home of the Cubs.

Many fans did not want Comiskey Park to go away. A crowd gathered on that March 1991 morning when the demolition was about to begin. As soon as the wrecking ball started to swing, a few people started to boo. Others joined them until a low, droning "Booooooooo" continued as the wrecking ball took its first few swings.

Meanwhile, on the opposite side of the ballpark, people started a demolition project of their own. They started to pry the park apart with crowbars and hammers. Mostly just bricks were taken, but one man was spotted carrying a door with "Players Entrance" stenciled on it. Signs were also a popular item to get away with. The police were there, but as long as the people didn't use their tools on one another, they let it go.

SOURCES

In addition to the sources cited in the Notes, the author also consulted:

Leventhal, Josh. **Take Me Out to the Ballpark** (New York: Black Dog & Leventhal Publishers, 2011).

Lowry, Philip J. **Green Cathedrals** (New York: Walker & Company, 2006).

Sullivan, Floyd. **Old Comiskey Park** (Jefferson, North Carolina: McFarland, 2014).

NOTES

1 Warren Brown, **The Chicago White Sox** (Kent, Ohio: Kent State University Press, 2007), 11.

2 "Comiskey Buys New Grounds for White Sox," **Chicago Tribune**, December 29, 1908: 4.

3 "Work Is Started on New Sox Park," **Chicago Tribune**, May 9, 1909: 8.

4 "Ironworkers Back at Park," **Chicago Tribune**, June 9, 1910: 10.

5 "Sox in 7-2 Defeat Leave Old Home," **Chicago Tribune**, June 28, 1910: 10.

6 "Night Baseball Inaugurated by Chicago White Sox Club," Logansport (Indiana) **Pharos-Tribune**, August 15, 1939: 2.

7 Arch Ward, "Comiskey Park Awarded Game of the Century: White Sox to Accept Ticket Orders June 1," **Chicago Tribune**, May 27, 1933: 19.

8 "Operate on Ted Williams' Elbow Today: Boston Ace's Arm Broken as All-Star," **Chicago Tribune**, July 13, 1950: 21 (Part 4, 1).

9 James Crusinberry, "World Series Opens Here on Sept. 4: Cubs May Play Red Sox on South Side," **Chicago Tribune**, August 25, 1918: 17.

10 Larry Lester, **Black Baseball's National Showcase: The East-West All-Star Game 1933-1953** (Lincoln: University of Nebraska Press, 2001), 21-22.

11 Lester, 64-66.

12 Scott Merkin, "White Sox Host Double Duty Classic," mlb.com, mlb.mlb.com/news/print.jsp?ymd=20080707&content_id=2087166&vkey=news_mlb&fext=.jsp&c_id=mlb&affiliateId=CommentWidget.

13 Dan Helpingstein, **South Side Hitmen — The Story of the 1977 Chicago White Sox** (Charleston, South Carolina: Arcadia, 2005), 76.

14 Derek John, "July 12, 1979: 'The Night Disco Died — Or Didn't,'" National Public Radio, npr.org/2016/07/16/485873750/july-12-1979-the-night-disco-died-or-didnt.

15 Retrieved from: https://www.Baseball-Reference.com/bullpen/Bill_Veeck.

16 Retrieved from: sportsteamhistory.com/chicago-cardinals.

17 Ibid.

A BALLPARK AS A POLITICAL FOOTBALL: FLORIDA, ILLINOIS, AND A NEW HOME FOR THE WHITE SOX

By John Bauer

Comiskey Park opened during the summer of 1910,[1] and the Chicago White Sox broke in their new home with a 2-0 loss to the St. Louis Browns. After hosting decades of American League baseball on the South Side of Chicago, as well as three World Series, Comiskey Park indeed showed its age during the summer of 1988. As with many major-league baseball teams during that era, the White Sox advocated for a new ballpark. With a scarcity of major-league teams and several booming cities seeking teams of their own, the threat of relocation would provide ample leverage for public financing of new ballparks to ensure that existing teams stayed put. For the White Sox, that formula would be applied to the effort to replace Comiskey Park with a new palace suitable for the modern era of baseball.

Indeed, the formula had already been applied with an apparently successful result. The White Sox seemed to have been saved through a 1986 legislative package that established an authority to oversee construction of a new ballpark and authorized the sale of bonds and new hotel taxes to finance the deal. By the spring of 1988, however, Comiskey Park continued to crumble with virtually no progress having been made on its presumed replacement. St. Petersburg, Florida, sensed an opportunity and pounced. Unlike Chicago, there was a new ballpark on the rise in St. Petersburg as the 43,000-seat Suncoast Dome inched toward readiness for major-league baseball. Though the fourth largest state in population in 1988, Florida lacked major-league baseball. The Suncoast Dome served as the bait. Of existing teams seeking new homes, the White Sox appeared to be the most desperate. A native Chicagoan, Commissioner Peter Ueberroth, acknowledged the situation. He said, "The White Sox are No. 1 on my watch list. ... [I]f they can't get the stadium they need in Chicago by the time they need it, I would not stand in their way."[2]

The combination of a courtship from Florida and inaction in Illinois presented White Sox managing partners Jerry Reinsdorf and Eddie Einhorn with an opportunity to play off two states in search of the best deal. St. Petersburg was going all-in to secure the White Sox. One member of the local Chamber of Commerce sold dozens of "Florida White Sox" T-shirts with more on the way, and a local radio station commissioned and regularly played the song "Come on White Sox."[3] Governor Bob Martinez overcame initial reluctance and confirmed his support for a $30 million legislative package intended to ready the Suncoast Dome for Opening Day 1989. "Let's play ball," he said.[4] In Illinois, almost two years of inaction provided the White Sox with an opening to get a better deal. In particular, the club hoped to renegotiate the part of the 1986 deal that required annual rent payments of $4 million and establish firm deadlines for the construction of a new stadium. By early May 1988, there was no guarantee that a better deal would be good enough for the White Sox. The club paid $25,000 for a feasibility study on the use of venerable Al Lang Stadium as a temporary home until the dome was completed.[5] Reinsdorf and Einhorn said the right things about staying, but it was suggested that their business partners were ready to accept the financial benefits offered by moving.[6]

Illinois Governor James "Big Jim" Thompson, whose arm-twisting helped secure passage of the 1986 deal, jumped back into fray. He declared, "I will do everything in my power to keep the Sox in Chicago."[7] Thompson authorized Deputy Governor James Reilly to assemble the principals to hammer out a deal. Starting on May 2, 1988, Reilly hosted a series of meetings with Reinsdorf and Einhorn in addition to Al Johnson, a representative of Chicago Mayor Eugene Sawyer, and Thomas Reynolds Jr., chairman of the Illinois Sports Facilities Authority (ISFA). The authority had been created by the 1986 legislation to issue $120 million in bonds and oversee construction of a new ballpark. Reinsdorf and Einhorn remained coy about their specific demands, but Reynolds noted that White Sox rent payments might be reduced because hotel tax revenues were exceeding projections.[8] The group hoped to craft a deal that would not require legislative approval, but it became apparent that the Illinois General Assembly might have to vote on a revised package.

The parties reached a tentative deal on May 9, but the apparent solution unraveled shortly before a planned press conference. Reilly said the governor's office and ISFA agreed to the White Sox' financial demands to the savings of approximately $60 million, but Reinsdorf and Einhorn would not consent to a request to suspend negotiations with St. Petersburg until the Illinois legislature could act on the package. Reilly complained, "We never told them to kill St. Petersburg's deal. We just said stop talking until our legislature ends. They couldn't do that."[9] Reynolds said that no additional money would have been required, only changes to the statute that created ISFA. Still, Reinsdorf and Einhorn were naturally reluctant to leave their fate exclusively to the Illinois legislature at the risk of killing the chance the Florida legislature might appropriate the $30 million to accelerate the dome's readiness for Opening Day. An unnamed team official declared, "They wanted us to cut off one leg in exchange for a promise that Springfield would try and give us another. ... That's not good business."[10]

Despite the impasse, Thompson rallied Sawyer as well as legislative leaders from both parties to support the deal. He also cajoled Reinsdorf and Einhorn into releasing a statement on May 11, 1988, that the White Sox would stay if the legislature approved the deal. Thompson proclaimed, "Chicago deserves to keep the White Sox and the White Sox want to stay."[11] The terms of the agreement included provisions related to rent reductions if attendance thresholds were not met; splits in concession and parking revenues; increasing the bond authorization to $150 million (just in case); and penalties if the ballpark was not ready by the 1991 season. Democratic Senate President Philip Rock supported the deal but cautioned, "I told the governor I thought it would be very difficult to pass."[12] In the delicate game of playing off two states against each other, Reinsdorf and Einhorn managed to make missteps that irritated both. The day after declaring their intent to stay if the Illinois legislature approved the deal, Reinsdorf and Einhorn met with Florida legislators seeking a promise to move if they approved the $30 million package. Governor Martinez expressed irritation at having appeared in front of cameras wearing a White Sox jersey as the two announced their conditional intent to stay in Illinois.[13]

During the second half of May, the situation appeared to swing toward St. Petersburg. The Florida House voted 66 to 38 to approve the $30 million package on May 25. Meanwhile in Illinois, Thompson attended one meeting of Republican legislators with some donning blue Cubs caps and others wearing Cardinals red. Also, with Thompson pushing for an income-tax increase to fund education and public-health initiatives, the White Sox proposal became an

COMISKEY PARK

Comiskey Park aerial view (Photo by Mark Rucker/Transcendental Graphics, Getty Images)

even hotter political potato. Although the White Sox bill required no additional revenue, legislators were concerned about the optics of voting to help a baseball team without funding other important public-policy initiatives. Reinsdorf advised fellow baseball owners of his situation during the American League meetings in San Francisco on May 31. He commented afterward, "I'm still hopeful we can stay. But now it's out of our hands. It's up to the legislature."[14] With several AL teams facing challenging ballpark situations of their own, it seemed unlikely the owners would stand in the way of the White Sox relocating to Florida.

There appeared to be a brief respite from the relocation threat when the Florida Senate initially failed to act on the Suncoast Dome bill. On June 2, with the end of the session approaching, a Florida Senate committee cut the $30 million proposal in half. From his perspective at ISFA, Reynolds cautioned against assuming a weakening in the White Sox position. He believed a lease agreement was imminent, and added that "[i]f the people in Springfield don't support it, then the Sox will leave town."[15] As the two states maneuvered over the White Sox, *Chicago Tribune* columnist Mike Royko started a "personal war" on Florida.[16] Noting that 2 million Illinoisans visited Florida each year, he declared residents of the latter "lousy ingrates" and labeled St. Petersburg "an overgrown hick town."[17] Royko encouraged readers to mail a white sock to St. Petersburg Mayor Robert Ulrich; several hundred would oblige. With the Florida legislative session extended a few days to finalize the state budget, St. Petersburg advocates cobbled together the votes on June 7 to pass the $30 million bill. St. Petersburg Assistant City Manager Rick Dodge gushed, "It's a wonderful invitation for the Chicago White Sox to become the Florida White Sox."[18] Reinsdorf and Einhorn issued their own anodyne statement: "Florida's political leaders have made a progressive statement to bring major-league baseball to their state by passing this legislation. Their commitment is most impressive."[19]

Back in Illinois, the likelihood of something similarly "impressive" seemed to diminish by the day. In addition to the generally tepid legislative reaction, Sawyer faced pressure as he looked to the 1989 Chicago mayoral election. Sawyer had become mayor upon Harold Washington's death in December 1987, and his position within the African-American community was not assured. The fact that African-Americans would be disproportionately displaced through condemnation proceedings in the South Armour Square neighborhood, an area near the current ballpark that would host the new one, provided an opening for political opponents to exploit. That Washington was understood to favor that location appeared not to matter. Sawyer's aloofness during the negotiations was noted. Moreover, of 67 Democrats in the House majority (versus 51 Republicans), only six were understood to support the stadium plan.[20] Support seemed similarly lacking among Republicans with Assistant House Minority Leader Gene Hoffman, who favored the package, adding, "I haven't found much support for the stadium at all."[21]

With a notable lack of support from the 32 Chicago-area House Democrats, Thompson prodded House Speaker Mike Madigan to bring his fellow Democrats into line. Thompson argued, "I think members of the General Assembly, especially the members from Chicago, who been dragging their feet and setting a poor example for their Downstate brothers, had better think very long and hard about whether they want to wear the jacket as the guys who lost the team."[22] Days later, Madigan announced he had 36 Democrats prepared to support the deal and challenged Thompson to find 24 GOP votes to ensure passage. The speaker pronounced, "If Governor Thompson can now convince the other legislative leaders and a comparable number of legislators from the other sectors, then we'll be able to pass the bill and keep the White Sox in Chicago."[23] Not to take Thompson's barbs lightly, Madigan added about the governor, "If he does his job, the White Sox will stay in Chicago. If he fails, the White Sox will leave."[24]

Progress was slow going in the state Senate. GOP leader James "Pate" Philip claimed only eight of his minority 28-member caucus supported the plan; property-tax relief was a higher priority.[25] Senate President Rock struggled to round up votes among the Democratic majority. In fact, some Democratic members had other ideas. One influential senator, William Marovitz, pushed a West Side complex that would house the Bears and White Sox, an idea with little appeal to the Bears.[26] Another Democratic senator, Greg Zito, pushed a plan to authorize the sale of $60 million in Build Illinois bonds to purchase the team from Reinsdorf and Einhorn and then sell $10 shares to the public. Zito argued that his plan would provide the two with $40 million more than they paid for the team, and "[i]n light of the fact they portray themselves as good businessmen, they would be foolish to turn it down."[27] Marovitz mocked the plan, "I hope no one thinks this will solve the Sox problem with the stadium." Nevertheless, the Senate approved Zito's plan on June 23 by a 38-to-18 vote with everyone looking to the House to kill the idea.

ISFA's leaders, Reynolds and executive director Peter Bynoe, continued to press for a realistic legislative solution. With the June 30 closing of the legislative session approaching, new complications emerged. For one, the lease remained unsigned. Without a signed lease, there would be nothing to offer the legislature. Thompson summarized the dilemma, "If there is no lease, then there will be no stadium. If there is no stadium, they've said they will go to Florida. It's that simple."[28] Additionally, efforts to effect an income-tax increase collapsed. Rock noted the dilemma facing legislators: "The perception would be that we have left the kids and the university systems bereft of what they need and yet we are affording a subsidy for professional sports. It's just not going to equate."[29] Although Thompson and Madigan traded barbs — with Thompson referring to the "do-nothing legislature"[30] — both men agreed that a signed lease was a prerequisite for any passage. Thompson argued, "If the White Sox want to stay in Chicago, they have it within their power to do that by signing a lease."[31] The White Sox relented and signed the lease on June 29, but also had a backup plan with St. Petersburg ready to take effect on July 1 if the legislature failed to act.[32] Reinsdorf defended the backup plan: "It would not be prudent for us to not have a backup waiting in the wings."[33]

With the arrival of June 30, the prospects for keeping the White Sox in Illinois appeared bleak. One Chicago Democratic representative lamented, "The income tax had to be there. But it's not, and Florida is going to get the White Sox."[34] Thompson continued to emphasize the revenue neutrality of the plan in relation to the 1986 deal and the exclusivity of this legislation in relation to those public services that went unfunded.[35] With the session in its final hour, Thompson and Madigan got to work on the floor of the Illinois House. In "an animated display of political arm-twisting,"[36] Madigan pushed three more Democrats to vote for the proposal and Thompson garnered six more GOP votes. Madigan implored the chamber, "There are risks, but there is an upside. Let's keep the Sox in Chicago."[37] In the end, minutes after passing the Illinois Senate 30 to 26, the White Sox stadium bill passed the Illinois House by a 60-to-55 vote. The time of the vote became the subject of legend. The Illinois Constitution required that the session end at midnight. The published roll of the vote read 12:03 A.M., which would have required a super-majority for passage, but Madigan noted, "By my watch, it was 11:59."[38]

Despite passage, there remained several steps to complete to consummate the deal. Specifically, ISFA was required by the lease agreement to acquire 80 percent of the necessary land by October 15. To obviate political concerns, Sawyer announced plans to meet with neighborhood residents and conceded, "I'm not going to suggest that anybody is going to enjoy losing their homes."[39] Further, ISFA faced significant financial penalties if the ballpark was not ready for the 1991 season. Flanked by Reinsdorf, Einhorn, and Sawyer, Thompson signed the legislation behind home plate at Comiskey Park on July 6. The governor announced, "I want to send the message that Chicago is most American of all cities and Illinois is the most American of all states."[40] Regardless of Chicago's status among American cities, it would remain both an American League city and a two-team major-league city. St. Petersburg would wait until 1998 before the Tampa Bay Devil Rays began play in what was then called Tropicana Field.

NOTES

1. The ballpark was known as White Sox Park when it opened in 1910. It became Comiskey Park in 1913.

2. Bob Verdi, "Will Sox Have Their Day in the Sun (Coast)?" **The Sporting News**, April 11, 1988: 5.

3. Robert Davis, "St. Pete Longs to Be Big League," **Chicago Tribune**, May 2, 1988: sec. 3; 1, 3.

4. Ibid.

5. "Chisox Eye Al Lang," **The Sporting News**, May 9, 1988: 25.

6. Jerome Holtzman, "Thompson Tells Sox He'll Do All He Can," **Chicago Tribune**, May 1, 1988: sec. 3; 3.

7. Ibid.

8. John Kass, "Thompson Jumps Into Sox Stadium Fray," **Chicago Tribune**, May 3, 1988: sec. 1; 1.

9. Kass, "State Halts Talks with Sox," **Chicago Tribune**, May 10, 1988: sec. 1; 1.

10. Kass and Tim Franklin, "Thompson Tries to Revive Sox Deal," **Chicago Tribune**, May 11, 1988: sec. 2; 1, 9.

11. Kass and Daniel Egler, "Sox Will Stay if Legislature OKs Proposal," **Chicago Tribune**, May 12, 1988, sec. 1; 1.

12. Ibid.

13. Kass and Egler, "Sox Owners Hold Talks in Florida," **Chicago Tribune**, May 13, 1988: sec. 2; 1, 2.

14. Holtzman, "At Least Reinsdorf and Einhorn Have AL Owners' Support," **Chicago Tribune**, June 1, 1988: sec. 4; 3.

15. Kass, "Florida Legislators Lobbying to Lure White Sox," **Chicago Tribune**, June 5, 1988: sec. 2; 1.

16 Mike Royko, "Look Out Florida: This Means War," **Chicago Tribune**, June 6, 1988: sec. 1; 3.

17 Ibid.

18 "Florida Legislature Approves $30 Million to Lure Sox," (Springfield, Illinois) **State Journal-Register**, June 8, 1988: 18.

19 Kass, "Florida Lawmakers OK Sox Funding Bill," **Chicago Tribune**, June 8, 1988: sec. 2; 1.

20 Kass, "Florida Legislators."

21 Kass, "Sox Owners in Pitch to Legislators," **Chicago Tribune**, June 9, 1988: sec. 2; 1.

22 Ibid.

23 "Madigan: Democrats Will Back Proposal to Keep Sox in Illinois," **State Journal-Register**, June 11, 1988: 15.

24 Ibid.

25 Kass and Egler, "Progress Seen on Sox Stadium Deal," **Chicago Tribune**, June 17, 1988: sec. 2; 3.

26 Ibid.

27 Doug Finke, "New Legislation Could Put White Sox in State's Hands," **State Journal-Register**, June 24, 1988: 19.

28 Kass, "Unsigned Lease May Doom White Sox Bill," **Chicago Tribune**, June 26, 1988: sec. 2; 2.

29 "Tax Increase May Doom Aid for White Sox," **State Journal-Register**, June 29, 1988: 27.

30 George Papajohn and Egler, "Governor Fears Tax-Hike Loss," **Chicago Tribune**, June 27, 1988: sec. 1; 1.

31 Egler and Kass, "Governor and Madigan Agree on Need for Sox Stadium Lease," **Chicago Tribune**, June 28, 1988: sec. 2; 2.

32 Egler and Kass, "Rock Holds Little Hope for Sox," **Chicago Tribune**, June 29, 1988: sec. 1; 1.

33 Finke, "Sox Owners Agree to Lease, Await Stadium Package," **State Journal-Register**, June 30, 1988: 22.

34 Kass and Egler, "Sox Sign Lease, but Deal May Be Doomed," **Chicago Tribune**, June 30, 1988: sec. 1; 1.

35 Finke, "Sox Owners."

36 Kass and Egler, "Bipartisan Rally Pushes Deal Through," **Chicago Tribune**, July 1, 1988: sec. 1; 1.

37 Ibid.

38 Ibid.

39 Kass and Cheryl Duvall, "Mayor Will Visit Site of Stadium," **Chicago Tribune**, July 6, 1988: sec. 2; 1.

40 "Thompson: We Are a Two-Team City," **State Journal-Register**, July 7, 1988: 17.

NEGRO BASEBALL AT COMISKEY PARK

THE EAST-WEST GAME (1933 - 1960)
AN ALL-STAR LEGACY

By Alan Cohen

"It makes no difference if the nation is in the midst of a major depression or riding the wave of prosperity, the East-West game is always a rousing success. It is the biggest sporting event ever promoted by Negroes and has been a box office hit from the start."

— Wendell Smith, **Pittsburgh Courier**, 1949.[1]

"The game itself is more than a mere promotion. It's our connecting link with organized baseball. It's our big opportunity to show, under perfect conditions, just what we are capable of producing through the years."

— Bill Nunn, **Pittsburgh Courier**, 1937.[2]

The story of the 28 years of Negro League East-West All-Star Games at Comiskey Park was documented by the great black writers who covered the event over the years, especially in the *Pittsburgh Courier* and *Chicago Defender*. Wendell Smith of the *Pittsburgh Courier* relayed the reminiscences of J.B. Martin, longtime president of the Negro American League, when Martin spoke on the eve of the 1954 game.

"The first East-West game, twenty-one years ago, opened the eyes of millions of people, and each year thereafter, more and more fair-minded people came to realize that it was sheer hypocrisy to pretend that there weren't any Negro players capable of playing in the major leagues. We were fortunate in that the players we had on exhibition (in the early years) were magnificent performers. There was for example Josh Gibson, one of the greatest hitters in the history of baseball; Willie Wells, the shortstop supreme; Ray Dandridge, the peer of all second basemen; James (Cool Papa) Bell, the swiftest outfielder in the game; and pitchers like Satchel Paige Willie Foster, Ray Brown, Leon Day, Joe Rogan, and others."[3]

In 1933 the first game between representatives of the East (Negro National League) and the West (Negro American League) was played at Comiskey Park. It was the brainchild of Pittsburgh restaurateur Gus Greenlee, who owned the Pittsburgh Crawfords (NNL). Others involved in launching the enterprise were owner King Cole of the Chicago American Giants (NAL), writer Fay Young of the *Chicago Defender*, and writers Bill Nunn, Chester Washington, John Clark, and Roy Sparrow of the *Pittsburgh Courier*.[4]

The score was West 11, East 7. Cool Papa Bell of the East squad led off the game with a fly ball to left field. The wall between Negro League baseball and Organized Baseball was totally insurmountable and scant attention was paid to the exploits of Bell and the others in the predominantly white mainstream press. But the games went on and ultimately the players would get their due recognition. Ten players from the 1933 game went into the Hall of Fame, as did the East manager, Pop Lloyd.

George "Mule" Suttles played for the Chicago American Giants. The West won the games in 1933 and 1935 and Suttles homered in each game, his homer in 1935 winning the contest in the 11th inning. He was always among the top vote-getters, but when his career ended in 1944 — he was 43 — he was little known outside of the Negro Leagues. He was inducted at Cooperstown in 2006.

More than 20 players who participated in the 28 games at Comiskey Park have been enshrined at Cooperstown, but others have escaped long-term fame. Jim West of the Washington Elites was batting .419 on the eve of the 1936 game. The *Kansas Whip* introduced the player to its readers on August 21, 1936. As a first baseman, he "ranks head and shoulders above any man modern baseball has produced for color. He was known for his "floppy old glove, his halting stumbling stride, his Houdini tactics as he spears a high one or digs a low one out of the dirt." The article's author concluded by saying that "the shadows of (George) Sisler, (Lou) Gehrig, and others will hang their heads in shame over the almost unbelievable feats of Jim West."[5]

West first played in the Negro Leagues in 1930 and continued to play until 1947. He, like so many others, would be denied the opportunity to play in Organized Baseball.

In 1936 the East team, stocked with future Hall of Famers from the Pittsburgh Crawfords, including Satchel Paige, Josh Gibson, Cool Papa Bell and Judy Johnson, romped to a 10-2 win to even the series at 2-2. Bell, had three hits, including a double, and Paige pitched the game's final innings as his team broke the game open.

In 1937 several players, including Satchel Paige, elected to play in the Caribbean and Central America for bigger paychecks. Nevertheless, there was an abundance of talent, including eight Hall of Famers. Hall of Fame pitchers Hilton Smith (West) and Leon Day (East) contended with the Hall of Fame bats of six players. Buck Leonard anchored the East Squad along with Mule Suttles. Suttles was accompanied by Newark Eagles teammates Ray Dandridge and Willie Wells. The West outfield included Turkey Stearnes in center and Willard Brown in left.

Leonard took center stage, clouting a second-inning homer to start the scoring as the East won, 7-2. With one out in the fifth inning, Bill Wright, the East's center fielder, made a great catch robbing the West's Newt Allen, diving headlong to grab the Texas Leaguer. This was on the heels of an equally remarkable play by East shortstop Wells an inning earlier. Wells, appearing in his fifth straight East-West game, sprinted into center field to grab a fly ball off the bat of Ted Radcliffe. Leonard, well past his prime, played briefly, at age 45, in the Piedmont League in 1953.

On August 23, 1938, the West evened the series at three games apiece with a 5-4 win. The key blow was a three-run inside-the-park homer off the bat of the West's Neil Robinson. *Chicago Daily News* sports editor Lloyd Lewis compared the Negro game to its white counterpart.

"The game was afire with speed. The bases were run with a swiftness and daring absent from the white man's game for 20 years. Crafty runners kept pitchers worried, catchers throwing hastily, and infielders darting in and out to hold them to the bags. They stretched singles into doubles; they went down to first so fast that no infield double play succeeded on a ground ball."[6]

The 1939 season marked the return of the "Bronze Abolisher of Peerless Pitchers."[7] Josh Gibson had rejoined the Pittsburgh Crawfords. The West Squad was led by Alex Radcliffe of the Chicago American Giants, the only player to appear in each of the first seven East-West Games. He appeared in 11 All-Star games at Comiskey Park in all, the last being at age 40 in 1946. By the time integration came to baseball, Radcliffe was too old to play.

Seventeen-year-old Connie Johnson was in his first year of professional baseball when he was selected to play in the 1940 game. He was with the Toledo Crawfords and was one of the pitchers victimized when the East scored four runs in the sixth inning en route to a 12-0 win.[8] He signed with the Kansas City Monarchs the following season and was with them, except for three years in the military, through 1950, appearing in his second and last East-West Game in 1950. On August 20, 1950, he pitched the middle three innings and hit a triple at Comiskey Park. He was credited with the win as the West won 5-3. After three seasons in the minor leagues, Johnson made his major-league debut in 1953 with the Chicago White Sox.

On July 27, 1941, more than 50,000 fans came through the turnstiles, with a paid attendance figure of 47,865.[9] There were a couple of new names on the East team that year, and they each contributed to an 8-3 win that gave the series lead to the East. Catcher Roy Campanella of the Baltimore Elite Giants and infielder Monte Irvin of the Newark Eagles were in the forefront as the East broke the game open with a six-run fourth inning. The big inning was topped off with a homer off the bat of Buck Leonard of the Homestead Grays.

In 1942 Campanella participated in an exhibition at Cleveland, playing for the Cincinnati Buckeyes of the Negro American League against a group of local sandlot players. He was suspended from that year's East-West game, but Josh Gibson had returned to the Homestead Grays and was behind the plate for the East squad. Ted Radcliffe, known as "Double-Duty," was a catcher for the West squad in 1942. It was his second appearance behind the plate in an East-West Game. He appeared in three other All-Star games as a pitcher.

Another big crowd (estimated by the *Pittsburgh Courier*'s Wendell Smith at 48,000)[10] was on hand on August 16, 1942. The encounter was one of the harder-fought contests in the series. Through six innings, the score was 2-2. Satchel Paige entered the game in the seventh inning for the West and the East solved him for three runs during his three innings of work, winning their third straight game, 5-2, and taking a 6-4 lead in the series. The winning pitcher that day was Dave "Impo" Barnhill. Barnhill was with the New York Cubans at the time and was sold in 1949 to the New York Giants organization. Barnhill spent three seasons at Triple-A Minneapolis, but never got to pitch in the majors.

On August 1, 1943, a record crowd of 51,723 saw Satchel Paige, in his first East-West starting appearance, hold the East hitless and scoreless in the first three innings (the only batter to reach was Josh Gibson on a walk) as the West won, 2-1. In his only plate appearance, Paige doubled and left the game for a pinch-runner in the third inning. The East's only tally came on a ninth-inning homer by Buck Leonard.

On August 13, 1944, the West beat the East 7-4. A five-run fifth-inning rally by the West was keyed by a two-run homer by catcher Ted Radcliffe. Josh Gibson of the East hit the longest shot of the day, but it was ruled a double. In the seventh inning, his 440-foot drive hit atop the public-address system in center field and bounced back on to the playing field.[11] Satchel Paige did not play. He was angered that receipts from the game did not include a fair distribution to soldiers during World War II. He had promised to withdraw if management did not "give all the money, 100 per cent, to war relief."[12] Despite these statements, there were those who felt that Paige's absence stemmed from the unwillingness of event organizers to meet his fee demands.[13]

Lorenzo "Piper" Davis played in his first East-West game in 1944. He was the player-manager of the Birmingham Black Barons when he made his fifth Comiskey Park East-West appearance in 1949. He was 32 at the time. In 1950 Davis was the first black player to be signed by the Red Sox. He batted .333 in 15 games at Class-A Scranton in the Eastern League but was let go by Boston after the season. He had several good seasons with the Oakland Oaks in the Pacific Coast League. From 1952 through 1954 Davis played in 416 games and batted .296. In 1953 he had 13 homers and 97 RBIs. But by then he was 35. There would be no call from the big leagues. A similar fate awaited Ray Dandridge who in 1944 was playing in this third East-West game. In 1949, at age 35, he joined the New York Giants organization and was shipped to Triple A. In four years at Minneapolis, he played in 501 games and batted .318. In 1950, at age 36, he had 36 extra-base hits and 80 RBIs. But the Giants felt he was past his prime. He was inducted into the Hall of Fame in 1987.

THE BASE BALL PALACE OF THE WORLD

Comiskey Park regularly hosted the Negro League East-West All-Star Games from the 1930s through the 1950s. Hall of Famer Josh Gibson of the Homestead Grays slides home in a pile of dust in the 1944 contest. (Photo by Mark Rucker/Transcendental Graphics, Getty Images)

Also playing in 1944 was Sam Jethroe. He had first been selected in 1942. In 1948 he signed with Brooklyn and played in their minor-league system in 1948 and 1949. The Dodgers traded Jethrow to the Boston Braves before the 1950 season and he was selected Rookie-of-the-Year in 1950.

Most of Martin Dihigo's career was spent in the Mexican League. He played with the New York Cubans in 1935-36 and in 1945, at the age of 40, he rejoined the New York Cubans. He was selected to play in the East-West game for the first time in 1945. Everyone who saw him play marveled at his abilities and he was enshrined in Cooperstown in 1977.

Phillip J. Schupler is not known to many baseball fans. So why does his name come up here? On the eve of the 1945 East-West Game, in mid-July 1945, Schupler, a New York State Assemblyman representing part of Brooklyn, wrote to Branch Rickey of the Brooklyn Dodgers. On the heels of the Dodgers' signing of Babe Herman, then 42, who had taken his last competitive swing in 1938, the assemblyman, whose constituency was exclusively white, wrote:

"If you are so desperate in your search for talent, I might suggest a source which would be more productive than the various homes for the aged which you have been scouting. There are many talented and able Negro ball players available who would insure the pennant for the Dodgers. You would enhance not only the efficiency and ability of the team by hiring some colored ballplayers, but that you would also increase the prestige of the Brooklyn Ball Club by showing that you relieve believe in the letter and spirit of the Ives-Quinn law (a New York law that established a State Commission Against Discrimination)."[14]

One week and one day after this letter appeared in the *Pittsburgh Courier*, the 1945 East-West Game was played at Comiskey Park. At shortstop for the West squad was Jackie Robinson of the Kansas City Monarchs.

COMISKEY PARK

The West took a 9-1 lead and withstood a last-inning rally by the East to win 9-6 in front of 31,714 spectators. As reported in the *Chicago Tribune*, "The game ended with a slick fielding play by Jackie Robinson, former UCLA football star. He went far to the left of his shortstop position to throw out Rogerio Linares."[15] At the plate, Robinson was 0-for-5. Roy Campanella, playing for the East, was 2-for-5 with two RBIs. Campy also gunned down a runner trying to steal.

Three weeks later, on August 24, the Chicago American Giants, playing at Comiskey Park, hosted the Kansas City Monarchs in the first game of a three-game series. Clyde Sukeforth of the Brooklyn Dodgers introduced himself to Jackie Robinson. On Tuesday, August 28, the Monarchs were in Davenport, Iowa. Robinson was in Brooklyn meeting with Branch Rickey. Campanella met with Rickey on October 13. The signing of Robinson was announced later in October and the signing of Campanella was announced on April 4, 1946.[16]

In the aftermath of the signings of Robinson and Campanella, the East-West games continued and would do so for 15 more years at Comiskey Park.

By the time of the 1946 game, only five black players had been signed to play in Organized Baseball (all by the Dodgers). The squads that played on August 18, 1946, were brimming with talent. Dan Bankhead, one heralded player, pitched three scoreless innings in the East-West Game. The next season, less than a month after he appeared in the 1947 East-West Game, he was sold to the Brooklyn Dodgers. When he made his major-league debut on August 26, 1947, he was the fifth player of color to appear in the big leagues in the twentieth century.

Against a formidable East lineup that included Josh Gibson (in his last East-West Game), Buck Leonard, and future big leaguers Larry Doby and Monte Irvin, the West prevailed 4-1, the only East run coming in the eighth inning on a fly ball by Doby. The most exciting play of the game was a double steal engineered by the West for their third run. In the fifth inning, with one out, Artie Wilson was at third and Sam Jethroe was at first. Jethroe took off for second. Catcher Josh Gibson's throw was cut off by Silvio Garcia who was unable to throw the scurrying Wilson out at home plate.[17]

By the time the 1947 East-West Game was played on July 27, with the West winning for the fifth straight game, 5-2, the color line was broken but, as had been the case in 1946, the bulk of Black talent was playing in the Negro Leagues. That was beginning to change. On the eve of the 1947 game Hank Thompson and Willard Brown, who had been scheduled to play, were with the St. Louis Browns. There were far more major-league scouts and mainstream (white) newspapers at the game, which drew 48,112 spectators. New faces were on the teams that year, most notably Orestes "Minnie" Miñoso of the New York Cubans and Luis Marquez of the Homestead Grays, both of whom made it to the majors. But there was one old face. Biz Mackey managed the East team. The game was played on his 50th birthday and, for a moment the former catcher turned back the clock, inserting himself into the game as a pinch-hitter. He was intentionally walked and left the game for a pinch-runner. The pinch-runner was one of the team's coaches, Vic Harris, who began playing professionally in 1923. Mackey was inducted at Cooperstown in 2006.

In 1948, although Jackie Robinson, Larry Doby, and Satchel Paige were in the major leagues, there was still great talent on exhibit at Comiskey Park. The West won the game 3-0 and the East was limited to three hits. Buck Leonard doubled and Minnie Miñoso singled, as did newcomer Junior Gilliam, who later became a fixture with the Brooklyn and Los Angeles Dodgers.

The 1949 game was played in the aftermath of the Negro National League folding after the 1948 season. Ten teams remained playing Negro baseball at the highest level, in the Negro American League, and those teams were represented when the players took to the field on August 14,

THE BASE BALL PALACE OF THE WORLD

1949. By this point, more than 35 players of color were in Organized Baseball.

Comiskey Park continued to host the East-West game through 1960 with a decline in interest and talent with each passing year. Nevertheless, a new generation of black players dreamed the dream of escaping the buses and the dust and the obscurity of the fading Negro leagues. For several, minor-league ball was on the horizon. A lucky few made it to the majors, and one player would take center stage at Cooperstown.

Prior to the 1949 game, the media praised Lenny Pearson. He was a big first baseman from the Baltimore Elites. At the age of 31, he was appearing in his sixth East-West Game at Comiskey Park. In 1950 he batted .305 in 63 games at Milwaukee of the Triple-A American Association, but he never made it to the majors.

Throwing out the first pitch in 1949 was Commissioner A.B. "Happy" Chandler. J.B. Martin said the "presence of Mr. Chandler at the contest will give added importance to the annual game. With a number of our players now going into Organized Baseball, we thought it proper and fitting to invite the commissioner to pitch the first ball."[18] Eight of the players in the game would make it to the majors.

Ralph J. Bunche, a diplomat known for his Nobel Peace Prize and his work with the United Nations, threw out the first ball in 1950 and 24,614 spectators saw the West win, 5-3. Junior Gilliam, playing in his last East-West Game, homered for the East, and future Dodgers teammate Joe Black was the starting pitcher for the East.

The 20th Annual East-West game was staged at Comiskey Park on August 17, 1952. The number of teams in the Negro American League had fallen to six, and three teams were represented on each squad. A leading vote-getter for the East squad was Henry Kimbro of the Birmingham Black Barons.[19] He was appearing in his seventh East-West game, but like most of the players in the game did not possess the talent to escape the buses and dust of the Negro Leagues.[20]

By 1953 there were only four teams represented at Comiskey Park. Indianapolis and Birmingham supplied the East players and from Kansas City and Memphis came the West team. These two players are worth remembering.

It was the last East-West Game for Lloyd "Pepper" Bassett, the starting catcher for the West. It was his fourth appearance in an East-West Game at Comiskey park. He was 43 and had begun his professional career in 1934 with the Crescent Stars, an independent team. His next season was in the Negro National League with Philadelphia. In 1948 the then 37-year-old had been a key part of the Birmingham Black Barons squad that played in the last Negro League World Series. In 1954 he played his last season with the Detroit Stars. He never got to play a game of integrated ball.[21]

It was the only East-West Game for the young shortstop of the Kansas City Monarchs. A month and four days after appearing in the August 13 game at Comiskey Park, Ernie Banks made his major-league debut Chicago's other big-league park.

In 1954 the managers were Negro League legends Oscar Charleston and Buck O'Neil. Charleston appeared in the first three East-West games and was elected to the Hall of Fame in 1976. Just how good was Oscar Charleston? Here is Honus Wagner's assessment:

"Oscar Charleston could have played on any big-league team in history if he had been given the opportunity. He could hit, run, and throw. He could do everything a great outfielder was supposed to do. I've seen all the great players in the many years I've been around, and yet to see anyone greater than Oscar Charleston."[22]

Buck O'Neil played in three East-West Games at Comiskey Park and first managed the West in 1950. He managed in five games and was introduced to a new generation of fans when Ken Burns' *Baseball* aired in 1994.

Francisco "Pancho" Herrera's seventh-inning homer was the big blow, breaking the game open as the West won its fourth game in succession, 8-4. Herrera made it to the majors, starting with the Phillies.

John Kennedy played shortstop for the West team. He was named to the team in 1955 but did not play. In 1957 he broke the color barrier with the Philadelphia Phillies, playing in five games. He was the second player of color and first African-American to play for the Phillies.

"Do you mean to tell me that old string bean can still throw good enough to pitch in a big game like that?"
— Casey Stengel, 1955.[23]

Satchel Paige first appeared in the East-West Game at Comiskey Park in 1934, hurling four shutout innings in relief for the win. After he closed out the 10-2 East win in 1936, his travels took him far and wide. He did not return to the event until 1941. He appeared in 1942 and 1943 as well, before sitting out the 1944 game. In 1955 he signed on with his former team, the Kansas City Monarchs. In the East-West Game, Paige pitched the first three innings and allowed no hits. The West defeated the East 2-0 with two seventh-inning runs.

J.C. Hartman was only 21 when he took over at shortstop in 1955. He was signed by the Cubs the next year. After a stint in the Army, he spent three years in the Cubs organization before being drafted by Houston. Midway through the 1962 season, he joined the Colt .45's.

In 1959, the West's starting pitcher was Willie Smith. In the game on August 9, won by the West 8-7 in 11 innings, Smith had a three-run inside-the-park homer. "Wonderful" Willie Smith was sold to the Detroit Tigers in 1960 and made it to the majors, as an outfielder, in 1963. In nine major-league seasons, he batted .248 with 46 homers and 211 RBIs.

The 1960 game was the last hurrah at Comiskey Park. The West won 8-4. It was the 18th win for the West in 28 games.

The National Baseball Hall of Fame began honoring sportswriters with the J.G. Taylor Spink Award in 1962. In 1993 it got around to honoring Wendell Smith. Two years later, they honored Sam Lacy of the *Chicago Defender*.

SOURCES

In addition to the sources cited in the Notes, the author used Baseball-Reference.com, and was especially fortunate to have discovered accounts of the East-West Games in the Bullpen section of Baseball-Reference.com. He also accessed Newspapers.com, the **Chicago Tribune**, and the following:

Einstein, Charles. "Major League Scouts Will Swarm on Negro Star Tilt," **Miami News**, July 23, 1947: 13.

Lester, Larry. **Black Baseball's National Showcase: The East-West All-Star Game, 1933-1953**, (Lincoln: University of Nebraska Press, 2001).

Washington, Chester L. Jr. "Sez Chez: East WILL Meet West," **Pittsburgh Courier**, August 20, 1938: 16.

NOTES

1. Wendell Smith, "Dream Game Is the No. 1 Sports Attraction," **Pittsburgh Courier**, August 13, 1949: 22.

2. William G. Nunn, "'Don't Kill the Goose that Lays the Golden Egg,' Nunn Warns Moguls; Lauds Game's Stars," **Pittsburgh Courier**, August 14, 1937: 16.

3. Wendell Smith, "The East-West Game Reaches Maturity," **Pittsburgh Courier**, August 15, 1953: 14.

4. Smith, "Dream Game Is the No. 1 Sports Attraction."

5. "Why the East-West Game Is Played in Chicago This Year," **Kansas Whip** (Topeka), August 21, 1936: 7.

6. Lloyd Lewis, "Lloyd Lewis Says Negro Baseball Is Faster Than That Shown in Majors," **Pittsburgh Courier**, August 27, 1938: 1, 4 (Originally appeared in the **Chicago Daily News** on August 22, 1938).

7. Chester L. Washington Jr., "'Dream' Teams Set for Classic," **Pittsburgh Courier**, August 5, 1939: 1, 17.

8. "East's Colored All-Stars Beat West, 12-0," **Chicago Tribune**, August 19, 1940: 21.

9. Nunn, "East Crushes West Before Record Throng, 8-3: East Batters Radcliffe in Fourth to Win Ninth 'Dream Game' Before 47,865 in Chicago," **Pittsburgh Courier**, August 2, 1941: 17.

10. Smith, "West Bows to East Before 48,000 Fans, 5-2," **Pittsburgh Courier**, August 22, 1942: 16.

11. Smith, "West Bombs East in 'Dream Game,' 7 to 4," **Pittsburgh Courier**, August 19, 1944: 12.

12. United Press, "Paige to Lead Strike if Game Isn't Benefit," **Cleveland Plain Dealer**, August 2, 1944: 12.

13 Neil Lanctot, **Negro League Baseball: The Rise and Ruin of a Black Institution** (Philadelphia: University of Pennsylvania Press, 2004), 189.

14 "Assemblyman Asks Brooklyn to Hire Negro Ballplayers," **Pittsburgh Courier**, July 21, 1945: 12.

15 Edward Prell, "West's Negro All-Stars Win 3d in Row, 9-6," **Chicago Tribune**, July 30, 1945: 17-18.

16 Neil Lanctot, **Campy: The Two Lives of Roy Campanella** (New York: Simon and Schuster, 2011), 129.

17 "45,474 Fans See West Wallop East, 4-to-1," **Pittsburgh Courier**, August 24, 1946: 16.

18 "Chandler to Throw Out First Ball at Negro Baseball Game," **Chicago Tribune**, August 6, 1949, Part 2: 4.

19 "Dream Classic Set for Chi, August 17," **Pittsburgh Courier**, July 26, 1952: 16.

20 "Negro All-Stars Ready," **Hammond Times** (Munster, Indiana), August 15, 1952: 18.

21 Frederick C. Bush, "Lloyd 'Pepper' Bassett," in **Bittersweet Goodbye: The Black Barons, the Grays, and the 1948 Negro League World Series** (Phoenix: Society for American Baseball Research, 2017), 7-11.

22 Smith, "Sports Beat," **Pittsburgh Courier**, August 21, 1954: 22.

23 Smith, "Sports Beat," **Pittsburgh Courier**, July 30, 1955: 12.

THE "BASEBALL PALACE OF THE WORLD" OPENS

JULY 1, 1910
ST. LOUIS BROWNS 2, CHICAGO WHITE SOX 0

By Bob LeMoine

On a sweltering summer afternoon on July 1, 1910, the ballpark that would one day be known as Comiskey Park hosted its first official game. At the time, the ballpark was known as White Sox Park. The Chicago White Sox would play 6,247 major-league games there before it closed on September 30, 1990. Charles Comiskey, the White Sox owner, was hailed by I. E. Sanborn of the *Chicago Tribune* as the "noblest Roman of them all" and as the architect of the "greatest baseball plant in the world" which "combines every perfection of its predecessors in other cities and in which no expense has been spared to remove all imperfections of other plants of similar nature."[1] Officially, 24,900 paid spectators came to see this opening extravaganza, but two Chicago newspapers agreed that the number was in reality closer to 30,000 than 25,000, with the entire musical accompaniment. And it probably seemed as if the entire city had been there that day, yet the mammoth ballpark still appeared to have room for more as the "great stands smilingly held out their bunting clad arms and gathered them all into their capricious laps without crowding anywhere," wrote Sanborn.[2]

The stadium was a remarkable feat, considering that it was assembled in just four months, minus the five weeks of stalled labor because of a steelworkers strike. The huge electrical scoreboard was still being completed just days before the game, and painters were still busy right up to game time. "Electricians have already have strung their wires from the press stand to the working devices on the board," the *Tribune* reported.[3] That new press box was located in the front of the second deck behind home plate. Home plate was new, but the flagpole from South Side Park was unearthed and placed in the northwest corner of the field.[4]

The grandstand and pavilion entrances were at 35th and Shields Avenue, where you could pass through one of the 14 turnstiles on your way to your 50-cent, 75-cent, or $1 seat. The 25-cent seats had an entrance on 34th and Shields, and the 50-cent seats in the third- and first-base pavilions had separate entrances. Reserved seating in the upper deck and box seats were 75 cents.[5] If you were one of the few fans with an automobile, you entered at 33rd and Shields. At 1 P.M. on July 1, 1910, the gates of the sparkling new ballpark were opened for the first time, and more than 1,000 eager fans rushed in to be the first to experience the new structure. As they dashed in, they passed departing construction workers who had been working right up to the last minute.[6]

The inaugural crowd was treated to the playing of "My Country 'Tis of Thee," "Has Anybody Here Seen Kelly?" and "Cheer! Cheer! The Gang's All Here" by five different bands. The Chicago Automobile Club led a parade of streamer- and banner-bedecked automobiles that made their way to the park.[7] A floral display of bats and a ball were placed on the field with white socks hanging beneath.

THE BASE BALL PALACE OF THE WORLD

At 3 P.M. Comiskey marched to home plate to thunderous applause and Mayor Fred A. Busse presented him with a purple banner that read, "The City of Chicago Congratulates Comiskey." American League President Ban Johnson and August "Garry" Herrmann, owner of the Cincinnati Reds and chairman of the National Commission, were also present at home plate. The American flag was raised, and the band played "The Star Spangled Banner." "Out across the mighty field in the great grand stand and in the pavilions and in the sun bleachers the 30,000 devotees of the national sport roared and shouted and screamed and sang in unison with that piece the band was playing," wrote Harry Daniel of Chicago's *Inter-Ocean*.[8]

The temperature at game time was officially 92 degrees, but the unofficial thermometers on the street hit 96. Ten people died of heat-related causes in Chicago that day.[9]

The White Sox emerged in new uniforms of dazzling white and blue trim. Chicago had on the mound Big Ed Walsh, one of the Deadball Era's greatest pitchers and a future Hall of Famer. (His 1.82 career ERA still ranks number one all-time.[10]) Going into the 1910 season, Walsh was 110-63 with a 1.68 ERA, and in 1908 he led the league in many pitching categories. Billy Sullivan made his first start of the season as catcher. The veteran Sullivan had been recovering after stepping on a rusty nail in spring training and nearly losing his leg when a quack physician recommended that he receive a nearly lethal dose of turpentine. The "grand little backstop" received tremendous ovations throughout the day.[11]

The Browns sent veteran Barney Pelty to the mound. Pelty, who would spend nine years of his 10-year major-league career with the Browns, was 11-11 with a 2.30 ERA in 1909. Tommy Connolly umpired behind the plate while Bill Dinneen handled the field.

The Browns' George Stone, known for his small crouch at the plate, led off with a double to left, the first hit in Comiskey Park history, and Roy Hartzell sacrificed him to third. Bobby Wallace grounded to second baseman Rollie Zeider, who threw home. Stone was tagged out in a rundown. During the rundown, Wallace took off for second but was beaten by a strong throw by Sullivan.

The clubs remained scoreless until St. Louis scored both of its runs in the third inning. Frank Truesdale reached when third baseman Billy Purtell could only deflect his scorching grounder. Purtell had to decide to "let it go by or lose a hand. Billy decided to keep the hand," Harry Daniel wrote.[12] Truesdale stole second and made his way to third on a groundout. Stone smashed Walsh's first pitch for a single along the left-field line, scoring Truesdale with the first run in the park's history. The new turf was troublesome for Patsy Doherty in left, as he "slipped and slid around like a man who is afraid to go home in the dark," wrote Daniel. Doherty finally threw the ball in as Stone dug for second. He slid hard, spiking Zeider's hand, knocking the ball free and forcing the rookie second baseman to leave the game, replaced by Charlie French. (Zeider would miss a couple of weeks.) Hartzell walked and Stone scored when Sullivan attempted to pick off Hartzell but threw "over [Chick] Gandil's upstretched anatomy."[13] Hartzell tried for third on the play but was thrown out by Shano Collins.

The Browns tried to tack on more runs in the fourth against Walsh. Bobby Wallace singled to right and scampered to third on Pat Newnam's hit. Walsh came back, striking out Al Schweitzer and Danny Hoffman. Wallace was nabbed at the plate in an attempted double steal with Newnam, and an opportunity was wasted.

Chicago had more problems with the new turf as Sullivan "fell headlong over some new laid sod" that snagged his spikes while he was attempting to corral a foul popup.[14] The tough-luck catcher avoided serious injury, but the same couldn't be said for the battered sod, which the *Chicago Examiner* said was the size of a washtub.[15]

In the fifth, Chicago's George Brown brought the crowd to its feet with a spectacular diving catch. "It is too bad for Browne that high dives do not figure in the percentage column," wrote

Daniel.[16] He was a century too early, it seems.

Pelty had allowed Chicago only two singles through six innings, both by rookie Lena "Bearcat" Blackburne, the first two Chicago hits in the history of Comiskey Park. The crowd finally had something to cheer about when Doherty slammed a triple to deep right. But Gandil was retired on a roller in front of the plate and the eager Doherty was thrown out at the plate when he tried to score on a "skimpy infield hit" by Purtell. "That was about as dangerous as those White Sox ever got on the first day in their new park," Daniel commented.[17]

Stone led off with a triple to right in the ninth, but Hartzell flied to Browne, and Stone had to hold at third. Wallace struck out, and when Stone tried to sneak home on a passed ball, he was thrown out, ending the game.

Pelty finished the game for the Browns, striking out three of his total five in the last two innings, scattering only five hits as he spoiled the White Sox' new home opener, 2-0. Walsh struck out six and allowed seven hits, with Stone (single, double, and triple, run, RBI) being the hitting star of the game.

Comiskey invited several of the out-of-town guests already mentioned, as well as Chicago baseball legends Cap Anson and Frank Isbell, to a banquet at the Chicago Automobile Club that evening.

"The game was distinctly not the thing yesterday," quipped the *Tribune*. As Sanborn appropriately wrote, it was "Charles A. Comiskey's big housewarming party."[18]

SOURCES

In addition to the sources cited in the Notes, the author consulted the following:

Baseball-Reference.com.

Dryden, Charles. "Sox Open New Park With 2-0 Defeat by Browns Before 30,000," **Chicago Examiner**, July 2, 1910: 10.

Retrosheet.org.

NOTES

1 I.E. Sanborn, "Commy to Greet Sox Fans Today," **Chicago Tribune**, July 1, 1910: 12.

2 I.E. Sanborn, "Big Army of Fans Greets 'Commy,'" **Chicago Tribune**, July 2, 1910: 10.

3 "New Park Awaits Fans' Onslaught," **Chicago Tribune**, June 30, 1910: 12.

4 Ibid.

5 "Commy to Greet."

6 "Big Army of Fans."

7 Ibid.

8 Harry Daniel, "30,000 Hail Sox in Modern Arena; Browns Win, 2-0," **Chicago Inter-Ocean**, July 2, 1910: 13.

9 "Ten Die of Heat as City as City Sizzles," **Chicago Tribune**, July 2, 1910: 1.

10 With a minimum of 1,000 innings pitched.

11 Trey Strecker, "Billy Sullivan Sr.," SABR BioProject. sabr.org/bioproj/person/d0d341b0 Retrieved November 22, 2017.

12 Daniel.

13 Ibid.

14 Ibid.

15 "Notes of the Sox," **Chicago Examiner**, July 2, 1910: 10.

16 Daniel.

17 Ibid.

18 "Big Army of Fans."

AN EXTRA-INNING SCORELESS PITCHERS' DUEL FOR THE AGES: COOMBS AND WALSH

AUGUST 4, 1910
PHILADELPHIA ATHLETICS 0, CHICAGO WHITE SOX 0
(16 INNINGS)

By Gregory H. Wolf

It was an epic pitchers' duel between the Philadelphia Athletics' Jack Coombs and the Chicago White Sox' Big Ed Walsh. "Sixteen scoreless innings of desperate pastiming with dusk the winner,"[1] declared the *Philadelphia Inquirer*, while the *Chicago Tribune* opined, "[N]either side had the shadow of a right to win against such pitching."[2] Windy City sportswriter Fred J. Hewitt of the *Inter Ocean* wrote that "One got powerfully tired of eyeing those ciphers as they crept along on two continuously growing lines on the top of the scoreboard."[3]

Skipper Hugh Duffy's Pale Hose squad was reeling as they prepared to conclude a four-game series with the AL-leading A's as part of a five-team, 20-game homestand in White Sox Park, inaugurated just five weeks earlier, on July 1, and immediately advertised as the Base Ball Palace of the World. The White Sox had lost 23 of their last 29 games to fall to 36-57 and land in seventh place, 26 games off the A's pace. Connie Mack, the owner-skipper of the A's, was none too pleased about his club's recent performance despite its first-place position (62-31) and 5½-game lead over the Boston Red Sox. The A's had won only seven of their last 15 games, with one tie.

Toeing the rubber for the White Sox was Ed Walsh, a 29-year-old right-hander and one of the most durable and best hurlers in baseball. Two years earlier, he had won a big-league-most 40 games, entered the season with a 110-63 slate, and had thrice paced the circuit in shutouts, which accounted for his minuscule 1.68 career ERA. Big Ed's 11-15 slate thus far in '10 reflected the sorry state of his team, not his pitching, as he went on to lead the majors with a 1.27 ERA despite 20 losses. Mack countered with Coombs, a 27-year-old righty who was emerging as the most dominant pitcher in baseball, at least for one season, and was making his 12th start in the last 35 days. Colby Jack (so named for his pitching success at Colby College in Maine) was one of the reasons the Mackmen were in first place. On the heels of a mediocre 35-35 slate in his first four seasons, Coombs boasted a 17-6 record and had registered shutouts in four of his last seven starts.

On a warm Thursday afternoon, 5,100 spectators settled in White Sox Park, located at the intersection of 35th Street and Shields Avenue on Chicago's South Side, for a 3:30 start time. [The ballpark was renamed Comiskey Park, after the owner Charles Comiskey, for the start of the 1913 season.] Their first chance to cheer probably occurred when Patsy Dougherty led off the second with a double. It was the White Sox' first hit — and last until the 12th inning. Possessing what Hewitt described as a "deceiving selection of baseball curveatures," Coombs whiffed two of the next three batters and had six punchouts through three innings.[4] The White Sox' best scoring chance for the game came when Coombs walked Freddy Parent and hit Paul Meloan to begin the fourth. After fanning Dougherty, Coombs uncorked a wild pitch, enabling both runners to advance. Lee Tannehill hit a hard grounder to second baseman Eddie Collins, who threw home to catcher Paddy Livingston. In a costly baserunning blunder, the runners had already committed; as Parent raced back to third, he met Meloan. Livingston, meanwhile, had thrown to Home Run Baker, who tagged both runners; Meloan was ruled out. The inning ended a few moments later when Tannehill was thrown out at second on a delayed double steal. Through nine innings, Coombs had fanned 12, marking the first time in his career he had reached double-digit strikeouts in a game, and he was far from finished.

While Coombs mowed down the White Sox, Walsh's spitter was "working to perfection," gushed Hewitt, mesmerizing the Mackmen.[5] Two defensive miscues put pressure on Big Ed in the seventh. After second baseman Charlie French juggled Eddie Collins's grounder, Walsh threw Baker's bunt attempt into center field. Harry Davis moved both runners a station on a sacrifice bunt. Danny Murphy followed with a single to right field which "[p]robably would have settled it if Ed Collins had known it was going to fall safe," reported the *Tribune*.[6] Meloan fielded the ball on one hop and his throw held Collins at third. Walsh, keeping "infernally busy" (according to the *Inter Ocean*), retired to the next two batters.[7]

The crowd got a laugh in the 11th when a dog jumped from the grandstand and delayed the game for five minutes until "heroic work by Donahue finally resulted in his banishment," reported the *Tribune*.[8] For the second time in three innings, the A's Home Run Baker reached second base, where he was stranded.

After holding the White Sox hitless for 10⅓ innings, Coombs yielded a one-out single to Meloan in the 12th. The robust 6-foot, 190-pound hurler "seemed to be groggy," opined the *Tribune*, "and was walking around out there as if he knew not what was expected of him."[9] After Dougherty's single, Baker scooped up Tannehill's grounder at third to initiate an inning-ending twin killing.

While the *Tribune* lamented that the "pressbox supply of cigarettes ran out" in the 13th inning, both hurlers traded punches like heavyweight boxers Jack Johnson and James L. Jeffries in their championship bout a month earlier in Reno, Nevada.[10] As overpowering as Coombs was, the A's defensive wizardry was the unsung key of the game. In the 13th, Eddie Collins saved his hurler when he snared Billy Sullivan's sharp liner and doubled Billy Purtell off second to end the frame. Collins had a repeat performance two innings later with Meloan and Tannehill on base via Coombs' fifth and sixth free passes of the game. Collins caught Purtell's liner and doubled Tannehill off first to end the inning.

Remarkably durable, Walsh was back on the mound to start the 16th. It was the seventh time in 25 starts thus far in '10 that Big Ed had hurled at least 10 innings, including two 15-inning and one 14-inning victories. With dusk arriving, Walsh led off the fateful last frame with his third and final walk, to Rube Oldring. Collins followed with what seemed to be a routine double-play grounder, but Walsh's throw sailed into second base, putting runners on the corners with no outs. The future Hall of Famer extracted himself by inducing two infield foul outs and a grounder.

As Jimmy Dygert warmed up in the bullpen, Coombs was back on the mound in the 16th, just the fourth time in his career that he had pitched at least 10 innings in a game. It was "so dark that hitting was more or less a matter of guess work," opined the *Tribune*, as home-plate umpire Bill Dinneen announced that the game would be over after this frame no matter what. Catching a second wind, Coombs unleashed a torrent of fastballs, which the *Tribune* claimed looked like "polka dots in the [catcher's] glove"[11] and, according to the *Inquirer*, "fast breaking curves, balls which whistled through the gloaming at tantalizing speed."[12] In overpowering fashion, Coombs whiffed Charlie Mullen, Sullivan, and Walsh in succession to end the game in a 0-0 tie after 3 hours and 28 minutes to the disbelief of the few remaining spectators.

In their remarkable pitchers' duel, Coombs and Walsh pitched arguably the best games of their careers, and certainly the longest. Walsh faced 60 batters, surrendered just six hits, and fanned 10. In his three-hitter while facing 54 batters, Coombs set a major-league record with 18 strikeouts, including French and Walsh four times each.

Neither pitcher slowed down after their epic match. Three days later, Walsh tossed a two-hit shutout against the Washington Senators and fanned 10. On August 11, he blanked the Boston Red Sox on three hits and tied his career high with 15 punchouts. He finished the season with a misleading 18-20 record and led the AL in losses.

Combs was in one of the best stretches in baseball history. Three days later he blanked the St. Louis Browns on five hits at Sportsman's Park. From July 1 through the end of the season, he went 24-5, including 10 straight wins, completed 25 of 27 starts, and tossed 12 shutouts, including four straight in September as part of a then-record 53 consecutive scoreless innings. He capped off his 31-9 season by tossing three consecutive complete-game victories against the Chicago Cubs in the World Series, giving Connie Mack his first of five championships.

SOURCES

In addition to the sources cited in the Notes, the author also accessed Retrosheet.org, Baseball-Reference.com, SABR.org, and **The Sporting News** archive via Paper of Record.

NOTES

1 "Coombs Hurls Wonderful Ball Against White Sox," **Philadelphia Inquirer**, August 5, 1910: 10.

2 "Sox Tie Macks in 16 Innings, 0 to 0," **Chicago Tribune**, August 5, 1910: 8.

3 Fred J. Hewitt, "Sox and Athletics Go Sixteen Innings and Nary a Score," (Chicago) **Inter Ocean**, August 5, 1910: 5.

4 Hewitt.

5 Ibid.

6 "Sox Tie Macks in 16 Innings, 0 to 0."

7 Hewitt.

8 "Sox Tie Macks in 16 Innings, 0 to 0." Hewitt in the **Inter Ocean** reported that the incident happened in the ninth inning.

9 "Sox Tie Macks in 16 Innings, 0 to 0."

10 Ibid.

11 Ibid.

12 "Coombs Hurls Wonderful Ball Against White Sox."

BIG ED WALSH SLOBBERBALLS HIS WAY TO NO-HITTER

AUGUST 27, 1911
CHICAGO WHITE SOX 5, BOSTON RED SOX 1

By Gregory H. Wolf

The Chicago White Sox right-hander Big Ed Walsh "slobber-balled along," gushed Windy City sportswriter Henry David, "his flow of expectoration kept up round after round."[1] Beat reporter I.E. Sanborn of the *Tribune* was equally excited about the hurler's wet ones, declaring that Walsh pitched "steadily, deliberately, and carefully with his spitball breaking wonderfully."[2]

Big Ed had accomplished almost everything on the diamond when he took the mound at White Sox Park on the last Saturday afternoon in August 1911. [The ballpark was renamed Comiskey Park, after the team's owner and founder, Charles Comiskey, for the 1913 season]. Sportswriter Fred J. Hewitt of the *Inter Ocean* declared that Walsh "is one of those carefully developed instruments that has been good for years and never loses class."[3] Few could disagree. Considered among the best and most durable hurlers of his generation, the 30-year-old Pennsylvanian boasted a 23-14 record, which pushed his career slate to 151-97 in parts of eight seasons. Three years earlier, Walsh had won 40 games (the last big leaguer to win that many) while completing 42 starts, tossing 11 shutouts, and logging a staggering 464 innings. Among baseball's hardest throwers, he also led that majors that season with 269 strikeouts, and had twice punched out 15 batters in his career. He had three one-hitters to his credit, the last of which came just 12 days before his fateful start against the Red Sox, when he added the final notch in his eventual Hall of Fame résumé: his first and only no-hitter.

The "Base Ball Palace of the World" drew a robust crowd of 18,000 fans to the intersection of 35th Street and Shields Avenue on Chicago's South Side for the first contest of a three-game series between the White Sox and Red Sox. Skipper Hugh Duffy's fifth-place Pale Hose (59-59) were in the midst of a six-team, 21-game homestand that the former Boston Braves outfielder hoped would catapult his club into the first division. Pilot Patsy Donovan's Red Sox (61-56) were in third place, trailing the front-running Philadelphia Athletics by 15½ games.

The Chicagoans wasted little time taking their whacks against 24-year-old southpaw Ray Collins, who, according to Hewitt, did not appear to be the intended starter.[4] Smoky Joe Wood, the brilliant 21-year-old phenom who had won his 20th game in a start against the St. Louis Browns three days earlier, had been warming up in the bullpen. He was replaced shortly before the 3 P.M. start time by Collins (9-9), a trusty hurler in his own right, coming off a season in which he posted a minuscule 1.62 ERA. Perhaps Collins was not yet adequately loose and lathered up, because the White Sox "pounded him hard enough to have driven any one [*sic*] else to the woods," opined Sanborn in the *Tribune*.[5] Matty McIntyre led off with a triple and scored two batters later when former pitcher and two-time 20-game winner-turned-outfielder Nixey

Hall of Famer Big Ed Walsh (left), shown with skipper Jimmy Callahan and coach Kid Gleason, had an awe-inspiring six-year run (1907-1912) during which he averaged 25 wins, 33 complete games, and 375 innings pitched with a 1.69 ERA. (Photo by Mark Rucker/Transcendental Graphics, Getty Images)

Callahan, playing in his first game in 10 days after a severe case of the boils,[6] caught everyone off guard with a bunt. All infielders charged and first baseman Clyde Engle fielded the ball cleanly, but no one covered first, reported the *Tribune*.[7] After Ping Bodie singled, Amby McConnell cracked a double to right field, scoring Callahan. While Bodie stopped on third, McConnell overran second, but when shortstop Steve Yerkes muffed the relay throw, Bodie scampered home for the third run, according to the *Tribune*.[8] [No error was given on this play.]

A serious outfield collision interrupted the game for several minutes in the bottom of the third and sent the crowd into a collective gasp. With two outs, Lee Tannehill smacked a fly to deep right-center field. As Tris Speaker caught the ball, Danish-born rookie Olaf Henriksen, making just his 12th start in right field, barreled into him. A "terrific impact jarred the ball out of Speaker's hands," reported the *Tribune*, as both players crashed violently to the ground.[9] Second baseman Heinie Wagner sprinted to the orb and heaved it back to the infield and time was quickly called. As both Speaker and Henriksen lay momentarily unconscious, players from both benches rushed to them. The *Boston Globe* suggested that the impact was so vicious, it appeared to be fatal for Henriksen, who was carried off the field.[10] Both players were replaced. [Henriksen was ultimately diagnosed with a wrenched shoulder and bruised stomach and missed a week; Speaker was back in action the next day.] The Red Sox were gifted an out when the next batter, Charlie Mullen, hit a screaming grounder off third baseman Larry Gardner's arm into Yerkes's mitt for an easier throw to first.[11]

The Pale Hose tacked on two more late-game runs. Bodie's single plated Walsh in the seventh while Bruno Block's single drove in Lee Tannehill, who had led off the eighth with a double. Collins went the distance, serving up 11 safeties.

Given a first-inning lead, Walsh toyed with the Red Sox all afternoon. The Donovans batted .275 as a team in 1911 (fourth best in the AL), but had no answer for Big Ed's spitter, heater, and occasional curve. Walsh's only blemish was a fourth-inning walk to Engle.

The outfield scoreboard tracked only the score, not hits, and word gradually spread around the ballpark that Walsh was working on a no-hitter. By the eighth inning, reported the *Tribune*, the White Sox faithful were "rooting for

[Walsh] madly as if a world's pennant depended on his right arm."[12] After Walsh fanned Gardner, Bill Carrigan "almost broke up the party," opined Sanborn, when his grounder sped over the pitcher's mound.[13] In the defensive highlight of the game, shortstop Tannehill scooped up the ball behind second base and in one motion threw it to Mullen at first, beating the runner by "half an inch."[14] Mullen ended the frame by fielding Wagner's weak roller.

As the crowd stood for every pitch, Walsh began the ninth by retiring Yerkes on a meek grounder, then punched out rookie Les Nunamaker, pinch-hitting for Collins. Joe Riggert, who had replaced Henriksen in right field, hit an infield chopper that "looked a hit for sure," asserted Sanborn, perhaps with some dramatic exaggeration.[15] McConnell fielded it easily on the hop and fired to Mullen to end the game in 1 hour and 50 minutes. Walsh "seemed to do it with so little effort," declared scribe Henry David, noting the hurler needed only five pitches (three spitters) to retire the side in the ninth.[16]

As teammates rushed to congratulate Walsh for his no-hitter, hundreds of fans poured onto the field. The *Inter Ocean* reported that a throng of 1,000 fans greeted Walsh, then in street clothes, after the game.[17]

Walsh struck out eight and faced 28 batters en route to tossing the first no-hitter in Comiskey Park, and the fourth in franchise history. Nixey Callahan tossed the first, in 1902, at South Side Park, where the White Sox played from their inaugural season in 1901 through June 27, 1910. Frank Smith authored a pair, the first in Detroit's Bennett Park in 1905 and the latter in South Side Park in 1908. By the time Comiskey Park closed after the 1990 season, five more Pale Hose hurlers had added their names to the list of no-hit-game hurlers: Joe Benz (1914), Vern Kennedy (1935), Bill Dietrich (1937), Bob Keegan (1957), and Joe Horlen (1967).

Walsh continued his dominant pitching through the end of the season despite playing for a mediocre fourth-place team (77-74). Big Ed finished with 27 wins (one fewer than Jack Coombs, who hurled for the 101-50, world-champion Athletics), completed more games (33) than anyone in baseball except Walter Johnson, and led all big-league pitchers with 56 appearances (37 starts), innings (368⅔), and strikeouts (255) to finish runner-up to the Detroit Tigers' Ty Cobb for AL MVP.

SOURCES

In addition to the sources cited in the Notes, the author also accessed Retrosheet.org, Baseball-Reference.com, Newspapers.com, and SABR.org.

NOTES

1 Henry David, "Wild-Eyed South Side Fans, Overflowing With Happiness at Wondrous Work of Spitball King, Almost Lynch Him on the Spot," (Chicago) **Inter Ocean**, August 28, 1911: 5.

2 I.E. Sanborn, "Walsh in No-Hit Victory; Sox Win," **Chicago Tribune**, August 28, 1911: 9.

3 Fred J. Hewitt, "Walsh Shuts Out Boston Without a Hit or Run, Sox Winning Game, 5-0," (Chicago) **Inter Ocean**, August 28, 1911: 5.

4 Ibid.

5 Sanborn.

6 David.

7 "Sox Sydelights," **Chicago Tribune**, August 28, 1911: 9.

8 Sanborn.

9 Ibid.

10 "Red Sox Blanked Without a Hit," **Boston Globe**, August 28, 1911: 5.

11 "Sox Sydelights."

12 Sanborn.

13 Ibid.

14 Ibid.

15 Ibid.

16 David.

17 Ibid.

BENZ WAS HUMMING ON ALL CYLINDERS

MAY 31, 1914
CHICAGO WHITE SOX 6, CLEVELAND NAPS 0

By Gregory H. Wolf

The Chicago White Sox were happy to be back at home for a Sunday matinee at Comiskey Park, their four-year old stadium, dubbed the "Base Ball Palace of the World," located at the intersection of 35th Street and Shields Avenue on the South Side of the Windy City. The Pale Hose had just completed a 16-game road trip and had played 28 of their last 32 contests on opponents' turf. Skipper Jimmy Callahan's seventh-place squad (17-22) had little time to unpack their bags, however, as the players had to board a train later that same evening and head to Detroit for a pair before they could get reacclimated to their homes in Chicago on Wednesday.

The White Sox' struggling offense had scored two runs or less in six of their last seven games, leading the sportswriter I. E. Sanborn of the *Tribune* to quip that the club was "proving [its] claim to the world's championship in 'The Science of How Not to Make Runs.'"[1] Callahan hoped his team's luck would change against the cellar-dwelling Cleveland Naps (13-24), with whom they had split a twin bill the previous day and had traveled by Pullman coach from the metropolis on Lake Erie.

Toeing the rubber for the White Sox was 28-year-old right-hander Joe Benz, whose nicknames "The Butcher" and "Butcher Boy" derived not from his penchant to toss high and inside, but rather from his German immigrant family's meat-cutting business. A spitballer and occasional knuckler, Benz had an undistinguished 23-29 slate in his first three campaigns, but seemed to emerge from the shadows of teammates Eddie Cicotte, Reb Russell, and Jim Scott, early in the 1914 campaign. His 4-5 record was offset by the league's third best ERA (1.14). Naps skipper Joe Birmingham sent 21-year-old rookie Abe Bowman to the mound for his first career start and third appearance.

The Second City was the center of big-league baseball on the last Sunday of May. While an estimated 10,000 spectators enjoyed the sun and temperatures in the mid-80s at Comiskey Park, 6,000 were at Weeghman Park (later known as Wrigley Field) for a matchup between the Indianapolis Hoosiers and Chicago Chi-Feds in the inaugural season of the Federal League, while approximately 2,500 spectators were on hand at West Side Grounds, the home park of the Chicago Cubs, as they played the St. Louis Cardinals.[2]

After Benz cruised through a one-two-three first, barely having to shift gears, "the Callahans hammered Bowman," gushed Sanborn.[3] Gradually emerging from a season-long slump, Buck Weaver whacked Bowman's first pitch to right field for a single. Hal Chase hit a tailor-made double-play grounder to second baseman Nap Lajoie (the team's longtime star after whom it derived its moniker), but shortstop Rivington Bisland muffed the throw and both runners were safe. Bowman helped his own cause by fielding Ray Demmitt's tapper back to the mound and initiating a 1-5-3 twin killing. Shano Collins's double plated Chase for the game's first run.

The White Sox added two more tallies in the third. With two outs and Chase on second via a walk and stolen base as part of a double steal with Weaver (who was thrown out), Demmitt lined to left, but Jack Graney made an ill-advised throw to home plate. As Chase easily scored, the ball hit him in the back and caromed so far away that Demmitt reached third base. Collins drew a free pass, then attempted a daring delayed double steal. Catcher Steve O'Neill's throw to Bisland was late, and then Bisland's return heave flew over O'Neill's head while Demmitt slid across the bag.

Prior to this game, there had been 69 no-hitters in major-league baseball since the founding of the NL in 1876. In 11 of those games, the team that was held hitless scored at least one run. This game increased those totals by one, but Benz was free from blame. Roy Wood led off the fourth with a bounder over Benz's head; shortstop Buck Weaver scoped up the ball, but threw errantly over Chase, enabling Wood to reach second. Weaver seemingly atoned for his miscue by fielding Bisland's grounder and firing a strike to third baseman Scotty Alcock to nab a sliding Wood, but Alcock muffed the catch. According to the *Tribune*, "the whole outfit looked groggy" with defensive lapses; consequently, Callahan sent Russell to the bullpen to warm up quickly before things got out of hand.[4] Described by Sanborn as a "dazzling electrical display — code for lightning double play," keystone sacker Joe Berger fielded Graney's grounder, tagged Bisland on his way to second, and then fired to Chase, while Wood crossed the plate to put the Naps on the board. But the White Sox were not yet out of the woods. Shoeless Joe Jackson, entering the game in a 7-for-36 slump to drop his average from .379 to .331, hit a routine grounder to Berger, who dropped the ball, then fired wildly to Chase for the White Sox' third error of the frame.[5] Benz dispatched Turner to end the shenanigan-filled inning.

The Calls, as the *Tribune* called the White Sox, tacked on three more runs in the seventh off right-hander Fred Blanding, who had replaced Bowman to start the fourth. A one-time starter with a 43-43 career record, including

A valuable starter and reliever, Joe Benz played his entire nine-year career with the White Sox (1911-1919), posting a 77-75 record, including a no-hitter, with a 2.43 ERA. (Photo: public domain)

1-6 thus far in '14, Blanding had lost his spot in the rotation earlier in the month. Chase's double drove in Weaver, who had singled for the third time; Demmitt's single plated Chase, and Collins's infield single made it 6-1. The Pale Hose finished the game with 13 hits, their biggest offensive outburst since they collected the same amount and scored nine runs in a victory over the Washington Senators on May 13 in the nation's capital.

Since the fateful fourth, Benz had not allowed a baserunner and had not allowed a semblance of a hit. He walked his first batter, Graney to lead off the seventh, but stranded him on first.

Aware of the possible no-hitter, the Comiskey crowd cheered Benz as he took the mound in the ninth. Known for his excellent control (he walked 2.1 batters per 9 innings in 1914), Benz issued his second free pass, to Wood, with one out in the ninth. With spectators on their feet, Benz challenged Bisland, who grounded weakly to Weaver for a 6-4-3 game-ending double play, made possible only when Chase "hooked" Berger's low and outside throw out of the dirt, according to the *Tribune*.[6]

Benz fashioned the fifth no-hitter in White Sox franchise history, and the second in Comiskey Park following Big Ed Walsh, who held the Boston Red Sox hitless on August 27, 1911. Benz fanned three and faced 29 batters, completing the game in 1 hour and 45 minutes. After settling for a three-hitter in an eight-inning complete-game 1-1 tie with the New York Yankees in his next start, on June 6 at Comiskey Park, Benz came remarkably close to fashioning another no-hitter. In a ferocious pitching duel with Walter Johnson, Benz yielded what the Sanborn of the *Tribune* called a "scratch" single to Eddie Ainsmith to lead off the ninth and finished with a sparkling one-hit shutout.[7] Bill Lamb pointed out in his excellent SABR biography of Benz that many at the park, including AL President Ban Johnson, thought the hit should have been ruled an error.[8] Benz concluded the season for the eventual sixth-place White Sox (70-84) with 15 wins, an AL-most 19 losses, and a 2.26 ERA.

SOURCES

In addition to the sources cited in the Notes, the author also accessed Retrosheet.org, Baseball-Reference.com, SABR.org, and **The Sporting News** archive via Paper of Record.

NOTES

1. I.E. Sanborn, "No Hits Off Benz; Cals Pound Ball; Humble Naps, 6-1," **Chicago Tribune**, June 1, 1914: 13.

2. Attendance totals from "Only 18,500 at Three Games; White Sox Draw 10,000 Fans," **Chicago Tribune**, June 1, 1914: 13.

3. Sanborn, "No Hits Off Benz."

4. "The Break with the Game," **Chicago Tribune**, June 1, 1914: 13.

5. J.M. Waterbury, "Joe Benz Pitches No-Hit Game; Naps Are His Victims," **Detroit Free Press**, June 1, 1914: 8.

6. "Sox Sydelights," **Chicago Tribune**, June 1, 1914: 13.

7. I.E. Sanborn, "Benz Allows One Hit; Defeats Johnson in First Game, 2-0," **Chicago Tribune**, June 11, 1914: 17.

8. Bill Lamb, "Joe Benz," SABR BioProject. sabr.org/bioproj/person/8dc7bc65.

JIM SCOTT TOSSES SHUTOUT IN 68 MINUTES: SHORTEST GAME IN WHITE SOX HISTORY

AUGUST 29, 1915
CHICAGO WHITE SOX 5, PHILADELPHIA ATHLETICS 0

By Richard Riis

The White Sox had good reason to want to get this day's game over with as quickly as possible. The weary team had played eight games over the last six days, with five, including the last four, going into extra innings, as well as back-to-back doubleheaders on August 21 and 22. The 89 innings they'd labored in six days were believed to be a record.[1]

Then, too, there was the weather. A band of cold rain had settled across the upper portion of the country, shortening or washing out four major-league games on the 28th and threatening more contests on the 29th. But it was the last scheduled game at Comiskey Park this season for Connie Mack's Athletics and both hosts and visitors were eager to get the game in before the skies opened up. It had been prearranged that, to permit both clubs to catch eastbound trains, the game would be called, regardless of the score, at 3:00 P.M.[2]

Twenty-one-year-old rookie right-hander Tom Sheehan, with three wins and three losses, was Mack's pick to start for the Athletics. Choosing not to compete financially with the free-spending Federal League, Mack had conducted a fire sale of his best players. The defending league champion A's had collapsed to a last-place club; except for aging second baseman Nap Lajoie, first baseman Stuffy McInnis, and first baseman-outfielder Amos Strunk, Mack's current roster was stocked primarily with rookies, castoffs, and players of less than major-league caliber. A July call-up from Peoria of the Three-I League, Sheehan was one of 24 pitchers to take a start on the mound for the Athletics in 1915.

White Sox owner Charles Comiskey plucked Mack's highest-priced star in the sale, second baseman Eddie Collins. Collins, the previous season's winner of the Chalmers Award as the AL's most valuable player, was purchased in December for a record $50,000.[3] The White Sox picked up a second A's regular, right fielder Eddie Murphy, in mid-season for $11,500. With Murphy leading off and Collins batting third, Chicago had risen from sixth place in 1914 to challenge the formidable Boston Red Sox for the pennant. Nine days before this gray, drizzly Sunday, the White Sox had pulled off another headline-making deal, acquiring outfielder Shoeless Joe Jackson from the Cleveland Indians for pitcher Ed Klepfer, outfielders Braggo Roth and Larry Chappell, and $31,500.[4] Since installing Jackson in center field and at cleanup in the batting order, the White Sox had won 10 of 15, and were in third place, seven games behind the Red Sox.

Some of the credit for Chicago's rise was also owed to their 27-year-old ace, right-hander

Jim Scott, who entered the game with a 20-7 record. If anyone on the White Sox might have been pleased at the prospect of playing in wet weather, it likely would have been Scott, known to sportswriters as "the curve ball wizard of the White Sox,"[5] and "the best curve ball pitcher in baseball,"[6] but to American League hitters as a purveyor of the mudball.[7]

Sources disagree on who introduced the mudball, although many credit Ed Reulbach[8] as far back as 1905; others said Irvin "Kaiser" Wilhelm[9] of the Federal League's Baltimore Terrapins or Jack Ryan of the Pacific Coast League's Los Angeles Angels[10] popularized the pitch after the emery ball was banned following the 1914 season. Scott reportedly adopted the pitch during the White Sox' spring training in Paso Robles, California,[11] in 1915.

In throwing the mudball, Scott would moisten a portion of the surface of the ball — a squirt of tobacco juice in the glove worked quite nicely — then rub a little dirt on the spot. Pitching the ball so that the muddy side remained in the same relative position to the ground as it sailed to the plate, an able practitioner could make the ball break up, down, to either side, or in a combination of any two. Scott's mudball, delivered with his trademark side-arm "clockspring" delivery,[12] had confounded opposing batters all season, and helped Scott compile 20 victories, six by shutout, against seven losses through August 28. His top victims? The lowly Athletics, against whom Scott had won five decisions without loss, two of them by shutout.

Although the mudball was legal (except in the Federal League, where it was banned on August 9, 1915[13]), the pitch had an ugly reputation. "[The mudball] is the most dangerous ball that has ever been introduced in the game," said Doc White, a former major leaguer now pitching for the Vernon Tigers of the Pacific Coast League. "You can't hit it, because it breaks four ways. I don't know who discovered the mudball, but we found out about it through Jim Scott, the White Sox hurler, when the Sox were here on their spring training trip. ... Somebody will get killed. It is far more dangerous than the emery ball because a pitcher can do far more with it. It breaks so fast that it will get some player sooner or later."[14]

Although contemporary accounts fail to comment on whether Scott was relying heavily on the mudball against the Athletics on August 29, it's a fair conclusion that, considering his success with the pitch all year and the conditions under which the game was played, the Athletics saw more than a few sudden drops and swerves at the plate that day. The hapless A's flailed away at Scott's deliveries, managing but three hits, singles by Lajoie and Rube Oldring and a double by Jack Lapp, spaced so far apart as to be "not even second cousins."[15] Scott struck out six and walked one. No Philadelphia baserunner but Lapp reached as far as second base.

The game was effectively over in the White Sox' half of the third inning. Catcher Ray Schalk singled and Scott bunted him to second. Murphy singled to score Schalk, and first sacker Shano Collins followed with another single, putting runners on first and second. Eddie Collins walked, loading the bases, and a long single by Jackson drove Murphy and Shano Collins home. Left fielder Happy Felsch followed with the White Sox' fifth base-hit in the span of seven batters, scoring Eddie Collins and Jackson.

With a five-run lead, the White Sox hustled to get the game in the books. "Every batter took a good healthy swing at nearly everything that could come over the pan and hit it if he could."[16] Sheehan scattered three more hits over the remainder of the game, all singles, and walked three more White Sox, but none figured in any scoring. No Chicago batter struck out, and aside from stolen bases by Murphy and Schalk, there were no accounts of daring play on the basepaths or overt attempts to get another rally going.

When the final out was recorded, the game was officially clocked at 68 minutes.[17] The elapsed time set a major-league record for the shortest regulation nine-inning game,[18] eclipsing a 70-minute contest between St. Louis and Brooklyn on September 29, 1904.[19]

The record would stand but 65 days. On October 4, 1915, the Brooklyn Superbas required only 63 minutes to dispatch the Philadelphia Phillies, 3-2, at Brooklyn.[20]

Today, the major-league record stands at 51 minutes, set by the Giants and Phillies on September 28, 1919. The Brown and Yankees surpassed the White Sox' and Athletics' record for brevity in the AL with a 55-minute game in 1926.

SOURCES

In addition to the sources listed in the notes, the author also consulted:

Atlanta Constitution.

Ithaca (New York) Journal.

Los Angeles Times.

The Sporting News.

Topeka Daily Capital.

NOTES

1. "All Around the Texas League," **Houston Post**, August 29, 1915: 17.

2. "Comiskey Park," **Chicago Tribune**, August 29, 1915: 46.

3. Rick Huhn, **Eddie Collins: A Baseball Biography** (Jefferson, North Carolina: McFarland, 2008), 116.

4. Kelly Boyer Sagert, **Joe Jackson: A Biography** (Westport, Conn.: Greenwood Publishing Group, 2004), 58.

5. "Frank Isbell Sold Jim Scott to the Chicago White Sox," **St. Louis Star and Times**, November 3, 1915: 11.

6. "How the Curve Became Baseball's Greatest Discovery," **Ogden (Utah) Standard**, September 25, 1915: 14.

7. "Scott First to Use Mud Ball," **Salt Lake Telegram**, August 29, 1915, 5.

8. "'Mud Ball' Dances Right Up to Batter," **Philadelphia Evening Public Ledger**, August 11, 1915: 11.

9. "'Mud Ball' Is Banned by Federal League," **Bridgewater (New Jersey) Courier-News**, August 14, 1915: 10.

10. "'Tobacco Ball' Newest from Coast," **Elmira (New York) Star-Gazette**, August 25, 1916: 8.

11. "'Mud Ball' Dances."

12. Jim Scott biography, sabr.org/bioproj/person/c679f80c [accessed March 6, 2018].

13. "Reulbach's 'Mud Ball' Banned by Fed League," **St. Louis Post-Dispatch**, August 9, 1915: 12.

14. "The 'Mud' Ball Controversy," **Sporting Life**, September 11, 1915: 11.

15. Ibid.

16. "Baseball," **The (Chicago) Day Book**, August 30, 1915: 22.

17. Ibid.

18. Ibid.

19. "Superbas Will Soon Be in Last Place," **Brooklyn Daily Eagle**, September 30, 1904: 12.

20. "Phillies on Edge for Start of World Series," **Brooklyn Daily Eagle**, October 5, 1915: 24.

ANOTHER COMISKEY PARK FIRST: THE WORLD SERIES ARRIVES

OCTOBER 6, 1917
CHICAGO WHITE SOX 2, NEW YORK GIANTS 1
GAME ONE OF THE WORLD SERIES

By John Bauer

Oh, how it rained. The day before the first World Series game ever hosted at Comiskey Park, the skies opened. The National League champion New York Giants had hoped for a practice that would have allowed them to acclimate themselves to the quirks of an unfamiliar ballpark. Instead, manager John McGraw kept his team at the hotel. Fans, some of whom had traveled from as far away as Los Angeles, began queuing the night before the game for the bleacher tickets to be placed on sale in the morning. They were soaked. By morning the rain stopped, but the dampness in the air, along with the brisk winds from Lake Michigan, provided the setting for Game One of the 1917 World Series. I.E. Sanborn of the *Chicago Tribune* advised fans accordingly: "Fair warning is given the fans to wear the warmest clothes they have and not be afraid to replace their B.V.D.s, temporarily at least, with something better designed to turn the lake winds from the skin."[1]

As the 2:00 P.M. first pitch approached, a festive atmosphere began to take hold. The fans had filled the stadium to its 32,000-seat capacity an hour before game time. A band provided entertainment.[2] Reflecting the United States' entry into the Great War earlier in 1917, Comiskey Park was adorned with red, white, and blue streamers and the White Sox players wore patriotic-themed stockings. In the crowd were over 1,500 members of the Officers' Reserve Corps from nearby Fort Sheridan, and "their khaki uniforms and sunburned faces supplied a background which contrasted sharply with the civilian gathering."[3] McGraw commented, "It always has been my wish to meet Charley Comiskey's White Sox for the world's title."[4] Comiskey exuded confidence about his club: "They are in perfect condition and will have no alibis."[5]

As the Giants prepared for the game, the only question appeared to be which pitcher would get the ball from McGraw. Ferdie Schupp (21-7, 1.95 ERA) was expected to start and the bookies were giving 2-to-1 odds on that choice.[6] At 26, however, Schupp was considered "the greenest man on the Giant staff."[7] Although he led the team in wins, McGraw opted for experience and selected 32-year-old Slim Sallee (18-7, 2.17); Schupp would be afforded time to study the White Sox hitters. Chicago manager Clarence "Pants" Rowland was reluctant to commit publicly, but as most expected, Eddie Cicotte (28-12, 1.53) took the mound for the home team. I.E. Sanborn wrote, "Cicotte has beaten even his own high standard of efficiency this year."[8] Cicotte's reputed "shine ball" caused some consternation among the Giants for its break, which was characterized as "like the course of a flying pigeon, just after a shot has been fired."[9]

Hall of Famer Eddie Collins played 12 seasons for the White Sox (1915-1926), batting .331 with a .425 on-base percentage, and helped the South Siders to the World Series title in 1917 and the pennant in 1919. (Photo Reproduction by Transcendental Graphics/Getty Images)

The contest opened with George Burns batting against Cicotte. Burns worked a full count before rapping a single over second base. Shoeless Joe Jackson pulled down fly balls from Buck Herzog and Benny Kauff for the first two outs, and Happy Felsch hauled in Heinie Zimmerman's ball in center field for the final out of the Giants first with Burns on second after a steal. Against Sallee, Shano Collins matched Burns' leadoff single by lining his own into right field. Sallee collected Fred McMullin's sacrifice bunt, which he flipped to Walter Holke at first base. With his namesake Shano now at second, Eddie Collins grounded sharply to shortstop Art Fletcher for the second out but advanced the runner to third. Jackson lifted a low fly toward right field that appeared likely to land for a hit and a run, but Herzog quickly backpedaled "in brilliant fashion after a hard run back into short center"[10] to claim the ball and end the inning. Herzog, the Giants captain, had missed most of the season's final month resting from a summer off-field injury, but appeared back to his usual standard at the most important time of year.

The second inning was scoreless. Ray Schalk led off the White Sox third with a "stinger" toward Zimmerman. The Giants third baseman "stabbed the bound with one hand" and delivered a clean throw across the diamond for the first out.[11] Cicotte singled to center, and Shano Collins followed with a single to right; however, the play ended with only Collins still on the basepaths after right fielder Dave Robertson's bullet to Zimmerman nailed Cicotte at third. With Collins on second and two out, McMullin lined Sallee's pitch over second. From center field, Kauff "came tearing in and tried to make a shoestring catch of it."[12] Kauff's father had traveled to Comiskey Park from Ohio to see his son play in a major-league game for the first time. Dad witnessed Benny dive for the ball … and miss. Collins scored easily for the first run of the Series as the ball rolled to deep center. Kauff's judgment was questioned later, the thought being that letting the ball bounce in front of him might have provided the chance to gun down

Collins at the plate.[13] Eddie Collins popped up to Fletcher in foul territory but the White Sox had the lead through three, 1-0.

In the Giants fourth, Robertson's two-out double was the only blemish for Cicotte as New York failed to tie. During pregame warmups, Felsch had blasted a ball into the left-field bleachers.[14] He equaled the feat with a pitch that counted in the bottom of the fourth. Seeing a favorable pitch coming his way with one out, Felsch "met it squarely with every ounce of power in his muscles, backed by the full swing of his body."[15] The result was "a drive of remarkable power and length"[16] that Burns and Kauff could only stand and watch as the ball landed in the left-field bleachers for a 2-0 White Sox advantage. After the game, Felsch was rewarded with a $50 Liberty bond, a prize offered by entertainer Al Jolson to any player who clouted a home run during the Series.[17] Chick Gandil's grounder and Buck Weaver's fly ball ended the frame.

The Giants struck in the fifth, and their pitcher was instrumental in clawing back a run. Before Sallee batted, catcher Lew McCarty led off the inning. McCarty had missed three months of the season with a broken leg[18] and struggled at the plate after his return on September 5. In fact, McCarty accounted for zero extra-base hits during that time. Against Cicotte, however, McCarty slammed the ball into right-center field for a triple that might have been a round-tripper but for his "game leg."[19] His batterymate, however, helped get McCarty across the plate. After staring at two pitches from Cicotte, Sallee dropped a short fly behind Eddie Collins to score McCarty. Hopes for a sustained rally were damaged when Weaver scooped up Burns's grounder to start a double play. Herzog struck out to end the inning.

With Chicago leading 2-1, the pitchers settled into a groove. The White Sox went down on three groundballs in the bottom of the fifth and neither team reached base in the sixth. After the game, Rowland observed of Cicotte that he "was stronger against the Giants at the finish than he was at the start."[20] Opportunity presented itself for the Giants in the seventh and defensive heroics preserved Chicago's lead. After McMullin gathered Robertson's roller for the first out, Holke hit a bullet to right for a single. As McCarty strode to the plate, White Sox defenders spread out in recollection of his earlier triple. McCarty's liner over Weaver's head appeared likely to drop fair. Like Kauff in the third inning, Jackson raced in, hoping to make the catch before the ball hit the turf. Unlike Kauff, Jackson's effort proved successful. Diving head-first, Jackson made the catch, turned a somersault, and "bobbed up on his feet again and the ball was firmly clutched in his grasp."[21] Rowland called the catch one of Jackson's best — and a likely game-saver.[22]

After Gandil's one-out single in the bottom of the seventh, Weaver struck out, but Gandil stole second and then claimed third on McCarty's bad throw. Schalk's grounder to Fletcher ended the inning, however. In the top of the eighth, Burns and Herzog accounted for the first two outs, but Weaver's throw on Kauff's grounder pulled Gandil off the bag. Sensing a possible hit-and-run play, Cicotte pitched out twice against Zimmerman. With Kauff again off the base, Cicotte fired to Gandil. Kauff raced for second, and Eddie Collins reeled in Gandil's high throw to apply the tag. After Cicotte grounded out to open the White Sox eighth, Shano Collins doubled down the line into left field. Sallee threw Collins out at third on McMullin's grounder for a fielder's choice, and McMullin was nailed trying to steal second with Eddie Collins batting.

Cicotte made quick work of the Giants to close out the game. Zimmerman's tapper back to the pitcher suggested such an easy out that Zim did not even bother running to first base. Weaver hauled in Fletcher's pop-up for the second out, then Shano Collins claimed the third out on Robertson's fly ball. Game One to the home team.

Rowland calmly summarized the result: "The boys went through in great shape, and we won a close one."[23] His owner was overcome with emotion; a tearful Comiskey grasped Cicotte's hand in congratulations.[24] Indeed, Cicotte's pitching appeared to confound the New Yorkers. For their part, the Giants promised revenge. "Wait till he faces us again. He'll be driven off the rubber before four innings have been played."[25] The Giants would have to wait until the Series reached the Polo Grounds before getting their next shot at Cicotte's "shine ball."

SOURCES

In addition to the sources cited in the Notes, the author consulted Baseball-Reference.com.

NOTES

1. I.E. Sanborn, "Over the Top for White Sox Today!" **Chicago Tribune**, October 6, 1917: 15, 16.
2. James Crusinberry, "Crowd Handled at Sox Contest Like a Machine," **Chicago Tribune**, October 7, 1917: 2, 1.
3. "Three Sox Big Figures in Winning First Game," **The Sporting News**, October 11, 1917: 3.
4. "Before the Battle," **Chicago Tribune**, October 6, 1917: 16.
5. Ibid.
6. James Crusinberry, "Confidence of Foe Supreme; Schupp Starts," **Chicago Tribune**, October 6, 1917: 15.
7. Sanborn, "Over the Top": 15.
8. Ibid.
9. Crusinberry, "Confidence."
10. I.E. Sanborn, "Felsch's Homer Wins First, 2-1," **Chicago Tribune**, October 7, 1917: 2, 1-2.
11. Ibid.
12. Ibid.
13. "Home-Run Hit Defeats Giants as Series Opens," **New York Times**, October 7, 1917: 1.
14. "Gossip of First Game," **The Sporting News**, October 11, 1917: 6.
15. Sanborn, "Felsch's Homer."
16. "Three Sox Big Figures."
17. Ring W. Lardner, "In the Wake of the News," **Chicago Tribune**, October 7, 1917: 2, 1.
18. Sanborn, "Over the Top": 16.
19. Sanborn, "Felsch's Homer."
20. Clarence Rowland (as told to James Crusinberry), "Sox In Front!" **Chicago Tribune**, October 7, 1917: 2, 3.
21. "Home-Run Hit."
22. Rowland.
23. Ibid.
24. "Home-Run Hit."
25. "Here Are Views on Mr. Cicotte," **Chicago Tribune**, October 7, 1917: 2, 1.

FABER'S PITCHING, NOT BASERUNNING, LEAD TO VICTORY

OCTOBER 7, 1917
CHICAGO WHITE SOX 7, NEW YORK GIANTS 2
GAME TWO OF THE WORLD SERIES

By Jacob Pomrenke

Before his first career World Series start, Red Faber was mostly known for the way he got his job in the big leagues: by impressing John McGraw on the world tour organized by the New York Giants manager and Chicago White Sox owner Charles Comiskey back in 1913.

Faber was an unproven minor leaguer then, but Comiskey took the pitching prospect along for the ride as an extra arm in case one of his stars got hurt on the four-month adventure around the globe.[1] McGraw took a liking to the White Sox recruit and helped him work on his spitball, which Faber used to earn a spot on Chicago's major-league roster the following spring.

In 1917 Faber got his chance to show McGraw just how much he had learned. No White Sox player would play a more important role in the fall classic against New York's National League champions.

Back in the World Series for the first time in 11 years, the White Sox had won 100 games in the regular season largely on the strength of their deep pitching staff, which posted a major-league-leading 2.16 ERA. Ace Eddie Cicotte held the visiting Giants to seven hits to win the World Series opener, 2-1, and now it was Faber's turn to stop an explosive offense that had led the NL in runs scored, home runs, and stolen bases.

The 29-year-old right-hander from Cascade, Iowa, was in his fourth big-league season but he had yet to make much of a name for himself. His career-best 1.92 ERA was marred by an inconsistent 16-13 record and he was used by manager Pants Rowland nearly as much out of the bullpen as in the starting rotation until the season's final weeks.

In Game Two against the Giants in front of about 32,000 fans at Comiskey Park, Faber became almost as much of a World Series goat as a hero.

New York opened the scoring in the second inning on a two-run single by Lew McCarty to score Dave Robertson and Walter Holke. When Robertson kicked away left fielder Joe Jackson's throw home, which was scored as an error on catcher Ray Schalk, Holke came scampering home for a second run. "Things became so quiet in the grandstand that one could hear the sparrows chirping in the rafters," the *Chicago Tribune* reported.[2]

But the White Sox quickly returned serve against Giants starter Ferdie Schupp with two runs of their own in the bottom half of the inning, thanks to consecutive hits by Jackson, Happy Felsch, Chick Gandil, and Buck Weaver, all singles. After Schupp walked the light-hitting Faber, McGraw had seen enough. He lifted his starter after just 1⅓ innings. His strategy of using southpaws like Schupp, Rube Benton, and

Game One starter Slim Sallee against the White Sox offense, led by the left-handed-hitting Jackson and Eddie Collins, was quickly backfiring.

After relieving Schupp, right-handed spitballer Fred Anderson deftly escaped a bases-loaded jam by striking out Nemo Leibold and inducing Fred McMullin to ground out. But he could hold off the White Sox onslaught for just one more inning. In the fourth, the home team's bats came alive to break the game open.

Weaver led off with a bunt single and moved up on Schalk's single. After Faber popped out, Leibold singled in Weaver with the go-ahead run and McMullin doubled the White Sox' lead with another base hit. That ended Anderson's day and another right-hander, Pol Perritt, came in to limit the damage. Collins greeted him with an RBI single and Jackson added another to make the score 7-2. Felsch mercifully ended the Giants' misery with a line drive to second baseman Buck Herzog, who turned an unassisted double play.

The collapse of the Giants' pitching "was one of the most pitiful incidents imaginable," wrote Grantland Rice.[3] "The Giants were supposed to have a fairly well-rounded staff, while the White Sox were supposed to be entirely dependent on Eddie Cicotte. … It was one of those occasions when one side does all the fighting and the other side is only beaten."

Rice credited manager Rowland with calling for successful hit-and-run plays — one of McGraw's signature strategies — on five of the White Sox' seven run-scoring hits. "This stealing of their stuff has pained the Giants not a little," he wrote.[4]

With Faber masterfully shutting down the Giants — only one New York baserunner got as far as second base in the final seven innings — the outcome was no longer in doubt. That set the stage for a little bit of levity and an all-time World Series blunder.

After reaching base in his first plate appearance, a rare occurrence for someone with only four hits in the regular season, Faber received an ovation from the Chicago fans when he stepped

In his 20-year big-league career, spent entirely with the White Sox (1914-1933), Red Faber, won 20-plus games in four seasons, and ranks second in franchise history in wins (254), innings pitched (4,086⅔), and complete games (273). (Photo by Mark Rucker/Transcendental Graphics, Getty Images)

to the plate for his third plate appearance in the fifth. With two outs and Buck Weaver on second base, Faber promptly earned another round of applause by knocking a single to deep right field. Weaver must have been too surprised to get a good jump and only advanced to third base. Meanwhile, Faber moved up to second on the throw home.

On the next pitch, Faber surprised everyone in the ballpark by taking off for third base "without rhyme or reason or warning."[5] Weaver, taking a big lead, slid back into the bag at the same time as Faber arrived. Catcher Bill Rariden had the presence of mind to throw the ball to third baseman Heinie Zimmerman, who placed a tag on both runners in the dirt. Faber's out was recorded to end the inning.

The play led to an oft-repeated, possibly apocryphal quote that still makes the rounds in baseball history books. When Faber reached third base only to find his teammate already there, a bewildered Weaver asked him, "Where in hell do you think you're going?" Red looked up and supposedly replied: "Back to pitch."[6]

White Sox beat writer I.E. Sanborn predicted that Faber's blunder would be "dug up by the historians as the feature of the 1917 world's series … a thousand, thousand years from now."[7] But by the end of the Series, it wasn't even the most notable mistake on the basepaths that week, having been overshadowed by Zimmerman's ill-fated footrace with Eddie Collins in Game Six.

Faber's adventures at the plate and on the bases provided some amusement, but the Giants were stifled by his steady work on the mound. He threw an efficient 99 pitches, 63 for strikes, according to an analysis by the *Chicago Tribune*.[8] The Giants swung early and often, allowing the White Sox pitcher to get out of the sixth inning on just six pitches. The ninth inning lasted only eight pitches.

In a game that epitomized the small-ball nature of the Deadball Era, the teams set a World Series record that still stands by combining for 22 singles and no extra-base hits.[9]

The White Sox were brimming with confidence heading to New York, having thrashed the National League champions two days in a row. "They knocked us silly," one Giants player said.[10] In a syndicated column written under Collins's name, the Chicago team captain said, "The game showed we are capable of hitting all kinds of pitching: southpaws, spitters, fast and curveballs. I cannot see how they ever expect to stop us now."[11]

SOURCES

Box scores for this game can be found at Baseball-Reference.com and Retrosheet.org:

Baseball-Reference.com/boxes/CHA/CHA191710070.shtml.

Retrosheet.org/boxesetc/1917/B10070CHA1917.htm.

NOTES

1   Brian Cooper, "Red Faber," SABR BioProject, accessed online at sabr.org/bioproj/person/a6dff769 on January 16, 2018.

2   James Crusinberry, "It's All Over but Shouting, Fans Believe," **Chicago Tribune**, October 8, 1917: 13.

3   Grantland Rice, "Teams Hurrying Eastward With Sox Two Games Ahead," **Brooklyn Eagle**, October 8, 1917: 20.

4   Ibid.

5   Ibid.

6   For two of many examples over the years, see Irving Vaughan, "Faber Attributes Long Diamond Life to Spitter," **Sioux Falls (South Dakota) Argus-Leader**, February 17, 1929: 8; and Daniel Okrent and Steve Wulf, **Baseball Anecdotes** (New York: Oxford University Press, 1989), 73-74.

7   I.E. Sanborn, "White Sox Whale Giants, 7-2," **Chicago Tribune**, October 8, 1917: 1.

8   "Red Faber Pitches 99 Balls at Giants," **Chicago Tribune**, October 8, 1917: 13.

9   In 1971, the Baltimore Orioles tied the White Sox' team record with 14 singles and no extra-base hits in Game Two against the Pittsburgh Pirates. But no World Series game has come close to the 22 combined singles that the White Sox and Giants had in 1917. See: Baseball-Reference.com/tiny/QxOkA.

10 Damon Runyon, "Defeat Dazes McGraws," **Chicago Examiner**, October 8, 1917: 9.

11 Eddie Collins, "Sox Have the Punch — Collins," **Chicago Examiner**, October 8, 1917: 8.

"BIG PUSH" BRINGS BEDLAM

OCTOBER 13, 1917
CHICAGO WHITE SOX 8, NEW YORK GIANTS 5
GAME FIVE OF THE WORLD SERIES

By Kevin Larkin

Game Five of the 1917 World Series was back in Chicago and the winner would be on the cusp of a championship. Skipper Pants Rowland's White Sox had taken the first two games of the fall classic in the Windy City, but John McGraw's Giants came back to take Games Three and Four at the Polo Grounds. Despite playing on the road, the Giants were favored by bettors.[1]

On the hill for the visiting Giants was southpaw Harry "Slim" Sallee, who had lost Game One to Eddie Cicotte on October 6. Sallee was a 10-year veteran who had after the 1917 regular season a record of 138 wins and 118 losses. Making his first start in the Series for the White Sox was Ewell Albert "Reb" Russell. Russell, like Sallee, was a left-hander and during the 1917 regular season he finished fourth on the White Sox with 15 wins, behind Cicotte (28), Lefty Williams (17), and Red Faber (16).

The 27,323 fans in attendance watched Russell walk the leadoff hitter, George Burns, with four pitches wide of the plate.[2] A double by second baseman Buck Herzog advanced Burns to third base and he scored on Benny Kauff's double that had Herzog going to third base. Kauff continued his hot hitting; he had hit two home runs in Game Four on Thursday.[3] Rowland wasted little time and replaced Russell on the mound with Cicotte. A fielder's choice by Heinie Zimmerman resulted in Herzog being thrown out at the plate by Buck Weaver. Kauff advanced to third base and he too was thrown out at the plate when Art Fletcher grounded to third baseman Fred McMullin, who threw home to catcher Ray Schalk. Dave Robertson hit for Jim Thorpe (the former Gold Medal-winning athlete from the 1912 Summer Olympics), and he singled to score Zimmerman, giving the Giants a 2-0 lead. Chicago came back with a run in the third inning on a walk to Eddie Collins and Happy Felsch's two-out double.

In the fourth inning the Giants broke through the White Sox lines with Cicotte in trouble and his supporting cast in danger of breaking into countless fragments.[4] Bill Rariden singled through the hole between second baseman Collins and first sacker Chick Gandil. Then after a round of applause as he approached the plate,[5] Sallee sacrificed Rariden to second base. He scored when Shano Collins erred trying to pick up a ball hit to him by Burns. Burns scored the second run of the inning when Weaver fumbled Herzog's groundball and Gandil made a throwing error to Cicotte on a grounder by Kauff; it was Chicago's third error of the game. Zimmerman grounded to McMullin at third base to end the frame with the Giants ahead 4-1. Sallee had allowed the White Sox just two hits at this point.

Neither team scored in the fifth inning, and after a scoreless top of the sixth, the White Sox hit three straight singles that had Weaver scoring their second run of the game.

Swede Risberg had pinch-hit for Cicotte in

the sixth inning and Claude "Lefty" Williams, in only his second full major-league season, took over in the top of the seventh. Williams gave up a double to Fletcher to lead off the inning. Williams made an error (Chicago's fourth of the game) on a bunt by Robertson and the Giants had runners on first and second with no outs. Williams struck out the side, but not before Rariden's single scored Fletcher and made the score 5-2.

Sallee was still on the mound for the Giants when Chicago came to bat in the bottom of the seventh inning. Sallee got Eddie Collins out easily, on a popup to shortstop. It then got interesting when Shoeless Joe Jackson stepped to the box. Home-plate umpire Silk O'Laughlin called Sallee's first pitch a ball. That brought about loud protests from both Sallee and Rariden.[6] Shoeless Joe singled on Sallee's next pitch, and Felsch sent him to second with another single. Both scored on Gandil's double to center field. Weaver's grounder to shortstop sent Gandil to third base and a walk to Schalk put runners at first and third with two outs. Schalk stole second base and when Herzog muffed Rariden's throw, Gandil scored the tying run and Schalk advanced to third base. Sallee struck out Byrd Lynn, pinch-hitting for Williams, to end the inning with the scored tied, 5-5.

Red Faber replaced Williams on the mound in the top of the eighth and retired the Giants in order. In the bottom of the inning Shano Collins singled and went to second on a sacrifice by McMullin. Shano Collins scored on Eddie Collins's single to center. Jackson singled to center; Kauff's throw to third attempting to cut down Eddie Collins was late, and when Heinie Zimmerman threw wild to second, Collins scored. The White Sox led 7-5. Sallee was replaced on the mound by Pol Perritt, who gave up a single to Felsch that made the score 8-5.

Now the game went into the ninth. Faber came back to the mound to close it out. He got Fletcher on a grounder to shortstop and Robertson on a fly to left, and faced Giants first baseman Walter Holke with a chance to give the White Sox a three-games-to-two lead in the Series. Holke fouled off several pitches and then hit a groundball to McMullin at third base. McMullin gloved it and threw to Gandil at first base for the final out of the game.[7]

Now both teams were headed back to the Polo Grounds for Game Six with Chicago needing just one more win to clinch the Series title.

There was an interesting side note to Game Five. It was the first time McMullin, Jackson, Felsch, Gandil, Weaver, Cicotte, Risberg and Williams all played in the same game. These were the infamous Black Sox, who were all banned from baseball on August 3, 1921, by Commissioner Kenesaw Mountain Landis. A ninth player in Game Five was also banned by Landis: the Giants' Benny Kauff. Landis ruled Kauff ineligible for his part in a scheme with his brother involving stolen cars received at a Manhattan automobile accessory business they owned. Kauff was acquitted on the charges but Landis called the acquittal a miscarriage of justice and banned Kauff from baseball in 1921.

SOURCES

In addition to the game story and box-score sources cited in the notes, the author consulted the Baseball-Reference.com and Retrosheet.org websites.

NOTES

1 "Giants Favored Over White Sox in Series Betting on Eve of Fifth Game," **New York Times**, October 13, 1919:10.

2 Ibid.

3 Ibid.

4 Grantland Rice, "Giants Routed After Leading Up to the Seventh," **New York Tribune**, October 14, 1917: 17.

5 "Detailed Account of Game by Innings," **New York Times**, October 14, 1917: 20.

6 Walter Trumbull, "Umpire's Ruling a Factor," **Chicago Tribune**, October 14, 1917: 17.

7 "Detailed Account of Game By Innings."

BABE RUTH TOSSES SHUTOUT AS PATRIOTISM PREVAILS IN OPENING OF FALL CLASSIC

SEPTEMBER 5, 1918
BOSTON RED SOX 1, CHICAGO CUBS 0
GAME ONE OF THE WORLD SERIES

By Mike Huber

With the war in Europe two months from the Allies' victory, the 1918 World Series began. A meager yet patriotic crowd of 19,274 fans was on hand at Comiskey Park, "the smallest that has witnessed the diamond classic in many years."[1] The minds of the spectators were clearly on the overseas conflict, yet they came to see "an unusually brilliant exhibition of baseball."[2] The first game had originally been scheduled for September 4, but rain had caused a delay. Further, the venue was moved from the Cubs' home ballpark, Weeghman Park (later renamed Wrigley Field), to Comiskey Park, "because it held more fans."[3] Many "believed that the Weeghman machine would win without allowing the American League club a single victory."[4]

For the Red Sox, Joe Bush had been warming up to take the mound, but Boston skipper Ed Barrow surprised the Cubs as "the Baltimore mauler [Babe Ruth] was named for the task."[5] The Cubs countered with their ace, Hippo Vaughn. In a battle of southpaws, "these two giants fought it out all the way"[6] in a classic pitchers' duel.

Chicago threatened in the opening frame, "with victory within their grasp."[7] With two outs, Les Mann singled and motored to third when Dode Paskert hit a Texas leaguer to left field (Paskert advanced to second on the throw to third). Ruth then walked Fred Merkle to load the bases. With the game possibly depending "on his next offering, Ruth served up a low fastball to [Charlie] Pick, at the same time waving his outfielders back toward the bleachers."[8] Pick lifted the ball high into left, but George Whiteman made the catch to end the inning.

They may have taken Ruth's pitching for granted, but the Cubs feared Ruth's bat. When he hit the first ball in batting practice "into the right field bleachers, the crowd roared with appreciation."[9] And as the Babe strode to the plate in the top of the third inning, "Max Flack simply turned about and marched about forty paces toward the right wall,"[10] while the crowd cheered, expecting some action. Ruth sent a deep line drive to right-center, and "the Cubs rooters groaned the moment their tympanums registered the sound of the bat and ball contact. It seemed a potential home run, but, as was the case throughout the afternoon with both sides, the high wind blowing directly against the batter, held back the swat and dropped it right into the mitt of the centerfielder" Paskert, who had stumbled at first, recovered quickly, and ran down the ball for a long out. In his two other at-bats, Ruth fanned and "struck out in such a manner that the crowd tee-heed audibly."[11] Throughout the game, the Cubs "successfully stifled the perilous home-run bat of Ruth, but they overlooked the menace of his pitching arm."[12]

Boston "did all of its stick execution in the first four innings, getting one hit in each of the first three, then grouping two for the winning tally in the fourth."[13] In the fourth, Vaughn allowed a leadoff walk to Dave Shean. Amos Strunk tried to bunt Shean to second but popped the ball up and Vaughn caught it. Whiteman did advance Shean to second, when he looped a single over short, bringing up Stuffy McInnis, "a notorious left-field hitter."[14] McInnis took Vaughn's first offering for a ball, "but the second pitch came across to suit him and he dropped a rather indifferent rap into left field along the foul line. Proper preliminary coaching would have placed [Cubs left fielder] Mann directly in line for an easy catch on this ball and a resulting out, with no score."[15] Instead, this proved to be the game-winner. The *New York Times* reported that the "one lone run grew larger as the pitchers battled along, both displaying an impenetrable mysticism of curves."[16]

The Cubs presented another opportunity in the sixth inning. With one down, "Paskert stung a hit to centre and Merkle slapped one to the same bailiwick, and Ruth was becoming plainly worried."[17] Boston's Barrow waved to the bullpen and Bush started warming up again. Pick rolled a sacrifice down the first-base line and both runners advanced. When Ruth got Charlie Deal to fly out to left, the threat ended.

And then something happened during the seventh-inning stretch that was "far different from any incident that has ever occurred in the history of baseball. As the crowd ... stood up to take their afternoon yawn,"[18] a band from the Navy training station just north of Chicago began to play "The Star Spangled Banner." This was the first time the song was played at a World Series game. "The yawns were checked and heads were bared as the ball players turned quickly and faced the music."[19] A few in the crowd began singing, then more joined in, until "a great volume of melody rolled across the field."[20] The crowd then "exploded into thunderous applause,"[21] and the beginning of a new tradition was being witnessed. "Certainly the outpouring of sentiment, enthusiasm, and patriotism at the 1918 World Series went a long way to making the (song) the national anthem," wrote John Thorn, the official historian of Major League Baseball.[22] It would be another 13 years before President Herbert Hoover officially designated the song as America's national anthem.[23] From the *New York Times*: "If the greatest reason for playing this world's series this year was to give the boys overseas something to talk about besides war, this game today will serve the purpose."[24]

The Cubs made one last attempt in the bottom of the ninth. With two outs, Deal dragged a bunt down the third-base line and beat the throw from Thomas for a single. Bill McCabe came on as a pinch-runner. Then Bill Killefer "took one last grand slam at the ball and shot a high ballooner between right and centre fields," but Hooper raced to the ball for the final out of the game. The Red Sox, behind Ruth's pitching, had won, 1-0.

Several accounts of the game mentioned how few occasions there were for the fans to cheer. The *Chicago Tribune* commented, "From the ball player's standpoint it was a great game, because of its proximity to perfection. From the rooter's view point it was tame and monotonous because there were so few tense moments."[25] Further, "[T]he crowd present sat through the entire game, all primed to burst forth when the proper time came. But it never came, because Ruth never allowed an attack to go far enough to do damage."[26] Ruth allowed six hits and one walk in the win, striking out four. Vaughn yielded only five hits, all singles. He struck out six and walked three. Neither team made an error, and perhaps the difference came down to the Red Sox getting one hit with men in scoring position (1-for-7) while the Cubs were 0-for-5

SOURCES

In addition to the sources mentioned in the notes, the author consulted Baseball-Reference.com and Retrosheet.org.

NOTES

1 "Red Sox Beat Cubs in Initial Battle of World's Series," **New York Times**, September 6, 1918: 14.

2 Ibid.

3 Don Babwin (Associated Press), "1918 World Series Key in US Love Affair with National Anthem," found online at bostonglobe.com/sports/redsox/2017/07/03/world-series-key-love-affair-with-national-anthem/J4XmvKVNXp69P4EQEU8piK/story.html. Accessed September 2017. Weeghman Park was the home of the Federal League's Chicago Whales in 1914 and Chicago Chi-Feds in 1915. The Cubs started playing there in 1916 and have stayed. The name was changed to Cubs Park in 1920 and then to Wrigley Field in 1926.

4 John E. Wray, "Vaughn's Defeat in World Series Opener Puts Bruins on Defensive in Pitching," **St. Louis Post-Dispatch**, September 6, 1918: 20.

5 **New York Times**.

6 "Sox Take First Game at Chicago," **Burlington** (Vermont) **Free Press**, September 6, 1918: 1.

7 **New York Times**.

8 **Burlington Free Press**.

9 Edward F. Martin, "McInnis' Smash Beats Cubs, 1-0," **Boston Globe**, September 6, 1918: 4.

10 James Crusinberry, "All Primed to Yell, But Precise Hurling Gives Fan No Chance," **Chicago Tribune**, September 6, 1918: 9.

11 Wray.

12 **New York Times**.

13 I.E. Sanborn, "Red Sox Grab First World's Series Battle From Cubs, 1-0," **Chicago Tribune**, September 6, 1918: 9.

14 "Crowd Present Seemed to Take Little Interest in Work of Rival Athletes," **St. Louis Post-Dispatch**, September 6, 1918: 20.

15 Ibid.

16 **New York Times**.

17 Ibid.

18 Ibid.

19 Ibid.

20 Ibid.

21 Ibid.

22 Babwin.

23 Ibid.

24 **New York Times**.

25 Sanborn.

26 Crusinberry.

TYLER'S PITCHING AND BATTING TIE SERIES

SEPTEMBER 6, 1918
CHICAGO CUBS 3, BOSTON RED SOX 1
GAME TWO OF THE WORLD SERIES

BY BILL PEARCH

Prior to the start of Game Two of the 1918 World Series, Fred Mitchell, manager of the National League pennant-winning Chicago Cubs, recalled George "Lefty" Tyler's previous World Series appearance. Mitchell earned his current position at the helm of the Cubs from successful work with his pitchers, especially Tyler, during his tenure in Boston. During Game Three of the 1914 World Series, he watched as Tyler surrendered four earned runs in 10 innings. Though Tyler failed to record the win, the Braves outlasted Philadelphia Athletics starting pitcher Bullet Joe Bush by plating the winning run in the bottom of the 12th inning to claim a 3-0 Series lead. The two pitchers matched up again nearly four years later with Tyler donning the Cubs' home whites and Bush the Boston Red Sox' road grays.

With war raging across Europe, the escalating international conflict cast a dark shadow over the 1918 season. Major-league club owners debated whether the regular season should end in early September.[1] Ban Johnson, the president of the American League, contemplated opening dialogue with President Woodrow Wilson's administration for guidance about baseball's role.[2] Ultimately, the issue was decided by Secretary of War Newton Diehl Baker Jr., who ruled in late July that major-league players were officially exempt from the government's "work or fight" mandate until September 1. The season would end then and be followed immediately by the World Series.[3] In the shortened season, the Cubs won the National League pennant with a record of 84-45 with 2 ties after 131 games, 10½ games ahead of John McGraw's New York Giants (71-53).[4]

Winning four World Series in four chances (1903, 1912, 1915, and 1916), the Red Sox owned more championships than any other major-league team. The Cubs were looking for their third World Series title after securing the franchise's fifth pennant. The Cubs had earned both previous championships more than a decade earlier (1907 and 1908).

In addition to the World Series opening on its earliest date, the best-of-seven format would change to eliminate unnecessary rail travel.[5] The Series would open with three games in Chicago and the final four games (if necessary) in Boston. The Cubs' home since 1916, Weeghman Park, was not capable of accommodating more than 16,000 spectators; all games in Chicago would relocate to the South Side's American League venue, Comiskey Park. With a seating capacity of 30,000, Charles Comiskey's ballpark previously hosted three games of the 1917 World Series between the White Sox and Giants.[6]

On Thursday, September 5, the Red Sox won the World Series opener behind George

Herman "Babe" Ruth's six-hit, 1-0 shutout. The Cubs needed to win Game Two if they wanted to seize a Series lead before games shifted to Fenway Park. Tyler knew that Chicago's hopes rested on his 28-year-old left arm. During his debut season with the Cubs, Tyler won 19 games and lost 8, and compiled a radiant 2.00 ERA in 269⅓ innings. He wrestled with control issues as a Boston neophyte, but when Mitchell became the Braves' pitching coach, Tyler blossomed.[7] When asked about his rotation, Mitchell said, "The pitching staff is what has carried the Cubs through a successful season, and will, I hope, enable them to still retain the championship of the world in the city of Chicago."[8]

At game time, Chicago's temperatures reached the mid-60s and the ballpark was only two-thirds full. Despite the demand for greater seating capacity, only 20,040 fans passed through Comiskey Park's turnstiles for the game.

Tyler opened the game by walking Harry Hooper, the Red Sox right fielder, on five pitches. He discovered his groove against Dave Shean and fanned the second baseman. Home-plate umpire George Hildebrand called Shean out for interference with Cubs catcher Bill Killefer, and Killefer doubled off Hooper attempting to swipe second base. Amos Strunk popped up to shortstop Charlie Deal to retire the side.

Bush, despite yielding a leadoff single to right fielder Max Flack, successfully navigated the bottom of the first. Bush nailed Flack advancing to second on a Hollocher groundball back to the mound. Center fielder Strunk intentionally dropped Les Mann's fly ball and nailed Charlie Hollocher for the second out attempting to advance to second. Center fielder Dode Paskert ended the inning by flying out to left field.

In the second, the Red Sox's first two batters reached base: George Whiteman walked and when Stuffy McInnis bunted, batterymates Tyler and Killefer collided. Everett Scott's sacrifice moved both runners to scoring position. Second baseman Charlie Pick fielded Fred Thomas' groundball and nailed Whiteman racing for home. Tyler escaped the inning with no runs scoring by inducing Sam Agnew to pop out to Flack in foul territory down the right-field line.

Chicago's first baseman, Fred Merkle, labeled for an absent-minded play 10 years earlier that cost his Giants the pennant, walked to lead off the Cubs' second.[9] Pick beat out a bunt toward third base. With runners on first and second, Deal, the Cubs third baseman, popped out to Shean at second. Killefer slammed Bush's pitch into right field, plating Merkle to give the Cubs a 1-0 lead and advancing Pick to third.

During his first regular season with the Cubs, Tyler had 21 hits in 100 at-bats with 8 RBIs. In the 1914 World Series, he had three plate appearances against Bush and failed to get a hit. This time, with two runners in scoring position, Tyler singled to center field driving home Pick and Killefer. Strunk's throw to the plate was too late to nail Killefer, but Agnew's relay to Shean nabbed Tyler advancing to second. The Cubs led, 3-0. Flack singled with two outs, but Shean ended the rally when he tagged Flack on an attempted steal.

Tempers erupted after the inning. Rather than vent his frustration toward the umpires, Red Sox coach Heinie Wagner, spewed venom at Tyler and Cubs coach Otto Knabe. Knabe, who loved to dispute during his playing days, accepted Wagner's challenge. As a player, Knabe's trademark was his trickiness and aggressiveness, and he seemingly could not take the field without wrangling with one of his opponents.[10] Words turned to fists as the two coaches approached the Cubs' dugout.[11] Cubs pitcher Claude Hendrix and teammates separated Knabe and Wagner.[12] The two teams rapidly doused the skirmish with the sole result being "a badly soiled uniform for Wagner."[13]

From the third inning through the eighth, Tyler and Bush hung zeros on the scoreboard. Bush allowed only four baserunners during those innings. Merkle reached base on an error in the fourth and advanced to second, but failed to score. Hollocher started the sixth inning with a triple, but was thrown out at the plate on Paskert's grounder. Bush walked two in the bottom of the seventh, but kept the Cubs scoreless.

Tyler matched his mound counterpart's production. He walked Bush in the third, but ended the frame unscathed. Bush again reached first in the fifth, on an infield error, but failed to advance beyond the initial sack. Shean singled and failed to score in the sixth, and Wally Schang and Hooper singled in the eighth. For those six innings, the Cubs hurler did not allow a runner to advance beyond second base.

Needing only three outs to even the Series at a game apiece, Tyler surrendered a leadoff triple to Strunk in the ninth. Boston finally ended the shutout when Whiteman also tripled. Whiteman held at third when McInnis grounded out to Tyler. Tyler walked Scott to place runners on the corners. Red Sox manager Ed Barrow inserted Jean Dubuc as a pinch-hitter for Thomas, but Tyler fanned him for the second out. Schang popped out to shortstop to end the game.

"Today's game was a tough one to lose, especially as we nearly broke it up in the ninth inning," said Barrow. "The Cubs had the better of the breaks, I think, and piled up a lead in the second inning too great for us to overcome."[14]

Mitchell expressed relief. "We are on even terms with Boston," he said. "The Cubs certainly recovered their batting eye, and they are confident of retaining it. Tyler pitched a wonderful game, and never was in danger, except in the ninth, when he grooved them over for Strunk and Whiteman. Those two triples saved Boston from a shutout."[15]

SOURCES

In addition to the sources cited in the Notes, the author also accessed Retrosheet.org, Baseball-Reference.com, and SABR.org.

NOTES

1. "World's Series Planned," **Boston Post**, July 27, 1918.

2. "May Ask President," **Boston Post**, July 20, 1918.

3. Peter Golenbock, **Wrigleyville: A Magical History Tour of the Chicago Cubs** (New York: St. Martin's Press, 1996), 172.

4. Chicago Tribune Staff, **The Chicago Tribune Book of the Chicago Cubs: A Decade-by-Decade History** (Midway: Chicago, 2017), 37.

5. James Crusinberry, "Cubs May Play Red Sox Squad on South Side," **Chicago Tribune**, August 25, 1918.

6. "Open Series in Comiskey Park," **Decatur (Illinois) Herald**, August 29, 1918.

7. Sean Deveney, **The Original Curse: Did the Cubs Throw the 1918 World Series to Babe Ruth's Red Sox and Incite the Black Sox Scandal?** (New York: McGraw Hill, 2010), 64.

8. Fred Mitchell, "The Strength of the Cub Machine: Why I Believe We Are Capable of Making a Powerful Bid for the World's Championship," **Baseball Magazine**, Volume 21, Issue 6, (October 1918): 463.

9. "Fred Merkle has Succeeded in Living Down Famous Boner While With Giants," **Chicago Eagle**, August 3, 1918.

10. "Knabe's Famous Rough Tactics," **Honolulu Star-Advertiser**, July 8, 1918.

11. Raymond Phelon, "Free-for-All Fight in World Series Battle," **St. Louis Star and Times**, September 7, 1918.

12. "Cubs Check Foe in Second Game of Title Series," **New York Times**, September 7, 1918.

13. I.E. Sanborn, "Drumfire Blows by Locals Force Foe to Retreat," **Chicago Tribune**, September 7.

14. "Cubs' Task Now Easier," **New York Times**, September 7, 1918.

15. Ibid.

COMISKEY PARK

CARL MAYS OUTDUELS HIPPO VAUGHN

SEPTEMBER 7, 1918
BOSTON RED SOX 2, CHICAGO CUBS 1
GAME THREE OF THE WORLD SERIES

By Brian M. Frank

Chicago Cubs ace James "Hippo" Vaughn had a dream regular season in 1918. Vaughn led the National League in numerous categories, including wins, ERA, and strikeouts.[1] But Vaughn's postseason was not going as well. Despite pitching spectacularly in Game One of the World Series, he lost to young left-hander Babe Ruth and the Boston Red Sox, 1-0. After the Cubs bounced back to win Game Two, it was expected that Cubs manager Fred Mitchell would give the ball to 20-game-winner Claude Hendrix for Game Three.

Even when Vaughn warmed up alongside Hendrix before Game Three, it was "supposed that the appearance of the port sider was only a bit of camouflage to scare the Red Sox."[2] However, Mitchell surprised everyone when he sent his ace back out on only one day's rest. Boston countered with Carl Mays, whose submarine delivery had helped him to a 21-13 record and a 2.21 ERA, as well as a league-leading 30 complete games and eight shutouts.

As Vaughn took the Comiskey Park mound, there were reminders throughout the ballpark that the country was at war.[3] Thousands of uniformed soldiers and sailors filled the stands. A sign in the outfield asked fans to "Buy War Savings Stamps and Do It Now." Throughout the game, airplanes "soared about" and "entertained the fans with a mock battle 10,000 feet, more or less, in the air and finished the exhibition with a tail spin."[4]

The game remained scoreless through the first three innings. To begin the fourth, Vaughn struck out Amos Strunk looking, "driving over a third strike with the speed of a cannon ball," but hit the next batter, George Whiteman.[5] This brought Stuffy McInnis to the plate.[6] Vaughn later recounted what he believed was a pivotal moment in the game, saying, "I got the first two past McInnis for strikes and had all the best of it, but wanted to drive him back from the plate, so intended to shoot the next one close to his bean. My control was bad, and I got it almost over the plate, just where he likes 'em, and he hit to left field for a single."[7]

With runners on first and second, Wally Schang singled home Whiteman to give Boston the first run of the game and send McInnis to third base. Everett Scott laid down a squeeze bunt up the first-base line. As the *Boston Globe* told it, Vaughn "came in for the tap and the agate just scooted up his sleeve like trained mice. This prevented him from getting 'Stuffy' from going into the plate, but when he turned to make a play at first Fred Merkle was out somewhere in No Man's Land. ..." All hands were safe on the botched fielding play.

Fred Thomas then hit a sharp single to right. As Wally Schang headed home, right fielder Max Flack fired the ball to catcher Bill Killefer, "who tagged Schang out as non-chalantes as he would have bitten off a chew."[8] Carl Mays lined out to center to end the rally, but the damage had been done, and the Red Sox led, 2-0.

Carl Mays dominated the early innings, as his "eccentric delivery" puzzled Chicago batters.[9] *The Sporting News* wrote: "For the first four innings, the Cubs were completely mystified by the slants of Mays. Carl deliberate and cool ducked his hand almost to mother earth just before letting loose of each pitch. ..."[10] The Cubs didn't get a hit off Mays until the fourth, when Les Mann doubled on a ball just fair down the right-field line. Dode Paskert then launched a fly to deep left. The *New York Sun* wrote that "Whiteman, at the crack of the bat, turned and started to run like a hungry greyhound. He didn't seem to pay attention to the ball, he just lengthened his stride and flew. Just before crashing into the low fence he suddenly shot up his gloved mitt, grabbed the ball out of the air and hung on to it."[11] Fred Merkle grounded to short to end the inning.

Charlie Pick led off the Cubs half of the fifth with a groundball that shortstop Everett Scott couldn't handle. The *Chicago Tribune* opined, "It was the ground's fault, not his, as the ball skittered under his hands hugging the dirt." The ball rolled into left-center field and Pick wound up at second base. He scored two batters later on Bill Killefer's single, cutting the lead to 2-1.

The Cubs entered the bottom of the ninth still trailing by a run. Mays easily retired the first two batters, bringing Charlie Pick to the plate with Chicago facing a Series deficit of two games to one. Pick hit a groundball that second baseman Dave Shean knocked down, but Pick beat it out for a hit. Left-hand-hitting Turner Barber pinch-hit for Charlie Deal. With a ball and two strikes on Barber, Pick stole second, beating Wally Schang's throw. Then, a pitch "filtered through Schang's mitt a couple of yards behind the plate," and Pick raced toward third.[12] Schang recovered the ball and fired it to third, where, according to the *New York Times*, "Ball and runner arrived at about the same time, and in the mêlée at the cushion the ball trickled from (Fred) Thomas's hands and rolled away toward the Chicago bench."[13] Cubs fans held their breath as Pick raced home with the potential tying run and Thomas fired the ball to the plate. "Straight and true and as swift as a bullet the ball went from Thomas's hand and into the waiting mitt of Schang. ... As Pick came tumbling into the final bag, stretching his left foot far out so as to hook the corner of the rubber platter, the ball clapped against the catcher's glove, and Schang tagged the runner with the ball."[14] As umpire Bill Klem's out call echoed through the ballpark, the Cubs' hopes of taking the lead in the Series died with it. The *Chicago Tribune* noted that "Boston's victory was won by a considerably smaller margin than one run, for the Cubs came within a long step of tying the count in the last half of the ninth."

After struggling in the fourth, Hippo Vaughn dominated the final five innings of the game, allowing only a walk and a single. Despite his stellar performance on just one day's rest, Vaughn took responsibility for the loss, stating: "It was my fault. They gave me one run, and that one should have been enough to win for us."[15] Vaughn may have been hard on himself in his assessment, as he'd been given almost no run support in either of his World Series starts. As the *Boston Globe* wrote, in recognition of Vaughn, "[E]verybody should doff their kellys, for he has pitched two sweet ball games and is deserving of considerable sympathy when a view of the vital statistics reveal that the Cubs have pushed only one run over the pan for him in 18 frames."[16]

SOURCES

In addition to the sources mentioned in the notes, the author consulted Baseball-Reference.com and Retrosheet.org.

NOTES

1. Vaughn led the league in wins (22), ERA (1.74), strikeouts (148), games started (33), innings pitched (290⅓), and shutouts (8).

2. "Finish One of the Most Dramatic Yet Seen in Baseball Classic," **New York Sun**, September 8, 1918: 4.

COMISKEY PARK

3   The season had ended early due to World War I's "Work or Fight" order and the Cubs chose to play their World Series home games at the larger Comiskey Park, rather than their home ballpark, Weeghman Park (later known as Wrigley Field.)

4   "Red Sox Earn Edge in Series," **New York Sun**, September 8, 1918: 4.

5   "Red Sox Earn Edge in Series."

6   McInnis's RBI single off Vaughn in the fourth inning of Game One had provided the only run of that contest.

7   "Jim Vaughn Blames Himself for Defeat; Poor Control Cause," **Chicago Tribune**, September 8, 1918: A5.

8   "Red Sox Earn Edge in Series."

9   I.E. Sanborn, "Crisp Onslaught in Fourth Beats Vaughn, Cub Ace," **Chicago Tribune**, September 8, 1918: A5.

10 "Carl Mays Takes His Turn in Baffling Cubs in Third Game," **The Sporting News**, September 12, 1918: 2.

11 "Finish One of the Most Dramatic Yet Seen in Baseball Classic," **New York Sun**, September 8, 1918: 4.

12 I.E. Sanborn, "Crisp Onslaught in Fourth Beats Vaughn, Cub Ace."

13 "Red Sox Check Rally in Ninth and Take the Game," **New York Times**, September 8, 1918: 32. Even Red Sox third baseman Fred Thomas was a reminder of the war. Thomas hadn't played a major-league game after joining the Navy in June, but was granted a two-week furlough from the Great Lakes Naval Training School in order to play in the World Series.

14 "Red Sox Check Rally in Ninth."

15 "Jim Vaughn Blames Himself."

16 "Red Sox Big Fourth Undoing of Vaughn," **Boston Globe**, September 8, 1918: 1.

WHITE SOX CLINCH AL PENNANT ON SHOELESS JOE JACKSON WALK-OFF SINGLE

SEPTEMBER 24, 1919
CHICAGO WHITE SOX 5, ST. LOUIS BROWNS 4

By Jacob Pomrenke

With 29 wins under his belt, Chicago White Sox ace Eddie Cicotte took the mound at Comiskey Park on September 24, 1919, just shy of a milestone victory — and with an opportunity to clinch the American League pennant.

The White Sox' march to the World Series was taking a little longer than they expected after spending most of the regular season in first place. Except for a brief swoon in late June, the White Sox had cruised comfortably atop the AL standings all year. They had been alone in first place since July 9. But the Cleveland Indians were coming on strong, having won 10 in a row, and Chicago's eight-game lead was cut in half with just five more to play. A win over the St. Louis Browns, plus a Cleveland loss to the Detroit Tigers, would finally put the pennant in Chicago's hands.

Chicago manager Kid Gleason called on his veteran right-hander Cicotte for the series opener. "Knuckles" had been on a roll, winning his last six starts and even picking up two wins in relief since his last loss on August 14. He entered this game with a 29-7 record and a 1.69 ERA.

Cicotte was making just his second start since Gleason gave him two weeks off in early September to rest before the World Series. At the time, Cicotte's break was widely rumored to be because of a sore arm.[1] At age 35, Cicotte was closing in on 300 innings for the season. Due to the absence of future Hall of Famer Red Faber, who was suffering from nagging injuries and a lingering bout of influenza, Cicotte and teammate Lefty Williams had been carrying the load for the White Sox. The two pitchers had started, and won, more than half of the team's games all by themselves.

Later, Cicotte's long layoff down the stretch would fuel speculation that White Sox owner Charles Comiskey had ordered him benched so he would not reach the 30-win milestone, thereby reneging on a promised $10,000 bonus.[2] This slight was seen as the pitcher's primary motivation for agreeing to help throw the coming World Series, a conspiracy that became known as the Black Sox Scandal.[3] But there is no evidence that Comiskey promised that large a bonus to his pitcher[4] — and besides, Cicotte did take the mound on September 24 with a chance to win his 30th game. All he had to do was beat the Browns, who came in with a 65-70 record, 22 games behind the first-place White Sox.

St. Louis manager Jimmy Burke sent spitballer Allan Sothoron to the mound. The 26-year-old right-hander was enjoying his finest season, with a 20-11 record and a 2.13 ERA, fourth-best in the American League. He had allowed just one earned run in his last 28⅔ innings against the White Sox.

The Browns jumped on Cicotte early with three runs in the first inning, on RBI singles from Baby Doll Jacobson and Ray Demmitt. Jack Tobin singled home Jacobson for another

Shoeless Joe Jackson, implicated in the 1919 Black Sox World Series-fixing scandal, went 12-for-32 against the Cincinnati Reds in the fall classic as the Pale House lost the best-of-nine Series five games to three. (Photo Reproduction by Transcendental Graphics/Getty Images)

run in the third to increase the lead to 4-0.

The White Sox countered with two runs in the fifth, when Swede Risberg doubled and scored on a throwing error and Ray Schalk came home on Nemo Leibold's double to right field. Before Risberg's at-bat, he asked home-plate umpire George Hildebrand to inspect the baseball. Sothoron's array of trick pitches had held Chicago to two hits up until that point. The ball was "so badly scarred" that Hildebrand threw it out and the White Sox were able to rally "before [Sothoron] could doctor up another one."[5]

The Browns scored again in the seventh, as Jimmy Austin and Jacobson hit back-to-back triples off the struggling Cicotte, who had allowed five earned runs in a start only twice before during the season. Jacobson tried to stretch his hit into a home run, but strong relay throws by center fielder Happy Felsch and shortstop Risberg helped keep the score 5-2 as Cicotte departed for a pinch-hitter. The White Sox starter allowed 11 hits and five runs in his seven innings pitched. As the *St. Louis Star* reported, the Browns "had little trouble in solving his shoots and they could have gathered more runs … if they had been a little more discreet in running the bases."[6]

White Sox team captain Eddie Collins cut the deficit to 5-4 with a one-out triple in the bottom half of the seventh, bringing home Leibold and Eddie Murphy, who had walked in Cicotte's spot. But Collins was thrown out at the plate on a close play and he argued so vigorously with umpire Hildebrand that he was "banished from the scrap."[7]

Long before relief pitchers were considered to be specialists, Dickey Kerr had developed into a bullpen ace for manager Gleason. The rookie left-hander from Texas was often called on in the late innings to hold the opposition until the White Sox' explosive offense could take over; he recorded a 7-1 record and a 1.78 ERA in 22 relief appearances in 1919.[8] On this day, after pitching two scoreless innings in relief of Cicotte, Kerr started the winning rally all by himself.

With the Sox down by one run entering the bottom of the ninth inning, Kerr led off with a single to left field and moved to third on a base hit by Leibold. Fred McMullin, who had come in to replace the ejected Collins, worked Sothoron for a walk to load the bases. Buck Weaver lifted a long sacrifice fly to center field, scoring Kerr and tying the game at 5-5. Leibold advanced to third base after the catch.

Shoeless Joe Jackson stepped to the plate against Sothoron with a chance to win the pennant on one swing of the bat. No American League team had ever clinched a World Series berth with a walk-off victory before.[9] Chicago's star slugger took a "vicious swat" and lined a hit to right-center field that would have gone "for two or three bases under ordinary circumstances."[10] One was all that was needed for Leibold to come home with the winning run. The White Sox mobbed Jackson in celebration and began to look ahead to their World Series matchup with the Cincinnati Reds.

One of the headlines in the *Chicago Tribune* sports section the following day offered an ominous preview of what was to come: "Bookies Favor Sox."[11]

SOURCES

Box scores for this game can be found at Baseball-Reference.com and Retrosheet.org:

Baseball-Reference.com/boxes/CHA/CHA191909240.shtml.

Retrosheet.org/boxesetc/1919/B09240CHA1919.htm.

Quinn, John M. "Lefty Kerr Stars Against Brownies as Sox Land Flag," *St. Louis Star*, September 25, 1919.

Sanborn, I.E. "White Sox Crown Themselves American League Champs," **Chicago Tribune**, September 25, 1919: 23.

Sanborn, I.E. "Cicotte Routed in Clash That Nails Flag For Sox, 6-5," **Chicago Tribune**, September 25, 1919: 23.

Wray, John E. "Cicotte's Weakness Alarms White Sox Supporters; Hard Hitting Clinches Pennant," **St. Louis Post-Dispatch**, September 25, 1919: 31.

NOTES

1. "Kerr Will Outdo Cicotte Against Reds, Fan Wagers," **St. Louis Post-Dispatch**, September 20, 1919: 8.

2. Bob Hoie, "1919 Baseball Salaries and the Mythically Underpaid Chicago White Sox," **Base Ball: A Journal of the Early Game**. (Jefferson, North Carolina: McFarland & Co., Spring 2012): 29-30. Hoie explains the genesis and evolution of the "Cicotte bonus" story, which began with a December 1919 report in **Collyer's Eye** and was embellished by Eliot Asinof in **Eight Men Out**. In 1990 Rob Neyer began dismantling the myth in Bill James's **The Baseball Book**, and other writers have followed with even more evidence to disprove the theory. See, for example, David Marasco, "Cicotte's 29 Wins in 1919," The Diamond Angle, accessed online at thediamondangle.com/marasco/hist/cicotte.html on December 3, 2006; and Lowell D. Blaisdell, "Legends as an Expression of Baseball Memory," **Journal of Sport History 19** (Winter 1992).

3. Regardless of the reasons for Cicotte's long layoff, just about everyone involved agreed that his involvement in the plot to fix the World Series had already begun before then. Cicotte himself testified that the fix was first discussed at a meeting of the players on September 10 or 12 at the Ansonia Hotel in New York. He returned to the field to win his 29th game on September 19 against the Boston Red Sox and then faced the Browns five days later. See William F. Lamb, **Black Sox in the Courtroom: The Grand Jury, Criminal Trial, and Civil Litigation** (Jefferson, North Carolina: McFarland & Co., 2013): 49-51.

4. Hoie, op. cit. As Hoie writes, "The amount of the ($10,000) bonus and its structure were … highly improbable." Contract cards acquired at the turn of the 21st century by the National Baseball Hall of Fame Library show that Cicotte was one of the highest-paid players in baseball, making a total of $8,000 in 1919 — second highest among all pitchers in the American League to Walter Johnson. Comiskey did promise a much smaller bonus to Lefty Williams in 1919: $375 for winning 15 games and an additional $500 if he won 20, both of which he earned. It seems extremely unlikely that Comiskey would have promised such a large bonus to Cicotte — more than his annual salary — for a similar performance milestone.

5. I.E. Sanborn, "Cicotte Routed in Clash That Nails Flag for Sox, 6-5," **Chicago Tribune**, September 25, 1919: 23.

6. John M. Quinn, "Lefty Kerr Stars Against Brownies as Sox Land Flag," **St. Louis Star**, September 25, 1919: 16.

7. Sanborn, op. cit.

8. Dickey Kerr 1919 season splits, Baseball-Reference.com, accessed online at Baseball-Reference.com/players/split.fcgi?id=kerrdi01&year=1919&t=p on January 13, 2018.

9. After Jackson's winning hit, no other AL team would clinch a pennant on a walk-off victory for a quarter-century. A full list of all 20 walk-off pennant clinchers in the World Series era can be found in the author's article, "Walking Off to the World Series," at The National Pastime Museum: thenationalpastimemuseum.com/article/walking-world-series.

10. Sanborn, op. cit.

11. "Bookies Favor Sox," **Chicago Tribune**, September 25, 1919: 23.

ROOKIE HURLER DICKEY KERR TURNS TABLES ON REDS, GAMBLERS

OCTOBER 3, 1919
CHICAGO WHITE SOX 3, CINCINNATI REDS 0
GAME THREE OF THE WORLD SERIES

By Mike Lynch

After the Chicago White Sox lost the first two games of the 1919 World Series to the Cincinnati Reds in Cincinnati, the Series shifted to Chicago's Comiskey Park for the next three tilts. Though Reds manager Pat Moran admitted his team was lucky to have beaten Lefty Williams in Game Two, he also insisted the Reds were "brimming over with [confidence]" and had "nothing to fear of the other pitchers of Gleason's staff."[1]

Gleason, of course, was White Sox manager William "Kid" Gleason and one of the pitchers they had no fear of was diminutive left-hander Dickey Kerr, a 26-year-old rookie who was once described by legendary writer Damon Runyon as being "too small for too much of anything, except, perhaps, a watch charm ..."[2] Standing only 5-feet-7 and tipping the scales at just over 150 pounds, Kerr was hardly an imposing figure, but he was a very good pitcher who went 13-7 with a 2.88 ERA in 17 starts and 22 relief appearances in 1919, and he'd be getting the ball in Game Three.

Kerr had two opponents to face on October 3, 1919 — the Reds and his own crooked teammates, who swore to gamblers that they'd never win for a "busher."[3] Rumors had swirled even before the Series began that the fix was in and several members of the White Sox had sold their souls for a massive payday. All they had to do was lose convincingly to the Reds. First baseman Chick Gandil and ace pitcher Eddie Cicotte were at the fore of a group that also included superstar left fielder Shoeless Joe Jackson, center fielder Happy Felsch, shortstop Swede Risberg, infielder Fred McMullin, Williams, and, allegedly, third baseman Buck Weaver.[4]

Cicotte, who had gone 29-7 with a 1.82 ERA during the regular season, plunked Reds second baseman Morrie Rath with his second pitch of Game One, which allegedly signaled gamblers that the fix was on, and lasted only 3⅔ innings in a 9-1 drubbing that was the most lopsided Game One rout in World Series history.[5] Then Williams, a 23-game winner, lost 4-2 in the second contest to put the White Sox in a two-games-to-nothing hole. Both losses raised eyebrows — Cicotte had hit only two batters all year before drilling Rath, and Williams' regular-season high in walks was four before he walked six Reds in Game Two.

Opposing Kerr in Game Three was Ray Fisher, a nine-year veteran who was in his first year with the Reds after spending his first eight big-league seasons with the Yankees. Dubbed "The Vermont Schoolmaster," the spitball artist went 14-5 with a 2.17 ERA in 26 games, and his experience against the White Sox and in Comiskey Park was supposed to give him an edge. But the afternoon belonged to Kerr, who was about to pitch the game of his life.

Kerr and Fisher traded goose eggs in the first — Kerr disposed of Rath on an easy grounder to Risberg and Jake Daubert on a fly ball to Felsh, and fanned Heinie Groh on four pitches; Fisher retired Nemo Leibold on a liner to right that Greasy Neale snared off his shoetops before turning a somersault, Eddie Collins grounded back to the box, and Weaver popped to first. Kerr dispatched the Reds with relative ease in the top of the second, but not before a questionable play by Risberg turned what should have been a double play into a single out that kept the inning alive. After Pat Duncan dropped a Texas League blooper in for a hit with one out in the inning, Larry Kopf grounded to Risberg, who "messed the ball around until too late to get Duncan at second," but Kerr coaxed Neale to ground out to Collins to end the frame.[6]

The White Sox struck first in the bottom of the second and plated two runs to take a 2-0 lead. "The climax, which happened all too prematurely, came as the wind from the stock yardes [sic] laden with life-giving balsam to the White Sox wafted over the diamond," waxed the *New York Tribune's* W.O. McGeehan. "It tickled the nostrils of Joe Jackson, the first of the White Sox to bat in the second inning. Joseph drove a hit to left."[7] Felsch followed with a sacrifice bunt that Fisher fielded and threw into center field, and the White Sox had runners at second and third with no outs.

That brought up Gandil, who rapped a single to right that scored both runners and advanced to second on Neale's throw to the plate. Risberg worked a walk to keep the rally going, which brought Groh to the mound to settle Fisher down. It worked. Ray Schalk hit a roller toward third that Fisher scooped up and tossed to Groh to nip Gandil, who went in standing up. Then Kerr grounded to Fisher, who threw to third again for another force out.[8] Leibold grounded to Groh to end the threat.

Kerr allowed a one-out single to Fisher in the top of the third on a bounder that the pitcher reached before he fell down, but retired the others with relative ease. Fisher got himself into another jam in the bottom of the frame when he surrendered hits to Eddie Collins and Weaver to put runners at first and second with nobody out, but Jackson bunted into an out thanks to a nifty play by Daubert, and Felsch grounded into an around-the-horn double play to end the inning.

Despite being up by two with Kerr seemingly in control, the hometown throng could be forgiven for getting a little antsy heading into the next inning. "In the fourth inning the Chicagoans were breathing their own odorous air in short anxious gasps," wrote McGeehan. "In the first two games it was the fourth that proved the fatal inning for the White Sox."[9] Indeed, Cicotte was lifted from his start in the fourth with his team down 6-1 and Williams allowed three runs on two hits and three walks in that frame in his turn on the mound.

Kerr gave the Windy City crowd a brief scare when he walked Groh to lead off the inning, but he recovered nicely to get Edd Roush on a grounder to short that advanced Groh to second. Duncan clubbed Kerr's fourth offering toward Risberg, who snared the drive and flipped to Collins for a double play. As if to ensure that they exorcised the curse of the fourth inning forever the White Sox tallied their third run on a Risberg three-bagger that got past Neale, who was "depressed and befogged by the local ozone," and a Schalk base knock.[10]

Schalk topped a grounder toward Fisher, but as the pitcher was about to make the play, the ball hit something and bounced over his head. Risberg scooted in with the third and final run of the game. Kerr allowed a leadoff single to Kopf in the fifth and the Reds reached second base after two groundouts by Neale and Bill Rariden, but that was as close as Cincinnati would get to home plate for the rest of the game.

Kerr retired the last 15 batters in order and cruised to a 3-0 victory, and the Sox pulled to within a game of Cincinnati going into their fourth tilt.

SOURCES

In addition to the sources mentioned in the notes, the author consulted Baseball-Reference.com and Retrosheet.org.

NOTES

1 "Eller Will Pitch Today Against Kerr or Cicotte," **Des Moines Register**, October 3, 1919.

2 Eliot Asinof, **Eight Men Out** (New York: Simon & Schuster, 1963), 108-109.

3 Gene Carney, "New Light on an Old Scandal," **Baseball Research Journal #35**: 77.

4 Along with seven of his teammates, Weaver was banned from the major leagues for life by Commissioner Kenesaw Mountain Landis for throwing the World Series to the Reds, except that Weaver's crime was having "guilty knowledge" of the fix and not reporting it. Despite attending some meetings in which the plot to throw the World Series was discussed, Weaver maintained his innocence until the day he died and still has strong support to clear his name.

5 The Milwaukee Brewers topped that with a 10-0 victory over the St. Louis Cardinals in Game One of the 1982 World Series.

6 W.O. McGeehan, "White Sox With Kerr in Box Win Third Game of World Series by a Score of 3 to 0," **New York Tribune**, October 4, 1919.

7 Ibid.

8 Claims were made that Gandil slowed up just enough to be thrown out and that proved he was trying to throw Game Three, but there's no evidence he did that. Had he slid, the play would have been closer, but it wouldn't have guaranteed he'd be safe. He also insisted in a 1956 interview with writer Melvin Durslag that the fix was off before the Series even began, but that has to be taken with a grain if salt.

9 McGeehan, "White Sox With Kerr in Box."

10 Ibid.

RING'S PITCHING, CICOTTE'S ERRORS LEAD REDS OVER WHITE SOX

OCTOBER 4, 1919
CINCINNATI REDS 2, CHICAGO WHITE SOX 0
GAME FOUR OF THE WORLD SERIES

By Mike Lynch

Thanks to Dickey Kerr serving his teammates a dose of rejuvenating elixir in Game Three, the White Sox had regained their confidence and were ready to take Game Four at Comiskey Park. "Reassured by yesterday's shutout of the Reds, the White Sox today declared they were ready to back up Eddie Cicotte ... and even up the series 2-2," announced the *Elmira Star-Gazette*.[1] The Reds were equally buoyant and insisted they were merely familiarizing themselves with Comiskey Park's "breezes, shadows and sunspots," the day before and this time would be different.[2]

With the fourth tilt scheduled for a Saturday, fans began lining up for tickets before midnight Friday and the crowd of 34,363 was more than 5,000 fans stronger than Friday's horde of 29,126. Cicotte was looking to redeem himself after a terrible outing in Game One that saw him allow six runs in 3⅔ innings. He'd allowed five or more runs only three times during the regular season and only twice did he throw fewer innings in a start, the latter being a planned two-inning tune-up for the World Series in his last regular-season start on September 28.

The Reds countered with 24-year-old right-hander Jimmy Ring, who bounced between the rotation and bullpen en route to a 10-9 record and 2.26 ERA that fell just out of the top 10 in the National League.

The park was full by noon and the bugs enjoyed an enthusiastic round of practice by the Reds featuring a long blast by Pat Duncan that cleared the left-field pavilion and a circus catch by Greasy Neale that brought a round of applause from the packed house.

Not surprisingly, the loudest cheers were reserved for the White Sox. "The stands got to their feet with a tremendous roar when the Gleason tribe took over the field for practice," reported the *Buffalo Evening News*. "Sirens, bells, and horns were brought into play. Two enthusiasts in the stands battered shiny dish pans with metal spoons."[3] But Cicotte was all business, his cap pulled down low, a smile nowhere to be found.[4]

Moments before Morrie Rath stepped to the plate to start the fray, a strong wind carried a cloud bank from Lake Michigan, lowering the temperature by several degrees and bringing the threat of rain. Cicotte tossed his first pitch and cut the heart of the plate with a curveball for strike one. Rath went down 0-and-2, but battled back and lined a single over Buck Weaver on the pitcher's sixth slant. Cicotte buckled down and got Jake Daubert to shoot a grounder to Eddie Collins, who started a 4-6-3 double play, then coaxed a popup off Heinie Groh's bat for the third out.

Nemo Leibold led off for the White Sox in the bottom of the first and worked the count to

2-and-2 before popping up to Daubert in short right field. Eddie Collins swung wildly at a Ring curveball and skied it to Rath for the second out, and Weaver poked a Ring heater to Neale to end the frame. Ring "showed a world of speed and his fast one was hopping in fine shape. ..."[5]

Cicotte was working "very slowly and cautiously," mixing his fastball with a sweeping curve, and the tactic worked to perfection.[6] National League batting champ Edd Roush began the second with an easy fly ball to Joe Jackson, Duncan popped to Collins, and Larry Kopf swung feebly at strike three.

As dominant as Ring was in the opening stanza, he was equally wild in the second, but he tiptoed out of a bases-loaded situation and escaped without allowing a run. Jackson led off with a shot to center that should have been an out had Roush not misjudged it into a double, then moved to third on a sacrifice by Happy Felsch. Chick Gandil poled a high pop in front of the plate that the wind grabbed before Groh hauled it in, and the White Sox had only one more chance to get Jackson in from third.

Swede Risberg worked a seven-pitch walk, then stole second base easily on a pitch that catcher Ivey Wingo dropped. Ray Schalk drew a free pass on four straight balls to load the sacks and there's little doubt it was by design with the weak-hitting Cicotte on deck. The Sox hurler almost spoiled the strategy when he battled to a full count, which actually had Ring grinning, but Rath made a nice play on Cicotte's hard grounder to second and he tossed to Daubert to end the threat.[7]

Cicotte looked nothing like the man who'd been battered about in Game One and cruised through another fairly uneventful inning in the third. Neale slammed Cicotte's first pitch down the third-base line, but Weaver picked it and threw the right fielder out. Wingo took a called strike before dropping a hit beyond Collins's reach, but Ring fouled three straight pitches before fanning on the fourth and the Reds had two out with a man on first.

Rath took a ball, then fouled one to left, where Jackson almost made a spectacular play when he snared the ball, but dropped it when he crashed into the wall. Wingo took off for second on the next pitch, but Schalk's throw was so strong Wingo didn't even bother to slide and the Reds were done. Ring had to work his way out of another jam, not entirely of his own making, when the Sox had runners at first and third with two outs — he hit Collins in the ribs with a curveball and Jackson was safe on Rath's error — before he coaxed Felsch to ground out to third.

Rath stepped to the plate again in the top of the fourth and this time shot a fly right at Jackson, who didn't have to move to record the out. Cicotte was working "easily and confidently" and his curve was "breaking nicely" as he dispatched Cincinnati with ease in the fourth, using only eight pitches to retire Rath, Daubert, and Groh.[8]

Unfortunately for the home team, Ring was finding his groove again, "burning the ball across in dazzling fashion," and needed only seven tosses to retire the White Sox in the bottom of the fourth.[9] Gandil hit an anemic popup to Daubert for the first out, Neale caught Risberg's fly ball on the right-field foul line after a long run, and Schalk popped up to Kopf to send the game into the fifth with neither team able to put a crooked number on the scoreboard.

That was about to change. Schalk recorded another assist when he deftly fielded a Roush tapper in front of the plate and threw him out for the first out of the fifth inning. The second out should have come soon after when Cicotte knocked down Duncan's shot up the middle, but his attempt to throw the runner out was wild and Duncan landed at second base on the error. Kopf followed with a single to left and Duncan lit out for home on what looked to be a close play at the plate. "Jackson rifled a perfect throw to the plate to cut off the run," wrote Eliot Asinof in *Eight Men Out*. "But Cicotte interceded. He stepped in front of the ball to cut it off. Artfully, as if to hurry his throw to second base, he allowed the ball to deflect off his glove for his second error of the inning. It rolled to the stands behind home plate."[10] Duncan scored and Kopf went to second on the muff.

Neale took two balls and a strike before driving the ball over Jackson's head for a run-scoring double; and the game, for all intents and purposes, was in the bag for Cincinnati. Cicotte was brilliant the rest of the way and faced the minimum 12 batters over the final four innings, allowing only a single in the eighth to Wingo, who was erased on a double play. But the White Sox couldn't crack Ring despite putting a runner on base in every inning from the fifth to the ninth.

Only one reached second base and the Reds went up three games to one on Ring's three-hit shutout in the 2-0 win.

SOURCES

In addition to the sources cited in the Notes, the author also accessed Retrosheet.org, Baseball-Reference.com, and SABR.org.

NOTES

1 "White Sox Confident of Victory Today While Reds Expect Some Easy Pitching," **Elmira Star-Gazette**, October 4, 1919

2 Ibid.

3 "Loose Fielding by Cicotte Gives Cincinnati Two Runs," **Buffalo Evening News**, October 4, 1919.

4 Ibid.

5 Ibid.

6 Ibid.

7 Ibid.

8 Ibid.

9 Ibid.

10 Eliot Asinof, **Eight Men Out** (New York: Simon & Schuster, 1963), 115. In an interview with Melvin Durslag that appeared in the September 17, 1956, issue of **Sports Illustrated**, Chick Gandil claimed he yelled to Cicotte to intercept the throw because they had no chance to get Duncan at the plate, but still had a shot at Kopf going to second.

HOD ELLER SCATTERS THREE HITS, FANS 9 TO LEAD REDS TO VICTORY

OCTOBER 6, 1919
CINCINNATI REDS 5, CHICAGO WHITE SOX 0
GAME FIVE OF THE WORLD SERIES

By Mike Lynch

Boasting a three-games-to-one lead after four tilts, the Reds had all but started counting their share of the World Series take. "With three victories to our credit, nothing will stop the Reds now of winning the world's championship," Cincinnati skipper Pat Moran declared before they were to face the White Sox at Comiskey Park in Game Five.[1]

Moran also insisted his pitching staff was "vastly superior" to Chicago's and, as if to prove it, he sent 19-game winner and shine-ball artist Hod Eller to the mound to face Lefty Williams instead of ace and Game One winner Dutch Ruether.[2]

Eller had gone to spring training with the White Sox in 1916 and legend was that he learned the shine ball from Eddie Cicotte and Dave Danforth. But according to biographer Stephen V. Rice, Eller learned the pitch accidentally while trying to get a better grip on the ball during a game against the New York Giants in 1917.[3] Eller mastered the pitch and went 45-26 with a 2.37 ERA for the Reds from 1917 to 1919.

The White Sox had spent part of the previous day, a soggy Sunday that pushed Game Five back a day, criticizing themselves and each other for plays they should have made in their three losses. But when a reporter remarked that the loser's share would be close to $4,000, he was told to go to hell.[4]

Monday was sunny and the game was played under a cloudless sky, but it was cold and the field was still damp and slippery even after the best efforts of laborers, who did all they could to get it in playing shape. Despite the chill in the air, attendance was 34,379 and would prove to be the highest of the Series. Once again the masses were treated to a brilliant pitching performance and once again Chicagoans would be sent home without a win. In a pattern that was becoming all too familiar in Chicago's losses, the White Sox suffered through a tumultuous inning that would lead to their downfall. This time it was the sixth.

Williams took the hill and fired his first pitch to Morrie Rath, a ball that was a foot outside. Five pitches later, Rath was on first with a walk, the seventh free pass issued by Williams in only 32 batters. Jake Daubert followed with a perfectly executed sacrifice bunt that sent Rath to second, but Williams got Heine Groh to fly to Happy Felsch, and Edd Roush to ground to Chick Gandil to end the inning.[5] According to the *Buffalo Evening News*, Williams' curve was breaking "very sharply" and he "worked the corners repeatedly."[6]

Eller struggled in his half of the inning and only a call that went against the White Sox kept them from loading the bases with one out. Nemo Leibold led off for Chicago and drew a seven-pitch walk that had the crowd responding with great enthusiasm.[7] Eddie Collins took two balls before Daubert went to the mound to settle Eller down. Collins took a strike, then grounded to shortstop Larry Kopf, who barely nipped the speedy runner at first. Collins thought he was safe and "protested vigorously," to no avail.[8] Leibold advanced to second on the play and might have scored had Eller not knocked down Buck Weaver's hit up the middle, but he stopped at third and the White Sox had runners at the corners with the heart of the order coming up. Moran took no chances and ordered ace reliever Dolf Luque to warm up.

It proved to be unnecessary. Joe Jackson hit a towering popup to Groh at third, Felsch followed with a fly ball to Pat Duncan in left, and the threat was over. So were the White Sox' hopes; they would put only two men on base the rest of the way. Of course the fans didn't know that and they continued to cheer their boys on, especially when Williams fanned Duncan and Greasy Neale in the top of the second, which brought the fans to their feet "with a great roar."[9] The southpaw was mixing his curve with a "slow one" with great success.[10]

Eller did Williams one better in the bottom of the frame and struck out Gandil, Swede Risberg, and Ray Schalk with a "wicked" shine ball that had Risberg so fooled he dodged out of the way of a pitch that swerved over the heart of the plate.[11] Williams continued mixing his pitches effectively, but changed things up in the third and relied heavily on a combination of fastballs and "underhand floaters" to retire the Reds easily.[12]

Not to be outdone, Eller made history when he struck out Williams, Leibold, and Collins in succession, giving him six straight punchouts, a World Series record, and thousands of new fans, who "rose with a mighty cheer" after his third strike sizzled past Collins's bat.[13] The Reds put a man at second in the top of the fourth when Roush reached first on shortstop Risberg's miscue with two outs, then advanced on a steal attempt made easier when Schalk dropped the pitch. But Duncan flied out to Jackson and the game went to the bottom of the inning still scoreless.

Weaver broke Eller's strikeout streak with a weak tap to the pitcher, but the 25-year-old righty continued to mesmerize White Sox batters and shut down Jackson on a grounder to the box before fanning Felsch on three pitches. Cincinnati had no answers for Williams in the fifth, but catcher Bill Rariden and an ingenious fan entertained the throng when Rariden skied a foul to right that was caught in the mouth of a megaphone, much to the crowd's delight.[14]

The White Sox put a man on first thanks to a two-out single to left by Schalk, but Eller struck out Williams to send the game to the fateful sixth. Eller led off the inning and he was no slouch at the plate, having batted .280 with a .409 slugging percentage during the regular season. "Eller was … known as a dead pull hitter to left," wrote William A. Cook. But when Eller came up in the third inning White Sox manager Kid Gleason "pulled Happy Felsch over toward right leaving a gap between center and left."[15]

Gleason waved Felsch toward right again in the sixth and Eller made the White Sox pay with a double to left center made worse when Felsch heaved wildly to the infield and Risberg deflected the ball far enough away for Eller to go to third. Rath sent Eller home with a sharp single to right on a two-strike pitch and the Reds went up 1-0. Daubert sacrificed again and Rath was on second with one out. Williams was careful with Groh and walked him on four pitches, the second of which Williams and Schalk argued was a strike.[16]

Accounts of what happened next differ somewhat depending on who's telling the story, but the result was the same regardless. Roush sent a fly to center that Felsch misplayed before racing back, catching up to it, and snagging the ball out of the air only to drop it. What followed was a comedy of errors that had Felsch slipping, falling, and dropping the ball again before he fired it to the infield where Collins corralled it and heaved to Schalk in an effort to nab Groh at home.[17] The latter slid past Schalk and umpire

Cy Rigler called him safe, sending Schalk into a rage and out of the game after he bumped Rigler during his tirade.

By the time the dust settled, the Reds had plated three runs. Duncan's sacrifice fly four pitches later gave the boys from the Queen City a 4-0 cushion before Williams could escape the inning. Eller continued to be largely unhittable and retired 12 of the last 13 White Sox, the lone blemish being Weaver's triple with two outs in the ninth. Cincinnati manufactured a run in the top of the ninth against Erskine Mayer on an error, walk, sacrifice bunt, and groundout to put the finishing touches on the 5-0 victory.

SOURCES

In addition to the sources mentioned in the notes, the author consulted Baseball-Reference.com and Retrosheet.org.

NOTES

1 "Can't Stop Reds … Moran," **Baltimore Sun**, October 5, 1919.

2 Ibid.

3 Hod Eller biography, Society for American Baseball Research, sabr.org/bioproj/person/32e0ca8c.

4 Eliot Asinof, **Eight Men Out** (New York: Simon & Schuster, 1963), 117.

5 "Reds Win Again," **Buffalo Evening News**, October 6, 1919.

6 Ibid.

7 Ibid.

8 Ibid.

9 Ibid.

10 Bill James and Rob Neyer, **The Neyer/James Guide to Pitchers: An Historical Compendium of Pitching, Pitchers, and Pitches** (New York: Fireside, 2004), 21. According to Rob Neyer, a slow ball was most commonly linked to the palm ball based on how contemporary pitchers demonstrated their grip.

11 "Reds Win Again."

12 Ibid.

13 Ibid.

14 Ibid.

15 William A. Cook, **The 1919 World Series: What Really Happened?** (Jefferson, North Carolina: McFarland & Company, Inc., 2001), 60-61.

16 "Marvelous Box Work of Eller Cops for Reds," **Moline** (Illinois) **Daily Dispatch**, October 6, 1919.

17 Cook wrote that Felsch was inexplicably playing shallow with slugger Edd Roush at the plate and that his first step was forward before he raced back and caught up to the ball, only to drop it as he slipped and fell. Eliot Asinof wrote in **Eight Men Out** that Roush's fly was a "towering shot to deep center field," that Felsch turned "at the crack of the bat and tore after it" while the crowd anticipated a typical Felsch grab, except that the outfielder turned too soon, slowed down, started again, turned again, lost sight of the ball, located it again, sped up and tracked it down, only to drop it. Then he slipped, fell, got up and grabbed the ball, dropped it, and grabbed it again.

REDS WIN FIRST CHAMPIONSHIP IN FRANCHISE HISTORY

OCTOBER 9, 1919
CINCINNATI REDS 10, CHICAGO WHITE SOX 5
GAME EIGHT OF THE WORLD SERIES

By Mike Lynch

After wins in Games Six and Seven in Cincinnati by scores of 5-4 and 4-1, respectively, it was clear the White Sox were no longer playing to lose. Dickey Kerr wasn't as brilliant in Game Six as he was in Game Three, but he went the distance in a 10-inning affair that saw the White Sox erase a four-run deficit before plating the go-ahead and eventual winning run in the top of the 10th on a double by Buck Weaver, Shoeless Joe Jackson's bunt single, and a hit by Chick Gandil.

Eddie Cicotte took the ball in Game Seven and enjoyed a second straight dominant start, allowing only one run on seven hits to earn his first World Series win and bring the White Sox to within a game of tying the Series at four games apiece. All they needed was for Lefty Williams to resemble the pitcher who had won 23 games during the regular season and not the one who'd lost twice to the Reds while allowing eight runs in 16 innings.

But Williams' performance in Game Eight would be his worst one yet and it's still surrounded by mystery, rumors, and conjecture. Legend has it that the southpaw's life was threatened before the game and he had no choice but to pitch poorly.[1] Some claim it was Williams' wife, Lyria, who was threatened, but she later said that the pitcher was afraid of retaliation if he pitched to win.[2] Williams insisted in his grand-jury testimony in 1920 that he had pitched to win all three of his starts.[3] He looked more like a man pitching for his life.

Cincinnati skipper Pat Moran gave Hod Eller the ball for Game Eight, hoping the spitballer could replicate his Game Five performance, a three-hit shutout in which he fanned nine White Sox, including six straight to set a World Series record. Some, however, believed Chicago would continue their comeback and win the next two games. "You tell 'em the dopesters are up against it now," wrote Fred R. Coburn in the *Minneapolis Star Tribune*, "there is no question that the Sox ... are hitting on all eight cylinders with prospects excellent for their eventual triumph."[4]

Morning clouds that brought the threat of rain were chased away from Comiskey Park by a blustery wind blowing away from home plate that had flags above the ballpark "straightened out flat against the breeze."[5] As usual, the place was packed with 32,930 fans, some of whom were still lined up outside the park when the game began.

Wary of Happy Felsch's miscues in center field, White Sox skipper Kid Gleason moved him to right field, where he hadn't played since 1915 and would amass only eight career games there. Nemo Leibold was in center and had experience there, but had played center field only once all season and that as a late-inning replacement for

Best known for receiving a lifetime ban from Organized Baseball for his knowledge of the 1919 World Series fix, in which he did not participate, Buck Weaver played his entire nine-year career with the South Siders, batting .272. (Photo by Mark Rucker/Transcendental Graphics, Getty Images)

Felsch in an August 2 game against the Boston Red Sox. It wouldn't matter.

Reds leadoff man Morrie Rath was greeted by a pitch that split the heart of the plate for strike one.[6] He fouled off the next offering, then popped to Swede Risberg at shortstop. Jake Daubert dropped a hit that touched down in the outfield grass before Leibold could grab it. Heinie Groh made Williams work before poling the southpaw's sixth offering just over Gandil's head and into right field.

With runners at first and second, Edd Roush ripped a double past first to score Daubert and send Groh to third. Sensing a repeat of Williams' first two starts of the Series, Gleason wasted no time and ordered Big Bill James to get warm. Reds left fielder Pat Duncan sealed Williams' fate with a line drive over third baseman Buck Weaver's head that went into the left-field corner for another double that plated Groh and Roush and gave Cincinnati a 3-0 lead.

"At this juncture Kid Gleason came up to the pitcher's box," wrote the *New York Tribune's* W.O. McGeehan, "and after a brief and torrid conference Claude Williams was told to go anywhere he wanted for the remainder of the afternoon."[7] Williams was sent to the bench only five batters into his outing. In the press box, legendary hurler Christy Mathewson asserted that Williams had thrown nothing but fastballs.[8] True or not, the southpaw tossed only 16 pitches.

James entered the contest, making his first appearance of the series, and immediately walked Larry Kopf, then fanned Greasy Neale for the second out of the inning before surrendering a run-scoring Texas League single over first base by Bill Rariden to give the Reds a 4-0 cushion. With Eller at the plate, Rariden stole second base to put runners at second and third, but James got the Reds hurler to fly out to end the inning.

The White Sox gave the home crowd hope in the bottom of the first when Leibold led off with a single and went to third on a Eddie Collins's two-bagger to left to put runners in scoring position with no outs. Moran stole a page out of Gleason's playbook and sent Jimmy Ring to the bullpen to warm up, but Eller struck out Weaver, got Jackson to pop to third, and fanned Felsch.

Cincinnati struck again in the top of the second on a two-out single by Groh followed by Roush's second double of the game, but the latter was erased in a rundown after overrunning the base, and the Reds had to settle for one run. Chicago cut the lead to 5-1 in the bottom of the third when Jackson blasted the Series' only home run, a deep drive to right field, but James couldn't hold the Reds back and they kept on scoring, sending Kopf across in the fifth, then three more against him and Roy Wilkinson in the sixth to go up 9-1.

The Reds plated their final run in the top of the eighth inning when Roush was plunked by a Wilkinson pitch to lead off the frame, went to second on a Duncan bunt, and came around to score on Rariden's single to left. Down 10-1, the White Sox finally showed life and rallied in the bottom of the inning.

Leibold led off with a drive to deep right field that was tracked down by Neale, but Eddie Collins shot one through the box for a base hit and Weaver sent him to third with a double to right. Jackson smoked a hard line drive to right for a two-bagger that scored Collins and Weaver. Felsch popped out to first, but Chicago got lucky when Gandil's drive to right got lost in the sun and landed 30 feet from Neale. By the time the dust settled, Gandil was on third with a triple and the White Sox had cut the lead to 10-4.

Roush also had trouble with the sun on Risberg's fly, but seemed to have recovered before dropping the ball, and Gandil scampered home with Chicago's fourth run of the inning. Eller got Schalk to ground out to second and the game went into the ninth. Wilkinson survived a leadoff single by Rath and kept the game at 10-5 with one more chance to at least pull even. Eddie Murphy pinch-hit for Wilkinson and took first when Eller's third offering hit him. Leibold poled what looked to be a hit to center but Roush made a spectacular catch, "barely getting to it, and turning a somersault, holding the ball."[9] Murphy had to hold first, but made second on Collins's third hit of the game, then went to third on a long fly to right by Weaver.

That brought up Shoeless Joe Jackson with a chance to get the Sox closer, and when Collins stole second all it would take was a base hit to pull them to within 10-7, but Jackson grounded out to Rath and the Cincinnati Reds were world champions for the first time in franchise history.

SOURCES

In addition to the sources cited in the Notes, the author also accessed Retrosheet.org, Baseball-Reference.com, and SABR.org.

NOTES

1 Jacob Pomrenke, Lefty Williams biography, Society for American Baseball Research, sabr.org/bioproj/person/0998b35f. Eliot Asinof, **Eight Men Out**, (New York: Simon & Schuster, 1963), 128. Asinof wrote that Boston gambler Sport Sullivan wanted to ensure that Williams was "in the bag" so he hired a man named Harry F. to threaten Williams, which he did, telling him that Cincinnati needed to be assured of a victory by the end of the first inning. Asinof later admitted that Harry F. was a fictional character.

2 Pomrenke, Williams biography.

3 William F. Lamb, **Black Sox in the Courtroom: The Grand Jury, Criminal Trial and Civil Litigation** (Jefferson, North Carolina: McFarland & Company, Inc., 2013), 59.

4 Fred R. Coburn, "Short Squibs on the Game," **Minneapolis Star Tribune**, October 9, 1919.

5 Damon Runyon, "Chicago Now Graciously Permits Cincinnatians to Hold That Jollification," **Salt Lake Tribune**, October 10, 1919.

6 W.O. McGeehan, "Play by Play Story of Game," **New York Tribune**, October 10, 1919.

7 W.O. McGeehan, "Cincinnati Reds New Baseball Champions — White Sox Beaten in Eighth Game 10 to 5," **New York Tribune**, October 10, 1919.

8 Asinof, **Eight Men Out**, 133.

9 McGeehan, "Cincinnati Reds New Baseball Champions."

HARRY HOOPER FIRST CHISOX BATTER TO HOMER TWICE IN COMISKEY PARK

JUNE 22, 1921
CLEVELAND INDIANS 3, CHICAGO WHITE SOX 2

By Gordon Gattie

The Chicago White Sox and Cleveland Indians experienced completely different kickoffs to their 1921 campaigns. The 1920 season ended with Cleveland capturing their first World Series, over the Brooklyn Robins, after a season-long battle with the White Sox and the New York Yankees for the American League pennant. The White Sox were constantly battered by gambling-related rumors arising from the 1919 World Series. A grand jury delivered indictments against 13 people in October 1920,[1] including eight accused players,[2] and the major leagues named Kenesaw Mountain Landis their first commissioner the following month.[3]

In March 1921 Landis suspended all eight Chicago players suspected of participating in the 1919 World Series fix, and White Sox owner Charles Comiskey added that regardless of the grand jury's verdict, the indicted players would never play for him again.[4] White Sox manager Kid Gleason needed replacements for 20-game winners Eddie Cicotte and Lefty Williams; left fielder Joe Jackson, who finished fourth in OPS during 1920 (1.033); center fielder Happy Felsch, who finished sixth in OPS (.923); shortstop Swede Risberg, third baseman Buck Weaver; and utility infielder Fred McMullin; first baseman Chick Gandil had retired from major-league baseball the previous year.[5] Consequently, fans and local sportswriters were hardly optimistic about the White Sox' coming 1921 campaign. Although starting pitchers Red Faber and Dickey Kerr were expected to deliver solid seasons and win 40 games between them, one local prognosticator commented, "[T]he young and untried members of the staff must accumulate 50 victories. It can't be done."[6] Manager Gleason, heading into his third season guiding Chicago, commented that he had a well-balanced lineup and expected his young pitchers to gain experience during the season.

The White Sox lost their season opener to the Detroit Tigers, 6-5, and ended April with a 4-6 record, four games behind first-place Washington; the Senators were percentage points ahead of Cleveland. The White Sox continued struggling in May, compiling a 13-17 record and falling more than 10 games behind the first-place Indians. As suspected, their young pitchers struggled with their control; as one sportswriter noted, "Between watching the opposing batsman stroll to first on passes and the Sox get picked off the cushions for lack of alarm clocks the south side fans are beginning to like the movies."[7] Although the White Sox lost four of five in an early June matchup with Washington, they rebounded to win their next three series. Heading into the June 21 series opener with Cleveland, the White Sox took three of four from the Yankees and rose to a fifth-place tie with Detroit, ahead of the St. Louis Browns and Philadelphia Athletics.[8] However, the Indians won the first game of the series, 6-3, behind several successful bunts.[9] (On the same newspaper page, three columns over, it was disclosed that the 1919 Black Sox trial before Judge Hugo Friend would start the following Monday.[10])

Cleveland, winner of the 1920 World Series, was led by Tris Speaker, in his third year as manager, and expectations were high for the Tribe to repeat as World Series champions.[11][12] The team started strong, finishing April with an 11-5 record that included a six-game winning streak, and ended the month percentage points behind Washington. Their good play continued in May and as June arrived, an eight-game winning streak had solidified their first-place standing, three games ahead of New York.[13]

Chicago's starting pitcher on Wednesday the 22nd was future Hall of Famer Faber, who was 14-3 with a 2.52 ERA over 139⅓ innings heading into the matchup. Uninvolved with the Black Sox scandal, Faber had won 12 of 13 decisions, including his last six in a row, going back to a May 5 two-hit shutout of Cleveland. Faber's repertoire included a spitball, sinking fastball, and curveball;[14] although the spitball was banned after the 1920 season, Faber was one of the 17 pitchers allowed to continue throwing the pitch.[15] Faber was credited with throwing a speed spitter, receiving credit for his effectiveness in spite of a downgraded defense behind him.[16] In a 1922 *Baseball Magazine* article, Faber noted, "Of course I depend a great deal on the spit ball. But I do not use spitters exclusively. I throw a lot of fast balls and some curves."

Jim Bagby, Cleveland's starter, was struggling with a 7-7 record and 4.85 ERA. Although he started the season strong by winning his first four decisions, Bagby hadn't been able to replicate his previous season's success, when he led the AL with 31 wins, 30 complete games, 339⅔ innings pitched, and a 2.89 ERA. Bagby was well-known for his fadeaway pitch, which he developed after suffering a broken arm while playing outfield for the minor league New Orleans Pelicans during the 1913 season.[17]

The White Sox crossed the plate first when future Hall of Famer Harry Hooper delivered his second homer of the season a vicious solo

Acknowledged as one of the best defensive right fielders in baseball history, Harry Hooper played the last five seasons (1921-1925) of his 17-year Hall of Fame career with the White Sox, hitting .302, including a career-best .328 at the age of 36 in 1924. (Photo by Mark Rucker/Transcendental Graphics, Getty Images)

shot into the right-field bleachers in the first inning.[18] After spending the first 12 seasons of his career with the Boston Red Sox, the popular Hooper had been traded to Chicago for Shano Collins and Nemo Leibold. Although most fans were shocked by the trade, those familiar with Boston's management were hardly surprised. A Boston sportswriter wrote, "For Harry Hooper, most popular player ever to wear a Boston uniform, the greatest right fielder of the past decade and the bulwark of the nearly denuded championship tree, has been handed over to Chicago in an eleventh hour trade and his passing marks the loss of the last great player to bring glory to Boston under the leadership of the stalwart Bill Carrigan."[19] Hooper was glad to leave the Red Sox; 70 years later he told author Lawrence

Ritter that once Harry Frazee acquired the club and needed cash, "before long he sold off all our best players and ruined the team."[20] Hooper provided a much-needed offensive boost to his new team; through Chicago's first 56 games, he was hitting .319 with 35 runs and five triples in 253 plate appearances. After spending April as the leadoff batter, he was moved to the cleanup spot by Gleason, then, just before the Cleveland series, into the number-3 position in the batting order.

In the top of the second, Cleveland first baseman Doc Johnston hit a catchable fly ball to left-center that fell between outfielders Bibb Falk and Amos Strunk for a double after missed communications. The next hitter, Les Nunamaker, singled home Johnston to tie the score, 1-1. In the sixth, Indians shortstop and future Hall of Famer Joe Sewell tripled, and Nunamaker drove him in with a sacrifice fly to right field, giving the Indians a 2-1 lead.

In the bottom of the sixth, Chicago catcher Ray Schalk walked, reached second on Faber's sacrifice, and moved to third on Ernie Johnson's bunt single. Eddie Mulligan hit a grounder to Cleveland second baseman Bill Wambsganss, who prevented Schalk from scoring by keeping him planted at third base. Hooper followed Mulligan with an infielder grounder to short, and was narrowly thrown out at first by Sewell to end the inning. The hometown White Sox still trailed by a run.

Cleveland's Johnston benefited from another fortunate outfield bounce in the eighth, and he reached second base with his second double. Once again, Nunamaker followed with a single to right field, scoring Johnston as Nunamaker drove home his third run.[21]

In the bottom of the ninth inning, the White Sox were trailing 3-1. Mulligan grounded to shortstop for the first out. Hooper strode to the plate and delivered his second homer, a blast to right that "also landed among the sun-kissed fans."[22] Falk singled to center field off Bagby and Strunk walked to put the tying and winning runs on base. First baseman Earl Sheely launched a long fly to deep left field that landed foul, then flied out to center fielder Tris Speaker for the second out. Pinch-hitter Johnny Mostil grounded out to second base, ending Chicago's threat.

The White Sox finished June with a 9-15 record, managed a .500 record during July, and then struggled for the remainder of the season. Chicago ended the 1921 campaign with a 62-92 record, 36½ games behind pennant-winning New York. Although Faber's winning streak was snapped with the loss to Cleveland,[23] he delivered a sensational season, leading American League pitchers in ERA (2.48), and compiling a 25-15 record over 330⅔ innings, including a league-leading 32 complete games. Hooper led the White Sox in OPS (.876) and slugging (.470) while finishing second on the team in homers (8) and tied for second best in stolen bases (13). He also led the junior circuit in fielding percentage for right fielders (.975).

Footnote: The Cleveland game was the first in which Hooper hit two home runs in a game. He hit eight round-trippers that season. Remarkably, he smacked two in a game again that season, against the Yankees on September 13. This time the White Sox won, 6-2.

SOURCES

Besides the sources cited in the Notes, the author consulted Baseball-Almanac.com, Baseball-Reference.com, Retrosheet.org, and the following:

Asinof, Eliot. **Eight Men Out: The Black Sox and the 1919 World Series** (New York: Owl Books, Henry Holt and Company, LLC, 1987).

Thorn, John, and Pete Palmer et al. **Total Baseball: The Official Encyclopedia of Major League Baseball** (New York: Viking Press, 2004).

Zingg, Paul J. **Harry Hooper: An American Baseball Life** (Champaign, Illinois: University of Illinois Press, 1993).

Retrosheet and Baseball-Reference accounts of this game as well as those in some newspapers differ as to who drove in Cleveland's runs. Retrosheet credits Cleveland first baseman Doc Johnston with all three of the team's RBIs. Baseball-Reference gives Johnston two RBIs and catcher Les Nunamaker one. Retrosheet presents the box score and play-by-play of the game; Baseball-Reference has only the box score. Some newspapers agree with Retrosheet;[24] a headline in the **Sandusky Star-Journal** reads, "Catcher Drove in All Indians' Runs; Hooper Made 2 Homers."[25]

THE BASE BALL PALACE OF THE WORLD

NOTES

1. "Baseball Jury Indicts Burns, Chase and Attel," **Chicago Tribune**, October 23, 1920: 17.

2. J.G. Taylor Spink, **Judge Landis and 25 Years of Baseball** (St. Louis: The Sporting News Publishing Company, 1974), 79.

3. Lawrence Richards, "Judge Kenesaw Mountain Landis," National Pastime Museum, May 24, 2016, thenationalpastimemuseum.com/article/judge-kenesaw-mountain-landis.

4. I.E. Sanborn, "Commy Through With Black Sox Despite Verdict," **Chicago Tribune**, March 14, 1921: 13.

5. Daniel Ginsburg, "Chick Gandil," SABR Biography Project, sabr.org/bioproj/person/945ce343.

6. Irving Vaughan, "How Teams of Major Circuits Size Up in Chase for Pennants and Then — World Series Glory," **Chicago Tribune**, April 10, 1921: 17.

7. "Sox Notes," **Chicago Tribune**, June 1, 1921: 25.

8. I.E. Sanborn, "White Hose Home After Good Trip to Battle Indians," **Chicago Tribune**, June 2, 1921: 19.

9. I.E. Sanborn, "Bunting Indians Lay 'Em Down; Beat the Sox, 6-3," **Chicago Tribune**, June 2, 1921: 21.

10. "Baseball Trial to Be Started Monday Morning," **Chicago Tribune**, June 2, 1921: 21.

11. Irving Vaughan, "How Teams of Major Circuits Size Up."

12. Wilbur Wood, "Indians Get Their Tough Ones Early," **The Sporting News**, April 13, 1921: 2.

13. Indians Put It Over in Twelfth Inning," **Detroit Free Press**, June 1, 1921: 14.

14. Bill James and Rob Neyer, **The Neyer/James Guide to Pitchers** (New York: Fireside Books, 2004), 197.

15. Brian Cooper, "Red Faber," SABR Biography Project, sabr.org/bioproj/person/a6dff769.

16. "Only Fast Spitters Are Getting By," **Olean** (New York) **Times Herald**, June 23, 1921: 20.

17. Jack Troy, "Bagby, Jr., Just Like His Pop, Even to Ability to Sock, Happy With Tribe for Whom Father Had 31 Wins in '20," **The Sporting News**, February 27, 1941: 3.

18. I.E. Sanborn, "Hooper's Homers Sox Only Runs as Indians Cop, 3-2," **Chicago Tribune**, June 23, 1921: 15.

19. Paul M. Shannon, "Hooper Traded to White Sox," **Boston Post**, March 5, 1921: 11.

20. Lawrence S. Ritter, **The Glory of Their Times: The Story of the Early Days of Baseball Told by the Men Who Played It** (New York: Quill William Morrow, 1992), 151.

21. "Nunamaker Aids Tribe to Victory," **Sandusky** (Ohio) **Star-Journal**, June 23, 1921: 7.

22. "Hooper Makes 2 Circuit Clouts but Hose Lose," **Moline** (Illinois) **Dispatch**, June 23, 1921: 12.

23. "Jim Bagby Victor Over Urban Faber, Shattering Streak," **Buffalo Courier**, June 23, 1921: 11.

24. "Indians Trip Up Faber and Cop Second Game, Too," **Mansfield** (Ohio) **News-Journal**, June 23, 1921: 8; I.E. Sanborn, "Hooper's Homers Sox Only Runs as Indians Cop, 3-2," **Chicago Tribune**, June 23, 1921: 15; Baseball-Reference.com, "June 22, 1921 Indians 3 — White Sox 2 Box Score", Baseball-Reference.com/boxes/CHA/CHA192106220.shtml; Retrosheet.org, "June 22, 1921 Indians 3 — White Sox 2 Box Score," Retrosheet.org/boxesetc/1921/B06220CHA1921.htm.

25. "Nunamaker Aids Tribe to Victory."

THE LINE DRIVE THAT CHANGED HISTORY

MAY 29, 1925
DETROIT TIGERS 13, CHICAGO WHITE SOX 9

By Matthew M. Clifford

In late June of 1978 baseball historian Eugene Converse Murdock traveled to Albany, Oregon, to interview an old-time baseball player named Wes Schulmerich. During his chat with Schulmerich, the retired player asked Murdock if he was going to meet with any other baseball retirees from Oregon. Wes reminded the historian that his old friend and baseball teammate Sylvester "Syl" Johnson lived 90 minutes away from Albany, in the small city of Gresham. Murdock recalled the name Syl, but he had not scheduled any detours to visit Gresham or Johnson. Schulmerich's suggestion proved fateful as Murdock made his way to Gresham to find Johnson. With an audio-cassette tape recorder and a microphone, Murdock and Johnson spent the balmy afternoon discussing Johnson's time in the majors.

During their conversation, Murdock listened patiently as the 77-year-old pitcher recalled his personal memories of the game. The interview took an interesting turn when Johnson explained details of a horrific and exciting story that took place at Chicago's Comiskey Park on May 29, 1925. On that date, Johnson was pitching for the Detroit Tigers under the watchful eye of his ferocious player-manager, Ty Cobb. Johnson remembered, "He's was a fightin' manager, if you know what I mean. He'd cut his own mother to get on base. Anyway I was with him in 1922, '23, '24. And then '25, the spring of the year 1925, I was pitching in Chicago. ..."[1] As Johnson's story began to unfold, Murdock learned how one line-drive hit changed a man's life, career, and address while making an indelible mark in the baseball history books.

On May 26, 1925, Cobb's Detroit Tigers took up residency at Chicago's Cooper Carlton hotel for a four-game series against Charlie Comiskey's White Sox. Johnson didn't pitch in the first three games. Two of the three games were won by Detroit while Chicago claimed one victory over the Tigers. Cobb insisted on taking another win from the White Sox before his team headed back home to play the Cleveland Indians. Around 2:30 P.M. on May 29, the fourth game began with a quiet first inning handled by Chicago pitcher Hollis "Sloppy" Thurston and Detroit hurler, George "Hooks" Dauss. No runs developed from either side until the top of the second when Cobb stepped up to the plate and singled. Cobb and his reliable right fielder Harry Heilmann, who had doubled, crossed home plate with assistance from Detroit first baseman Luzerne "Lu" Blue and shortstop Jackie Tavener. Dauss smacked a double to bring Blue and Tavener home.

With Detroit leading 4-0, White Sox manager Eddie Collins took Thurston off the hill and sent in Leo Magnum to finish the inning. Chicago came back in the bottom of the second" Bibb Falk singled off Dauss. Chicago's Harry Hooper doubled to advance Falk to third base, and Willie Kamm singled, bringing Falk home. Dauss cleaned up the second inning with ease and Detroit held a 4-1 lead. It was interesting that Falk broke Chicago's silence. Falk, a Texas native known by his sharp epithet, "Jockey," had earned a reputation as a fierce competitor who would "ride" or "jockey" opposing players with verbal taunts. Falk had become the White Sox' left fielder in 1921, succeeding Shoeless Joe Jackson, who was banned from the game for his role in the 1919 World Series fix.

Jackson occupied Comiskey's left field until the Black Sox investigation closed in October 1920. When the 1921 season opened, Falk stepped into Jackson's shoes and he stayed there for eight years. Falk created his own personal hitting strategy during his time at Comiskey Park. In June 1974 (four years before he interviewed Syl Johnson), Murdock had stopped in Austin, Texas, to interview Falk. As the conversation turned, Falk complained, "When you play in a big park like White Sox, 352 both ways and 400 and something center and crosswind messing you up, you had to cut down. I used to hit a lot of long flies and then I cut down and started hitting line drives and that's where I hit doubles."[2] Falk's ability to hit line drives was uncanny, yet strangely precise — especially on May 29, 1925.

The third inning was uneventful. Magnum let Detroit's third sacker Fred Haney score in the top of the fourth while Dauss felt the revenge of the Sox as they brought in three runs. Chicago trailed, 5-4. Cobb and his crew came back swinging in the fifth, collecting four runs off Magnum before skipper Eddie Collins gave him the hook and sent in Frank Mack to stop the bleeding. Mack had his hands full with two Detroit employees on the sacks and Cobb stepping in the batter's box. Ty hit a triple to bring both Tigers home and the top of the fifth ended with Detroit leading 11-4. Tavener scored in the top of the sixth and the Tigers upped their lead to 12-4. The score stayed unchanged until the top of the ninth when Detroit third baseman Haney scored another run, bumping the Tigers ahead of Chicago, 13-4.

The bottom of the ninth inning appeared to be a game of child's play for Cobb. The confident boss took Hooks off the hill and sent in Syl Johnson to finish the game. Johnson, a pitching weapon that Cobb used carefully, joined Detroit in 1922. During his four years as a Tiger, Johnson suffered the bad luck of a broken wrist, a broken rib, and torn ligaments in his arm. Johnson let two Chicagoans score before Falk stepped up with a Texan grin on his face. Falk aimed up and smashed a lightning line drive at Syl. The ball came back like a boomerang to the pitcher, headed directly at his face. The hit crashed against his skull, coating one side of the ball with blood. The bloody sphere rolled toward Blue on first and Falk was tagged out. Johnson was credited with an assist — for stopping the ball with his face. The pitcher fell to the ground unconscious as the Comiskey fans gasped in horror.

While he recalled the event to Murdock, Johnson said, "We had a big lead going in the ninth inning. Bibb Falk hit a line drive hit me right there. Fractured eight bones. Knocked me down. Just a line drive. A flash. Fred Haney was on third base and he come over and Bassler was catching and he got ahold of me. Blood was just a-pouring out. After that happened, they thought I was through."[3] Johnson was taken to Mercy Hospital in Chicago, where he stayed for 11 days to heal. The Tigers beat the White Sox 13-9 with the game closed by Detroit's left-handed ace, Bert Cole. Johnson, cited by Cobb as a jinx, was sent down to the minors to play for the Vernon Tigers after his facial injuries healed. In 1926, he signed with the St. Louis Cardinals. It appeared that Falk's liner had literally knocked Johnson from the American League into the National League. Johnson remained a National Leaguer until he retired from the majors 14 years later.

Prior to his exit in 1940, Johnson achieved two interesting feats for the record books. On May 29, 1935, exactly one decade after experiencing the trauma of Falk's line drive, Johnson struck out Babe Ruth twice at the Baker Bowl in Philadelphia.

Johnson recalled purposely throwing easy pitches to Ruth. He told Murdock, "Struck out the last two times. Second to last time up, he comes by the pitcher's mound and he says, if I can't hit those kind, kid, I've gone blind. So I threw him my high fastball, you know. And he never hit a home run in the Baker Bowl … and it was just a bandbox."[4]

Ruth (who played for the Boston Braves at the time) appeared in his last major-league game on May 30, 1935. Four years later, Johnson got another chance to face Ruth during the first Hall of Fame game at Cooperstown, on June 12, 1939. Ruth popped up Johnson's easy pitch during the exhibition and it was caught by the catcher, Orville Jorgens, as an easy out.

Today, Sylvester Johnson's name, his distinction as "The Last Pitcher to Strike Out Babe Ruth" and the date of his fateful feat are displayed on a brass plaque at Main City Park in Gresham, Oregon.

SOURCES

Baseball-Reference.com.
Retrosheet.org.
Baseball Almanac.
SABR Encyclopedia.

The Sporting News (1925).
Brooklyn Daily Eagle (1925).
Detroit Free Press (1925).
The Oregonian, Portland (1925).
New York Post (1925).

Somonauk Public Library, Somonauk, Illinois.

The City of Gresham (Mayor Shane Bemis, Assistant Ashley Graff).
Baseball Hall of Fame Library and Museum, Cooperstown, New York.

Danielle R. Clifford (Research).

NOTES

1   Eugene Converse Murdock Audio Interviews. Recorded June 27, 1978 in Gresham, Oregon. Mears-Murdock Exhibit, Cleveland Public Library.

2   Eugene Converse Murdock Audio Interviews. Recorded June 3, 1974, in Austin, Texas. Mears-Murdock Exhibit. Cleveland Public Library.

3   Eugene Converse Murdock Audio Interviews. Recorded June 27, 1978, in Gresham, Oregon. Mears-Murdock Exhibit. Cleveland Public Library.

4   Ibid.

LYONS HURLS 21-INNING COMPLETE GAME; UHLE GOES 20 IN EPIC STRUGGLE

MAY 24, 1929
DETROIT TIGERS 6, CHICAGO WHITE SOX 5
(21 INNINGS)

By Gregory H. Wolf

The staggering, awe-inspiring numbers point to an era in baseball that seems unfathomable from a modern perspective. Ted Lyons of the Chicago White Sox and the Detroit Tigers' George Uhle combined to toss 41 innings, face 164 batters, and surrender 41 hits, as well as fashion streaks of 14 and 15⅓ scoreless innings, respectively, in a 21-inning contest that was completed in 3 hours and 31 minutes. It was "superb pitching that beggars description," gushed Motor City sportswriter Harry Bullion, who extolled the suffering of the loser as much as the glory of the victor in this epic struggle of wills. "The injustice of it all was that Lyons, as brilliant as Uhle was, was obliged to lose, although the fate, if it had befallen Uhle, would have been just as severe."[1]

The scene of Lyons and Uhle's "grueling duel" was Comiskey Park in the Windy City. Inclement weather had canceled the first game of the series the previous day, forcing the teams to play six games, including a pair of doubleheaders, in the next four days. Skipper Lena Blackburne's Pale Hose squad was floundering, and was in sixth place (12-20), headed for its ninth consecutive second-division finish since the Black Sox scandal decimated the once-proud franchise. Manager Bucky Harris' fourth-place Bengals (19-15) were an early-season surprise, and trailed the eventual pennant-winning Philadelphia Athletics by five games.

Right-handers Lyons and Uhle were among the decade's best pitchers and biggest names. A future Hall of Famer, Lyons was not yet the "Sunday Teddy" once-a-week hurler, but rather a durable workhorse, who tied for the AL lead in victories in 1925 (with 21) and 1927 (with 22). He entered the season with a sparkling 90-67 slate despite playing for horrible clubs, and was 3-2 thus far in '29. Acquired by Detroit in the offseason, Uhle had anchored the Cleveland Indians' staff, posting a 147-18 record in 10 seasons. The former three-time 20-game winner, who led the big leagues in victories in 1926 with 27 and paced the AL with 26 in 1923, was considered washed up after two disappointing campaigns, but had emerged as the hottest pitcher in the circuit, beginning the '29 season with seven consecutive complete-game victories.

Both teams came out swinging. The White Sox' Alex Metzler tripled to lead off the bottom of the first and scored on Bill Hunnefield's single. Willie Kamm's triple accounted for the second run to put Uhle on the ropes with no outs. Two batters later, Carl Reynolds reached on third baseman Marty McManus' throwing error, the Tigers' only miscue of the game, and moved to second. In what proved to be one of the most decisive plays of the game, first sacker Dale Alexander fielded Dutch Hoffman's grounder and pegged out Kamm at home. Still shaky, Uhle walked Bill Cissell before Buck Crouse grounded to first to end the frame.

The Tigers roared back in the second, victimizing Lyons for five hits and three runs. Heinie Schuble's sacrifice fly with one out scored Alexander while Roy Johnson added an RBI single and Harry Rice a run-scoring double. Lyons was hit hard again in the third when Alexander belted a one-out triple and scored on Eddie Phillips' single, which according to sportswriter Irving Vaughan of the *Chicago Tribune*, fell between second baseman Hunnefield and right fielder Carl Reynolds in short right field.[2] Phillips advanced to third on Schuble's double, but both were left stranded.

Uhle had only two rough innings, the second of which occurred in the fifth. Four straight one-out singles led to a run (on Reynolds' liner), followed by Cissell's sacrifice fly for another to tie the game, and then Crouse's RBI single to give the Tigers a 5-4 lead. Crouse stole second to put two runners in scoring position, but Lyons grounded innocuously to Schuble at short to end the threat.

After the Tigers' Charlie Gehringer and Harry Heilmann led off the seventh with consecutive singles, resulting in a run on Alexander's sacrifice fly to forge a 5-5 tie, the game took an unexpected shift.

Up to this point, it was easily the two hurlers' worst outing of the season. In his first five innings, Uhle was clubbed for 10 hits; Lyons was roughed up for 11 in 6⅓, and then they embarked on the game of their lives.

Given the moniker "The Bull" for his heavy workload (he had twice led the AL in innings pitched and complete games), Uhle settled down and held the White Sox hitless from the sixth through 10th innings. He had pitched at least 10 innings in a game already nine times in his career (and eventually accomplished it 16 times). His previous high was 13 in a victory over the White Sox at Comiskey Park on August 30, 1923. From the 11th inning through the 20th, the Bull scattered seven singles, never more than

Hall of Famer Ted Lyons holds the White Sox record for most career wins (260), innings pitched (4,161), starts (486), and complete games (356). (Photo by Mark Rucker/Transcendental Graphics, Getty Images)

one in an inning, and no White Sox runner moved beyond second.

While Uhle mowed down batters and was never in danger, Lyons bent (and bent), but somehow did not break. Bullion gave credit to the Pale Hose defense, which he called "as staunch as Gibraltar."[3] Lyons was as bullish as Uhle. Short and stocky (5-feet-11 and 200 pounds), Lyons was a tightly-wound coil of power. He too had paced the AL in innings pitched and complete games, in 1927, and would do it again in 1930. In the post-1900 era, Lyons ranks first among all pitchers by completing 73.5 percent of his starts (356 of 484) and tossed at least 10 or more innings in a game an astounding 35 times.

As the game moved into extra innings, Lyons was seemingly always in trouble. The Tigers future Hall of Fame duo of Gehringer and Heilmann lined consecutive one-out singles in the 12th, but the Mechanical Man was caught in a rundown between third and home in a daring double-steal attempt. Alexander drew a free pass, but Lyons erased McManus to end the threat. The Tigers collected two more singles in the next frame, yet left the runners stranded on first and second. The 14th "was dizzier than anything that went before," opined Windy City scribe Vaughan.[4] Heilmann belted a one-out double and sped home two batters later on McManus' single to short right. According to Vaughn, Reynolds took the ball on one hop and nailed a sliding Heilmann at the plate.[5] With nerves of steel, Lyons worked around leadoff singles in the 16th and 20th innings.

Lyons and Uhle entered rarefied territory at the beginning of the 21st inning. Prior to this game, only nine twirlers since 1900 had hurled at least 20 innings in a game, and only three since the Live Ball, post-1920 era.[6] Astonishingly, three pairs of those pitchers were locked in marathons, led by Joe Oeschger and Leon Cadore's 26-inning 1-1 tie on May 1, 1920.

One of the best-hitting pitchers in baseball history with a .289 lifetime average, Uhle led off the 21st with a sharp grounder that "hopped just in front" of Hunnefield at second, wrote Vaughan, and "rolled up the front of his shirt."[7] Legging out his fourth single of the afternoon, Uhle was replaced with pinch-runner Emil Yde (himself a pitcher). Johnson followed with a shot over the mound. Lyons missed it, then Hunnefield "stumbled and sprawled," yet corralled the ball to save a possible run.[8] His throw to third was too late to erase Yde while Johnson took second. Adrenaline flowing, Hunnefield then scooped up Rice's grounder and fired a strike to catcher Moe Berg to cut down Yde at the plate. Gehringer's fly to deep right-center field broke the tie as Johnson scored.

Lil Stoner, the Tigers reliable swingman, relieved Uhle and made it interesting. Pinch-hitter Johnny Watwood led off with a single and moved a station on Lyons' sacrifice bunt, and then to third on Metzler's grounder. Needing a hit to tie the game, Hunnefield tapped meekly to the mound, and Stoner tossed to Heilmann (who had moved from right field to first in wholesale defensive replacements in the 20th) to secure the Tigers' victory.

One can only wonder how Lyons felt. He faced 85 batters and yielded 24 hits, while walking two and fanning four. His 21-inning outing is tied with four others for the fourth longest among post-1900 pitchers. He was given a few extra days' rest, but was back on the mound six days later, hurling another complete game, and lost again, 4-3, to the Indians. For a dismal 59-93, seventh-place team, Lyons went 14-20, completing 21 of 31 starts. He compiled a 260-230 lifetime record in 21 seasons, all with the Pale Hose.

In his 20-inning effort, Uhle faced 79 batters, surrendered 17 hits, walked three, and fanned four. Five days later, he tossed a complete game to beat the St. Louis Browns and win his ninth straight start. He struggled for much of the remainder of the season, finishing with a 15-11 slate, while completing 22 of 30 starts. He retired after the 1936 season with a 200-166 record.

SOURCES

In addition to the sources cited in the Notes, the author also accessed Retrosheet.org, Baseball-Reference.com, and SABR.org.

NOTES

1 Harry Bullion, "Gehringer's Long Fly Decides Game," **Detroit Free Press**, May 25, 1929: 17.

2 Irving Vaughan, 'Sox Fall Before Detroit, 6-5, in 21 Innings," **Chicago Tribune**, May 25, 1929: 19.

3 Bullion.

4 Vaughan.

5   Ibid.

6   Since 1900, the following pitchers have hurled at least 20 innings: Joe Oescher of the Boston Braves and Leon Cadore of the Brooklyn Robins each tossed 26 innings in a 1-1 tie on May 1, 1920. The Braves' Bob Smith threw a 22-inning complete game against the Cubs on May 17, 1927, and lost 4-3; in addition to Lyons, these four hurlers also tossed 21 innings: The Braves Art Nehf lost a complete game to the Pittsburgh Pirates, 2-0, on August 1, 1917; the Cubs Lefty Tyler went the distance to beat the Phillies, 2-1, on July 17, 1917; and Babe Adams of the Pirates beat Rube Marquard of the New York Giants, 3-1, on July 17, 1914. Uhle and three other twirlers tossed 20 innings: Oeschger, then with the Phillies, and Burleigh Grimes of the Robins went the distance in a 9-9 tie on April 30, 1919; and Milt Watson of the Phillies tossed 20 innings to lose to Tyler (and his 21 innings) and the Cubs, 2-1, on July 7, 1918.

7   Ibid.

8   Ibid.

A DREAM REALIZED

JULY 6, 1933
AMERICAN LEAGUE 4, NATIONAL LEAGUE 2
ALL-STAR GAME

BY LYLE SPATZ

In 1933, Chicago was celebrating its centennial by hosting a World's Fair, entitled *A Century of Progress Exposition*. Fair officials asked the local sports editors to think of an athletic event that would attract fans to Chicago from around the country.

Arch Ward, sports editor of the *Chicago Tribune*, suggested a baseball game to be played at Comiskey Park matching the best players in the American League against the best players in the National League. Labeling it "the game of the century," he was certain it would be a success. Fan interest was sure to be high, but to make it even more so, he would have the fans select the players. But before any announcement of such a game could be made, Ward had to ascertain if his dream was feasible. The first person he consulted was American League President Will Harridge.

Ward was prepared to drop the whole scheme if he could not get Harridge's approval. To Ward's delight, Harridge not only approved, he promised to recommend it to the eight American League club owners. The following day, Ward explained the plan to William E. Veeck, president of the Chicago Cubs. Veeck loved the idea and promised to lobby for the game with the other National League owners. A call by Ward to National League President John Heydler also elicited a promise to discuss the proposed game with those owners.

On May 9, at a special meeting in Cleveland, the American League owners enthusiastically voted in favor of the game and chose July 6 as the date. However, a few days later, Ward received a telegram from Heydler informing him that three NL owners — the Giants' Charles Stoneham, the Braves' Charles Adams, and the Cardinals' Sam Breadon — had turned down the idea.

Breadon based his opposition on the fear that any future games, as this one was doing, would be forced to donate the proceeds to charity. Stoneham and Adams opposed the idea because of the selected date. The Giants and Braves were scheduled to play a doubleheader in Boston on July 5, making it impossible for any chosen players to be in Chicago in time to play on July 6.

Breadon dropped his opposition after Ward convinced him that other cities, including St. Louis, could benefit by hosting a future All-Star Game. The only obstacle remaining was the July 5 Giants-Braves doubleheader. After National League owners persuaded Heydler to postpone that doubleheader, a contract was signed by Ward, representing the *Tribune*, Heydler, and Harridge.

Editors at the *Tribune* had thought it unlikely other newspapers would do anything to help publicize a rival newspaper, yet all 55 Ward had asked to join in, accepted. In a gesture of cooperation, they even volunteered to help in the polling. The idea captured the imagination of fans everywhere, who then took the opportunity to vote for the players they most wanted to see.

Chicago White Sox outfielder Al Simmons, tied with Washington manager-shortstop Joe Cronin for the league lead in batting, got the most votes, 346,291. Philadelphia Phillies outfielder Chuck Klein, the National League's leading hitter, was also its leading vote-getter, with 342,283.

The final rosters, 18 players per league, were determined by a combination of the fans' votes and the selections of the respective managers. The players would not be paid for participating, but would benefit indirectly by the net receipts of $46,506 the game raised for the Association of Professional Baseball Players of America.

The two most honored managers in the game, one from each league, were selected to lead their respective teams. John McGraw had stepped down in June 1932 after 30 years at the helm of the New York Giants, but the National League called him out of retirement to manage this one game. The Americans gave the managerial honors to Connie Mack, who had led the Athletics since the league's birth.

The regular season would resume the following day, although the owners had agreed that if the All-Star Game was rained out, they would cancel the next day's schedule and play it then. That precaution proved unnecessary; the weather was perfect and though the country was struggling through the worst economic crisis in its history, every seat was filled.

For all sections of the park, patrons had been allowed to buy only four tickets, and there was no standing room. All seats were priced the same as for regular-season games at Comiskey Park, and because they played the game under "World Series rules," no spectators would be allowed on the field. The crowd of 47,595, conducted itself in an exemplary manner, as if each fan knew he was witnessing something special.

The American League stars won the game, 4-2, but both sides offered strong pitching, solid hitting, and near-flawless defense. Yankees first baseman Lou Gehrig's drop of Philadelphia Phillies shortstop Dick Bartell's foul pop in the fifth inning was the game's only error.

Babe Ruth, 38 years old and nearing the end of his career, provided the AL's margin of victory with the first home run in All-Star competition, a third-inning two-run blast. It came off National League starter Bill Hallahan of St. Louis and increased the American League's lead to 3-0.

Five days before the game, McGraw and Mack had announced that the starting pitchers would be Carl Hubbell of the Giants and Lefty Grove of the A's, the game's two best left-handers. But both managers changed their minds on game day, although both stayed with left-handers: McGraw went with Hallahan (10-4), while Mack chose the Yankees' Lefty Gomez (9-6).

Current Giants manager Bill Terry captained the National Leaguers, who had the words "NATIONAL LEAGUE" on the fronts of their gray road uniforms with an "NL" emblazoned on their caps. Tigers second baseman Charlie Gehringer captained the Americans, each of whom wore his regular home uniform.

To help familiarize themselves with the other league, both teams used the other's ball during batting practice to acclimate themselves to the different constructions. An American League ball, reputed to be livelier, would be used for the first 4½ innings, before the teams switched to the thicker-covered National League ball.

At 1:15 P.M., home-plate umpire Bill Dinneen of the American League called "Play Ball!" and Cardinals third baseman Pepper Martin stepped in as the first All-Star batter. Gomez retired him on a groundball to shortstop Cronin, and the "dream game" had become a reality. In the second inning, the American Leaguers scored the first All-Star run, helped along by the wildness of Hallahan, who not for nothing was known as "Wild Bill."[1] After walking White Sox third baseman Jimmy Dykes and Cronin, he yielded a two-out single to Gomez, a historically weak batter, that scored Dykes.

When Hallahan walked Gehrig following Ruth's third-inning home run, McGraw replaced him with Cubs right-hander Lon

Charles Comiskey helped found the American League and was the founding owner of the Chicago White Sox. Under his guidance, White Sox Park, later renamed Comiskey Park, was built in 1910. (Photo: public domain)

Warneke. Meanwhile, Gomez held the National Leaguers scoreless in his three innings, as did Washington's Alvin Crowder in the fourth and fifth. The Nationals finally broke through in the sixth. Warneke hit a one-out triple, a long fly down the right-field line that was poorly handled by Ruth, and scored as Martin was grounding out. Frankie Frisch, manager-second baseman of the Cardinals, followed with a home run to cut the AL's lead to 3-2.

Warneke had already pitched three full innings, and had raced around the bases in the top of the sixth; nevertheless, McGraw sent him out to pitch the home half of the inning. The American Leaguers quickly got a run back on a single by Cronin, a sacrifice by Rick Ferrell, and a single by Cleveland's Earl Averill, batting for Crowder. Ferrell, the Red Sox' lone representative, caught the entire game, despite having finished third in the voting behind the Yankees' Bill Dickey and Philadelphia's Mickey Cochrane, both of whom were injured.

Hubbell and Grove came on in the seventh. Hubbell, who had shut out the Cardinals, 1-0, in 18 innings four days earlier, pitched two innings, blanking the American Leaguers on one hit. Grove pitched the final three innings for the AL, also allowing no runs, though the National Leaguers threatened in both the seventh and the eighth.

They had runners on second and third in the seventh, with just one out, but Grove struck out the Cubs' Gabby Hartnett and got Hartnett's Chicago teammate, Woody English, on a fly ball. Then in the eighth, with two out and Frisch, who had singled, on first, Hafey hit what would have been a game-tying home run in a park less spacious than Comiskey. Ruth ran it down and caught it with his back pressed to the right-field wall. Grove retired the National Leaguers one-two-three in the ninth, and the "game of the century" was over.

McGraw went to the winners' locker room to congratulate Mack, his longtime rival, and Ruth, whom he had often denigrated in the past.

Both managers said they hoped the game would be repeated annually.

Adapted from the author's article on the 1933 All-Star Game that appeared in *The Midsummer Classic: The Complete History of Baseball's All-Star Game*.

SOURCES

The author also accessed Retrosheet.org, Baseball-Reference.com, and SABR.org.

NOTES

1 Hallahan walked five in his two-plus innings, which remain the most walks given up by a pitcher in one All-Star Game.

THE "GAME OF GAMES": THE FIRST NEGRO LEAGUE ALL-STAR GAME

SEPTEMBER 10, 1933
WEST 11, EAST 7
NEGRO LEAGUE ALL-STAR GAME

By Bob LeMoine

> The East-West Game became the spirit and life of Negro League baseball, serving to entertain, educate, and ultimately provide a forum to integrate our national pastime many years later.
>
> — Larry Lester[1]

The idea for a Negro League all-star game is attributed to sportswriters Roy Sparrow of the *Pittsburgh Sun-Telegraph* and Bill Nunn of the *Pittsburgh Courier* in July of 1933. Gus Greenlee, owner of the Pittsburgh Crawfords, suggested that the writers contact Robert Cole, owner of the Chicago American Giants, and look into holding an East-West game at Comiskey Park in Chicago. The deal was made with Cole, the park was secured for a September 10 date, and publicity began in earnest. The game would annually prove to be "the pinnacle of any Negro League season," wrote Negro Leagues historian Larry Lester. "It was an all-star game and a World Series all wrapped in one spectacle."[2]

Fans could vote for their favorite players through African-American newspapers including the *Chicago Defender, Pittsburgh Courier, Kansas City Call,* and *Baltimore Afro-American*. The significance was monumental, as Negro League legend Buck O'Neil remembered. "While the big leaguers left the choice of players up to the sportswriters, Gus (Greenlee) left it up to the fans. After reading about great players in the *Defender* and *Courier* for so many years, they could cut out that ballot in the black papers, send it in, and have a say. That was a pretty important thing for black people to do in those days, to be able to vote, even if it was just for ballplayers, and they sent in thousands and thousands of ballots."[3]

With just over a million votes cast, Oscar Charleston of the Pittsburgh Crawfords received the most votes, 43,793, while Willie Foster of the Chicago American Giants was runner-up with 40,637. Each was joined by six teammates in the starting lineups.[4] The crowd of 19,568 braved the drizzly weather, many arriving on packed train cars. The Illinois Central Railroad needed a special coach to bring fans in from New Orleans, while others arrived by rail from Mississippi and Tennessee. The Sante Fe Chief brought fans from Kansas City and Wichita, while the New York Central brought fans from the East.[5] "The depression didn't stop 'em — the rain couldn't —and so a howling, thundering mob of 20,000 souls braved an early downpour and a threatening storm to see the pick of the East's baseball players battle the pick of the West," wrote Al Monroe in the *Chicago Defender*.[6] With such high stakes, the *Kansas City Call* thought Greenlee must have "lost 10 pounds worrying over the possibility that rain might ruin the game."[7]

Around 2:30 P.M. the umpires, Costello,

THE BASE BALL PALACE OF THE WORLD

Cusack, Baldwin, and Stack, "moved from beneath the home dugout like groundhogs searching for that proverbial shadow, only braving steady drizzle to yell the usual 'Play ball!'" West was the home team, and Foster stood on the mound in the drizzle staring in at Cool Papa Bell. The "Game of Games" was on.

Bell flied out to left, and both clubs went quietly in the first two innings, with Sam Streeter of Pittsburgh on the hill for the East. Jud Wilson's single in the second for the East was the first hit in the history of the East-West game. In the bottom of the third, Sam Bankhead of Nashville beat out an infield hit, the West's first hit of the game. Moving to second on a groundout, Bankhead scored the first run in the game's history, on a single by Chicago's Turkey Stearnes.

Trailing 1-0 in the top of the fourth, the East got its first two men aboard when Rap Dixon of the Philadelphia Stars walked and Charleston was hit by a pitch. They performed a double steal while Biz Mackey of Philadelphia struck out. Wilson, also of Philadelphia, grounded to second. Leroy Morney of the Cleveland Giants threw wildly to the plate and both Dixon and Charleston scored, with Wilson taking second. Dick Lundy of Philadelphia walked and Vic Harris of the Homestead Grays grounded to Morney, who booted an easy double-play opportunity. The bases were loaded. John Henry Russell laid down a perfect suicide-squeeze bunt along the first-base line, scoring Wilson. The East now led, 3-1.

The lead changed quickly in the bottom of the inning. Chicago's Willie Wells doubled and scored on teammate Steel Arm Davis's double to cut the East's lead to 3-2. Chicago's Mule Suttles received a strong ovation from the crowd "because Mule, to colored fandom," wrote William Nunn of the *Pittsburgh Courier*, "is what Ruth is to major-league baseball."[8] Suttles smashed a home run into the upper deck in left-center to give the West a 4-3 lead. "With hardly any effort he swung," Nunn wrote. "Like a bullet from a rifle. 'Cool Papa' Bell started to run. Suddenly he stopped. Pandemonium reigned. Straw hats filled the air ... worth the price of admission any day."[9] The first home run in the East-West game was indeed a memorable one. Naturally, it was Ruth who hit the first home run in the major-league All-Star Game two months earlier, in the same park.

The East countered with two runs in the top of the fifth when Dixon reached on a checked-swing roller in front of the plate. Charleston was again hit by a pitch and Mackey blooped a single to load the bases with one out. Wilson singled to left, scoring Dixon and Charleston to give the East a 5-4 lead. Lundy hit a fly ball to right that scored Mackey, but an appeal play resulted in Mackey being called out for leaving third too soon. In the bottom of the fifth, Larry Brown of Chicago tripled to center but was tagged out when he overran third base.

The West struck again in the bottom of the sixth. Wells singled and scored on a double by Alex Radcliffe of Chicago to tie the score, 5-5. As the rain came down, Bertram Hunter of Pittsburgh came in from the bullpen to pitch for the East. Suttles was clutch again, doubling to right, scoring Radcliffe, and then he too scored on single by Morney. Brown singled to right but Morney was out on an appeal play when he failed to touch second base on the way by. Despite the blunder, the West now led, 7-5.

Josh Gibson was now catching for the East in the bottom of the seventh. A leadoff single by Foster, the first such by a pitcher in the game's history, led to a pitching change; George Britt of the Homestead Grays came in to pitch. Stearnes doubled to right, sending Foster to third. A fly ball by Wells scored Foster. Davis doubled to right, scoring Stearnes. Radcliffe's single and a misplay by Harris in left field scored Davis. The West led, 10-5.

In the top of the eighth the East put the first two runners on when Gibson and pinch-hitter Judy Johnson singled, but both were stranded when Foster got Lundy to line out, Fats Jenkins to ground out, and Russell to pop out. The West added a run in the bottom of the eighth. The East scored two in the top of the ninth on flies by Dixon and Charleston, but Gibson lined out to Davis in left for the final out of the West's 11-7 victory.

Every player in the lineup for the West had at least one hit, with six players having two each of the 15 total. Foster pitched the entire game, allowing the East only seven hits and three earned runs. While Nunn called it "a game which produced thrills galore," one of the game's greats didn't show.[10] Satchel Paige declined the invitation and remained in the hills of North Dakota, pitching for his integrated Bismarck semipro team.[11]

The only mention of the game in the *Chicago Tribune* was a two-paragraph item under a *Dick Tracy* comic strip.[12] *The Sporting News*, the self-proclaimed "Baseball Paper of the World," didn't mention the "Game of Games." Undeniable, however, was the conversation around baseball that resulted from it.

Henry L. Ferrell of the *Chicago Daily News* quipped that Charleston, Suttles, and Lundy would each get a major-league contract if the they "were of a lighter shade."[13] Ferrell also believed some cities wanted to see a winner, no matter the color of their skin. The East team, he said, "might well be moved as a unit into Cincinnati or Boston, where the long suffering patrons of the Reds and the Red Sox have been praying for a magic rod to strike a rock and appease their thirst for a team."

The *Chicago Defender* wrote in its September 16 issue, "If the white club owners of the National and American leagues would surrender their prejudices and recognize fitness and ability instead of color, baseball would be established firmly on the grounds of clean and wholesome sport." The East-West game reportedly outdrew the crowd across town watching the Cubs play a doubleheader at Wrigley Field.[14] "Professional baseball has been and is losing thousands of dollars yearly by its narrow and asinine prejudiced attitude in the operation of the national game," the *Defender* wrote. "We ask again: What is the matter with baseball? The answer is, plain prejudice — that's all."

It would be several years before baseball dealt with its "prejudiced attitude," but the "Game of Games" was an early sign of better days ahead.

SOURCES

Dickson, Paul. "The Negro Leagues East-West All-Star Game," The National Pastime Museum. March 12, 2017. Retrieved August 19, 2017. thenationalpastimemuseum.com/article/negro-leagues-east-west-all-star-game#_edn2.

NOTES

1   Larry Lester, **Black Baseball's National Showcase: The East-West All-Star Game, 1933-1953.** (Lincoln: University of Nebraska Press, 2001), 25.

2   Lester, 1.

3   Lester, 3.

4   Lester, 37. The rest of the top 10 in voting: Turkey Stearnes 39,994; Willie Wells 39,136; Newt Allen 39,092; Jud Wilson 37,681; Alec Radcliffe 36,712; Josh Gibson 35,376; Mule Suttles 35,134; John Henry Russell 29,846.

5   Lester, 3.

6   Al Monroe, "20,000 See West Beat East in Baseball 'Game of Games,'" **Chicago Defender**, September 16, 1933. Reprinted in Lester, 30-31.

7   "Heavy Hitting Beats East in Classic," **Kansas City Call**, September 15, 1933. Reprinted in Lester, 30.

8   William G. Nunn, "West's Satellites Eclipse Stars of the East in Classic," **Pittsburgh Courier**, September 16, 1933. Reprinted in Lester, 32.

9   Ibid.

10 Nunn.

11 "Satchel Paige and Barney Brown are Expected to Pitch," **Bismarck Tribune**, September 9, 1933: 6; Lester, 42.

12 "West Victor, 11-7, in Negro All-Star Game," **Chicago Tribune**, September 11, 1933: 21.

13 "Charleston, Lundy, Suttles Ranked as 'Major League Timber,'" **Pittsburgh Courier**, September 16, 1933: 5.

14 Attendance numbers are not available for that game.

THE BASE BALL PALACE OF THE WORLD

THE HOTTEST SHOW IN TOWN

AUGUST 26, 1934
EAST 1, WEST 0
NEGRO LEAGUE ALL-STAR GAME

By Will Osgood

The summer of 1934 was a scorcher in Chicago. It was one of the hottest summers in Chicago on record. But for Negro League All-Stars like Alex Radcliffe and Satchel Paige, who both grew up in Mobile, Alabama, it was nothing out of the ordinary.

Luckily for them, and for the fans attending the matchup of the best black baseball had to offer that season, the temperatures cooled slightly from the record-setting 105 of July 24, or the 100 on August 8.

The date August 26, 1934, didn't show up on any Chicago weather records. As one observer put it, "Sunday was one of those perfect baseball days. Not a cloud in the sky to mar the perfect azure-blue of the heavens."[1]

We know, however, that what the weather may have lacked in heat, the Negro League All-Star Game played at Comiskey Park made up for. That is to say, it was hotly contested.

Negro League All-Star Games weren't played like the modern midsummer classic. Yes, it was an exhibition. Yet both teams wanted nothing more than to win. And the score showed it.

A pitcher's duel if there ever was one. The East team won 1-0 on a run that crossed the plate in the next to last inning. The teams would have been willing and able to play extra innings if the score required it.

Cool Papa Bell made sure it was unnecessary, scoring the game's only run in the top half of the eighth inning. Bell was known throughout the Negro Leagues as an excellent baserunner.

According to Ted "Double Duty" Radcliffe, Bell was "so fast, he'd run out of sight."[2] (Double Duty was the brother of Alex Radcliffe, who started at third base for the West team.)

Just how did Bell score? The way he often did. More specifically the way he was instructed to. In an interview at the Hall of Fame in 1996, Bell told journalists, "I was a long-ball hitter too. But they didn't want me to hit no long balls. They wanted me to get on base."

He was a reach-base artist extraordinaire, working counts, being a pest. But the pesky ways only got more annoying for opposing pitchers, catchers, and managers when Bell got on base. And that was most certainly the case in the eighth inning of this game.

Bell used that legendary speed to steal second on a swinging strikeout by Pittsburgh Crawfords catcher Cy Perkins. The pitcher who secured the strikeout was hometown pitcher Willie Foster of the Chicago American Giants.

As the third and final pitcher (following Ted Trent and Chet Brewer) used by West manager Dave Malarcher, Foster would take the loss in the contest. The man who drove Bell in and pinned the loss on Foster was Philadelphia Stars third baseman Jud Wilson, one of the least recognizable All-Stars in the game.

Wilson's Philadelphia Stars would go on to win the 1934 Negro League championship, defeating the Chicago American Giants, the team's only championship. Perhaps the way he collected the winning hit in this game was a hint of what was to come.

With Bell attracting so much attention at second base, Wilson looped a ball into a Bermuda Triangle made up of West shortstop Willie Wells, second baseman Sammy T. Hughes, and center fielder Turkey Stearnes.

There were two outs when Wilson put wood on the ball, after Pittsburgh first baseman Oscar Charleston lined out. Thus Bell was running at the crack of the bat, making his successfully crossing home plate a certainty, bordering on an afterthought.

The big news was that Wilson would play the role of hero in a game with stars like the aforementioned Wells, Charleston, Stearnes, and Josh Gibson. But it should be noted that Wilson was batting cleanup for the East. If anyone was to bring in the run, Wilson was responsible, hitting in the game's traditional power spot in the batting order.

Though the Negro Leagues played a slightly different style of baseball than the white professional leagues, it still held to traditional lineup construction and overall roster composition. Wilson was second in vote-getting among East position players, so he was not quite as unlikely a hero as his name recognition, or lack thereof, might suggest.

Then again, it is not as if Wilson was the only hero in the East team's victory. Credit must also be shared by the three pitchers used by East manager Dick Lundy (who doubled as the starting shortstop). Slim Jones from Philadelphia was the starter.

His day got off to an inauspicious start as he walked the leadoff hitter Wells, and then balked him to second. He quickly settled down, though, retiring Alex Radcliffe, Turkey Stearnes, and Chicago first baseman Mule Suttles.

Jones pitched two more innings, allowing just one more baserunner. He struck out four West All-Stars in his three innings.

Jones was followed by Pittsburgh Crawfords right-hander Harry "Tin Can" Kincannon. The 5-foot-10, 190-pound curveball artist was not as sharp for the East squad as his predecessor and successor. In two innings of relief, he gave up four hits. But he bridged the gap to the most dominant Negro Leagues pitcher of the era, Leroy "Satchel" Paige.

Paige received the nickname "Satchel" back home in Mobile working alongside many of his baseball teammates literally carrying satchels. As "Double Duty" Radcliffe explained in a SABR interview, Paige "was so big and tall, he could carry five satchels."

Pitching in this contest against the best competition he could face in the Negro Leagues, Paige powered through with his blazing, heavy fastball for four shutout innings to record the win for the East squad.

According to both Bell and Double Duty Radcliffe, Paige threw his fastball as fast as anyone in the Negro Leagues. Radcliffe caught him when they were teammates with the Crawfords in 1932. He recalled a doubleheader in New York in which he caught Paige in game one, then took the mound in the second game. Both pitched shutouts.

Was Paige fast? Radcliffe said, "When I had to catch Satchel, I'd go to the store to get a wrap."[3]

"Nobody who ever lived throw harder than Satchel. Closest was Bob Gibson." Satchel could throw so hard, looked like the ball disappeared."[4]

Paige was strong and nasty, much like his stuff. He used his fastball, curveball, change-up, and even occasional knuckleball to confuse and keep West hitters off balance. The usual starting pitcher came in as a reliever and dominated.

The lineup Paige mowed down over four innings included players of whom Radcliffe used such superlatives as "greatest ballplayer I ever saw (Wells)," and "hit some balls so far, it's a shame (Stearnes)." It also included Double Duty's brother Alex, whom he referred to as "a good .380 hitter," who could hit the ball out of any ballpark.

Similarly, the East team was built on all-time

hitting talent. Aside from Cool Papa Bell and Wilson, Oscar Charleston was one of the best players Double Duty ever saw as a player and manager. Josh Gibson wasn't shabby either.

In other words, the 1934 Negro League All-Star Game featured much of the best talent the Negro Leagues ever produced. In the midst of that conglomeration of talent, the individual standouts, who did not necessarily affect the final outcome of the game, were Pittsburgh second baseman Chester Williams for the East and Chicago first baseman Mule Suttles for the West, who collected three hits apiece.

For the 25,000 fans in attendance at Comiskey Park, the second annual East-West game did not disappoint. They got every bit of their money's worth. The East avenged an 11-7 loss in the inaugural East-West All-Star Game from the year before. This contest was played close to the vest in comparison to the prior year's contest.

The newspaper coverage of the game was apropos of the times. The day after, August 27, the *Pittsburgh Press* had just a brief blurb in a column of sports items.[5] The *Pittsburgh Post-Gazette*, Pittsburgh's largest paper had nothing on the game in its August 27 issue.

The *Pittsburgh Courier*, the newspaper for African-American readers, ran two pieces on the game in its Saturday, September 1, issue. Writer William G. Nunn described the game thusly: "No diamond masterpiece was this game! No baseball classic! Those words are relegated into the limbo of forgotten things in describing the titanic struggle for supremacy…"[6]

SOURCE

"East-West All Star Game: Summaries," cnlbr.org/Portals/0/RL/East-West%20All%20Star%20Game%20Summaries.pdf.

Mandel, Ken, MLB.com. Slim Pitcher: Jones Dominated Negro League Baseball for a Short Time. mlb.mlb.com/mlb/history/mlb_negro_leagues_profile.jsp?player=jones_stuart.

Thorn, John, Black Ball, Part 2. "Our Game," ourgame.mlblogs.com/black-ball-part-2-1dcade51cdf6.

NOTES

1. William G. Nunn, "'Satch' Stops 'Big Bad Men' of West Team," **Pittsburgh Courier**: 15.

2. Ted "Double Duty" Radcliffe, interviewed by Fay Vincent, Society of American Baseball Research, July 5, 2002. oralhistory.sabr.org/interviews/radcliffe-ted-double-duty-2002/.

3. Ibid.

4. Ibid.

5. "East Beats West," **Pittsburgh Press**, August 27, 1934. news.google.com/ers?nid=djft3U1LymYC&dat=19340827&printontpage&hl=en.

6. Nunn.

THE MULE KICKS THE MAESTRO

AUGUST 11, 1935
WEST 11, EAST 8 (11 INNINGS)
NEGRO LEAGUE ALL-STAR GAME

By Frank Amoroso

At a time when a pint of Kentucky bourbon cost $1.25[1] and a round-trip train ticket between Chicago and Niagara Falls, the honeymoon capital of the world, cost $8,[2] the stars of the Negro Leagues played one of the most dramatic ballgames ever. On a sunny Sunday afternoon in Chicago, 30,000 fans gathered to watch the best black baseball players compete in the third annual East-West Negro League All-Star game. Thirteen future Hall of Famers participated.[3] They bore memorable nicknames like Cool Papa, Devil, Mammy, Submarine, Slim, and Turkey; but it was the battle between the Maestro and the Mule that determined the outcome. The fans were treated to an epic contest that featured two comebacks from four-run deficits and culminated in an 11th-inning walk-off home run by the game's strongest power hitter off the best pitcher not named Satchel Paige.[4]

An All-Star game featuring black players was the brainchild of A.W. "Gus" Greenlee as a response to the severe anti-black repression that barred black athletes from the major leagues. Dire economic conditions of the 1930s precluded the Negro League World Series between 1928 and 1941,[5] thereby making the All-Star Game the premier event for black players to showcase their skills. As noted in an announcement promoting the game, it was a battle between "teams which could enter either the American or National League and show their heels to the leaders."[6]

The game, hosted by R.A. Cole, owner of Chicago American Giants, was played in the spacious Baseball Palace of the World, Comiskey Park. When it was built in 1910, the ballpark was the first symmetrical field in the major leagues — 362 feet down the foul lines and 420 feet in center. Designed to blend with the surrounding area, the exterior of Comiskey Park incorporated red brick archways similar to nearby factories. Built of steel and concrete, it was a departure from previous wooden structures. Innovations like turnstiles and ramps, instead of open gates and stairs, helped facilitate the safe flow of fans entering and exiting the facility. On the field, foul lines were old fire hoses pressed flat and painted white. The pitcher's mound was like a jewel in the center of a diamond-shaped cutout in the infield grass.

In contrast to the major leagues, where sportswriters chose the All-Stars, fans elected the Negro League players using ballots distributed by weekly and daily newspapers and at Negro League games. The East team was chosen from the Brooklyn Eagles, Newark Dodgers, Philadelphia Stars, and New York Cubans. The West team was selected from the Chicago American Giants, Columbus Elite Giants, Pittsburgh Crawfords, and Homestead Grays. The fans cast over 150,000 ballots.[7]

Webster "Submarine" McDonald managed the East team that included Paul Arnold, Leon Day, Ray Dandridge, Martin Dihigo, Robert

Evans, George Giles, Fats Jenkins, Slim Jones, Richard Lundy, Biz Mackey, Alejandro Oms, Dick Seay, Jake Stephens, Ed Stone, Luis Tiant Sr., and Jud Wilson.

Oscar Charleston managed the West team. His players were Cool Papa Bell, Larry Brown, Raymond Brown, William "Sug" Cornelius, James Crutchfield, Josh Gibson, Bob Griffith, Sammy T. Hughes, Buck Leonard, Leroy Matlock, Alex Radcliffe, Ted Trent, Felton "Mammy" Snow, Turkey Stearnes, Mule Suttles, Willie "Devil" Wells, Chester Williams, and Burnis Wright.

Known as The Maestro, Cuban-born Martin Dihigo was a tall, powerful switch-hitter who played every position, including pitcher. "He was the best ballplayer of all time, black or white," a competitor said.[8] In his best season he posted a 0.90 ERA and went 18-2 while hitting a league-leading .387. In addition to being enshrined in the National Baseball Hall of Fame in Cooperstown, Dihigo is the only player also inducted in the baseball halls of fame in Cuba, Mexico, the Dominican Republic, and Venezuela.

George "Mule" Suttles was a gentle giant. He did not seek the limelight like his more famous contemporaries; he let his 50-ounce bat do the talking. Over a 25-year period, Suttles averaged 34 homers and compiled a .327 career batting average. Where Josh Gibson hit vicious line drives, Mule was known for gargantuan blasts. In a game played in Havana, Mule crushed a ball over the center-field fence that witnesses swore cleared the 60-foot-high wall and traveled over the heads of the mounted policemen patrolling outside the ballpark — a distance of 600 feet.[9] In a game against the Memphis Red Sox, he hit three homers in the same inning. On this day in 1935, he saved his best for last.

Over the first six innings, the East built a 4-0 lead on the strength of timely hitting, including an RBI single by Dihigo to plate the first run. East pitcher Slim Jones mesmerized the West during his three-inning stint. He helped his cause by blasting a homer into deep right field. His successors on the hill did not fare as well.

Leon Day was roughed up for three runs in the home sixth and another in the seventh to tie the score. Lefty Luis Tiant followed Day and held the West until he faltered in the 10th.

Meanwhile, the West's pitching held until Bob Griffith entered the tie game to pitch a disastrous 10th in which he yielded four runs. His outing would have been much worse without a great shoetop catch by Mule Suttles. With the East's seemingly commanding lead, fans began to head for the exits.

Their exodus did not last long. In the bottom of the 10th, Luis Tiant Sr. ran into trouble. With one run in and the bases loaded with none out, manager McDonald turned to Dihigo, who stopped the carnage. Fans who returned to their seats were treated to a storybook ending.

In the home 11th, Martin Dihigo made a grievous mistake; he walked Cool Papa Bell, the legendary speedster. The inimitable Satchel Paige once remarked that Bell was so fast that when he switched off the light, he was in bed before the room got dark.[10] No doubt both teams recalled how in the All-Star Game a year earlier, Bell had plated the game's only run by scoring from second base on an infield hit.[11] In this game, East catcher Biz Mackey had gunned down three baserunners attempting to steal and picked Ray Dandridge off third to end the West's threat in the 10th, and manager Charleston signaled for a sacrifice. Hughes executed a bunt perfectly, advancing Bell to scoring position. One down.

As the number-three hitter, Chester Williams approached the plate, Dihigo glanced at the on-deck circle. The imposing figure of Josh Gibson settled onto one knee to watch the confrontation. Gibson had already collected four hits, including a ringing double in the sixth inning that Dihigo tried to catch before crashing into the center-field wall. Whether later in the game Dihigo suffered from the effects of the collision is a matter for conjecture.

The pitcher made quick work of Williams, striking him out. Two down.

In the West's dugout, Mule counseled the relief pitcher Sug Cornelius.

"Go up there and kneel in the on-deck circle, Cornelius, they'll think you're up next."[12]

With so many substitutions in an All-Star Game, Suttles counted on confusion in the opposing dugout regarding the proper batting order at this point. As Cornelius hefted a couple of bats in the on-deck circle, Mackey signaled for an intentional walk to Gibson. The walk to Gibson was imperative. Why give one of the greatest batters of all time a chance to win the game when a walk would set up a force play at any base?

As Gibson ambled to first, Suttles emerged from the dugout. The PA announcement crackled over the speakers:

"Now batting for the West squad, THE MULE!"[13]

Dihigo shot a contemptuous look at the West's dugout for the gamesmanship. With two out and two on, Dihigo was confident he could get Mule out. The hometown fans rose to their feet, exhorting the local star with his trademark cheer: "Kick, Mule! Kick, Mule!"

Suttles who had already walked four times, relished the opportunity to hit. In the on-deck circle, Mule swung five bats before entering the batter's box.

The Maestro was the epitome of determined concentration as he glared toward the plate. After checking the runners, he unleashed a ball that sizzled as it bore in on Mule. Thwapp!

"Inside. Ball one," shouted the umpire, barely audible over the noisy crowd.

The next pitch was a perfect strike at the letters. Mule nodded, exhaled, and stepped back. He bent, grabbing some dirt to dry his hands. He practiced a half-swing with his fearsome black bat. Settling back in the box, Mule locked his eyes onto the area next to Dihigo's right ear where the ball would soon appear.

What happened next is best described in a poem entitled "Lament on the East-West Game" that appeared in the *Philadelphia Tribune*.

The bat met ball, the ball passed the fence
And with it went the East team's chance
Turn back, oh time, but the deed is done
Mule Suttles' homer the game has won.
And so, my friends, Mac knows full well
That managing, like war, is hell. [14]

NOTES

1   Chicago Tribune, August 10, 1935: 15.

2   Chicago Tribune, August 5, 1935: 16.

3   Members of the National Baseball Hall of Fame in Cooperstown, New York: Cool Papa Bell, Raymond Brown, Oscar Charleston, Ray Dandridge, Leon Day, Martin "The Maestro" Dihigo, Josh Gibson, Buck Leonard, James "Biz" Mackey, Turkey Stearnes, Mule Suttles, Willie "Devil" Wells and Jud Wilson.

4   Instead of attending the East-West All-Star game, Satchel Paige accepted a better monetary offer to play for an integrated team called the Bismarck Churchills and led them to victory in the semipro National Baseball Congress Championship at Wichita, Kansas. nbcbaseball.com/about-us/history/ (retrieved February 4, 2018).

5   Larry Lester, Black Baseball's National Showcase (Lincoln: University of Nebraska Press, 2001), 1. (hereinafter cited as Lester Compilation).

6   "Expect 30,000 at All-Star Game Sunday," Chicago Defender, August 10, 1935, reproduced in Lester Compilation, 69.

7   "Colored All-Star Nines Meet in East-West Game Today" Chicago Tribune, August 11, 1935: 2, 4.

8   National Baseball Hall of Fame website page for Martin Dihigo. Quote attributed to Buck Leonard baseballhall.org/hof/dihigo-mart%C3%ADn (retrieved February 4, 2018).

9   John B. Holway, Blackball Stars (Westport, Connecticut: Meckler Books, 1988), 267. (hereinafter cited as Holway).

10 William Gildea, "On Today's Scene: Paige Admits He's Feeling His Age" Washington Post, April 29, 1969: D2.

11 William G. Nunn, " 'Satch' Stops 'Big Bad Men' of West Team," Pittsburgh Courier, September 1, 1934, reproduced in Lester Compilation, 57.

12 Holway, 276-77.

13 Holway, 270.

14 Ed Harris, Lament on the East-West Game, Philadelphia Tribune, August 29, 1935, reproduced in Lester Compilation, 77.

VERN KENNEDY'S NO-HITTER KO'S CLEVELAND

AUGUST 31, 1935
CHICAGO WHITE SOX 5, CLEVELAND INDIANS 0

By Gregory H. Wolf

The Chicago White Sox were in unusual territory. Not since the days of Hall of Fame player-manager Eddie Collins had the Pale Hose sported at least a .500 record on the last day of August; however, Jimmy Dykes, in his first full season as player-manager, had the fifth-place White Sox (61-60) in position for their first winning season in nine years as they took on the Cleveland Indians for a two-game series to conclude a 24-game homestand. The ChiSox had struggled during their extended stretch in Comiskey Park, having won just nine of their last 22 games. And to make matters worse, they were coming off an embarrassing 6-2 loss in an exhibition game to the Milwaukee Brewers of the American Association at Milwaukee's Borchert Field the day before.[1] The third-place Tribe, on the other hand, was playing its best ball of the campaign under Steve O'Neill, who had replaced manager Walter Johnson on August 5. He had guided the team to 18 wins in its last 28 games to move into third place (64-58), though well behind the streaking Detroit Tigers. The Indians had just concluded a 20-game homestand and were scheduled to play 20 of their next 22 games on the road.

Toeing the rubber for the White Sox was 28-year-old right-hander Vern Kennedy, in his first full season in the big leagues. A former decathlete, Kennedy was hailed by his one-time coach Tad Reid as "the greatest athlete ever produced" by Central Missouri Teachers College (now known as the University of Central Missouri, in Warrensburg), but chose the ball and glove instead of a classroom.[2] He began his professional baseball career in 1930, failed in subsequent look-sees with the Pittsburgh Pirates and the Philadelphia Athletics, and was acquired by the White Sox in 1934 after going 15-18 and 17-18 in 1933 and 1934, respectively, for the Class-A Oklahoma City Indians of the Texas League. One of the biggest surprises on the Chisox in 1935, Kennedy had completed eight of his last nine starts and sported a 9-7 slate (4.11 ERA). On the mound for the Indians was a longtime reliable right-hander, 29-year-old Willis Hudlin, who had tossed one of the best games in his career in his last appearance, a 15-inning shutout of the Philadelphia A's on August 24 to improve his record to 12-9 and 122-114 in parts of 10 seasons, all with the Indians.

The weather was perfect with clear skies and temperatures around 70 degrees for a Saturday afternoon of baseball at the Base Ball Palace of the World on the South Side of the Windy City. After a one-two-three first, Kennedy got the only run he needed in the bottom of the frame. Jocko Conlan led off with a single and then scored on Luke Appling's two-out single.

The White Sox scored four more runs in the game, but they were just gravy given Kennedy's gem. In the fourth, Dykes' one-out single drove home Zeke Bonura, who had doubled. George Washington followed with another single, but

Luke Sewell hit into inning-ending 6-4-3 twin killing. The most exciting play of the game took place in the sixth. Hudlin loaded the bases on singles to Bonura and Dykes and a walk to Sewell with two outs. Kennedy, a competent hitter, spanked a liner that rolled all the way to the wall in center field, clearing the bases for a 5-0 lead. (Kennedy batted .244 in his 12-year career.)

Kennedy "sent a sinking assortment of curves, snow balls and dazzlers across the plate," gushed the United Press.[3] At no time was the hurler in trouble and his teammates played flawless, error-free defense. The first Indians baserunner was Eddie Phillips, who led off the third with a walk. He was forced by the next batter Roy Hughes, who subsequently stole second, the only time in the game that a Tribe player advanced that far. Kennedy also issued a walk in the sixth and one in the seventh.

Kennedy began the ninth three outs away from becoming the third White Sox hurler to toss a no-hitter in Comiskey Park. The immortal Ed Walsh tossed the first, turning the trick on August 27, 1911, against the Boston Red Sox in the 14-month-old park, known then as White Sox Park. Joe Benz was the second, on May 31, 1914, beating the Indians, 6-1. Kennedy fanned Kit Carson, pinch-hitting for Hudlin, for the first out. To the plate stepped streaking Milt Galatzer, who began the day batting .393 (22-for-56) in his last 16 games to raise his season average to .317. In what sportswriter Edward Burns of the *Chicago Tribune* called the only "hair raiser" of the game, Galatzer hit a ball to short left.[4] "It looked like a certain hit," continued Burns. Rip Radcliff had started every game thus far in left field, but was out with an injury (and eventually missed six games). In his place was center fielder Al Simmons, who had considerable experience in left field when he played for the A's. Bucketfoot Al made a "diving catch," wrote Burns, to save the no-no. Perhaps shaken from the only close play of the game, Kennedy issued his fourth and final walk of the game, to Earl Averill. Only Joe Vosmik, who entered the game as the AL's

After his years with Chicago, Vern Kennedy played for Detroit, Cleveland, and four other teams in his major-league career. (Photo: National Baseball Hall of Fame)

leading hitter (.352 batting average), stood between Kennedy and baseball immortality. On a 3-and-1 count, Vosmik hit a screeching liner down the right-field foul line, but it was "foul by a foot," declared Burns. On the next pitch, Kennedy caught Vosmik looking to record his fifth and final punchout and secure the no-hitter in 1 hour and 41 minutes.

Kennedy's no-no was the first in the AL since Bobby Burke held the Boston Red Sox hitless on August 8, 1931. Paul Dean of the St. Louis Cardinals fashioned the last one in the big leagues, defeating the Brooklyn Dodgers, 3-0, on September 21, 1934. (There weren't any no-hitters in the majors in 1932 or 1933.) Kennedy struggled in his next five starts, going 0-4 with a 5.08 ERA in 33⅔ innings, and finished the season with an 11-11 slate (3.91 ERA in 211⅔ innings). He won a career-best

21 games the next season and earned his first of two All-Star berths. Kennedy never achieved the stardom that season might have predicted, nor flirted again with a no-hitter. Three seasons later, he led the AL with 20 losses, splitting his time with the Detroit Tigers and St. Louis Browns. In parts of 12 major-league seasons with seven teams, he posted a 104-132 record.

Like Kennedy, the White Sox slumped in September, doomed by an 8-17 skid to finish in fifth place with a 74-78 record. The next season, led by Kennedy, Dykes's squad not only had a winning record (81-70), the fourth-place club also finished in the first division for the first time since 1920, a year marked by the lifetime ban of eight White Sox players implicated in the 1919 World Series betting scandal.

SOURCES

In addition to the sources cited in the Notes, the author also accessed Retrosheet.org, Baseball-Reference.com, SABR.org, and **The Sporting News** archive via Paper of Record.

NOTES

1 Charles Nevada, "White Sox Lose Exhibition at Milwaukee, 6-2," **Chicago Tribune,** August 31, 1935: 15.

2 United Press, "Kennedy's Old Coach Hails Him as Star Athlete," **Chicago Tribune,** September 1, 1935: A3.

3 United Press, "Vernon Kennedy Pitches No-Hit, No-Run Game for Chisox," **Arizona Republic** (Phoenix), September 1, 1935: 12.

4 Edward Burns, "Kennedy Pitches No-Hit Game for White Sox," **Chicago Tribune,** September 1, 1935: A3.

"BULLFROG" DIETRICH RESUSCITATES CAREER WITH A NO-HITTER

JUNE 1, 1937
CHICAGO WHITE SOX 8, ST. LOUIS BROWNS 0

By Gregory H. Wolf

The Chicago White Sox' bespectacled 27-year-old right-hander Bill Dietrich's five-year big-league career was at a crossroads when he took the mound against the St. Louis Browns on June 1, 1937, in the Windy City. In his last start, just two days earlier, Dietrich was "battered almost beyond recognition," opined *Chicago Tribune* sportswriter Irving Vaughn, surrendering 10 runs in just 3⅓ innings to the Cleveland Indians.[1] With an ERA of 10.12, Dietrich probably recognized that his days on skipper Jimmy Dykes' staff were numbered.

The last year had been a trying one for Dietrich. The previous June Philadelphia Athletics owner Connie Mack, who had signed the local phenom out of high school in 1929, finally gave up on the erratic hard-thrower and sold him to the Washington Senators in a waiver transaction. When Washington attempted to send Dietrich outright to Albany in the International League after five relief appearances and just three weeks, Chicago blocked the move. Dykes and his trusted coach, former big-league catcher Muddy Ruel, were known to take chances on pitching reclamation projects, and acquired Dietrich despite his 22-33 career record and ERA well in excess of 5.00. Dietrich, whom coaches and teammates called "Bullfrog" because of his round face and slightly protruding eyes magnified by his glasses, split his eight decisions for the White Sox in '36, but had thus far struggled in '37 while battling the flu and sinus problems.

Undoubtedly suppressing the memories of his last start, Dietrich enjoyed a 1-2-3 inning against manager Rogers Hornsby's Browns on a warm Tuesday in Comiskey Park. Chicago had kicked off a 14-game homestand the day before by sweeping last-place St. Louis (10-24) in a doubleheader to increase its winning streak to three games and move a game over .500 (18-17). The White Sox wasted no time pummeling 33-year-old left-hander Chief Hogsett, owner of a 53-66 record in his nine-year career, including 1-4 with a 5.79 ERA thus far in '37. Leadoff hitter Rip Radcliff drew a walk and scampered to third on "Iron Mike" Kreevich's double to left; both scored on Dixie Walker's double to right. After retiring Zeke Bonura and Luke Appling, Hogsett walked Jackie Hayes and Tony Piet to load the bases. His third consecutive walk, to Luke Sewell, resulted in the third run of the game. Hogsett dispatched Dietrich to end the frame.

Following another three-up-three-down inning by Dietrich, Hogsett returned to the mound, still smarting from his rude welcome in the first inning. Hogsett "started to work himself into another spasm of wildness," wrote Irving Vaughn, and walked Radcliff again. A seemingly perpetually perturbed Hornsby yanked Hogsett in favor of swingman Russ Van Atta, who had led the AL in pitching appearances in each of the previous two campaigns. The 31-year-old left-hander with a 28-32 record in five seasons induced Kreevich to hit a grounder that forced Radcliff at second, before he "was bitten by the control bug." Van Atta walked Walker, then received a boost from shortstop Bill Knickerbocker, who fielded Bonura's lazy grounder to initiate an inning-ending 6-4-3 double play.

After Dietrich retired his 12th straight batter, Chicago's leadoff hitter reached base for the fourth consecutive time when Sewell drew a walk in the fifth. [Appling had singled to start the third but was erased in a failed stolen-base attempt]. Sewell took off on contact as Dietrich attempted a sacrifice bunt. Third baseman Harlond Clift fielded the ball and "foolishly attempted a force play at second," opined Vaughn. Both runners were safe and subsequently advanced on Radcliff's sacrifice bunt. Kreevich, who had gone 26-for-73 in his previous 17 games to raise his batting average from .176 to .322, singled to drive in Sewell and Dietrich, and advanced to second when left fielder Joe Vosmik fumbled the ball. Bonura drew a two-out walk, but Appling failed to pad Chicago's 5-0 lead, flying out to right.

Dietrich's perfect game ended in the sixth inning when he walked the leadoff batter, Rollie Hemsley, on four pitches. The slow-footed catcher was retired one batter later when Tom Carey hit a bouncer to shortstop Luke Appling, who started a 6-4-3 twin killing. Dietrich committed a cardinal sin by walking his mound counterpart, Van Atta, then ended the inning by inducing Harry Davis to ground out to first baseman Zeke Bonura.

Sam West led off the top of the seventh with what Vaughn called the "most treacherous" hit of the game, a screeching liner to first base. But fourth-year veteran Bonura, who had led AL first sackers in fielding percentage in two of his first three seasons, made a leaping catch to keep the no-hitter intact. It was his second spectacular defensive play of the game. In the fifth inning he snared Knickerbocker's slashing liner. Hot-hitting Beau Bell, who eventually led the AL in hits (218) and doubles (51) while batting .340 in 1937, smashed a two-out liner to third baseman Tony Piet, who juggled the ball just long enough to permit Bell to reach first safely. Piet was charged with an error. Unshaken by Bell's presence on the basepaths, Dietrich fanned Clift to close out the seventh.

The White Sox battered Van Atta for three more runs in the eighth. Sewell led off with a double. Kreevich connected for his third hit, a two-out single to left field, to drive in Sewell. The fleet-footed, 5-foot-7, 165-pound Kreevich stole second and moved to third on Hemsley's errant throw. Dixie Walker took advantage of the situation by singling Kreevich home. After Bonura singled, Appling slapped Chicago's fourth consecutive two-out single, driving in Walker and increasing Chicago's lead to 8-0.

Known throughout his career as a hothead whose temper often got the better of him, Dietrich took the mound in the ninth just three outs from becoming the first big-league pitcher to toss a no-hitter since his Chicago teammate Vern Kennedy held Cleveland hitless on August 31, 1935, at Comiskey Park. An unusually calm Dietrich revealed to Irving Vaughn after the game that he was not nervous in the last two-plus innings because he had a feeling that the error charged to Piet in the seventh would be overturned and Bell credited with a hit. Nonetheless, Dietrich knew the pressure of a no-hitter. In just his fourth professional start, in 1931, the Bullfrog spun a no-hitter against Wilkes-Barre in the Class-B New York-Pennsylvania League as a member of the Harrisburg Senators.

Dietrich began the ninth by retiring Sunny Jim Bottomley, in the final campaign of a 16-year Hall of Fame career, on a routine fly to center fielder Kreevich. Given his recent struggles, Dietrich was in unusual terrain. He had not hurled a nine-inning complete game since defeating the Browns at Sportsman's Park on August 6 of the previous year. The knock against Dietrich was his lack of command and his frustrating inconsistency. But when the stout, 6-foot, 185-pound hurler could harness his fastball, he enjoyed moments of brilliance, and had

Hall of Famer Luke Appling played his entire 20-year big-league career with the White Sox. He led the AL in batting average twice (1936 and 1943) and collected 2,749 hits despite missing almost two complete seasons serving in the US Army during World War II. (Photo by Mark Rucker/Transcendental Graphics, Getty Images)

tossed six shutouts, including two two-hitters, in just 54 career starts entering the '37 campaign. Dietrich retired Harry Davis on an "easy bounder" to second baseman Jackie Hayes for the second out. As the White Sox faithful stood cheering, Dietrich threw a fastball by Sam West, who swung and missed to end the game in one hour and 48 minutes.

Mobbed by teammates, Dietrich finished with five punchouts. "His fastball was on the inside corner for both right- and left-hand hitters," said batterymate Luke Sewell, who caught his third no-hitter. "As a result, they were hitting the ball with the handle of their bats and easy fly balls followed."[2] Undoubtedly aided by Dykes and Ruel, Dietrich pitched consistently enough to maintain his spot in the rotation, and concluded the campaign with an 8-10 record and 4.90 ERA in 143⅓ innings. Plagued by myriad injuries throughout his 16-year career (1933-1948), Dietrich enjoyed his greatest success in the war years with the White Sox, retiring with a 108-128 record.

Dietrich's gem was the White Sox' fourth of 10 consecutive victories that catapulted the club from sixth place on May 29 into a tie with the New York Yankees for first place on June 8. It was the first time Chicago had been at the top of the AL standings that late in the season since August 31, 1920, just four weeks before former White Sox players Eddie Cicotte and Shoeless Joe Jackson confessed their participation in a scheme to fix the 1919 World Series to a grand jury. Manager Jimmy Dykes' '37 club ultimately finished in third place with an 86-68 record, their best marks since their fateful and history-altering 1920 season.

SOURCES

In addition to the sources cited in the Notes, the author also accessed Retrosheet.org, Baseball-Reference.com, SABR.org, and **The Sporting News** archive via Paper of Record.

NOTES

1 All quotations are from Irving Vaughn, "Dietrich Hurls No-Hit Game; Sox Win, 8-0," **Chicago Tribune**, June 2, 1937: 23.

2 Joe Wancho, "Luke Sewell," SABR BioProject; sabr.org/bioproj/person/3fcde47d. In addition to Dietrich's no-hitter, Sewell also caught Vern Kennedy's in 1935 and Wes Ferrell's as a member of the Cleveland Indians on April 29, 1931.

STEINBACHER'S PERFECT SIX-FOR-SIX

JUNE 22, 1938
CHICAGO WHITE SOX 16, WASHINGTON SENATORS 3

By Adam Klinker

In a three-year big-league career, Chicago White Sox rookie right fielder Hank Steinbacher amassed a grand total of 170 hits. He got 3.5 percent of them (five singles and a double) one afternoon in 1938.

That June 22 in front of just 500 fans at Comiskey Park, Steinbacher's record-tying six hits in six at-bats saw the White Sox, 19-32, and just 1½ games out of the American League cellar and ahead of the St. Louis Browns, pound the fourth-place Washington Senators (31-29, 16-3).

Records aside, Steinbacher's offensive effort may have been overshadowed by his teammate, left fielder Rip Radcliff, who was 4-for-5 with a double, triple, and six RBIs. As it happens, Radcliff had entered the game as the last American Leaguer to rap six hits in a nine-inning contest, having done so against the Philadelphia Athletics on July 18, 1936, though he needed seven at-bats to do the trick. Steinbacher would be the last to do it for the next six seasons, until George Myatt accomplished the feat in 1944.

White Sox second baseman Jackie Hayes and pitcher Monty Stratton added three hits apiece to the 17-hit carousel, with Stratton's two RBIs backing his pitching performance. The emerging ace scattered eight hits to notch his fifth win of the season.

Steinbacher endured his share of rookie riling, but took it in stride. According to Henry P. Edwards of the *Cleveland Plain Dealer*, the outfielder was given the nickname "Sammy" sometime in the 1938 season and was assigned the role of clubhouse scapegoat.

"No matter what he did, if the Sox lost, his team mates blamed 'Sammy,'" Edwards wrote in 1939. "Even when he made six for six, they grumbled because he scored only three runs and drove in two others. Why the Sox so pick on Henry? Because they knew he was good natured and could take it without it affecting his work. … He just grins when they gang up on and pan him for not hitting a triple when he hit a mere double or why he did not throw out a runner at the plate on a ball hit way to the Comiskey park score board."[1]

By the time June 22, 1938, rolled around, however, Steinbacher looked well on his way to proving himself as the regular right fielder on skipper Jimmy Dykes's White Sox squad, even as he'd suffered some slippage after a hot start — his average falling from .381 on May 27 to a season-low .316 on June 21. He wasn't alone in tumbling production. Since May 26, Chicago had gone 7-20, outscored in the losses by a count of 114-43.

"Skipper James Dykes of the White Sox yesterday came out of dugout hiding, took an it's-about-time hint from his big boss, Lou Comiskey, shook up his lineup and ended the day happier than he's been in weeks," *Chicago Tribune* mainstay Ed Burns wrote in his lead on June 23. "… Hank Steinbacher, who had been fading fast in the third spot in the batting order, was moved up to second and went base hit crazy."[2]

Indeed, that afternoon Dykes performed a wholesale restructuring of a White Sox lineup that had been battered through much of June, including a 7-0 shutout authored by Washington's Harry Kelley (fresh off a 21-loss season in 1937) the day before.

The new-look White Sox ranged up against Wes Ferrell for the third time in the 1938 season, having split the earlier two contests, knocking the right-hander around in a 9-2 win on May 22 and falling, 5-1, on June 3. It was to be one of the last times Ferrell and his brother, catcher Rick Ferrell, would team up as batterymates and, as it turned out, one of their shorter tandem outings.

After Stratton easily retired the visitors in the first inning, the White Sox sprang to life. Newly installed leadoff man Hayes tapped an infield single and Steinbacher followed with the first of his six knocks, a single moving Hayes to second. Rather inauspiciously, Hayes was picked off, but center fielder Mike Kreevich's groundout pushed Steinbacher to second, where he was driven in by Radcliff's single to right — the White Sox' first run in 15 innings.

Stratton held Washington scoreless in the second, then sparked a fire in the home half. Shortstop Boze Berger walked with one out and the pitcher banged what the *Washington Post*'s Shirley Povich called a "juicy two-bagger" to left-center to score Berger.[3] Hayes walked and Steinbacher singled to center for hit number two, plating Stratton. Kreevich's flyout brought up Radcliff, who doubled. Robbed of an RBI by Hayes' baserunning gaffe in the first, Radcliff brought his second baseman home this time but was denied a third RBI when Steinbacher — the team's good-natured whipping boy — was thrown out at the plate.

The 4-0 lead prompted the removal of the Ferrell brothers. Wes, who ultimately took the loss to fall to 9-5, was replaced on the mound by Monte Weaver, and Tony Giuliani came out to catch. Weaver's initial troubles were not of his own making as Buddy Myer made two errors on groundballs by third baseman Marv Owen and catcher Tony Rensa in the inning's bottom half, but then the hurler's control was piqued. He uncorked a wild pitch, moving the runners up 90 feet. Weaver induced a popup by Joe Kuhel, but a fly ball by Berger brought home Owen before Stratton was retired to end the inning with a 5-0 lead.

Stratton continued to hold the Senators at bay, putting up a fourth straight blank frame and holding the five through nine batters hitless.

In the White Sox' half of the fourth, Steinbacher collected his third hit, another single, and Kreevich, Owen, Rensa, and Kuhel all walked to score two more Chicago runs, bringing the score to 7-0. In the fifth, Hayes walked and moved to third on Steinbacher's fourth knock, a double, his only extra-base hit of the game. Kreevich popped out and Radcliff was intentionally passed, but Weaver let fly another wild pitch to score Hayes, and issued his sixth base on balls, to Owen, loading the bases again. Rensa worked a full count before grounding out to end the inning with the White Sox up 8-0.

Stratton showed a brief lacuna in his otherwise flawless arsenal in the top of the sixth, surrendering back-to-back doubles by Myer and Sam West, the former scoring on the latter's hit.

After sharpening their claws on Weaver for three innings, the White Sox turned their attentions to his relief, lefty Chief Hogsett, who retired the first man he faced in the sixth. But walks again proved costly for the Senators' pitchers as Hogsett passed Berger and gave up an infield single to Stratton. Hayes singled to plate Berger and Steinbacher notched his fifth hit, a single, to score Stratton. Radcliff's third hit, a single, plated Hayes for the left fielder's third RBI of the afternoon, and by the end of the inning, the White Sox were firmly in control, 11-1.

Though the home half of the seventh started promisingly enough with Rensa's double and a walk to Kuhel, Berger grounded into a double play. Rensa moved to third. With Stratton next, it appeared the White Sox would suffer their first blank frame of the contest. But the pitcher delivered his third hit and second RBI as Rensa strolled home. Hayes followed with a walk, bringing the 5-for-5 Steinbacher to the plate with a chance to write himself into the record books. The lefty's sixth hit bounded out to Goose

Goslin (making his final career start that day in right) to load the bases. Kreevich walked, forcing in Stratton, and Radcliff knocked a three-bagger to unload the sacks, making it 16-1.

Stratton blanked Washington again in the eighth, and finally, Hogsett managed to hold Chicago scoreless in the home half — the first frame without a run for a Senators pitcher all day.

In the ninth Washington's Buddy Lewis doubled and came home on Al Simmons' eighth homer of the season. Cecil Travis then lined a single, but Stratton managed to silence the next three men in order and bring the game to its 16-3 conclusion in favor of Chicago.

As Ed Burns noted, just five White Sox accounted for the 17-hit total, including the pitcher Stratton who had 18 other hits for the season. (It was his last major-league campaign after he lost a leg in a hunting accident that offseason.)[4] Steinbacher singled in the first, second, and fourth, doubled in the fifth, and singled again in the seventh and eighth.[5]

As Shirley Povich waxed in the *Post*, "The Chicago Club's score by innings reads like a WPA grant: 1-3-1-2-1-3-5-0-x." He also provided Steinbacher, who would play just 126 more big-league games, with the Homeric epithet of "Big-legged."[6]

SOURCES

In addition to the sources cited in the Notes, the author also consulted Baseball-Reference.com, Retrosheet.org, and SABR.org.

NOTES

1 Henry P. Edwards. From a typewritten story distributed January 15, 1939, by the American League Service Bureau, appearing in the Hall of Fame file of Hank Steinbacher.

2 Edward Burns, "Steinbacher Gets Six for Six to Tie Record," **Chicago Tribune**, June 23, 1938: 19.

3 Shirley Povich, "Chisox Shake Slump, Trounce Nats, 16 to 3," **Washington Post**, June 23, 1938: X18.

4 Burns: 20.

5 "Chisox Rout Washington in 16-3 Tilt, **Decatur Herald**, June 23, 1938: 6.

6 Povich.

SEPTEMBER CALL-UP MERV CONNORS FIRST WHITE SOX TO BLAST 3 HOME RUNS IN GAME AT COMISKEY

SEPTEMBER 17, 1938
CHICAGO WHITE SOX 7, PHILADELPHIA A'S 4
(GAME TWO OF DOUBLEHEADER)

By Gregory H. Wolf

Home Runs and Comiskey Park. Those two didn't mix much for most of the ballpark's 80-year existence. When it opened it 1910, the Base Ball Palace of the World, as it was known, had dimensions of 420 feet in center field, 363 feet at the foul poles, and 382 feet in the power alley.[1] Though those distances were adjusted, in and out, in subsequent years, there were few cheap home runs like those in other ballparks, such as the pillbox Baker Bowl in Philadelphia or Ebbets Field in Brooklyn. White Sox teams were built around speedy contact hitters and good defensive players. Happy Felsch was the first Pale Hose player to club at least 10 home runs in a season, whacking 14 in 1920. That was a team record until Carl Reynolds hit 22 in 1930; 40 years later, Bill Melton became the first White Sox player to wallop 30 or more home runs in a season, with 33 in 1970. As baseball changed and the long ball attracted fans, the White Sox continued their Deadball-Era-inspired play through the 1920s and 1930s. While Hall of Famer Harry Hooper, in 1922, was the first member of the team to club a pair of round-trippers in one game at Comiskey, the first to connect for three in a game at the majestic ballpark was a little-known journeyman who hit just eight in his undistinguished career, which consisted of two September call-ups.

Chicago had baseball fever as the 1938 season counted down its final two weeks. That buzz, however, was focused on the Windy City's North Side team, the Cubs, who suddenly found themselves in an unlikely pennant race. The White Sox, well, let's just say they weren't evoking comparisons to the World Series squad of 1917, or the 1919 team either, for that matter.

Few things had gone as planned for skipper Jimmy Dykes's ChiSox in 1938. After a surprising third-place finish and 86 victories the year before, the sixth-place club (56-75) had struggled most of the season and trailed the New York Yankees by 35 games. Even the weather conspired against them. Saturday's doubleheader to conclude a four-game series with the Philadelphia Athletics was necessitated by the postponement of the game the previous day. It was also the 21st twin bill for the club since July 24 (and the A's 19th) as the Great Depression, in its eighth year, still had the nation in its grip, forcing the big leagues to schedule a record number of doubleheaders to reduce costs and attract fans. Connie Mack, owner and manager of the A's since 1901, was heading for his third last-place finish in four seasons. The halcyon days of the A's three consecutive pennants (1929-1931) and two World Series championships seemed an eternity away.

Only about 5,000 spectators ventured to

the intersection of 35th Street and Shields on Chicago's South Side to enjoy the national pastime on a pleasant, late-summer afternoon with temperatures in the low 60s. The Pale Hose emerged victorious in the first game of the doubleheader, 7-4, with "Sunday Teddy" Lyons making his typical once-a-week-start, and going the distance.

Toeing the rubber for the White Sox in the second game was 31-year-old right-hander Jack Knott, who had been acquired in a trade with the St. Louis Browns in mid-June. He had lost his last eight starts for the White Sox to drop his season slate to 4-12 (and 43-66 in parts of six big-league seasons). His mound opponent was 23-year-old Jim Reninger in his major-league debut.

In 1938, White Sox batters hit the fewest home runs (67) in the AL, as well as the fewest (24) of any AL team in their home ballpark. Only the Washington Senators' cavernous Griffith Stadium experienced fewer home runs than Comiskey (64 to 60). Those statistics aside, this game was about the long ball and the A's Wally Moses commenced the action by leading off the game with a solo blast to right field.

In the second inning, Merv Connors stepped to the plate for the White Sox with two on and no outs. The 23-year-old utilityman, who "has been touring various minor leagues at the expense of the White Sox," wrote sportswriter Irving Vaughan in the *Chicago Tribune*, was purchased from the Longview (Texas) Cannibals after leading the Class C East Texas League with 24 home runs in 1936.[2] The stout, 6-foot-2, 195-pound right-handed-hitting Connors pounded 24 more taters for the Cannibals in '37, finishing third in the circuit. He earned a September call-up and clubbed two home runs for the White Sox in 103 at-bats. He had another September look-see in 1938 after pacing the Class A-1 Texas League in home runs (22) and at-bats per home run (16.6) with the Shreveport (Louisiana) Sports. Just 2-for-13 with one home run since his recall, Connors blasted a ball to deep left field for a three-run clout to give the White Sox the lead.

Triples, and not home runs, were the story in the third inning. The A's Hal Wagner led off the inning with a three-bagger and scored on Billy Werber's one-out fly ball. In the bottom of the frame, Hank Steinbacher clouted one over center fielder Bob Johnson's head, reported Vaughan, driving in Boze Berger (who had singled) and easily reached third.[3] He subsequently scored on Rip Radcliff's deep fly to give the White Sox a 5-2 lead. A near-triple in the fourth led to the A's third run. Skeeter Newsome sent a blast down the left-center-field power alley, plating Bob Johnson; however, when he tried for three, he was thrown out on shortstop Johnny Gerlach's relay throw.

In the game of his life, the pull-hitting Connors supplied the final two Pale Hose runs of the game. He led off the fourth with a solo shot to left. With one out in the sixth, he made history when he walloped Reninger's first pitch over the left-field wall to become the first White Sox hitter to crank three home runs in one game. The only other player to hit three in a game at Comiskey Park was the Yankees' Lou Gehrig, who achieved the feat on May 4, 1929.

Connors led off the eighth with a chance to join a select group of sluggers with four home runs in a game. Bobby Lowe of the Boston Beaneaters was the first, on May 30, 1894, followed by Ed Delahanty of the Philadelphia Phillies on July 13, 1896. The first AL slugger was Gehrig on June 3, 1932; the Phillies' Chuck Klein was the most recent (July 10, 1936). Connors connected squarely with Reninger's offering. As the ball soared high into left field, it looked as though it could clear the wall, but it "hit the left field scoreboard," reported Vaughan.[4] Connors missed a home run "by a few feet," and settled for a double. Consecutive two-out walks by Reninger filled the bases, but the rookie recorded his third punchout of the game to end the inning.

Knott hurled a 1-2-3 ninth to finish the game in 1 hour and 43 minutes.

Connors' performance was the stuff of fairy tales: a record-setting three home runs, five RBIs, and 18 total bases. He continued to swat the ball over the next two weeks, finishing with a .355/6/13 line with a .710 slugging average. And then the clock struck midnight. Connors had tryouts with the White Sox in 1939 and 1940, but never made it back to the majors. He did, however, continue swatting home runs. After battling injuries in 1939 and 1940, he whacked a combined 29 in 1941 and 27 the following season. At the age of 38 in 1950, he slugged 47 with the Amarillo Gold Sox to lead the Class C West Texas-New Mexico League, and followed it up with 34, third-best in the Class C Longhorn League the next season, his last in professional baseball.

SOURCES

In addition to the sources cited in the Notes, the author also accessed Retrosheet.org, Baseball-Reference.com, Newspapers.com, and SABR.org.

NOTES

1 "Comiskey Park Historical Analysis," Baseball Almanac. baseball-almanac.com/stadium/stadiumi.shtml.

2 Irving Vaughan, "Connors Hits Three Homers as Sox Beat Macks, 8-4, 7-4," **Chicago Tribune**, August 18, 1938: 31.

3 Ibid.

4 Ibid.

THE EAST-WEST ALL-STAR GAME GOT THEIR VOTE

AUGUST 6, 1939
WEST 4, EAST 2
NEGRO LEAGUE ALL-STAR GAME

By Norm King

As the *Cheers* resident know-it-all Cliff Clavin might have said, "It's a little-known fact …" that the first major-league All-Star Game held at Comiskey Park in 1933 was not the only inaugural All-Star competition held that year at the ballyard that Charles built.

Following on the heels of the Comiskey classic, Pittsburgh Crawfords Secretary Roy Sparrow and *Pittsburgh Courier* editor Bill Nun discussed the idea of having a similar game pitting the best players from the newly constituted Negro National League against each other.[1] Their initial idea was to hold the game at Yankee Stadium, but after receiving a tepid response to that suggestion, Crawfords owner Gus Greenlee recommended that the game be held at Comiskey because it would appeal to the Windy City's large black population. The West won the first game, 11-7, on September 10, 1933, in front of approximately 20,000 rain-soaked fans. The game was a success and a new tradition was born.

With the organization of the Negro American League in 1937, the game pitted the best players from the two circuits against each other. Because Negro National League teams were based in the East, and Negro American League teams played in the Midwest, it was easy to continue calling the event the East-West All-Star game.

The game grew in popularity as the pressures of the Depression eased. It helped that neither league dominated, as the two sides split the first games evenly, with three wins apiece. The first six games set the stage for one of the classic matchups in the event's history. On August 6, 1939, the West used home-run power in the seventh and eighth innings to overcome a 2-0 East lead in front of 40,000 fans, a record attendance for the classic up to that time.

Fans voted for the players on each side from ballots available through America's three leading black community newspapers, the *Pittsburgh Courier*, the *Kansas City Call*, and the *Chicago Defender*. Even though they were only voting for baseball All-Stars, the right to do so was important to many African-Americans because many were denied the right to exercise their franchise under existing Jim Crow laws.

"(D)uring the 1930s, voting was so difficult for blacks that many did not bother," wrote Bo Smolka in his history of the Negro Leagues. "So the chance to vote for the East-West All-Star Game players was a big deal. More than 17 million ballots were submitted for the 1939 East-West Game."[2]

"That was a pretty important thing for black people to do in those days, even if it was just for ballplayers," said Hall of Famer Buck O'Neil.[3]

Those votes resulted in a lot of talented players participating in the game, including future

Theolic Smith was a three-league All Star, including the Negro Leagues, the Pacific Coast League, and the Mexican League (pictured here in 1947). (Photo: public domain)

Hall of Famers Willie Wells, Josh Gibson, Mule Suttles, Leon Day, and Buck Leonard for the East squad, and Hilton Smith for the West.

The weather was perfect as heavyweight boxing champion Joe Louis arrived wearing a snazzy gabardine suit to throw out the first pitch to Greenlee. Once the game started, the favored Easterners scored two runs in the second inning off starter Theolic Smith of the Memphis Red Sox. The rally started when Leonard was safe on an error by shortstop Ted Strong. Leonard advanced to third on Pat Patterson's single, and after Patterson stole second, both runners scored on a single by Sammy Hughes.

Both sides pitched well over the next several innings as the score remained 2-0. In fact, keeping East sluggers Gibson, Suttles, and Leonard hitless (the three went 0-for-10) allowed the West to mount their comeback.

"At this point (the second inning) the hopes of the thousands of Western rooters hit a new 'low,' but still the West's pitching continued on a high plane," wrote Chester L. Washington Jr. "Eastern base hits were as scarce as hen's teeth and soon the hopes of the West started to soar again."[4]

That soaring began in the seventh inning when Neil Robinson broke the East's shutout bid, blasting Roy Partlow's first offering 380 feet into the second tier of the left-field stands. The West completed their comeback in the eighth. Ted "Double Duty" Radcliffe singled to center, and was sacrificed to second by Parnell Woods. Dan Wilson followed that with a two-run homer that put the West in the lead to stay. After Bill Holland replaced Partlow, Double Duty's brother Alec greeted him with a base hit. Robinson then hit a fly ball that Suttles lost in the sun. Radcliffe reached third on the play while Robinson landed on second with a double. The West showed what small ball is about when Billy Horne hit a sacrifice that brought Double Duty home with an insurance run. Double Duty Radcliffe pitched a 1-2-3 ninth and earned the victory for the West while Partlow was tagged with the loss.[5]

"With one bold stroke of his bat, this artist of the diamond painted a picture before the astonished eyes of some 40,000 fans … a painting as dramatic in its highlights and shadows as Rembrandt's [sic] 'Blue Boy,'" wrote Bill Nun about Wilson's homer.[6] "Dan Wilson today stole the thunder of the vaunted power-hitters of the East."[7]

The West's victory gave them a 4-3 lead in the series, and helped them maintain a dominance they held for the duration of the series' existence. The East-West All-Star Game was held annually at Comiskey Park until 1960, with the West winning 16 of the 28 matchups. The last two Classics were held at Yankee Stadium in 1961 and at Kansas City's Municipal Stadium in 1962, with the West winning both contests, 7-1 in 1961 and 5-2 in 1962.

THE BASE BALL PALACE OF THE WORLD

SOURCES

In addition to the sources listed below, the author also used:

Negro League Baseball E-museum.

Thenationalpastimemuseum.com.

Finder, Chuck. "Negro Leagues Converged in an East Meets West Powerball Summit," **Pittsburgh Post-Gazette**, July 9, 2006.

Kleinknecht, Merl F. "East Meets West in Negro All-Star Game," **Baseball Research Journal** (SABR), 1972.

Lester, Larry. **Black Baseball's National Showcase** (Lincoln: University of Nebraska Press, 2001).

Newman, Roberta. **Shadow Culture, Shadow Game: The Negro Leagues**.

Sullivan, Floyd, editor. **Old Comiskey Park: Essays and Memories of the Historic Home of the Chicago White Sox, 1910-1991** (Jefferson, North Carolina: McFarland and Company, 2014).

NOTES

1. The first Negro National League, founded in 1920, could not survive the Great Depression and folded in 1931.

2. Bo Smolka, **The Story of the Negro Leagues** (Minneapolis: ABDO Publishing Company, 2013), 9.

3. Ibid.

4. Chester L. Washington Jr., "Sun Rises in the West," **Pittsburgh Courier**, August 12, 1939: 17.

5. Partlow later played briefly with the Montreal Royals in 1946, the same year Jackie Robinson broke the color barrier in Organized Baseball.

6. **Blue Boy** was painted by the Englishman Thomas Gainsborough.

7. William G. Nunn, "Homers by Dan Wilson, Robinson Decide Battle," **Pittsburgh Courier**, August 12, 1939: 17.

CHICAGO NATIVE JOHNNY RIGNEY PITCHES WHITE SOX TO HISTORIC FIRST NIGHT GAME VICTORY

AUGUST 14, 1939
CHICAGO WHITE SOX 5, ST. LOUIS BROWNS 2

By Mike Huber

On a warm August Monday night in Chicago, the sports news centered on baseball at Comiskey Park, where the White Sox would be playing their first night game at home. Afterward, the *Chicago Tribune* described the event: "In the inaugural of night major league baseball in Chicago more than 30,000 watched John D. Rigney of River Forest turn in a handsome three hit performance to beat the St. Louis Browns, 5 to 2."[1] Playing under the lights had been the ambition of J. Louis Comiskey, White Sox president-owner, but he had died a month before (July 18). Instead, "baseball under the stars was a hit from the moment young Charles Comiskey II [Louis's son] pressed two switches at 8.25 o'clock that brought out the green in relief. It was as though one had suddenly walked into bright sunshine."[2]

The crowd[3] was five to ten times bigger than in previous Chicago-St. Louis meetings in 1939 at Comiskey Park. In June, the first game of a three-game series between the two teams drew 3,000, while the next day's doubleheader brought just 6,000 to the ballpark.

Chicago's starter, 24-year-old Johnny Rigney, was in his third season with Chicago. He had his only winning season in 1939, and he brought a six-game winning streak into this contest against St. Louis. He was opposed by Bill Trotter, a 6-foot-2-inch righty for the Browns who had won four of his last five decisions.

The White Sox "started the scoring business in the second inning,"[4] when Rip Radcliff hit a single to left with one out. Eric McNair flied out, and with Mike Tresh batting, Radcliff swiped second base. Tresh then knocked an RBI single to left, plating Radcliff with the game's first tally.

With two outs in the bottom of the fourth, McNair launched a double to right-center. Tresh "sent McNair home with a single to center."[5] Rigney tried to help his own cause with a double, but Tresh stopped at third base. Both runners were stranded when Jackie Hayes hit a comebacker to Trotter for the third out.

An inning later, Chicago added another run. Joe Kuhel led off with a single to right. He stole second and then stopped at third when Mike Kreevich singled to center. Gee Walker hit a grounder that went off Trotter's hand and beat the pitcher's throw to first. Kuhel scored and Kreevich moved to second. Kreevich then stole third. Browns backstop Joe Glenn faked a throw toward third base but instead threw to first, as Walker had been lured off the bag by the fake. This put Walker in a rundown, during which Kreevich broke from third for home. St. Louis second baseman Johnny Berardino "threw to Glenn to harpoon Kreevich,"[6] for the inning's first out. Walker managed to get to second, but the White Sox would not score again in the inning.

Rigney, Chicago's big right-hander, faced the minimum through the first five innings, fanning six. A leadoff walk to Glenn in the sixth ended the perfect game. Then Chicago shortstop Luke Appling had "an almost unprecedented fit of the fumbles."[7] Obviously affected by the lights, Appling botched three grounders and a catch, each of which could have resulted in a double play. Instead, Appling's miscues resulted in two force outs and two errors, presenting the St. Louis squad with two runs "on a hit production of one single [by Berardino], the first hit off Rigney, some ten minutes after the inning should have been over."[8] Every one of the four balls hit into the infield during the top of the sixth was misplayed by Appling.

Chicago "pulled out of danger in the seventh."[9] With the score 3-2 and Roxie Lawson now pitching for the Browns, Kuhel singled and Kreevich doubled to start the action. Walker received an intentional pass, loading the bases. Appling forced Walker at second, with Kuhel scoring on the play. When Radcliff sent a grounder to second, Berardino fired home and Kreevich was declared out at the plate for the second time in the game. McNair then delivered a single to center, driving in Appling. The 5-2 score stood to the end.

The victory in the first night game at Comiskey Park "lighted the White Sox' way right back into third place a half-game ahead of the Cleveland Indians."[10] Rigney earned his 10th victory of the season, and Chicago scored its ninth win against St. Louis in 11 games to this point of the season.[11] Had Appling's defense been a bit more solid, Rigney would have pitched a shutout; both of the runs scored in the sixth inning were unearned. As reported in the *St. Louis Post-Dispatch*, "even the lights couldn't help [the Browns] see Johnny Rigney's fast one."[12] In the complete-game victory, his 10th of the season, Rigney struck out 10 Browns batters, scattering three hits with one walk. Trotter was saddled with the loss, his record dropping to 5-6.

It appeared that only Appling was affected by the new nighttime venue, although some players complained that "a ground ball makes a shadow as it skips across the turf, thus increasing the hazard of fielding."[13] Chicago's skipper, Jimmy Dykes, told reporters, "The umpires still look the same to me under the lights."

Four nights later, on August 18, the White Sox hosted the Cleveland Indians for the second home night game of the season. According to Retrosheet, 46,000 witnessed the White Sox' 1-0 victory, as Eddie Smith beat Cleveland's Bob Feller in 11 innings. Chicago played five night games at Comiskey Park in 1939, going 4-1 with a swarm of fans at each game. The only loss came on August 22, when the New York Yankees blasted the White Sox, 14-5, before a season-high crowd of 50,000. Johnny Rigney earned victories in three of the four night-game wins.

While the White Sox and Browns were making history at Comiskey Park on August 14, the two cities' other teams (Cubs and Cardinals) played each other in a day game at Sportsman's Park in St. Louis. The Cubs won, 4-0, extending their winning streak to five games. Members of the Cubs' front office were in attendance at Comiskey for the White Sox' historic event. Charles Drake, assistant to P.K. Wrigley, told reporters that "Wrigley Field would not be lighted until the Cubs were certain their fans wanted night baseball. He declared that under no circumstances would the Cubs join the night baseball movement next year [1940]."[14] That certainty took another 49 years, as the lights didn't go on at Wrigley Field until August 8, 1988, "breaking a 72-year tradition of sunshine baseball."[15] That game was rained out and the first official game was played the following night.

SOURCES

In addition to the sources mentioned in the Notes, the author consulted Baseball-Reference.com and Retrosheet.org.

NOTES

1. Edward Burns, "Sox Win 1st Night Game, 5-2, Before 35,000," **Chicago Tribune**, August 15, 1939: 15.

2. Edward Prell, "Cub Officials See Sox Play Under Lights," **Chicago Tribune**, August 15, 1939: 15.

3. The **Chicago Tribune** reported a crowd of 35,000. The **St. Louis Post-Dispatch** reported "slightly more than 30,000." Both Retrosheet.org and Baseball-Reference.com list the attendance as 30,000.

4. Burns.

5. Ibid.

6. Ibid.

7. Ibid.

8. Ibid.

9. Ibid.

10. Ibid.

11. The White Sox were 19-4 against the Browns in 1939.

12. "Browns Idle After Losing at Night in Chicago," **St. Louis Post-Dispatch**, August 15, 1939: 11.

13. Prell.

14. Ibid.

15. Jerome Holtzman, "Lights! Action! And then ...," **Chicago Tribune**, August 9, 1988: 37. The Cubs-Phillies game was rained out, delaying the first complete night game at Wrigley Field until the next night, August 9.

BOB FELLER'S OPENING DAY NO-HITTER

APRIL 16, 1940
CLEVELAND INDIANS 1, CHICAGO WHITE SOX 0

By C. Paul Rogers III

In all of baseball history through 2015, only one no-hitter was pitched on Opening Day. Perhaps not surprisingly, it was thrown by the 21-year-old prodigy Bob Feller on April 16, 1940, against the Chicago White Sox on a blustery 40-degree day in Comiskey Park. The masterpiece was the first of three no-hitters Feller threw in his illustrious career, along with a remarkable 12 one-hitters.

Feller was coming off his second dominant season, having gone 24-9 in 1939 for the third-place Cleveland Indians. They had, however, finished 20½ games in arrears of the powerful New York Yankees, who had blown away the rest of the league with 106 wins. The White Sox had finished fourth, two games back of the Indians, and both squads had high hopes for 1940.

The unseasonably cold day, even for Chicago, held the Opening Day crowd down to just over 14,000. Three of them, however, were Feller's father, Bill; his mother, Lena; and his sister, Marguerite, who had all traveled from Van Meter, Iowa, to take in the first game of the season.

Feller didn't feel particularly sharp warming up and wondered how the strong wind blowing in from center field would affect his curveball.[1]

He began by retiring leadoff hitter Bob Kennedy on a fly to right and then sandwiched a walk between two strikeouts to retire the side. The second inning proved more problematic. With one out, Taft Wright, who was something of a Feller nemesis, hit a fly ball to Roy Weatherly in center field that Weatherly dropped. The official scorer, Ed Burns of the *Chicago Tribune*, took a moment or two before ruling an error.[2] Feller struck out the next batter, but then issued consecutive walks to Mike Tresh and opposing pitcher Edgar Smith to load the bases with two outs. He then bore down to strike out Kennedy and escape the jam.

The weather was making it difficult for Feller to grip his curveball, and after the second inning he threw almost all fastballs. Joe Kuhel led off the third with a walk and stole second. Feller managed the first two outs on a flyball to right and a popup to first, bringing the dangerous Luke Appling to the plate. Appling connected solidly, driving a hard, low line drive to right field. But Ben Chapman, covering ground quickly, made a nice running catch to end the inning.

Meanwhile, the Indians had managed only an infield single and a couple of walks against Edgar Smith, a southpaw who had engaged in several duels against Feller in previous seasons. In the top of the fourth, however, Indians first baseman Hal Trosky smashed a mighty blast to right field that the wind knocked down enough for Taft Wright to catch against the fence. Jeff Heath followed with a single through the left side of the infield, and with two outs catcher Rollie Hemsley lined a long drive over Wright's head in right. Hemsley rumbled into third with a triple, scoring Heath for what would be the only run of the game.[3]

Feller had by now found his rhythm and after his walk to Kuhel he retired 20 White Sox in a row. Other than Appling's liner, the only other hard-hit ball was a similar line drive by

A South Side institution: the façade of Comiskey Park in the 1940s. (Photo by Mark Rucker/Transcendental Graphics, Getty Images)

Wright in the fourth, also run down by Chapman in right field. In the eighth second baseman Ray Mack made a nice play on a slow roller to nip the speedy pinch-hitter Larry Rosenthal by a step.[4]

Feller already had three one-hitters in his three-plus years in the big leagues and the crowd was by now hoping this would be the day he broke through, even against the home team. By the eighth inning the fans were standing, rooting for Feller to complete his gem, and in the ninth they were in an uproar. He managed to give them plenty of drama, beginning by running the count to Mike Kreevich to 2-and-2 before retiring him on a popup to second baseman Mack. Moose Solters was next and Feller retired him on the third pitch on a routine groundout to shortstop Lou Boudreau. Now only "Old Aches and Pains" Luke Appling stood between Feller and immortality. Appling was known for his bat control and his penchant for fouling off pitches. With two strikes, he fouled off four Feller fastballs before working a 10-pitch walk to become the first White Sox baserunner since the third inning.[5]

The free pass brought Taft Wright to the plate. Feller threw ball one and then, on the second pitch, Wright hit a screaming groundball to the left of second baseman Mack. He managed to lunge and knock it down with his glove hand, get up and retrieve it on the grass with his bare hand, and throw a perfect peg to Trosky at first to nail the speedy Wright by a half-step. Just like that, the game was over and Feller had his first no-hitter. His teammates rushed to congratulate him, shaking his hand and slapping him on the back, while leading him through the fans, who were racing onto the field.[6]

Surprisingly, Feller's first no-hitter wasn't one of his most dominating performances. He struck out eight, modest by his standards, and allowed five walks. After the game, his catcher, Hemsley, said, "I've seen Bob better, but he was plenty good enough."[7]

For his part, Feller thought his stuff was "just about normal." He related that he tired in the fourth, but got his second wind the next inning.[8]

The next day the Indians returned to Cleveland by train and an estimated 7,000 greeted them at Union Terminal. The throng included Mayor Harold Burton, a uniformed band, and Cleveland immortal Tris Speaker. The next day an article ran in a local paper about 8-year-old Paul Hauschultz, a huge Indians fan who had been in the hospital with spinal meningitis, a mastoid infection, and streptococcus for about a month. The article mentioned how much he'd improved while listening on the radio to Feller's no-hitter. As a result, Feller surprised the youngster with a visit in the hospital, armed with a ball signed by the entire team and another signed by himself.[9] According to Feller's 1990 memoir, the youngster was able to go home that afternoon.[10]

The Indians soon found themselves in a tight pennant race with the Detroit Tigers and New York Yankees. Their season, and Feller's, however, was tainted by a June player revolt against their caustic manager, Oscar Vitt. A number of Indians, Feller among them, went to Alva Bradley, the owner of the club, to try to get Vitt fired. Bradley refused but when the press got wind of the attempted revolt, they dubbed the team "the Crybabies."[11] Even with all the drama, the Indians led the league much of the first half of the season and finished in second place, just a game behind the Tigers.

Feller would go on to have a gargantuan season, winning 27 games and leading the league in wins, innings pitched, strikeouts, earned-run average, games started, and complete games while tying for the lead in shutouts. He finished second in the MVP voting to Hank Greenberg, but was voted the American League Player of the Year by *the Sporting News*.

NOTES

1. Bob Feller, **Strikeout Story — Bob Feller** (New York: A.S. Barnes & Co., 1947), 175.

2. Feller, **Strikeout Story**, 176.

3. Gordon Cobbledick, "Feller Hurls No-Hitter to Win, 1 to 0, **Cleveland Plain Dealer**, April 17, 1940: 21.

4. Charles Bartlett, "Indians Put on a Big Celebration After No-Hitter," **Chicago Tribune**, April 17, 1940: 27.

5. Cobbledick, 1. In his second autobiography, published in 1990, Feller claimed that after Appling fouled off four or five straight 2-and-2 pitches, he threw two fastballs outside on purpose to in effect intentionally walk him and get him out of the way. Bob Feller with Bill Gilbert, **Now Pitching — Bob Feller** (New York: Birch Lane Press, 1990), 96; Bob Feller with Burton Rocks, **Bob Feller's Little Black Book of Baseball Wisdom** (New York: McGraw-Hill, 2001), 29.

6. Cobbledick, 21.

7. John Sickels, **Bob Feller — Ace of the Greatest Generation** (Dulles, Virginia: Brassey's, Inc., 2004), 91.

8. Bartlett, 25.

9. John Phillips, **The Crybaby Indians of 1940** (Cabin John, Maryland: Capital, 1990), 5; Sickels, 91.

10. Feller with Gilbert, 97.

11. Franklin Lewis, **The Cleveland Indians** (New York: G.P. Putman's Sons, 1949, reprinted by Kent State University Press, 2006), 206-13; Phillips, 26-32.

THRILLS AND SURPRISES: 51,723 SEE SATCHEL PAIGE AND OTHER NEGRO LEAGUE GREATS

AUGUST 1, 1943
WEST 2, EAST 1
NEGRO LEAGUE ALL-STAR GAME

By Bob Lemoine

"If you were anybody, you were at the East-West Game."

— Buck O'Neil

"It was a great ball game," wrote Wendell Smith of the *Pittsburgh Courier*. "One packed with thrills and surprises. One cast in a setting as colorful and picturesque as any movie saga. One that will go down in history in brilliant lettering and stand in bold relief until the pages upon which it is written wither in the dust of time."[1] Fortunately, digital archives have preserved for us the accounts of this game from August 1, 1943, or they could have indeed withered "in the dust of time." While we are privileged to have technology that allows us to look back in time, we can never truly appreciate the significance of this game to the 51,723 who came to Comiskey Park to witness some of baseball's all-time greats who were overlooked due to the color of their skin.

While the national pastime remained segregated, both the white major leagues and the Negro Leagues faced a common barrier as men of all races had donned or soon would don military uniforms to serve their country in World War II. But in a time of uncertainty, fans turned out in what amounted to the largest crowd in the history of the East-West Game. An estimated 10,000 more were turned away at the gates.[2] Virgil Blueitt of Chicago was the home-plate umpire for the first four innings, and then he switched places with Fred McCrary of Philadelphia. Frank Forbes of New York City and Harry Walker of Cleveland completed the crew.

Satchel Paige of Kansas City started on the mound for the West, while David "Impo" Barnhill of the New York Cubans pitched for the East. Paige was already established as one of the all-time greats, but Barnhill, having the best season of his career to that point, wouldn't let the huge crowd or the legend get to him. "When I walked out of the clubhouse and saw all those people, then I wanted to put on my big show," said the man who learned the game playing stickball on the streets of Greenville, North Carolina. "That ain't no time to be nervous."[3]

Paige was dominant from the start, striking out Henry Kimbro of Baltimore and Buck Leonard of Homestead in the first inning. In the top of the second, Josh Gibson drew a walk; then with two out made it to second on a passed ball. But Paige struck out Sam Bankhead, also of Homestead, to end the threat.

In the bottom of the second, Neil Robinson of Memphis drew a walk from Barnhill. Buck

THE BASE BALL PALACE OF THE WORLD

O'Neil of Kansas City laid down a sacrifice bunt to get Robinson to second. Tommy Sampson of Birmingham singled to right, scoring Robinson and giving the West a 1-0 lead. Ted Radcliffe of Chicago lined into a double play to end the inning.

In the top of the third, Paige fanned Cool Papa Bell of Homestead to give him his fourth and final strikeout of the game. Surprisingly, with his pitching day completed, Paige still batted in the bottom of the inning. After looking overmatched with two Barnhill pitches, Paige laced a double to left, the only extra-base hit of the game until the ninth. Bubba Hyde of Memphis went in to run for Paige, who left to thunderous applause. "He left as he came — proud and cocky — still the most colorful player in baseball — still the 'Great One,'" wrote Smith.[4]

Jesse Williams of Kansas City laid down a bunt that Barnhill fielded and threw to Homestead's Howard Easterling at third. Easterling mistakenly thought it was a force play and failed to tag Hyde, which the official scorer later admitted should have been scored an error.[5] No damage was done, as Hyde was later thrown out attempting to score on a fly ball.

In the fourth, the West padded its lead against pitcher John Wright of Homestead. Willard Brown of Kansas City singled to center and stole second. He moved to third on a groundout, and then scored when O'Neil grounded back to the mound. Wright threw to Leonard to get the out at first, but Leonard's throw home was too late to get the sly Brown. The West held a 2-0 lead, but would score no more runs that day.

Gread McKinnis of Birmingham followed Paige and the lefty allowed only one hit, a single by Rabbit Martinez of New York, in three innings of work. Theolic Smith of Cleveland also pitched two hitless innings, but was mystified at trying to get that last out to finish the game. It was a nailbiting finish.

In the ninth, Smith was aided when Lloyd "Ducky" Davenport of Chicago robbed Bell of a hit to right field. Jerry Benjamin of Homestead pinch-hit for Juan "Tetelo" Vargas of the Cuban Stars. A slow roller to second was dug out at second by Tommy Sampson of Birmingham, who threw Benjamin out by a step. Next came Leonard, who drove the ball into Comiskey's upper deck in right field (Wendell Smith reported the blast being 352 feet) to give the East its first run and make the score 2-1. Smith now had to contend with the ever-dangerous Gibson, batting .550 for the season. Gibson slammed a shot to Williams at shortstop, who "tried to field the ball and almost got his hand torn off," wrote Frank Young of the *Chicago Defender*.[6] The tying run was now on base. Easterling singled to right to move Gibson to second. West manager Frank Duncan had lost confidence in Smith and waved in Memphis's Porter Moss from the bullpen. Vic Harris of Homestead, the manager of the East, countered by sending himself up to pinch-hit for Newark's Leonard Pearson. Moss threw two poor pitches nowhere near the plate, and the intensity grew. He then threw a submarine-style pitch that got over for a strike. Harris popped a fly to Brown in center to end the contest. Young wrote, "that jam-packed session was a humdinger."[7]

"This is not only the biggest Negro sports event," wrote Joe Bostic of *The People's Voice*, "but the largest proportion in the nation from the point of view of patron interest to the extent of paying an admission price. ... No other event begins to draw anything like this one. ... It is a great thing this classic, and I, for one, am proud to be a part of it."[8] Two years later, Bostic, an African-American sportswriter and pioneering radio broadcaster, escorted two Negro League players to the Brooklyn Dodgers' spring camp and demanded of team President Branch Rickey that they receive a tryout. It was, perhaps, a poorly executed attempt at breaking baseball's color barrier. It was Rickey himself who broke the barrier two years later with the signing of Jackie Robinson.[9]

Hope for racial equality on the baseball diamond was on the horizon. But even that day, as Wendell Smith concluded, "[O]nce again the sun is shining brilliantly on the baseball front in the rugged, Golden West!"[10]

SOURCES

Newspaper sources listed in the Notes are taken from:

Lester, Larry. **Black Baseball's National Showcase: The East-West All-Star Game, 1933-1953** (Lincoln, Nebraska: University of Nebraska Press, 2001).

NOTES

1. Wendell Smith, "Pitchers Star as West Beats East in Thriller," **Pittsburgh Courier**, August 7, 1943. Printed in Lester, 212.

2. United Press, "Satchel Paige Struts His Stuff in East-West Camp," printed in **Daily Notes** (Canonsburg, Pennsylvania), August 2, 1943: 6.

3. James A. Riley, "Dave Barnhill." Retrieved September 4, 2017. research.sabr.org/journals/dave-barnhill

4. Smith. Lester, 213.

5. Frank Young, "Satchel Paige and West Take East Into Camp," **Chicago Defender**, August 7, 1943. Lester, 217.

6. Ibid; Lester, 216.

7. Ibid.

8. Joe Bostic, "The East-West Classic, Top Sports Event," **The People's Voice**, August 14, 1943. Lester, 218-219.

9. George L. Hiss, **The Joe Bostic Story: First Black American Radio Announcer.** (Bloomington, Indiana: AuthorHouse, 2005), 72-73; Chris Lamb, "Two Who Tried Out Before Jackie Robinson," Retrieved September 4, 2017. espn.com/mlb/story/_/id/12691678/two-tried-jackie-robinson; The players Bostic promoted to Rickey were Terris McDuffie and Dave "Showboat" Thomas, who were 35 and 40 years old, respectively, and were unlikely to have made the team anyway.

10. Smith. Lester, 214.

JOSH GIBSON, COOL PAPA BELL, AND BUCK LEONARD STAR IN THE BASEBALL PALACE OF THE WORLD

SEPTEMBER 26, 1943
HOMESTEAD GRAYS 9, BIRMINGHAM BLACK BARONS 0
GAME FOUR OF NEGRO LEAGUE WORLD SERIES

By Bob LeMoine

A crowd of 6,000 turned out to Comiskey Park on September 26, 1943, at 2:30 P.M. for Game Four of the Negro League World Series between the Homestead Grays of the Negro National League and the Birmingham Black Barons of the Negro American League. The previous three games had been played in Washington, D.C., Homestead's home park, a 4-2 Birmingham win; Baltimore, a 5-5 tie; and in Washington again, where the Grays pulled out a 4-3 win. The remainder of the Series would be played in Columbus, Ohio, Indianapolis, Birmingham, and Montgomery, Alabama. Birmingham had defeated Chicago in a playoff series for the NAL, after Birmingham won the first half of the season and Chicago the second half. Winfield Welch's Birmingham squad was 51-42-2 overall, while Candy Jim Taylor's Homestead team easily won the NNL by 17 games over the New York Cubans, finishing 53-14-1.

Johnny Wright, with a NNL-best 20-4 record and a 2.33 ERA, took the mound for the Grays. Gready McKinnis (3-8) was his Birmingham opponent.

The Grays got on the scoreboard in the second inning. Josh Gibson, who had a monstrous year, batting .442/.541/.806, a league-leading 20 home runs, and 112 RBIs, walked. Howard Easterling doubled to left, sending Gibson to third. After a popout, Tommy Sampson knocked down a Jud Wilson grounder and threw him out, but Gibson scored for a 1-0 lead.

In the third, speedster Jerry Benjamin doubled and scored on Buck Leonard's triple, giving the Grays a 2-0 advantage.

Cool Papa Bell led off the fourth with a single. McKinnis fumbled Benjamin's bunt, and both runners were safe. Leonard dragged a bunt single and the bases were loaded. A fly ball by Gibson brought in Bell and the Grays had a 3-0 lead.

Bell made a great defensive play for the Grays in the bottom of the third when he speared a drive off the bat of Felix McLaurin and doubled off Ted "Double Duty" Radcliffe, who had ventured well off second base. The amazing catch "seemed to change the complexion of the entire game," wrote the *Pittsburgh Courier*.[1]

Radcliffe gave new meaning to his "Double Duty" nickname. He was the manager and catcher for Chicago of the Negro American League. Paul Hardy, Birmingham's regular catcher, was drafted into the US Army at the end of the season. Birmingham sought out Radcliffe to take his place, and the Grays granted permission. Wendell Smith of the *Pittsburgh Courier* cried foul over the entire process, and used the incident to push his belief in the need for a Negro League commissioner. "Despite the fact that the Grays approved the move," he wrote, "there is no justification for it. According to baseball rules, the Homestead Grays won the series when the first ball was thrown in the first game in Washington, D.C., because Birmingham was using an ineligible player." Since the Grays allowed the move, Smith sarcastically remarked, "[T]o hell with the rules and regulations."[2]

John Huber came in to pitch for Birmingham in the sixth, and the fireworks were just starting. Jud Wilson hit a slow grounder to Leonard Lindsay at first, but his throw was low to Huber covering the bag. Vic Harris drew a walk, and Wright beat out a bunt to load the bases. Bell doubled down the left-field line. Wilson and Harris scored. Wright scored on Benjamin's groundout. Leonard was intentionally walked to load the bases, and a single by Gibson scored Bell to make the score 7-0. Easterling singled, driving in Leonard. Matt Carlisle, who entered the game after Sam Bankhead was injured in a collision at second base with Piper Davis, grounded out, but another run scored, and the Grays led 9-0. Their six runs in the sixth blew the game wide open.

Wright allowed Birmingham only five hits and struck out two while walking six in the complete-game victory. Bell was the hitting star, going 3-for-5.

Cumberland Posey, the Negro League legend and owner of the Grays, writing in the *Pittsburgh Courier*, described the logistical problems in the Series. Negro League clubs did not own their own ballparks and often had to fit their schedules around the schedules of the white baseball clubs. The Series might have been played solely in the Midwest had it not been for Clark Griffith rearranging already scheduled games to fit the Negro League games in at Griffith Stadium in Washington.[3]

The Black Barons tied the Series with an 11-8 win in Game Five, but Wright threw a second shutout on September 29 in Game Six, winning 8-0. Playing Game Seven at home, Birmingham squeaked out a 1-0 win in 11 innings, and the Series was tied again. Homestead took the Game Eight clincher, 8-4. The Series left a bad taste in the mouths of fans. The final game was scheduled for October 10 in New Orleans. Wendell Smith was told several players had to report to their draft boards in the middle of the week, so the game was switched to Montgomery on October 5. Hayward Jackson, also of the *Courier*, believed it was a matter of poor communication. In either case, a highly publicized game that would likely have had a large crowd became a much smaller affair in Montgomery. "I wonder how long the men who are responsible for Negro baseball will continue to boot the public around and do as they please," Smith railed. "The entire promotion of the World Series was a farce."[4]

Management issues, however, have retreated into the shadows of time, and the sunset of the Negro Leagues themselves would soon descend. But for those at Comiskey Park on September 26, they saw five stars who would become Hall of Famers (Bell, Ray Brown, Gibson, Leonard, and Wilson) when the color of their skin was no longer an excuse to disregard their greatness.

SOURCES

Negro Leagues Database. seamheads.com/NegroLgs/index.php.

"Sox Park Is Site of Negro Game Today," **Chicago Tribune**, September 26, 1943: 34.

Staff Correspondent. "Wright Hurls 5-Hitter to Blank Birmingham," **Afro-American**, October 2, 1943: 18.

NOTES

1 "Barons Shut Out in Game at Chi," **Pittsburgh Courier**, October 2, 1943: 16.

2 Wendell Smith, " 'Smitty's Sports Spurts," **Pittsburgh Courier**, October 2, 1943: 16.

3 Cum Posey, "Posey's Points," **Pittsburgh Courier**, October 2, 1943: 16.

4 Wendell Smith, " 'Smitty's Sports Spurts," **Pittsburgh Courier**, October 16, 1943: 16; Hayward Jackson, "New Orleans Fans Score Cancellation of Series Game," **Pittsburgh Courier**, October 16, 1943: 16.

LOPAT SLINGS EXTRA-INNING GEM

SEPTEMBER 9, 1944
CHICAGO WHITE SOX 2, ST. LOUIS BROWNS 1
(14 INNINGS)

By Tom Pardo

Hopes were running high on this warm September night in 1944. In Western Europe, Allied forces crossed the Moselle River in northern France during the largest artillery exchange with the Nazis to date. For the first time, a redhead — 19-year-old Venus Ramey of Washington, D.C. — was crowned Miss America in Atlantic City.[1] Even on the South Side of Chicago, hearts were light as Steady Eddie Lopat gave his beleaguered White Sox a needed boost in outlasting ex-GI Jack Kramer and the pennant-chasing St. Louis Browns, 2-1, in a 14-inning marathon at Comiskey Park.

The 1944 campaign had not been kind to White Sox skipper Jimmy Dykes and his players. Like most teams at this time, Dykes' better players were serving in the military, including shortstop Luke Appling, right fielder Taffy Wright, infielder Dario Lodigiani and pitchers Johnny Rigney and Eddie Smith. Consequently, the quality of play on the diamond suffered. Offensively, the team ranked last in batting average and other hitting categories. Third baseman Ralph Hodgin sported the best average at .295. Defensively, the result was much the same; the White Sox finished sixth in fielding percentage. By the time the White Sox hooked up with the Browns in this series, the club sat in seventh place with no chance of advancing out of the second division.

The brightest light of this dreary White Sox season was rookie left-handed starter Eddie Lopat. Son of a shoe repairman, Lopat toiled in the minors for seven seasons before being called up for a 30-day trial in 1944 by the White Sox. Expectations were not high for this smallish hurler, who did not possess a commanding fastball. However, Lopat's deceptive pitching motion and excellent use of off-speed pitches, particularly his screwball, landed him a permanent spot in the White Sox' starting rotation.[2]

Coming into the Browns series, Lopat had won three consecutive outings and four of his last five starts to even his season record at 9-9. Despite this surge, Lopat's season record against the Browns was wanting. In his first major-league start on April 30, Lopat lost to the Browns, 5-4. On June 13 Lopat was defeated, 5-3, by his opponent on this day, Jack Kramer. A week later, on June 20, he had a no-decision as the White Sox lost once again to the Browns, 4-3.

Contrary to the White Sox misfortunes, St. Louis was pursuing the improbable — its first American League pennant! Long the laughingstock of the junior circuit, the 1944 edition of the Browns benefited from several players rejected for military service, including infielder Vern Stephens, first baseman George McQuinn, and outfielder Al Zarilla. Two key players, catcher Frank Mancuso and pitcher Sig Jakucki, returned from active duty to also contribute to the Browns' success.

St. Louis started the 1944 campaign with a bang, winning nine in a row which broke an

American League record of seven set by the 1933 Yankees. After the All-Star break, the Browns reeled off a 10-game winning streak and by mid-August they held a seven-game lead. Then reality set in as the Browns, hampered by poor defense, meek offense, and the inability to hold leads, surrendered all of that lead to the Yankees and Tigers by early September. A thrilling pennant race was now underway.

Jack Kramer was a major factor in the Browns' turnaround. The workhorse of manager Luke Sewell's starting corps,[3] right-hander Kramer was playing in his first full season after serving in the Navy's Seabees. A clotheshorse with the moniker of Handsome Jack, Kramer was a fastball pitcher who hated to be pulled from games. Coming into the White Sox series, he had a record of 1-2 over his last five appearances, but his most recent outing, on September 3 against the Tigers, resulted in a 7-1 complete-game victory.[4]

As the 9,325 spectators settled into their seats at Comiskey Park (some were St. Louis rooters including a contingent of players' wives[5]), it was apparent that this middle game of a five-game series was a must-win situation for the Browns.[6] The teams had split the first two games, the Browns coming out on top in the opener, 5-4, despite committing four errors and the White Sox returning the favor with a 9-5 thumping of the Browns in the second contest. By game time, St. Louis was a full game behind the Yankees in second place and could not afford to lose further ground.

The Browns were unable to draw blood in the opening round despite a two-out single to center by center fielder Mike Kreevich and an almost round-tripper to deep left-center by shortstop Vern Stephens that was hauled in by Sox center fielder Thurman Tucker.

Kramer was not so fortunate in the home half of the first. With one out, White Sox second baseman Ray Schalk smashed a grounder off Kramer's glove for an infield hit. After third baseman Ralph Hodgin took Kreevich deep in center for the second out, center fielder Hal Trosky connected for a double to the scoreboard in right, scoring Schalk for the game's first run.

After the first inning, the game turned into a classic pitching duel. Kramer allowed only one hit, a single in the fifth by catcher Mike Tresh, until the 10th, when Hodgin opened with a single to right-center. Lopat was equally effective as he scattered three hits through the next six innings.

White Sox fans were tasting victory as Lopat took the mound to begin the eighth. The crafty left-hander was able to get Browns catcher Red Hayworth to ground out to shortstop Skeeter Webb for the first out. Then the seemingly impossible happened and that White Sox win was put on hold. Kramer came to the plate and smacked his second home run of the season to deep left-center. (His first also came at the expense of the White Sox.)[7] The Browns were unable to capitalize on Kramer's dinger, but the damage had been done. Game tied, 1-1.

The ninth inning came and went like a whisper. As the game moved into extra innings, Lopat and Kramer showed no signs of tiring, but both teams were struggling to put together anything that resembled a rally.

In the Browns' 10th and 11th innings, opportunities to take the lead came and went. First baseman George McQuinn opened the 10th with a base hit to left. He moved to second on a sacrifice by Hayworth and went to third when Kramer grounded out to Lopat for the second out. Second baseman Don Gutteridge ended the inning with a line drive to White Sox left fielder Eddie Carnett.

In the top of the 11th, Browns right fielder Milt Byrnes drew the only walk off Lopat in the game. Kreevich sacrificed Byrnes to second. Byrnes had more ambitious designs. Seeing that White Sox third baseman Hodgin was standing away from the base, Byrnes made a wide turn at second. Suddenly he thought better of it but it was too late and he was tagged out by Webb in a desperate attempt to scamper back to second. With that threat extinguished, Lopat proceeded to retire the next 10 St. Louis batters.

Finally the White Sox bats came alive in the

home half of the 14th. With one out, Schalk lined a single to center, his third hit of the game. Hodgin sent his second single of the contest into left, moving Schalk to second. After Trosky grounded to Gutteridge for the second out, Tucker swung at the first pitch from Kramer and hit "a 5-and-10 cent single" between backpedaling Gutteridge and charging Byrnes in right to score Schalk and give the spoiler White Sox a much-needed victory.[8]

The game was a pitching masterpiece as both Lopat and Kramer went the distance. It was perhaps the best pitching performance in Comiskey Park during the 1944 season. Kramer scattered nine hits and yielded only one walk while fanning six. Lopat was equally outstanding. He gave up only seven hits, including Kramer's home run, and one walk. A week later, though, Kramer would get his revenge over Lopat when the Browns shut out the Sox, 9-0, at Sportsman's Park.

For the Browns, this game was one they could not afford to lose. It was the team's 15th loss in 21 games and it moved the Browns into third place for the first time since mid-May, percentage points behind the surging Tigers and still one game behind the Yankees. Eventually, the Browns righted the ship and clinched the American League pennant by a game over the Tigers.

For the White Sox, the win was only their sixth in the last 20 games. The team finished in seventh place, but the emergence of Eddie Lopat gave White Sox fans hope that there would be more victories like the one they were celebrating.

SOURCES

In addition to the sources cited in the Notes, the author consulted the following:

Burns, Edward. "Browns Beaten in 14th by Sox; Drop to 3rd," **Chicago Tribune**, September 10, 1944: Part 2, 1.

Drees, Donald H. "Yanks Lose; Browns Can Tie for Lead by Winning Tonight," **St. Louis Star-Times**, September 9, 1944: 5.

Otto, Wayne K. "Browns Battle Sox Under Arcs Tonight," **Chicago Herald-American**, September 9, 1944: 15.

Ryan, Jack. "Jakucki Out to Shake Off St. Louis Shakes," **Chicago Daily News**, September 9, 1944: 17.

Simons, Herbert. "Desperate Browns Try Kilowatt Shift," **Chicago Times**, September 9, 1944: 25.

------. "Sox Triumph, 2-1, in 14-Inning Battle," **Chicago Times** (Final Edition), September 10, 1944: 40.

Wallar, Glen L. "White Sox Nip Browns, 2-1, in 14th," **St. Louis Globe-Democrat**, September 10, 1944: C1.

Retrosheet.org.

NOTES

1 "Redhead 'Miss America,'" **Chicago Herald-American**, September 10, 1944: 3.

2 Zita Carno, "Eddie Lopat," SABR Baseball Biography Project (sabr.org/bioproj/person/e3a049be), undated, accessed December 5, 2017.

3 Kramer led the Browns pitching staff in games started (31), complete games (18), and innings pitched (257). His record was 17-13 in 1944, second only to Nelson Potter's 19-game winning mark. Baseball-Reference.com (Baseball-Reference.com/teams/SLB/1944.shtml), undated, accessed December 15, 2017.

4 C. Paul Rogers III, "Jack Kramer," SABR Baseball Biography Project (sabr.org/bioproj/person/ee60d53f), undated, accessed December 6, 2017.

5 "Browns Lose in 14 Innings and Fall to Third Place," **St. Louis Post-Dispatch**, September 10, 1944: 16a.

6 Browns manager Luke Sewell offered this sobering assessment of his team on the eve of the White Sox series: "The team is likely to continue to make errors and its batting attack is not the strongest in the league." Donald H. Drees, "Browns in Chicago to Resume Drive for Pennant Tonight," **St. Louis Star-Times**, September 7, 1944, 21.

7 A St. Louis sportswriter claimed, perhaps with a bit of hyperbole, that Kramer's home run was "one of the longest of the Comiskey Park season." "Browns Lose."

8 Wayne K. Otto, "Sox Nip Browns in 14th, 2-1; Yanks Lose as Tigers Win," **Chicago Herald-American**, September 10, 1944: Part Two, 1. Byrnes was playing "prevent" defense deep in right field when Tucker hit this Texas Leaguer. Immediately Byrnes streaked in and almost made a spectacular catch. However, first-base umpire Jim Boyer ruled that Byrnes had trapped the ball. "Browns Lose."

HILTON SMITH GOES THE DISTANCE AS MONARCHS ROLL

SEPTEMBER 25, 1946
KANSAS CITY MONARCHS 5, NEWARK EAGLES 1
GAME FIVE OF NEGRO LEAGUE WORLD SERIES

By Richard Cuicchi

Negro League team owners could see the handwriting on the wall when Jackie Robinson signed a contract with the Brooklyn Dodgers to play in Montreal in 1946. Additional Negro League players, particularly the stars, would be sought out by major-league owners for their own teams, and the Negro Leagues' competitiveness would decline. Despite the bleak outlook for the future, the Negro Leagues were able to compete for a few more years before folding altogether.

Since 1942, one of the league's highlights had been the Negro World Series, a postseason series between the champions of the Negro National League and Negro American League. In 1946 the series matched the Negro National League's Newark Eagles against the Kansas City Monarchs of the Negro American League.

The Series schedule called for the first game to be played at the Polo Grounds in New York and the second at Newark's home field, Ruppert Stadium, followed by two games in Kansas City's Blues Stadium. If necessary, a game in Chicago's Comiskey Park and then a return to Newark would follow in a best-of seven series. It wasn't uncommon then for African-American teams, including barnstorming teams during the offseasons, to pursue opportunities to play in major-league ballparks, where they could draw bigger crowds and showcase Negro Leagues talent.

The World Series reportedly attracted dozens of major-league scouts who came to identify the top African-American talent in anticipation of further steps toward integration.[1] Indeed, several of the stars of these two teams would eventually be among the first group of African-American players signed by Organized Baseball.

The Monarchs were without Jackie Robinson, who had played for them in 1945 before signing with the Dodgers organization for the 1946 season. However, Buck O'Neil, Hank Thompson, and Willard Brown rejoined the team in 1946 after returning from military service. Thirty-nine-year-old Satchel Paige, Connie Johnson, and Jim Lamarque were the star pitchers.

The Eagles' lineup featured a middle-infield combination of second baseman Larry Doby and shortstop Monte Irvin. Leon Day, Max Manning, and Rufus Lewis were the Eagles' best pitchers.

Newark had evened the series in Game Four in Kansas City on September 24 with an 8-1 victory. Irvin had four hits including a three-run home run.[2]

Game Five was played on September 25 at Comiskey Park, which had also been the site of one of two Negro Leagues East-West All-Star games in August.[3] Kansas City newspapers reported a crowd of 4,000 attended the Wednesday

A star with the Newark Eagles in the Negro Leagues and the first African-American player in the American League, with the Cleveland Indians in 1947, Larry Doby belted 24 home runs and knocked in 102 runs in 1956, his first of two seasons with the White Sox. (Photo by Kidwiler Collection/Diamond Images/Getty Images)

night game, in which Kansas City was designated the home team.

Manning drew the starting assignment for the Eagles. He had pitched a complete game in Game Two in Newark (heavyweight boxing champion Joe Louis threw out the first pitch), and held the Monarchs to two hits. Kansas City countered with 39-year-old Hilton Smith as its starter.

The Monarchs' regular right fielder, Ted Strong, was absent from the team; he had left to begin his Puerto Rican Winter League assignment.[4] Ford Smith, who was the starting pitcher in Game 2, took his place in the starting lineup.

Hilton Smith held Newark scoreless through the first four innings.

Thompson walked to lead off the bottom of fourth inning for the Monarchs. Brown fouled out to catcher Leon Ruffin and Thompson stole second base as O'Neil struck out. John Scott hit a hard drive to shortstop Irvin, who was unable to throw him out at first. Ford Smith singled to center field, scoring Thompson. Mickey Taborn lined out to right fielder Bob Harvey to end the inning.

Thompson again got things started for the Monarchs in the bottom of the sixth when he doubled to left field. Brown was retired on a grounder to second baseman Doby, with Thompson advancing to third base. O'Neil then executed a squeeze bunt to first baseman Lennie Pearson, which scored Thompson. Scott tripled down the left-field line. After an intentional walk to Ford Smith, Scott scored on Manning's wild pitch, making the score 3-0.

In the bottom of the seventh inning, the Monarchs scored two more runs. Hilton Smith opened with a single to right field. Chico Renfro drove a pitch that fell a foot within the left-field foul line for a single. Herb Souell fouled out to Irvin. Thompson struck out, but Brown doubled to right, scoring Smith and Renfro. O'Neil fanned to end any further threat.

Newark scored its only run in the top of the eighth when Irvin singled with one out and scored on Pearson's double to center. That ended the scoring; the Monarchs won, 5-1.

Winning pitcher Smith, who went the distance for the Monarchs, gave up 10 hits struck out eight and walked one. Manning took only his second loss of the season, yielding nine hits and three walks, while striking out seven in eight innings.

For the fourth time in five Series games, Newark had more hits than Kansas City but couldn't piece together enough of them to generate more runs. Jimmy Wilkes, Irvin, and Pearson accounted for six of the Eagles' hits, with two apiece. Monarchs shortstop Renfro played flawlessly in the field, handling six hard-hit chances.

The Eagles were facing elimination as the Series moved back to their home field, Newark's Ruppert Stadium, on September 27. But they evened the series again in Game Six with a 9-7 win and went on to capture the championship with a 3-2 victory in Game Seven on September 29.

Several of the players from the two teams went on to play in the majors. Doby became the first African-American player in the American League with the Cleveland Indians in 1947. Thompson and Brown made their major-league debuts that year, with the St. Louis Browns. Paige got to the big leagues in 1948 with Cleveland and Irvin in 1949 with the New York Giants, while Connie Johnson reached the majors in 1953 with the Chicago White Sox. O'Neil, Paige, Doby, Irvin, Hilton Smith, and Day have been elected to the National Baseball Hall of Fame.

Newark manager Biz Mackey and Monarchs owner J.L. Wilkinson were inducted into the Hall of Fame as early pioneers of the Negro Leagues.

Owned by businesswoman Effa Manley and her husband, Abe, Newark won its only Negro World Series title that year. Effa Manley became the first woman elected to the National Baseball Hall of Fame, for her leadership and vision in creating respect for Negro League baseball.

SOURCES

In addition to the sources cited in the Notes, the author consulted the following:

"Monarchs Take Lead," **Kansas City Times**, September 26, 1946.

Irvin, Monte, and James A. Riley. **Nice Guys Finish First** (New York: Carroll & Graf Publishers, 1996).

Luke, Bob. **The Most Famous Woman in Baseball** (Washington: Potomac Books, 2011).

O'Neil, Buck, Steve Wulf, and David Conrads. **I Was Right on Time** (New York: Simon & Schuster, 1996).

Overmyer, James. **Effa Manley and the Newark Eagles** (Metuchen, New Jersey: Scarecrow Press, 1993).

Seamheads Negro Leagues Database. seamheads.com/blog/category/negro-lgs/, accessed May 17, 2018.

Young, Frank. "Monarchs Win 5th Game of World Series Played in Chicago, 5-1," **The Call** (Kansas City), September 27, 1946.

NOTES

1. Baseball Reference Bullpen, Baseball-Reference.com/bullpen/1946_Negro_World_Series, accessed May 17, 2018.

2. Ibid.

3. James Segreti, "West Defeats East All-Star Negro Nine, 4-1," **Chicago Tribune**, August 19, 1946: 27.

4. Baseball Reference Bullpen.

FEW NOTICE AS THE NEGRO LEAGUE WORLD SERIES VISITS CHICAGO

SEPTEMBER 26, 1947
NEW YORK CUBANS 9, CLEVELAND BUCKEYES 2
GAME FIVE OF NEGRO LEAGUE WORLD SERIES

By Ken Carrano and Richard Cuicchi

The baseball world changed in 1947. This statement cannot be disputed. But changes almost always allow the Law of Unintended Consequences to be activated as well. The addition of Jackie Robinson to the Brooklyn Dodgers of the National League, and later Larry Doby to the Cleveland Indians of the American League, would start the demise of Negro baseball. This may not have been known when Robinson took the field on that April Tuesday in Brooklyn, but it would become apparent soon.

There is no good way to spot the beginning of the end. Perhaps it was in the early 1940s, when Bill Veeck supposedly planned to purchase the Philadelphia Phillies and stock it with Negro League stars. Perhaps it was in April of 1945, when the Boston Red Sox gave a tryout to Robinson, then of the Kansas City Monarchs, Marvin Williams of the Philadelphia Stars, and Sam Jethroe of the Cleveland Buckeyes. The politically influenced tryout was a sham, and the Red Sox became the last team to integrate in 1959 with Pumpsie Green. "We knew we were wasting our time," Robinson told the *Boston Globe* in 1972.[1] By the time Branch Rickey signed Robinson in October 1945, the change to the major leagues and the Negro Leagues had become inevitable.

When Robinson broke camp with the Dodgers in 1947 after his successful season in Montreal, the attention of the baseball press — both in the traditional and Negro papers — meant less coverage to the teams in the Negro Leagues. Every move Robinson made was chronicled by the *Pittsburgh Courier*, the *Chicago Defender*, and others. Every column-inch dedicated to Robinson was an inch that the Chicago American Giants, the Kansas City Monarchs didn't get.

The Newark Eagles were the defending World Series champions and started off the 1947 season as they finished 1946. But when Eagles owner Effa Manley sold Doby to the Indians in July, the Eagles season was effectively over, allowing the New York Cubans to win the Negro National League pennant. The Cubans, as their name suggested, were primarily made up of players from the island country and supplemented by a couple of pitchers and a backup catcher from the United States and a second baseman from the Dominican Republic.[2] The team was owned by former racketeer Alex Pompez and managed by Jose Maria Fernandez. The Cubans were led by Luis Tiant Sr., aged 41 at the time and the second oldest player in the league.[3] Tiant, father of longtime major leaguer Luis Tiant, was 10-0 for the Cubans in 1947, belying his advanced age.[4] Tiant Sr.'s screwball was his signature and ranked the seventh best screwball by Bill James and Rob Neyer.[5] From the plate, the Cubans were led by third baseman Saturnino Orestes Armas Miñoso Arrieta, whom most will know as "The Cuban Comet," or simply "Minnie." Miñoso, who would become a mainstay at Comiskey Park, playing there in parts of five decades, hit .354 for the Cubans in 1947[6] and was the starting third baseman for the East in the annual East-West All-Star Game. Second baseman Silvio Garcia and right fielder Claro Duaney joined Miñoso and Tiant on the All-Star Team.

The Cleveland Buckeyes were trying to rebound in 1947 after a subpar season the year before. Champions of the World Series in 1945, the 1946 Buckeyes struggled to a 36-40-3 record. Relying on catcher-manager Quincy Trouppe, first baseman Archie Ware, and the speedy Jethroe, the Buckeyes cruised to a 42-12 record and led the Negro American League from start to finish. An aging Chet Brewer, Webbo Clarke, and Genie Smith led the pitching staff that had been depleted since the 1945 season.

The Buckeyes clinched the NAL title early in September and expected to start the 1947 series at League Park in Cleveland.[7] The Cubans won their title soon after with a 2-1 victory over the Homestead Grays at Shibe Park in Philadelphia and announced that the Series would begin at the Cubans home, the Polo Grounds, on September 19. The Series had always been a traveling road show, and it would move from the Polo Grounds, then to Yankee Stadium before hitting the road for games in Cleveland, Philadelphia (Shibe Park), and Chicago (Comiskey). The sixth game of the Series would be back in Cleveland, and, if necessary, a Game Seven location would be determined.

The weather threatened the entire day of the first Series game but didn't claim victory until six full innings were played. The Buckeyes chased Cubans starter Dave Barnhill after plating five in the first two innings, but the Cubans battled back to tie the game in the fifth before the heavens opened up during the top of the seventh, causing Game One to be a 5-5 tie.

Moving across the Harlem River, Game Two saw the Buckeyes take the lead in the Series with a 10-7 triumph before 9,000 spectators. The Cubans made several errors during the game, and had overcome separate three- and four-run deficits, but couldn't overcome loading the bases with no one out in the ninth, and the Buckeyes finished off the Latins with three in the ninth.

The series moved to Cleveland on September 23 but the Buckeyes could not take advantage of their home field due to the pitching of Barney Morris, who shut them down, 6-0. The Cubans cruised to a 9-4 win in Game Four, thanks in part to Ray Noble's grand slam, sending the Series to Chicago.

The weatherman had promised a partly cloudy and warm day for Game Five, but Chicago is known for unpredictable weather and at first pitch, the temperature was an April-like 48 degrees. Because of this and the lack of a home team[8] only 2,048 came out to see if the Buckeyes could tie up the Series. The Cubans would not let this happen, battering Buckeyes starter Brewer for 11 hits and scoring all nine of their runs in the first six innings. Lino Donoso, loser of Game Two, picked up the win for the Cubans, scattering seven hits. Donoso was aided by the defense of Horatio Martinez, who made leaping catches of two line drives off the bat of John Cowan. The 9-2 victory gave the Cubans a 3-games-to-1 Series lead as they headed back to Cleveland. New York then captured the Series in Game Six, played on September 27 in Cleveland, in their third come-from-behind win. The hometown Buckeyes led 5-0 after five innings, but were error-prone again, including five misplays behind pitcher Genie Smith. The Cubans scored three runs in the sixth, one in the seventh, and two in the eighth. Pat Scantlebury pitched in relief of starter Tiant, silencing the Buckeyes' bats after the fifth inning, to record the winning decision in the Cubans' 6-5 victory.

As the better players continued to follow Robinson and Doby to the major leagues, the Negro Leagues tried to survive. There was only one more Negro League World Series, with the Homestead Grays defeating the Birmingham

Black Barons to win the final Series in 1948. The Negro National League folded shortly thereafter. Several of the combatants in the 1947 Series would go on to feature in the major leagues.

Tiant retired after the 1948 season, but Miñoso, Noble, Scantlebury, and Donoso eventually made it to the majors. Miñoso became a nine-time all-star in 17 major-league seasons. Cubans owner Pompez, who became the head of international scouting in Latin America for the New York Giants in 1950, was elected to the National Baseball Hall of Fame in 2006.

Al Smith, Jethroe, Trouppe, Clarke, and Sam Jones from the Buckeyes team would make it to major-league clubs. Jethroe was named the National League Rookie of the Year in 1950, while Jones won 102 major-league games and Smith was a two-time All-Star outfielder.

Shortly after winning the 1947 Series, the Cubans traveled to Cuba to play the Havana Cubans in a five-game exhibition series that was expected to draw 150,000 attendees. Since most of the members of the New York team played winter ball in Cuba, the Havana fans would be familiar with them. The Havana Cubans, an all-white team, played in the Florida International League with seven other teams from Florida.[9]

NOTES

1. Seth Maxon, "The Curse of Jackie Robinson," Slate.com, May 4, 2017.

2. "1947 Negro World Series," Baseball-Reference Bullpen. baseball-reference/bullpen/1947_Negro_World_Series. Retrieved July 26, 2018.

3. According to the **New York Amsterdam Times**, New York Black Yankees pitcher John Stanley was 42 during the 1947 season.

4. John Holway, **The Complete Book of Baseball's Negro Leagues** (New York: Hastings House, 2001), 448. Subsequent research complied and published by seamheads.com gives Tiant Sr. a record of 9-0.

5. Bill James and Rob Neyer, **The Neyer/James Guide to Pitchers, A Historical Compendium of Pitching, Pitchers and Pitches** (New York: Simon & Schuster, 2004), 52.

6. This figure is from seamheads.com., Holway has his average at .294.

7. **Pittsburgh Courier**, September 13, 1947: 13.

8. Seamheads.com shows the Chicago American Giants with a 20-51 record in 1947, good for last in the six-team circuit.

9. **Chicago Defender**.

SOURCES

In addition to the sources listed in the Notes, the authors accessed Baseball-Reference.com, SABR's BioProject via SABR.org, **The Sporting News** archive via Paper of Record, the Negro League database of seamheads.com, the **Chicago Tribune** and **Pittsburgh Courier** via newspapers.com, and the **Chicago Defender, New York Amsterdam News**, and **Cleveland Call and Post** via ProQuest Historical Newspapers. Ken Carrano would like to extend special thanks to the libraries at DePaul University and Northwestern University for their assistance.

RED SCHOENDIENST'S EXTRA-INNING HOMER GIVES NATIONAL LEAGUE DRAMATIC WIN

JULY 11, 1950
NATIONAL LEAGUE 4, NATIONAL LEAGUE 3
(14 INNINGS)
ALL-STAR GAME

By C. Paul Rogers III

The 1950 All-Star Game returned to Comiskey Park for the first time since the inaugural game in 1933. A capacity crowd of 46,127 witnessed the most suspenseful All-Star Game to date as the National League prevailed, 4-3, on Red Schoendienst's 14th-inning home run off Detroit's Ted Gray to end the American League's four-game winning streak. The game had everything: drama, clutch hitting, spectacular fielding, and overpowering pitching.[1] Although it was the first All-Star Game to go extra innings, even with five additional frames the game still took only 3 hours and 19 minutes.

The days leading up to the game had seen controversy stemming from the fact that the fans had neglected to elect a natural center fielder into the starting lineup when they chose Ralph Kiner, Hank Sauer, and Enos Slaughter. National League manager Burt Shotton wanted to substitute Duke Snider of his own Brooklyn Dodgers for Sauer and initially obtained approval from National League President Ford Frick. But after backlash from the fans, Commissioner Happy Chandler reversed course, forcing Shotton to start the 34-year-old Slaughter in center. The Chicago fans roundly booed Shotton in pregame introductions, since Sauer was a Chicago Cub,

but Shotton grinned good-naturedly and doffed his cap, turning many of the boos to applause.[2]

The pregame ceremonies celebrated the return of the All-Star Game to Comiskey with two events. First, the crowd stood for a moment of silence to honor Babe Ruth, whose home run in the 1933 game was the first in All-Star history. Second, Connie Mack, who was manager of the American League team in 1933 and at 87 was still the manager of the Philadelphia Athletics, threw out the first ball from the box seats, tossing it to starting pitcher Vic Raschi of the Yankees, who trotted it back to Mr. Mack.[3]

Raschi, who was 10-6 and had a run of six scoreless All-Star innings, was up against 23-year-old Robin Roberts, who was 10-3 and was the first All-Star starting pitcher in Philadelphia Phillies history.[4] Once the game began, so did the excitement and the first of many outstanding fielding plays. Ralph Kiner, the second batter of the game, lifted a ball to deep left field that sent Ted Williams crashing into the scoreboard to make a spectacular catch, saving an extra-base hit. Williams spent considerable time rubbing his left elbow after the catch, but stayed in the game until the ninth inning.[5] X-rays later taken in Boston revealed a fracture. He would miss the next 66 games for the fourth-place Red Sox, effectively ending their pennant hopes.[6]

The National League did break through first, scoring two runs in the top of the second in a matter of seconds. Jackie Robinson led off with a single to right field, quickly followed by Enos Slaughter's triple to left-center for one run. Hank Sauer's long fly ball to Hoot Evers in right soon plated Slaughter with the second run. The National League dodged a bullet in the bottom half of the inning when Slaughter made a fine outstretched running catch of rookie Walt Dropo's smash in front of the bullpen, 415 feet away from home plate, to keep the score at 2-0.[7] The catch confirmed Shotton's late decision to play Slaughter in center rather than the plodding Sauer, who could not have reached Dropo's drive.[8]

The American League did manage a run off Roberts in the third on a leadoff ground-rule double to left-center by Cass Michaels, sent to pinch-hit for Raschi by American League manager Casey Stengel. Phil Rizzuto, playing in his first All-Star Game in his seventh big-league season, laid a perfect bunt single down the third-base line, moving Michaels to third. After Larry Doby struck out, George Kell's fly to deep center plated Michaels to close the score to 2-1.[9]

Bob Lemon of the Indians and Don Newcombe of the Dodgers took over on the mound for their respective leagues in the fourth inning. Lemon retired the Nationals in order but Dropo greeted Newcombe with a triple that caromed off the bullpen wall in deepest center field at a crazy angle. Newcombe managed to squirm out of the jam after Evers grounded out to shortstop Marty Marion as Dropo held at third. Yogi Berra followed with a comebacker that hung Dropo out to dry off third for the second out. Bobby Doerr then forced Berra at second to end the inning.

Newcombe's luck ran out in the fifth, however, as the American League took the lead for the first time. Lemon, a converted third baseman who was always a good hitter, led off with a walk.[10] After Rizzuto struck out, Doby hit a sharp grounder up the middle that second baseman Jackie Robinson got a glove on but could not hold. The ball trickled into center field as Lemon advanced to third and Doby sped into second with an unconventional double. Kell followed with another deep fly to Andy Pafko in center to score Lemon with the tying run and send Doby to third.[11] Ted Williams was next and, batting with what turned out to be a broken elbow, smashed a clutch two-out single to right to put the Americans up 3-2.

Meanwhile Lemon had retired six straight National Leaguers. In the top of the sixth he surrendered a leadoff single to right to pinch-hitter Dick Sisler, who was immediately erased on Willie "Puddinhead" Jones's double-play grounder. Lemon then struck out Kiner to complete three near-perfect innings.

Jim Konstanty, premier relief pitcher for the Phillies,[12] threw a perfect sixth while the National League threatened to tie the score in the top of the seventh against Art Houtteman on a two-out walk to Slaughter and Pafko's infield single. Roy Campanella smacked a deep fly but Comiskey's cavernous center field held it as Doby made the putout to avert any damage.

Houtteman retired the National League in order in the eighth inning to bring about the ninth. Meanwhile, Larry Jansen had taken over for the National League in the seventh and proceeded to deliver perhaps the best pitching performance in All-Star Game history.[13] He began by retiring the first six batters he faced, four by strikeout.

The ninth inning saw the American League clinging to its one-run lead with Houtteman still on the mound. But on the second pitch of the inning, Ralph Kiner slammed a ball into the left-field seats to tie the score, 3-3, as the crowd sat stunned.[14] Jansen kept the game even in the home half with another overpowering inning, retiring Joe DiMaggio, who had replaced Evers in right, on a fly ball to center and punching out Jim Hegan and Jerry Coleman for his fifth and sixth strikeouts in three innings.[15]

Allie Reynolds took over for the American

League as the game went to the 10th inning and retired the National League in order. Because of the extra innings, the normal rule limiting pitchers to three innings was no longer in effect, and so Shotton could leave the dominant Jansen on the mound. Larry continued to throw goose eggs, allowing only a harmless two-out single to Doby in the bottom half.

The National League mounted a serious threat against Reynolds in the 11th that began with Kiner's one-out double to the gap in right. The Chief intentionally walked Stan Musial and retired pinch-hitter Johnny Wyrostek on a fly to Doby in center.[16] Slaughter hit a routine groundball to Jerry Coleman, in for defense at second, but Coleman booted it to load the bases with two outs. Pafko smacked a deep drive to left that promised to end the game, but Dom DiMaggio, also inserted for defense, made a fine catch with his back against the wall to end the inning. Jansen then sailed through the bottom of the inning, retiring the Americans in order.

Reynolds returned to form and retired the National League in order in the top of the 12th. To the relief of the American League, Duke Snider pinch-hit for Jansen in the inning. In five razor-sharp innings, Jansen had given up one single and no walks while striking out six. But the junior circuit jumped from the proverbial frying pan to the fire, as side-wheeling Ewell "The Whip" Blackwell replaced Jansen. He began by striking out Hegan and Coleman before Tommy Henrich, batting for Reynolds, lined out to Pafko in center.

Ted Gray, the only lefty among the 11 pitchers used, replaced Reynolds on the mound for the American League in the top of the 13th, and after allowing a leadoff single to Jones, retired Kiner, Musial, and Wyrostek on fly balls to the outfield.[17] Blackwell made quick work of the Americans in the bottom of the inning on a fly ball and two groundouts, setting the stage for the climactic 14th inning.

Red Schoendienst, who had entered the game at second base when Wyrostek batted for Robinson, led off. The 27-year-old was in the midst of his sixth major-league season and enjoying his fourth All-Star berth.[18] The switch-hitter batted righty against the southpaw Gray and was not known for his power, particularly from that side of the dish. But on a 2-and-2 pitch he walloped a no-doubter into Comiskey's second deck in left field to give the Nationals the lead, 4-3.

Pafko singled to left, suggesting that the senior circuit might not be through. Gray then struck out Campanella but Pafko advanced to second on a passed ball. Casey Stengel then waved in Bob Feller to pitch to the trio of right-handed batters to follow. Feller struck out Blackwell before walking Pee Wee Reese to put runners on first and second. But Willie Jones flied to center for out number three.

Blackwell still had to get the Americans out in the bottom half and proved up to the task, allowing only a one-out single to left to Ferris Fain. The Whip quickly induced Joe DiMaggio to hit into an around-the-horn double play to end a most memorable 14-inning thriller.

Blackwell was the winning pitcher and finished his work for the day by allowing one hit in three shutout innings. Together Konstanty, Jansen, and Blackwell had allowed two hits and no runs over the last nine innings of the game, while striking out 10 and walking no one.

There were reports that Schoendienst called his home run on his way up to bat.[19] In his memoirs, however, Schoendienst related that while shagging flies in pregame practice with Dick Sisler, Duke Snider, Walker Cooper, and others, they were all kidding about what they would do if they got into the game. Schoendienst said he just blurted out that he was going to hit one into the upper deck in right field, to the guffaws of the others since he was not a home-run hitter. When he went up to bat in the 14th, those same teammates reminded Red of his pregame boast. Walker Cooper asked, "You going to hit it up in the right-field stands?"

"No," Schoendienst answered. "Left field now," since he was batting right-handed, and of course that is exactly what he did, to the shock of everyone.[20]

THE BASE BALL PALACE OF THE WORLD

SOURCES

In addition to the sources cited in the Notes, the author also accessed Retrosheet.org, Baseball-Reference.com, and SABR.org.

NOTES

1 Edward Burns, "N.L. Finds Ball Lively — If Hit," **Chicago Tribune**, July 12, 1950: 44.

2 William J. Conway, "Schoendienst Hit Last Act in Big Drama," **Philadelphia Inquirer**, July 12, 1950: 37.

3 Conway, 37.

4 Raschi was the 10th starting pitcher from the Yankees in the 17 games. He was the winning pitcher in the 1948 game and racked up a save in the 1949 contest. Roberts would go on to start a total of five All-Star Games.

5 John Drebinger, "National League Beats American on Schoendienst's Homer in 14th," **New York Times**, July 12, 1950: 34.

6 David Vincent, Lyle Spatz, and David W. Smith, **The Midsummer Classic — The Complete History of Baseball's All-Star Game** (Lincoln: University of Nebraska Press, 2001), 106. The Red Sox finished four games behind the pennant-winning Yankees in 1950, playing without Williams until September 15. Donald Honig, **The All-Star Game — A Pictorial History, 1933 to Present** (St. Louis: The Sporting News Publishing Co., 1987), 81.

7 Drebinger, 34. Arthur Daley of the **New York Times** called it "one of the most spectacular catches in All-Star history, one worthy of a DiMaggio (either of them), or a Tris Speaker." Arthur Daley, "A Bit of Star-Gazing," **New York Times**, July 12, 1950: 35.

8 As evidence of Sauer's limited speed, he stole one base in 1950 and had 11 total steals in 15 major-league seasons. In any event, Slaughter had approached Shotton on the morning of the game, asking for the center-field assignment. Conway: 37.

9 Kell, who was hitting .365 to lead the American League at the break, was the top vote-getter in both leagues. Vincent et. al, 107.

10 Lemon frequently pinch-hit during the season for his Cleveland Indians and had a .232 lifetime batting average with 37 home runs. He hit .272 in 1950 with six home runs.

11 Pafko was now in center field, replacing Sauer in the lineup as Slaughter moved to right.

12 Konstanty would be named National League MVP based on his record-setting 74 relief appearances for the pennant-winning Phillies, along with 16 wins and 22 saves (although not yet an official statistic) and 152 innings in relief. The Phillies' four All-Stars (Konstanty, Roberts, Sisler, and Jones) were a club record. Hard to imagine today, but the rest of the Phillies, who were in first place by one game, spent the All-Star break playing exhibition games against Triple-A opponents. The Whiz Kids, as they were called, beat the Rochester Red Wings 8-7 in Rochester on July 9 and lost 5-3 to the Toronto Maple Leafs, their Triple-A affiliate, on July 10 in Toronto. Stan Baumgartner, "Phils Edge Leafs (sic) in 6 Innings, 8-7," **Philadelphia Inquirer**, July 11, 1950; Stan Baumgartner, "Leafs Defeat Phillies, 5-3," **Philadelphia Inquirer**, July 12, 1950: 37.

13 Of course, most would argue that Carl Hubbell's performance in the 1934 All-Star Game, when he consecutively struck out Babe Ruth, Lou Gehrig, Jimmie Foxx, Al Simmons, and Joe Cronin, future Hall of Famers all, tops Jansen.

14 Irving Vaughn, "National Wins on Home Run in 14th, 4-3," **Chicago Tribune**, July 12, 1950: 1.

15 It was DiMaggio's 12th All-Star Game. He was nursing a pulled muscle and had been expected to only pinch-hit. "AL All-Stars 9-5 Favorites Over NL; Roberts vs. Raschi," **Philadelphia Inquirer**, July 11, 1950.

16 Musial was playing first base after five starts and six All Star appearances in the outfield. Wyrostek, in a somewhat puzzling move by Shotton, was hitting for Jackie Robinson, who was batting .365 at the break. Of course, the move got Schoendienst in the game as Robinson's replacement at second base.

17 Jones set an All-Star Game record that still stood as of 2019 with seven at-bats in the extra-inning game. It was one of two All-Star Game appearances in his 15-year big-league career.

18 Schoendienst would play a total of 19 years in the majors and be selected as an All-Star 10 times.

19 Jim Dailey, "Pitch He Hit? Red Can't Say," **Philadelphia Inquirer**, July 12, 1950: 37.

20 Red Schoendienst with Rob Rains, **Red — A Baseball Life** (Champaign, Illinois: Sports Publishing, 1998), 64-65.

GUS ZERNIAL'S THREE HOMERS PROVIDE PREVIEW OF REST OF DECADE

OCTOBER 1, 1950
ST. LOUIS BROWNS 10, CHICAGO WHITE SOX 6

By Richard Cuicchi

The October 1, 1950, doubleheader between the Chicago White Sox and St. Louis Browns didn't have much to offer fans in its pregame billing. Both teams were ending dismal seasons in the second division of the American League. These final games of the season didn't have any consequence for the 1950 campaign in terms of the league standings, postseason play, or league honors. The relatively low attendance of 4,548 was perhaps the best evidence that the game offered little fan appeal.

But what actually emerged in the final contest of the season was a personal-best performance by Gus Zernial, who slammed three home runs in the second game of the doubleheader, after hitting a home run in the first game. The day's accomplishment would be a preview of seasons to come for Zernial, who wound up among the American League home run leaders of the 1950s.

Entering the three-game series that began on Saturday, September 30, the White Sox held a one-game lead over the Browns for sixth place in the American League. The White Sox took the Saturday game, 8-2, as the 6-foot-2, right-handed-batting Zernial contributed a home run and a single to the cause. Chicago took the first game of Sunday's doubleheader, 4-3, a walk-off victory, settling the issue of which team would finish in sixth place. Zernial again chipped in by slamming a two-run homer, his 26th of the season.

In the second game of the day, White Sox manager Red Corriden put 19-year-old rookie Gus Keriazakos on the hill for his major-league debut. The right-hander earned a call-up after finishing with an 11-8 record with Memphis.

Browns skipper Zack Taylor countered with eight-year veteran Stubby Overmire as his starting pitcher. The left-hander was 8-12 in his first season with the Browns, after having spent the previous seven years with Detroit. Five of Overmire's wins had come in his last eight starts.

Keriazakos gave up a single to Browns center fielder Ray Coleman in the top of the first inning without yielding a run, but then ran into a buzz saw in the second, as the Browns batted around, combining four singles and four walks to put across four runs. Singles by Bill Sommers and Overmire and a walk to Dick Kokos drove in the Browns' runs.

Zernial led off the bottom of the second inning with a home run. Keriazakos tried to help his own cause with a hit but was thrown out at second trying for a double, leaving the score 4-1.

In the top of the third inning, the Browns picked up where they left off on leadoff singles by Hank Arft and Tom Upton. Arft scored on a fielder's choice by Sommers and an out by Overmire. After Keriazakos issued his fifth walk of the game, Corriden replaced him with Marv Rotblatt, who was making only his ninth major-league appearance.

Overmire had his own problems in the bottom of the third inning. Gordon Goldsberry singled to score Nellie Fox, who had led off the inning with a single. Zernial then homered again, scoring Goldsberry, to close the gap to 5-4.

Kokos hit a solo homer for the Browns in the top of the fourth, making the score 6-4.

After scoreless fifth and sixth innings by both teams, the Browns widened their lead with two tallies in the top of the seventh. Singles by Don Lenhardt and Owen Friend preceded a run-scoring double by Sommers, and Friend scored an unearned run on Goldsberry's error to make the score 8-4.

In the bottom of the eighth, Zernial attempted to keep the White Sox in the game with his third home run of the day, this time off Jack Bruner, who had replaced Overmire in the sixth inning. Johnny Ostrowski, who had led off with a double, also scored on Zernial's blast.

However, the Browns scored two more runs in the ninth inning on a two-run home run by Friend, resulting in a final score of 10-6.

Overmire got the win, yielding four runs on nine hits in five innings pitched. Keriazakos took the loss, allowing seven hits and five walks in 2⅓ innings. He would pitch in only 27 more games during his major-league career. Even though the two teams combined for 30 hits, seven walks (all by White Sox pitchers), and 16 runs, the game lasted only 2 hours and 3 minutes.[1]

Two noteworthy players for the White Sox that day were shortstop Luke Appling, appearing in his last major-league game at age 43, and second baseman Nellie Fox, who was playing in his second full major-league season at age 22. Both players eventually were inducted into the Baseball Hall of Fame.

Zernial, then 27 years old, finished 1950 with 29 home runs, good for fifth place among American League batters. He set a White Sox record for most home runs in a season, surpassing the 27 hit by Zeke Bonura in 1934 and tied by Joe Kuhel in 1940.[2] Zernial led the American League with 110 strikeouts, but he also drove in 93 runs.

Years later in an interview, Zernial recalled his record-setting 1950 season. "I hit 29 home runs that year, but I was not really aware that anything special was going on until the season was over," he said. "Then I read that Zeke Bonura and Joe Kuhel had hit 27. I felt pretty good about it. I was bright-eyed, bushy tailed and a pretty naïve young kid. And here I set a record. It was not an easy park to hit homers in either."[3]

With four home runs for the day, Zernial became only the fourth player to accomplish the feat in a doubleheader. Stan Musial broke that mark with five homers in a twin bill on May 2, 1954.[4]

Zernial probably wished he could have played against the Browns every day of the season, since 11 of his 29 home runs in 1950 came at their expense.

His five-home run performance during the last three games of the season was a prelude to his overall performance in the decade of the 1950s. He led the American League in home runs (33) and RBIs (129) in 1951, when he was traded by the White Sox to the Philadelphia A's after only four games played as part of a monster 13-player transaction among the White Sox, A's, and Cleveland Indians.

He was one of only five American League players to hit 200 or more home runs (232) in the 1950s. The others were Mickey Mantle (280), Yogi Berra (256), Ted Williams (227), and Larry Doby (215).

Zernial is not as recognizable as other power hitters of his era. Part of that comes from the fact that he primarily played for second-division teams, and he was selected as an All-Star in only one season (1953). However, his historic game on October 2, 1950, is among the most memorable in Comiskey Park lore.

SOURCES

Baseball-Reference.com.

"Browns End It in Split; Zernial Hits 4 Homers," **St. Louis Post-Dispatch**, October 2, 1950: 6B.

Retrosheet.org box score: CHA195010012.

Westcott, Rich. "'Ozark Ike' Menaced Pitchers in the 1950s," **Baseball Hobby News**, October 1988: 51-52.

Baseball-Reference.com/boxes/CHA/CHA195010012.shtml.

Retrosheet.org/boxesetc/1950/B10012CHA1950.htm. (play-by-play deduced from newspaper accounts. Fielding credits are from Retrosheet event files).

NOTES

1. At the time of this writing in 2018, the length of games was being addressed as a concern by Major League Baseball for maintaining fan interest. With today's average in excess of three hours per game, it seems remarkable this White Sox-Browns game could be played in such a short amount of time.

2. "Zernial Hits 4 for New Sox Mark," **Chicago Tribune**, October 2, 1950: F4.

3. Herb Fagen, "The Forgotten Power Boy of the 1950s," **Oldtyme Baseball News**, Volume 5, Issue 6.

4. Mark Aaron, "Gus Zernial," SABR BioProject, http://sabr.org/bioproj/person/9e80ddce

MIÑOSO HOMERS IN FIRST SOX PLATE APPEARANCE, BUT MANTLE'S FIRST CAREER BLAST BOOSTS BOMBERS

MAY 1, 1951
NEW YORK YANKEES 8, CHICAGO WHITE SOX 3

By Mark S. Sternman

The long love affair between Minnie Miñoso, the first black player in White Sox history, and South Siders began with a bang in his first game with his new club. Traded as part of a three-team deal on April 30 that also involved the Athletics and the Indians,[1] Miñoso, called by Chicago manager Paul Richards "the kind of player you need to win pennants,"[2] homered in his first Chicago plate appearance to give the White Sox an early 2-0 lead, but the Yankees rallied for an 8-3 win in a game that also featured the first New York homer for another notable outfielder with double-M initials, Mickey Mantle.

The game served as a harbinger of a changing of the guard for the New York outfield. As Mantle starred, Joe DiMaggio, in his final season, missed the contest. He had "been troubled by a lame throwing shoulder, [and] turned up with an overnight development — a stiff neck. Instead of being started, he was carted to Mercy hospital for X-ray pictures and ... [was] diagnosed [with] a muscle spasm that might yield quickly to heat and massage."[3]

Pitcher Bob Cain (0-1) started for the White Sox. Two weeks later he would go to Detroit in a trade, and in August he would gain lasting fame while pitching for the Tigers and walking the diminutive leadoff pinch-hitter Eddie Gaedel. Cain got off to a better start in this game by retiring the first two batters. A two-out double by Gil McDougald proved harmless and positioned Chicago to strike first.

Facing Vic Raschi, the two newest Chicago acquisitions got their White Sox careers off to promising beginnings. Fresh from Philadelphia, Paul Lehner singled with one out to bring Miñoso to the plate for the first time in his White Sox career. Miñoso got off to a dream start with a home run measured at 425 feet.[4] Chicago led 2-0 after one.

At the beginning of another strong season that would lead to a third straight World Series championship, the Yankees replied quickly with a rally ignited by Cain's wildness. He plunked Yogi Berra to open the second and gave up an infield single to Phil Rizzuto to put two runners on with two outs. Cain only had to retire Raschi to escape the jam, but walked the pitcher to load the bases for Mantle, who hit leadoff in his rookie campaign. Mantle hit to Miñoso, whom the *Chicago Tribune* had described in an article that appeared on the day of the game as "a speedster who can operate in the outfield as well as in the inner defense,"[5] which suggested that the White Sox prized his versatility over his glove.[6] The recent acquisition "bobbled Mantle's grounder,"[7] and the error plated two runs to tie the game.

The score remained 2-2 until the fourth although Cain lost again control in the third. For

Among the most exciting yet most underrated players of his generation, nine-time All-Star Minnie Miñoso was a legitimate five-tool player, whose daring baserunning, timely hitting, and rifle arm in left field struck fear in opponents. (Photo by Mark Rucker/Transcendental Graphics, Getty Images)

the second straight inning, he hit the first batter he faced, plunking McDougald this time. Cain wild-pitched McDougald to second but stranded him by retiring Gene Woodling, Berra, and Jackie Jensen without the ball leaving the infield.

Raschi retired the White Sox in order in the second and third innings. Belying their "Bronx Bomber" reputation, the Yankees played small ball in the fourth to take the lead. Joe Collins reached on a bunt single and went to second on Rizzuto's single. Raschi moved both runners up with a sacrifice, and Mantle hit a fly ball to center to give New York a 3-2 lead. Jerry Coleman singled in Rizzuto and stole second, but Cain avoided any additional damage. Chicago now trailed 4-2.

Raschi set down nine straight White Sox until Rizzuto's error with two outs in the fourth put Jim Busby on first, but Nellie Fox hit into a fielder's choice to keep the Chicago deficit at two runs.

Both teams scored in the fifth. With one out, Berra hit the first homer of his 1951 MVP campaign to put the Yanks up 5-2.

Possibly belatedly feeling the pain after having been hit previously by Cain, Berra exited the game after his blast, and Charlie Silvera replaced him. Gus Niarhos singled. Batting for Cain, Bud Stewart singled to send Niarhos to second. Chico Carrasquel completed the trio of singles to load the bases with none out and the 2-3-4 hitters due. With Raschi reeling, Lehner gave him a lifeline by bunting. The squeeze play scored a run to get the White Sox within 5-3, but Chicago would draw no closer. Miñoso reached on a fielder's choice to Raschi, and Eddie Robinson's fly to Jensen ended the frustrating frame for Sox partisans.

Randy Gumpert came on to pitch for Chicago in the top of the sixth. Continuing his productive day at the plate, Raschi doubled. Then "Gumpert tried to fool Mantle with a changeup. Years later, he described what happened. 'Mickey smacked the ball in dead center field right into the bullpen ... it must have traveled 450 feet in the air!'"[8]

In recounting the long-ago event, Gumpert, who lived 90 years, apparently told different stories at different times. In another version, he recollected, "I threw Mantle a screwball. Evidently it didn't screw very well and he hit it into the bullpen in center field."[9]

Dan Daniel in *The Sporting* News had recently chided, "Mickey will have to learn that trying to knock the ball out of the park every time he comes up is a rough program."[10] Mantle's first homer gave New York a commanding 7-3 lead in the sixth.

In the seventh, Cliff Mapes came in for Mantle for defense, but the veteran Raschi needed little additional assistance from his teammates. Still, the Yankees added on in the eighth against Marv Rotblatt. Collins walked, Rizzuto moved him to second with a sacrifice, and pinch-hitter Johnny Mize plated Collins with a single to give New York an 8-3 lead.

Tom Ferrick replaced Raschi in the eighth. Ferrick yielded a single to Miñoso in the eighth and two other Chicago hits in the ninth, but none of the runners scored. Miñoso had a good day at bat with his two hits. Cleveland general manager Hank Greenberg rued the need to trade Miñoso for pitching. "He has the chance to become one of the real good players of our time," said Greenberg. "He already looks like a great hitter, and his defensive weaknesses can be corrected. We wanted to keep him."[11]

The White Sox had pursued Miñoso since 1950. "We tried to get Miñoso in December during the winter meetings at St. Pete," Chicago general manager Frank Lane said. "We failed because he was too valuable a prospect, but we've been thinking about it ever since."[12]

Miñoso may have hit well but, as so often happened in the 1950s, the big bats of the Bronx Bombers overpowered the popgun attack of the South Siders as the Yankees spoiled Minnie's dynamic debut with a comfortable road win.

SOURCES

In addition to the sources cited in the Notes, the author also accessed Retrosheet.org, Baseball-Reference.com, and SABR.org.

NOTES

1. The trade talks started between Chicago and Cleveland before expanding to include Philadelphia. "Richards and [general manager] Hank Greenberg of the Indians talked trade during the White Sox visit [to Cleveland.] But no one expected the negotiations to get far, because Hank was asking for Billy Pierce." Edgar Munzel, "What's Keeping Chisox Up? Why, a .317 Batting Average," **The Sporting News**, May 2, 1951: 16.

2. Art Morrow, "A's Get What They Needed — Lots of Help," **The Sporting News**, May 9, 1951: 7.

3. Irving Vaughan, "Cubs Lose, 11 Banished; Sox Beaten, 8-3," **Chicago Tribune**, May 2, 1951.

4. Warren Brown, **The Chicago White Sox** (Kent, Ohio: Kent State University Press, 2007), 228.

5. Irving Vaughan, "Sox Get Miñoso, Lehner; Play Yanks Today," **Chicago Tribune**, May 1, 1951.

6. The next day, Miñoso made another error that led to two more unearned runs in a 6-4 loss to New York. "Richards ... was quick to blame Miñoso's shaky fielding on the fact that he has been moved around ... so much in recent years. He played third, short and the outfield for San Diego last season and this year wound up at first base in his final few games for the Indians when Luke Easter was injured." Edgar Munzel, "Paul Tailors White Sox to Their Park," **The Sporting News**, May 9, 1951:

7. **The Sporting News**, May 9, 1951: 18.

8. Harold Friend, "Mickey Mantle's First Home Run Was His Most Memorable," **Bleacher Report**, bleacherreport.com/articles/743050-mickey-mantles-first-home-run-was-his-most-memorable (accessed March 9, 2018).

9. Victor Debs Jr., "Randy Gumpert," **The National Pastime** (Cleveland: Society for American Baseball Research, 1999): 94.

10. Dan Daniel, "Spec Gives Casey Rosier Outlook on Yankees' Pitching," **The Sporting News**, May 2, 1951: 6.

11. Ed McAuley, "Hank Finally Gets His Man — Lefty Hurler," **The Sporting News**, May 9, 1951: 7.

12. Milt Woodard, "Frank Lane Engineer of 3-Club, 7-Player Deal," **The Sporting News**, May 9, 1951: 7.

ROGOVIN GOES SEVENTEEN IN LOSING EFFORT

JULY 12, 1951
BOSTON RED SOX 5, CHICAGO WHITE SOX 4
(17 INNINGS, SECOND GAME OF DOUBLEHEADER)

By Greg Erion

Coming out of the 1951 All-Star break the White Sox were in first, percentage points ahead of the Boston Red Sox. This was heady stuff for a team that had not held the lead this late in the season since 1920 when the soon-to-be-labeled Black Sox were in a three-way race for the pennant. That year their effort was derailed at the end of the season when eight players were suspended for fixing the 1919 World Series.

Years in the second division followed, a couple of third-place finishes in the 1930s and 1941; never serious contenders and by the late 1940s they were back in the second division, finishing last in 1950. But in 1951 fortunes dramatically improved thanks to general manager Frank Lane and manager Paul Richards.

Lane joined the club after 1948 and proceeded to turn the franchise around through a series of shrewd trades — a signature activity of his that down through the years would garner him the nicknames Frantic Frank and Trader Lane. He obtained quality players Nellie Fox and Billy Pierce for next to nothing and engineered a complex trade in early 1951 to bring outfielder Minnie Miñoso to the White Sox. By the All-Star break, these and other transactions brought them to a precarious hold on first place.

Sitting in the stands to watch the doubleheader was the venerable Connie Mack, 88-year-old owner and former manager of the Philadelphia A's. Little did he know that he was in for 26 innings of play and 6 hours and 45 minutes of baseball. Showing his resolve, the baseball legend watched both games, not leaving Comiskey until 1:17 A.M. the following morning.[1]

After the All-Star break, Chicago resumed the season hosting Boston in a doubleheader. In front of 52,595 fans, the White Sox lost the first game to the Red Sox, 3-2, thanks to Mel Parnell's pitching and Clyde Vollmer's two-run homer in the seventh. A two-run rally by the White Sox in the ninth fell just short. Game two began with Boston rookie Leo Kiely starting, just his second major-league game. Ten days earlier, Kiely had debuted, throwing a complete-game 5-2 win over the Washington Senators. This appearance would further test his mettle.

Countering Kiely, Richards called on Saul Rogovin. Rogovin was another of Lane's acquisitions, having been traded by Detroit to Chicago just six weeks earlier. Rogovin was in his third year in the majors. His career record with the Tigers had been an unimpressive 3-3 with a 5.56 ERA. Richards had managed and caught Rogovin in the minors several years earlier and saw his potential. When he became available, doubtless at Richard's urging, Lane brought him to Chicago. The trade rejuvenated his career. His record with Chicago going into the game on July 12 was a deceiving 4-3, but all three losses were by one run. More to the point, his ERA with Chicago was an impressive 2.37. Overall, including his appearances with Detroit, it was 2.92, then second in the league only to Bob Feller.

Rogovin got through the first without Boston scoring. Not so with Kiely. Fox and Eddie Robinson were hit by pitches. Don Lenhardt drove Fox in, Robinson going to third. Then, before a stunned crowd, Lenhardt and Robinson performed a double steal, aided in part by catcher Les Moss's wild throw to second. Robinson's steal was unique — he pilfered just 10 bases in his 13-year major-league career — this was the only instance he stole home.[2] Kiely got out of the inning without further damage.

Boston came back to score in the second on two singles and Vollmer's run-scoring double play. When Chicago came to bat in the bottom of the inning it was without Ted Williams on the field for Boston. Williams had to leave with a strained muscle behind his left knee. It was a precautionary move; he returned to the starting lineup two days later. Charlie Maxwell replaced him in the lineup.[3] It would be a long night for the 24-year-old future slugger, as he went 0-for-6 dropping his batting average to a minuscule .118.

No further scoring took place until the seventh, when Red Sox' playing manager Lou Boudreau singled and Bobby Doerr's 12th home run of the season put Boston up 3-2, a lead that proved short-lived. In the bottom of the inning, Chicago catcher Gus Niarhos led off with a walk, Chico Carrasquel sacrificed him to second, and Rogovin, aiding his own cause, singled Niarhos to third. It was the second of three hits in the game for Rogovin. Bob Dillinger grounded out, sending Niarhos home, and Fox plated Rogovin with the tying run. Kiely was removed and succeeded by Ray Scarborough, who induced Robinson to pop out, ending the threat.

Boston came back immediately when Fred Hatfield singled and an error by Rogovin moved him to second. Dom DiMaggio drove Hatfield home to tie the game, 4-4, going into the eighth.

Ellis Kinder replaced Scarborough on the mound and with that a scoreless duel between Kinder and Rogovin commenced over the next eight innings.

In Kinder, Rogovin found a formidable opponent. The 36-year-old Kinder, just two years removed from being a starting pitcher who won 23 games, was now the league's premier reliever. In 1951 he led the league in games, games finished, and saves — the latter a then unrecorded statistic. He would end the year with an 11-2 record to go with a sparkling 2.55 ERA. Over the next eight innings, Rogovin gave up just three hits; Kinder five.

The closest either team came to scoring came in the 12th when the White Sox combined two singles and a walk to load the bases with just one out. But Floyd Baker's strikeout and Jim Busby's inning-ending grounder squelched the threat.

Boudreau opened the top of the 17th with his second hit of the game and went to third on Billy Goodman's single. Vollmer flied out to Miñoso in left for a run-scoring sacrifice. Kinder set the White Sox down quietly in the bottom of the inning, giving Boston a sweep of the doubleheader. The time of the game was 4:01.

Rogovin had gone 17 innings, allowing 10 hits and six walks along the way, giving him a 5-5 record. Kinder's 10 innings of five-hit, five-walk shutout ball earned him his fifth victory on the year with no losses. More important, their sweep put them into first place, one game over the White Sox and 1½ games over the Yankees. As dramatic as this game was, there was more to come when both teams trudged back to Comiskey for the next game, to be played later that day (July 13).

The game pitted Chicago's ace, Billy Pierce, against Boston's somewhat erratic Mickey McDermott. Before 25,211 fans, the teams locked into a 19-inning marathon. Boston scored one in the first and one in the fifth a home run by the hero of the previous game, Clyde Vollmer. Chicago countered with two in the bottom of the inning. In this appearance, McDermott proved outstanding, going 17 innings, giving up just eight hits before giving way to Harry Taylor in the 18th. Pierce threw seven-plus effective innings before Luis Aloma entered the game in the eighth, squelched a bases-loaded threat, and thereafter allowed just one hit over the next five plus innings.

Chicago's run at first place was basically done for the season. Tied with Boston for a day or so over the next few games, they slowly faded out of the picture as the Yankees, Indians, and Red Sox surged past them. Overall, though, Chicago's season was a success. The White Sox finished fourth but were in first for seven weeks in the middle of the season. Chicago set a franchise record for attendance (1,328,234), the first time over a million since the inception of their team in 1901, and the first of seven consecutive seasons over a million.

Chicago was a perennial contender in the 1950s, capping off the decade by winning the pennant in 1959 aided by the efforts of players like Fox and Pierce, who first gave them respectability during the 1951 season.

As for Rogovin, his 17-inning performance mirrored the solid season he gave Chicago. He won the ERA championship with a 2.78 mark and showed a 12-8 record. Seven of his defeats were by one run. He was the first pitcher in the American League to win the ERA title while with two teams, having started with Detroit.[4] Rogovin fashioned a 14-9 record in 1952, then was plagued by intermittent arm trouble thereafter. His career ended in 1957 after a few brief appearances for the Phillies.

SOURCES

In addition to the sources cited in the Notes, the author also accessed Retrosheet.org, Baseball-Reference.com, and SABR.org.

NOTES

1 Bob Ajemian, "White Sox and Red Sox Go Down on the Dawn Patrol," **The Sporting News**, July 25, 1951: 21.

2 Gene Mack Jr., "Red Sox Win in Seventeen Innings, Hold First Place," **Boston Globe**, July 13, 1951: 1.

3 Ibid.

4 Jim Hearn led the National League in ERA at 2.49 while pitching for the Cardinals, then Giants.

EDDIE ROBINSON KNOCKS IN SEVEN

JULY 3, 1952
CHICAGO WHITE SOX 12, ST. LOUIS BROWNS 3

By Stephen D. Boren

On the evening of July 1, 1952, the Chicago White Sox were in a three-way tie for second place with the season almost half over. They did win the last game of a three-game series in Detroit on the 2nd. And after two victories over the St. Louis Browns in a pair of games on July 3, they were in second place. A big part of the two wins was a pair of three-run home runs by Eddie Robinson in the first game and an RBI single in the second.[1]

William Edward Robinson, better known as Eddie Robinson, was a four-time All-Star first baseman who is not remembered by many baseball fans today, although he was involved in professional baseball for 65 years, most of them at the major-league level. His 29 home runs in 1951 tied him with Gus Zernial for the Chicago White Sox' single-season home-run record, which stood until Bill Melton hit 33 in 1970.

The White Sox won the first of the two games, 6-3, and the second one, 12-3. This was not a doubleheader sweep. The first game was actually the resumption of the second game of an April 27 twin bill that had been suspended after five innings because of darkness with the White Sox leading the Browns 3-1, after the teams went 19 innings in the first game.[2] The gap of over two months had given rise to the possibility of players on each team having played on both sides of this game. While it did not happen, it easily could have occurred. Leo Thomas had started the suspended game as the Browns' third baseman but was traded to the White Sox with Tom Wright on June 15 for Al Zarilla and Willie Miranda. However, White Sox manager Paul Richards did not use Thomas when the game resumed on July 3.

After the White Sox won the suspended game, they quickly found themselves behind 1-0 in the third inning of the scheduled contest after a single by Browns second baseman Bob Young and a triple by future White Sox fan favorite Jim Rivera. Robinson had grounded out to second baseman Bob Young in the first inning. After Nellie Fox opened the bottom of the third inning with a rare strikeout, St. Louis pitcher Earl Harrist hit Minnie Miñoso with a pitch. Bud Stewart singled to right field, sending Miñoso speeding to third base. Eddie Robinson, the next batter, hit a home run that "hit the upper balustrade of the right field stands."[3] Now the White Sox had a 3-1 lead. After Sam Mele flied out, Hector "The Line Drive Collector" Rodriguez singled, and Sherman Lollar followed with another single, the Browns' player-manager, Marty Marion, replaced Harrist with Dave Madison, who got Willie Miranda to ground out to first base.

In the fourth the Browns got a walk and two singles off White Sox starter Marv Grissom, but thanks to a double play from Fox to Miranda to Robinson, there was no scoring. However, after Grissom grounded out to start the bottom half of the inning, Nellie Fox doubled and Minnie Miñoso walked. Bud Stewart singled Fox home as Miñoso took third. Then Robinson faced Madison and lined another home run to right, this time into the seventh row of the seats in the upper deck of the right-field stands. This again drove in Miñoso and Stewart for a 7-1 White Sox lead·

In the sixth inning, Robinson grounded to first baseman Gordon Goldsberry, who threw to pitcher Tommy Byrne at first to retire him.

A single by Byrne, two walks, and a groundout by Al Zarilla gave the Browns another run in the seventh inning. In the eighth, a singles by Minnie Miñoso and Ray Coleman put Robinson at the plate again. This time he "merely" singled Miñoso home for his seventh RBI of the game. A wild pitch followed by a groundout by Tom Wright and a single by Rodriguez gave the White Sox two more runs. A home run by Lollar increased the lead to 12-2. An error by Rodriguez in the ninth allowed the Browns a meaningless final run and the game ended as a 12-3 victory for the Sox.

The seven RBIs by Robinson did not set a White Sox record. Carl Reynolds had eight against the New York Yankees on July 2, 1930. Despite multiple publications stating the contrary, Joe Jackson never had eight RBIs in a game in 1920 or in any other season for the White Sox.

The next day, the Fourth of July, the White Sox again defeated the Browns twice, 3-1 and 2-0. Eddie Robinson went only 1-for-6 in the two games. Since the 6-3 victory of July 3 was officially part of the White Sox' April 27 suspended game, the team had only a four-game winning streak (one game July 2 against Detroit, the regularly scheduled July 3 game, and both July 4 games), not five. The team finished in third place, behind the Yankees and Cleveland Indians, that year, for the first time they finished that high since 1941.

Despite Eddie Robinson's 22 home runs, 104 RBIs, 70 walks (including a league-leading 16 intentional walks), only 49 strikeouts, a .296 batting average and being the starting first baseman for the American League All-Star team, he was traded after the season to the Philadelphia Athletics with Joe DeMaestri for Ferris Fain and minor leaguer Bobby Wilson. While Fain had won the American League batting titles in 1951 and 1952, he had hit only two home runs and driven in a mere 59 runs in 1952. Getting rid of their only power hitter (Minnie Miñoso was a distant second with 61 RBIs) had White Sox fans questioning this decision.[9]

SOURCES

In addition to the sources listed below, the author also consulted Baseball-Reference.com, Retrosheet.org, and **The Sporting News**.

NOTES

1 Edward Burns, "Sox Whip Browns, 6-3, 12-3; Regain 2D," **Chicago Tribune**, July 4, 1952: 3, 1.

2 Edward Burns, "Sox Battle 19 Innings for 1 Victory, 7-6," **Chicago Tribune**, April 28, 1952: 4, 1.

3 "Sox Whip Browns, 6-3, 12-3."

"16" IS MAGIC NUMBER AGAIN FOR JACK HARSHMAN IN SHUTOUT DUEL

AUGUST 13, 1954
CHICAGO WHITE SOX 1, DETROIT TIGERS 0
(16 INNINGS)

By Richard Cuicchi

When Chicago White Sox pitcher Jack Harshman shut out the Detroit Tigers on August 13, 1954, it was the second time in less than three weeks that the number 16 would be significant for him.

Harshman outdueled the Tigers' Al "Lefty" Aber in an historic 16-inning contest that ended in a White Sox 1-0 victory. The left-handed rookie had pitched a complete-game gem against the Boston Red Sox on July 25, when he recorded 16 strikeouts for a White Sox record.

Before the 1954 season, Harshman had pitched in only two major-league games, in 1952 with the New York Giants. He had broken in with the Giants as a first baseman in 1948, but had been converted to a pitcher by the Giants after unsatisfactory performance at first.[1]

Harshman, 26, was a nice addition to the White Sox starting rotation, which included veterans Virgil Trucks, Bob Keegan, Sandy Consuegra, and Billy Pierce. Coming into the game against the Tigers, he had a 9-6 record, including two shutouts and six complete games. In his most recent outing, he threw a seven-hit shutout against the Washington Senators.

Aber entered the 1954 season having pitched in fewer than 25 games over two years. The left-hander had been traded to the Tigers in June 1953 in a deal with the Cleveland Indians that involved seven other players. His record was 4-6 before the game against the White Sox.

The day game at Comiskey Park was played before an attendance of 9,487. The White Sox were in third place, 7½ games behind the league-leading Cleveland Indians, while the fourth-place Tigers were a distant 20½ games behind the White Sox.

After Harshman retired the side in order in the first inning, he was less efficient over the next six innings; the Tigers got runners in scoring position in four innings. But they were unable to push across a run. Harshman held them at bay, and Detroit was 1-for-15 with runners in scoring position.

In the top of the ninth inning, the Tigers mounted their biggest threat to that point when they put runners on first and third with two outs on singles by Aber and Harvey Kuenn. But Harshman got out of the jam again when he retired Bill Tuttle on a pop fly to the catcher.

Aber was also pitching magnificently, allowing only five White Sox baserunners (three hits and two walks) through the first nine innings.

In the bottom of the 10th, Harshman nearly took matters into his own hands. Ex-Tiger Johnny Groth singled with two outs, the first White Sox hit since the fourth inning. Harshman, a decent hitter from his days as a former first baseman, sent right fielder Al Kaline to the wall in right-center. A wind blowing toward left field kept the ball in play, and Kaline made the catch.[2]

The White Sox threatened to end the game in the bottom of the 12th, when Matt Batts singled with one out. Pitcher Billy Pierce ran for Batts. Cass Michaels walked, putting runners on first and second.

White Sox manager Paul Richards sent up Ed McGhee to pinch-hit for Jim Rivera, who had struck out twice against Aber. But Aber induced a 6-4-3 double play to end the threat.

The Tigers took their turn at trying to rustle up a run in the top of the 13th. With one out, Walt Dropo walked. Kaline's groundball forced pinch-runner Reno Bertoia at second. Red Wilson's single moved Kaline to second base. A tired Harshman dug deep to make Bob Nieman fly out to end the inning.

The White Sox advanced Nellie Fox to third base in the bottom of the 14th inning with two outs, but Aber retired Carl Sawatski on a grounder to second to squelch the potential winning run.

By the top of the 16th Harshman had already faced 60 batters in the marathon game. He walked Wilson, who took second on Wayne Belardi's sacrifice. Aber hit a smash to shortstop Michaels, who threw out Wilson trying to advance to third base. After a walk to Kuenn put a runner at second base again, Tuttle failed for the second time to bring in the run.

Chico Carrasquel led off the bottom of the 16th, the 54th batter faced by Aber. He singled to left field. Fox bunted but catcher Sawatski grabbed the ball and forced out Carrasquel at second base. The triumph was short-lived: Minnie Miñoso tripled to right field for the walk-off victory for the White Sox. Miñoso's hit fell a few feet behind first base, just inches in fair territory, curved, and bounced off the wall in front of the right-field box seats. An usher stationed down the right-field line attempted to stop the ball, but it quickly zipped past him without his touching the ball. Right fielder Kaline mishandled the ball momentarily in his haste to get the ball back into the infield. Second baseman Bertoia relayed the ball home, but Fox beat the throw to the plate. Tigers manager Fred Hutchinson contested the play, claiming that the usher interfered with Kaline's fielding of the ball. But umpire Ed Runge rejected Hutchinson's argument.[3]

Harshman gave up nine hits and seven walks while striking out 12 in his third consecutive win. The Tigers' Ray Boone accounted for four of the punchouts.

Aber was the hard-luck guy on Friday the 13th. He pitched the best game of his career, scattering nine hits and three walks. The White Sox were 0-for-8 with runners in scoring position.

Counting his shutout on August 8 and two scoreless innings at the end of his complete game on August 3, Harshman now had pitched 27 consecutive scoreless innings. On the 15th he pitched two scoreless innings in relief in the second game of a doubleheader, and added four more in a start on August 19, for a total of 33 scoreless innings over the five-game stretch. The record for most consecutive scoreless innings pitched, established in 1988 by Orel Hershiser, is 59.

Harshman's outing was among the longest extra-inning shutouts in the major leagues. Since World War II, only Jerry Walker (1959) and Juan Marichal (1963) have equaled the 16-inning feat. Ed Summers (1909), Walter Johnson (1918), and Carl Hubbell (1933) hold the record for most shutout innings in a game, 18.

The White Sox led the American League with 21 shutouts in 1954. Harshman contributed four, while Trucks added five and Pierce four. Although the White Sox were in pennant contention on August 13, the Cleveland Indians wound up breaking the pennant race open with two substantial winning streaks, winning 111 games to win the American League pennant. The White Sox finished a distant third with 94 wins.

SOURCES

In addition to the sources mentioned in the Notes, the author also consulted:

Baseball-Reference.com.

Gabcik, John. "Jack Harshman," SABR BioProject, sabr.org/bioproj/person/8cffce43.

Smith, Lyall. "Tigers Go 16 Innings Before Losing for Aber," **Detroit Free Press**, August 14, 1954: 11.

NOTES

1 Edward Prell, "Harshman Quit Hitting Home Runs to Pitch," **The Sporting News**, September 1, 1954: 3.

2 Edward Prell, "Sox, Harshman Defeat Tigers 1-0, in 16th on Miñoso's Triple," **Chicago Tribune**, August 14, 1954: 2, 1.

3 Ibid.

THE MICK BELTS NUMBER 50 AS THE BOMBERS TAKE THE PENNANT

SEPTEMBER 18, 1956
NEW YORK YANKEES 3, CHICAGO WHITE SOX 2
(11 INNINGS)

By Gregory H. Wolf

When the Yankees took the field at Comiskey Park on Chicago's south side, the question wasn't whether the Bombers would capture their seventh pennant in eight years since Casey Stengel took over as skipper in 1949, but rather when they would clinch. Catapulted by a 27-6 run, which ended on July 30, the front-running Yankees (92-52) owned an 11-game lead over the Chicago White Sox (80-62), against whom they were wrapping up the season series in a one-game showdown.

The Yankees were an offensive juggernaut in '56, leading the majors in runs scored (857) and the AL in round-trippers (190). The team counted Yogi Berra, Moose Skowron, and Hank Bauer among its home-run threats; however, the star of the show was 24-year-old Mickey Mantle. Longtime *New York Times* sportswriter Arthur Daly gushed that "Mantle's hitting throughout the major part of the season was the single biggest factor" in the Yankees' pennant drive.[1] Already in his sixth full season, the Commerce Comet was coming off a stellar campaign in 1955, having led the AL in home runs (37), triples (11), slugging percentage (.611), and on-base percentage (.431). The 5-foot-11, 195-pound plug of power upped the ante in '56, entering the game leading the majors in round-trippers (49) and runs batted in (121); however, a slump since the beginning of September, during which he batted just .208 (11-for-53), dropped his batting average to .350, two points behind Boston's Ted Williams, and endangering the young slugger's quest to capture the Triple Crown.

The game's pitching matchup featured the "league's finest lefthanders," opined scribe Joe Trimble of the *New York Daily News*.[2] The Ol' Perfessor sent Whitey Ford, leading the majors at the time with a 2.58 ERA, to the bump. The 27-year-old was 18-5, which pushed his career slate to 79-27 in parts of five seasons. The Pale Hose skipper, Marty Marion, countered with 29-year-old Billy Pierce, who was coming off a 10-inning complete-game victory over the Red Sox five days earlier for his league-leading 20th victory, improving his career record to 114-97.

On a pleasant Tuesday evening with temperatures in the high 60s, a robust crowd of 31,694 packed the Base Ball Palace of the World for the eighth game of the White Sox' 13-game (and final) homestand of the year.

Pierce looked dominant to start the game, punching out Billy Martin and Mantle to roll through a 1-2-3 first. Ford registered two quick outs, then former two-time long-ball champ Larry Doby blasted a towering home run, sailing an estimated 420 feet and landing in the lower left-field stands.[3] It was Doby's 20th clout of the season and his sixth against the Yankees.

While Ford looked shaky, working around a

THE BASE BALL PALACE OF THE WORLD

1956 Triple Crown winner Mickey Mantle's 50th home run of the season secured the pennant for the Yankees that season. The Commerce Comet belted 30 of his 536 career round-trippers in Comiskey Park. (Photo by Kidwiler Collection/Diamond Images/Getty Images)

single and a walk in the second, Pierce cruised, retiring the first 10 batters he faced. That changed when Martin hit a bloop popup to shallow right that second baseman Nellie Fox bobbled and dropped after calling off right fielder Bubba Philips. It was a "difficult chance," admitted sportswriter Robert Cromie of the *Chicago Tribune*, who added that "Phillips probably could have handled [it] more easily."[4] Mantle tied the game on a run-scoring single to right.

Ford's struggles continued in the fourth when Walt Dropo led off with a single and moved to third on Sherm Lollar's double. But the Chairman of the Board escaped trouble by inducing two infield grounders sandwiched around a foul popup to end the frame.

In the eighth inning, Dropo's seventh home run of the season broke the 1-1 tie and gave the White Sox the lead, 2-1.

Pierce entered the ninth having allowed only five baserunners on three hits, a walk, and an error, then yielded his hardest-hit ball of the game. Described by sportswriter John Drebinger of the *Times* as "the Yanks' fiery second sacker and the apple of Stengel's' right ear," Billy Martin belted a long fly "off the wall in right center" for a triple.[5] According to Cromie, center fielder Larry Doby "barely missed catching [the ball] after a desperate run that ended with him crashing onto the wall."[6] After Mantle fanned, Berra hit what Cromie called a "fluke" popup down the left-field foul line, just out of the reach of shortstop Luis Aparicio and left fielder Minnie Miñoso, to tie the game. Coming off his third AL MVP Award in five seasons, Berra extended his hitting streak to 17 games. (It eventually ended at 19 contests.)

In an old-fashioned pitching duel, both aces took the mound in extra innings. After Pierce worked a 1-2-3 10th, Ford escaped a leadoff single by Aparicio when Doby grounded into an inning-ending 4-6-3 twin killing.

In the 11th Pierce retired Bauer on a fly to deep left and fanned Martin. Mantle, the "Oklahoma Muscle Man," mused Drebinger, swung at Pierce's first pitch and sent a mighty wallop into the upper deck in left field to give the Yankees a 3-2 lead.[7] A jubilant Mantle quipped after the game that he wasn't sure what kind of pitch it was, just that it "was high and either a fast ball or slider."[8] Mantle joined a very exclusive club of 50-home-run hitters, joining Babe Ruth (four times), Hack Wilson, Jimmie Foxx (two times), Hank Greenberg, Johnny Mize, Ralph Kiner (two times), and Willie Mays. Also, Mantle's home run was the Yankees' 182nd of the season, tying the AL record set by the '36 club, led by Lou Gehrig and rookie Joe DiMaggio.

Despite Mantle's dramatic clout, the excitement did not abate. After Berra fouled out to end the 11th, the Cuban Comet, Minnie Miñoso, led off the bottom of the frame with a single and moved up a station when Dropo walked, sending Ford to the showers. In came relief specialist Bob Grim, who two years earlier had won 20 games as a swingman and received the AL Rookie of the Year Award. He induced Lollar, one of the slowest men in the league, to hit into a crowd-hushing 6-4-3 double play while Miñoso reached third. Grim struck out the next batter, Jim Rivera, to preserve the Yankees' 3-2 victory and end the game in 2 hours and 55 minutes. More importantly, he clinched the Yankees seventh pennant in eight seasons and their 22nd since 1921.

The Yankees had little time to celebrate their pennant as they had to catch a midnight train from the 63rd Street Station. Scheduled to arrive back in New York City late the next night, the players surely had time to savor the victory in Pullman coaches.

The Ol' Perfessor was as feisty and confident as ever. "I don't care who wins the National League race," he quipped when asked about whom he preferred to play in the World Series. [The Brooklyn Dodgers and the Milwaukee Braves were tied after games on September 18, with Cincinnati Reds 4½ games back in a heated struggle.] "We beat Pierce tonight. Have they got anyone in that league who's as good as Pierce?"[9]

Postscript: Mantle emerged from his September slump and went 9-for-21 with 3 home runs and 9 RBIs to capture the ninth Triple Crown (52-130-.353) in the post-Deadball (1920) Era, joining Rogers Hornsby (1922, 1925), Jimmie Foxx (1933), Chuck Klein (1933), Lou Gehrig (1934), Joe Medwick (1937), and Ted Williams (1942, 1947). The Yankees avenged their World Series loss in seven games to the Dodgers the previous October by beating "Dem Bums" in Game Seven, 9-0, in Brooklyn, powered by four home runs.

SOURCES

In addition to the sources cited in the Notes, the author also accessed Retrosheet.org, Baseball-Reference.com, Newspapers.com, and SABR.org.

NOTES

1 Arthur Daly, "Sports of the Times," **New York Times**, April 20, 1956: 40.

2 Joe Trimble, "Yanks Clinch on Mick's 50th," **Daily News** (New York), September 19, 1956: 77.

3 John Drebinger, "White Sox' Pierce Bows in 11th, 3-2," **New York Times**, September 19, 1956: 42.

4 Robert Cromie, "Yankees Clinch Pennant on Mantle's 50th Home Run," **Chicago Tribune**, September 19, 1956: 55.

5 Drebinger.

6 Cromie.

7 Drebinger.

8 Trimble.

9 Associated Press, "Yankees Clinch Seventh Flag in 8 Yrs," **Decatur** (Illinois) **Daily Review**, September 19, 1956: 14.

THE SPLENDID SPLINTER SMASHES THREE IN THE WINDY CITY

MAY 8, 1957
BOSTON RED SOX 4, CHICAGO WHITE SOX 1

By Gregory H. Wolf

After Ted Williams belted three home runs in a game for the first time, in the opening game of a doubleheader against the Cleveland Indians on July 14, 1946, Tribe manager Lou Boudreau instituted his famous infield shift in the second game to defend against the left-handed hitter. The second and last time the Splendid Splinter belted three, he was 38 years old and the feat evoked a barrage of praise. He's "turned into an automatic cannon," gushed sportswriter Arthur Siegel in the *Boston Traveler*,[1] while Hub scribe Hy Hurwitz of the *Globe* described the accomplishment as "king-sized slugging."[2] Red Sox beat reporter Joe Cashman of the *Boston Record* opined that Teddy Ballgame's torrid start to his 16th big-league season was "the most famous slugging surge in baseball history."[3] All-Star left fielder Minnie Miñoso, whose Chicago White Sox squad Williams victimized added, "He makes 'em all look easy. Like he was bunting the ball."[4]

To say Williams was hot was an understatement. The day before his longball-trifecta, he reached base all five times (including three walks) he came to the plate, capped off by a ninth-inning two-run home run, an AL-best sixth round-tripper of the early season, to provide the BoSox with the deciding runs in their 4-3 victory over the White Sox to open a three-game set in the Windy City. Coming off a typical Williams-esque season, a .345 batting average, major-league-best .479 on-base percentage, and .605 slugging percentage, Williams upped those figures to a big-league leading .453/.586/.868 through the first 19 games of the '57 season while pundits wondered how long he could keep up the pace.

ChiSox skipper Al Lopez, whose club (11-6) had lost four straight games to drop out of first place and trailed the New York Yankees by a half-game, was in an ornery mood even before Wednesday's matinee with the Red Sox commenced. He called on Bob Keegan, a 36-year-old, injury-prone right-hander who had been actively shopped in the offseason, to stop the slide. An All-Star in 1954, Keegan (30-26 career slate) began the '57 campaign banished to the bullpen and had pitched sparingly, yielding five runs in 6⅔ innings. Pinky Higgins, manager of the third-place Red Sox (11-8), sent 27-year-old right-hander Frank Sullivan to the mound. The two-time All-Star, who had tied for the AL lead with 18 wins two years earlier, was 1-2 (2.61) and 48-33 in his career.

The Base Ball Palace of the World, located at 35th and Shields on Chicago's South Side, drew a sparse crowd of 4,529 spectators despite a gusty but beautiful late-spring day with temperatures hovering around 70. When Williams trotted to the plate with two outs, White Sox infielders initiated the shift. Second baseman Nellie Fox was "stationed in short right field," noted sportswriter Arthur Sampson in the *Boston Herald*, and shortstop Luis Aparicio settled where Fox normally played, between first and second.[5] The strategy didn't matter as Williams sent Keegan's slider into the lower deck in right-center. With that blast, Williams surpassed the total home runs he had whacked the entire 1956 season in Comiskey Park, netting just one in 55 at-bats, though he did manage a .345 batting average.

In a scene of déjà vu, Williams came to bat in the third with two out and none on. And again, he parked a Keegan offering in the lower deck, this time in left-center, for a 2-0 Red Sox lead. Al Lopez, who had played with and against some of baseball's best sluggers in his 19-year career, 18 of those spent in the NL, paid the Splinter his due, but also added, "He had a gale blowing for him this afternoon. The one he hit to left center [in the third] ... would have been caught if there hadn't been any wind."[6]

That pair of tallies proved all Sullivan needed. After yielding a leadoff single in the first to speedy Luis Aparicio, en route to leading the AL in stolen bases for the second of nine straight seasons to start his career, Sullivan retired the next 11 batters until Larry Doby doubled with two outs in the fourth. He then set down 11 more batters until Jim Landis's double with one out in the eighth snapped the streak.

Williams led off the sixth with a chance to hit his third consecutive home run of the game and fourth in two games, but flied out to left. Afterward he seemed more upset about that out than his trio of clouts. He told reporters that the first of his three rules to good hitting was "get a good ball to hit," and then offered a self-critique. "I went for a bad ball with a 3-and-1 count on me and I fouled it off. I could have had a walk, but I wanted to hit it. Then I swung at another bad ball and I popped it up."[7] Imagine Teddy Ballgame after going hitless in a game! Also in the sixth, Jackie Jensen and Frank Malzone singled with two outs to extend their hitting streaks to 10 games each.

Boston still held a precarious 2-0 lead when Williams came to bat in the eighth with Billy Klaus on first via a single and no outs. Williams swung at Keegan's first pitch and sent the ball "20 rows deep into the upper stands in right center," reported Sampson about the towering blast.[8] Mickey Vernon followed with his second hit of the game, a single, to send Keegan to the showers. Vernon went to third on Malzone's single off reliever Bill Fischer, who escaped the jam unscored upon.

Ordinarily Gene Stephens would have replaced Williams for defensive purposes in the bottom of eighth, noted Boston sportswriters, but with Teddy Ballgame due to bat fourth in the ninth, there was a chance that he could become just the ninth player to hit four home runs in a game. Those chances rose when Sullivan reached on third baseman Fred Hatfield's second error of the game, and moved up a station on Jimmy Piersall's sacrifice. "I ordered the bunt," said Higgins, wanting to avoid a double play, "because I wanted to make sure Ted would get to hit again."[9] After Klaus flied out, Williams strode to the plate, but Lopez was having none of it and called for an intentional walk, much to the chagrin of the few spectators still in Comiskey Park. "I don't care if it's Williams or Mantle or anybody else," said Lopez. "We're still in the ballgame. We're out to win. To hell with four home runs in a ballgame."[10] Williams departed for pinch-runner Stephens and the Red Sox failed to score.

The White Sox finally got on the board in the ninth when Miñoso doubled to drive in Fox, who had walked. Sullivan finished with a four-hitter with five punchouts, completing the game in 1 hour and 59 minutes. Still seething, Lopez order his men to stay in uniform and conducted batting practice.

Williams became the first Red Sox player to hit three home runs in a game twice. Besides Williams, Jim Tabor (1939), Bobby Doerr (1950), Clyde Vollmer (1951), and Norm Zauchin (1955) had achieved the feat once before.

Williams took an analytical approach after the game. "Keegan had real good stuff, but he made a couple of mistakes," Ted opined. "He served me two home runs that he did not mean to let go."[11] [Keegan had his moment in the sun later that season, tossing a no-hitter in the second game of a doubleheader on August 20 against the Washington Senators.] Williams harbored no ill will against Lopez for ordering the intentional walk in the ninth, adding that the White Sox weren't out of the game. Williams freely admitted, "I had some help with the wind" on his first two clouts; however, he noted that successful hitters make adjustments.[12] "The score, type of pitching you are facing, the wind, and other factors govern what a batter should do at the plate," said Williams, holding court in the Red Sox clubhouse. "Many people don't think I ever consider such things, but I do. That's why it isn't a good idea to set homer goal or a batting-average goal."[13]

Celebrating his 39th birthday during the season, Teddy Ballgame eventually slowed his astronomical pace, but not by much. In what is surely one of the most impressive seasons in baseball history, Williams batted .388 to capture his fifth AL batting crown, and led the majors with a .526 on-base percentage and .731 slugging percentage, as the Red Sox finished in third place.[14]

SOURCES

In addition to the sources cited in the Notes, the author also accessed Retrosheet.org, Baseball-Reference.com, Newspapers.com, and SABR.org.

NOTES

1. Arthur Siegel, "Ted Could Stay Hot Long Time," **Boston Traveler**, May 9, 1957: 33.

2. Hy Hurwitz, "Williams Hits 3 Homers as Sox Defeat Chicago, 4-1," **Boston Globe**, May 9, 1957: 1.

3. Joe Cashman, "Ted Slams 3 Homers, Beats ChiSox, 4-1," **Boston Record**, May 9, 1957: 28.

4. Hy Hurwitz, "'I Broke My Own Rule,' Why Ted Williams 'Failed' to Have Perfect Day," **Boston Globe**, May 8, 1957: 16

5. Arthur Sampson, "Williams Raps in All Runs, Sox Win, 4-1. Ted Crushes Three Homers," **Boston Herald**, May 9, 1937: 35.

6. Hurwitz, "'I Broke My Own Rule,' Why Ted Williams 'Failed' to Have Perfect Day."

7. Ibid.

8. Sampson, "Williams Raps in All Runs, Sox Win, 4-1. Ted Crushes Three Homers."

9. Ibid.

10. Mike Gillooly, "Ted's Dizzy Pace Stuns Baseball," **Boston American**, May 9, 1957: 50.

11. Bob Glass, "Keegan Errs on Homers," **Boston Record**, May 9, 1957: 28.

12. Hurwitz, "'I Broke My Own Rule,' Why Ted Williams 'Failed' to Have Perfect Day."

13. Arthur Sampson, "Ted Hopes for Health, Hits," **Boston Herald**, May 9, 1957: 1.

14. In 1957 Williams led the AL in on-base-percentage for the 11th of 12 times, and in slugging percentage for the ninth and last time.

SWEET BILLY'S GEM EXTENDS CHISOX LEAD

JUNE 8, 1957
CHICAGO WHITE SOX 2, BALTIMORE ORIOLES 0

By Tom Pardo

Mention the name of Billy Pierce and smiles cross the faces of older Chicago White Sox fans. The affable southpaw, whose No. 19 is retired and whose statue resides in the left-field bleachers at Guaranteed Rate Field, was the darling of the Sox starting corps in the 1950s. Whenever Billy took the mound, White Sox rooters knew their beloved team had a great chance to win. Such was the case on a warm Saturday afternoon in early June 1957 when Pierce threw an outstanding three-hit shutout of the Baltimore Orioles, 2-0, before only 5,642 of the White Sox faithful.

The '57 edition of the "Go-Go" Sox blazed a path to the top of the American League early in the campaign. Heading into this game, the team commanded a five-game lead over the New York Yankees. Such good fortune was not surprising given the abundance of talent on the White Sox roster. Under the tutelage of skipper Al Lopez, the leading sluggers on the South Side included future Hall of Famers Nellie Fox, Larry Doby, and Luis Aparicio, catcher Sherman Lollar and outfielders Minnie Miñoso and Jim Rivera. In addition to Pierce, the veteran starting rotation of Jack Harshman, Dick Donovan, and Jim Wilson had already accounted for 23 of the team's 31 victories. Their 21 complete games led the major leagues.

Without question the one who catapulted the White Sox to such lofty heights was Pierce. "Sweet Billy" did not pick up the game until he was 15, but right away he could throw hard in spite of his slight build.[1] Now in the prime of his career, Pierce was well on his way to achieving back-to-back 20-win seasons with a 9-2 record coming into this game. He had won six straight starts dating back to May 10, including five complete games and a scoreless streak of 16 innings.

The left-hander's success was attributed to three factors: durability, control, and pitch selection. Pierce was the workhorse of the White Sox starters, logging the most innings pitched since 1951. He had become a master of the strike zone, reducing his walks per nine innings steadily since breaking into the big leagues. But it was Pierce's pitch selection that made him special. He had a blazing fastball and an effective curve, but his mentor and first White Sox skipper, Paul Richards, transformed him into a truly great pitcher by teaching him to throw a wicked slider.[2] Richards summed up the source of his pupil's success: "Driving ambition and desire plus tremendous ability."[3]

Opposing the White Sox on this afternoon was a Baltimore Orioles team that had not yet escaped from the shadows of its previous incarnation as the St. Louis Browns. Since leaving the Gateway City for the Chesapeake Bay for the 1954 season, the Orioles had managed only one sixth- and two seventh-place finishes in the American League. The 1957 version was not faring any better given their seventh-place residency at game time.

Yet in spite of their record, the O's were victors in six of their last eight games and claimed some impressive early-season statistics under the direction of Paul Richards. Offensively, the team was second in batting (.263) and first in hits (443). Defensively, Baltimore was first in fielding average (.987), tied for first with the Yankees in double plays (56), and made the fewest errors of any major-league team (25).[4]

The Orioles starting corps was aging; four of its five pitchers were well into their 30s. Lefthander Bill Wight, who was 35 and already playing for his sixth team, was given the ball for this contest. At best it could be said that Wight was a mediocre thrower who possessed an above-average pickoff move. In his latest outing, though, on June 2, Wight finally picked up his first win of the season, 3-2 over the surging Yankees.[5]

In contemplating this matinee duel, Al Lopez faced two significant challenges: weak run production supporting Pierce and Pierce's sustainability. In the southpaw's previous four outings, White Sox hitters scored only seven runs. Furthermore, Lopez was starting Pierce on three days' rest in order to have him fully rested for a coming series against the Yankees.[6]

In contrast to Richards, who advocated the then standard four days' rest between starts, Lopez stressed flexibility based on scheduling circumstances. He conceded that Pierce's velocity might diminish in this game, "but control is the most important thing in pitching."[7] And Billy was the "king" of control.

Concern regarding Pierce's effectiveness seemed justified as he appeared a bit wobbly at the outset. With two out in the first inning, Orioles first baseman Dick Williams laid down a perfect bunt along the third-base line for an infield hit. Cleanup slugger Bob Nieman drew a pass; Pierce was unwilling to give the Orioles left fielder anything good to hit. The rally was snuffed out when catcher Gus Triandos hit a soft liner to White Sox shortstop Sammy Esposito for the final out.

The White Sox opened the scoring without generating a hit in their half of the second, a sure

In his 13 seasons with the South Siders, Billy Pierce was a seven-time All-Star, won 20 games twice, and posted a 186-152 slate. (Photo by Mark Rucker/Transcendental Graphics, Getty Images)

sign of continuing offensive woes. After Wight walked catcher Sherman Lollar and Dropo, right fielder Dave Philley sacrificed the runners up. Third baseman Bubba Phillips proceeded to hit a towering drive to center field; Jim Pyburn caught it for the second out, but threw offline to the plate, allowing Lollar to give the Sox a one-run lead.

Following their early-inning shakiness, both Pierce and Wight settled into a good rhythm during the middle frames. Wight had a no-hitter for 5⅓ innings, including retiring 11 White Sox in a row. Pierce set down eight Orioles before the sixth inning.

Baltimore had an excellent opportunity to equalize the contest in the sixth. Second baseman Billy Gardner, who had extended his hitting streak to 12 games with a single in the third, bounced a roller to shortstop Sammy Esposito, who fumbled the ball and threw wide to Dropo.[8] Gardner slid safely into first just under Dropo's tag, a call unsuccessfully disputed by Al Lopez. Gardner advanced to second on third baseman George Kell's sacrifice. After Williams flied out to Philley in right, Nieman hit the longest drive of the day, to the 415-foot sign in center. Rookie Jim Landis broke quickly and hauled it in to retire the side.

Pierce received some needed breathing room in the White Sox sixth. With one out, All-Star second baseman Nellie Fox extended his hitting streak to 13 games by smashing a double to right that Tito Francona misjudged. Fox moved to third on left fielder Minnie Miñoso's groundout to Gardner and trotted home with the White Sox' second tally on Lollar's hot single up the middle.

The Orioles' last chance for redemption came in the eighth inning. Bob Boyd, pinch-hitting for Wight, opened the frame by being called out after running into the ball he topped in front of the plate. Pierce walked Gardner and then yielded a single to Kell. Williams killed the rally by hitting into a double play.

After the White Sox went quietly in the eighth, Pierce completed his 2-0 masterpiece by setting the Orioles down in order in the ninth, and in record time.[9] With this victory and a Yankees loss to Detroit, the White Sox stretched their AL lead to six games, their biggest margin since clinching the pennant in 1919.

Although totally exhausted and again the victim of a weak offense, Pierce managed to put the team on his back in gaining his 10th win of the season, becoming the first major leaguer to hit that mark in 1957.[10] Continuing his dominance over the Orioles, he allowed only four runners as far as second base. Now his career record against the Orioles was an eye-popping 14-2.

Pierce attributed his success on this day to the slider Paul Richards taught him to throw.[11] That pitch worked to perfection. It was the southpaw's second straight shutout and third of the campaign. The win boosted Pierce's complete-game streak to six (eight overall for the season). His six strikeouts increased his season total to a league-leading 70. His consecutive scoreless streak now extended to 23 innings. Pierce had now allowed only one run in 47 innings, lowering his ERA to 1.79 As if these feats were not amazing enough, opponent hits against Pierce in his last five outings looked "like Ben Hogan's golf card as the string read 4-4-3-2-3."[12]

Despite Bill Wight's superb two-hit performance for the Orioles, Billy Pierce was the story of this game. His battery mate, Sherm Lollar, reflected on Pierce's mastery: "Billy has never been sharper. ... He now has poise and confidence and the ability to fool the best hitters in the league."[13] Just ask the Orioles!

SOURCES

In addition to the references cited in the Notes, the author consulted the following:

Baseball-Reference.com.

Retrosheet.org.

Brown, Warren. "Bill Outduels Wight, 2-0; Tops Yankees by 6," **Chicago American**, June 9, 1957: Final Edition, 15-16.

Brown, Warren. "Pierce Wins 10th, Sox Get Two Hits," **Chicago American**, June 9, 1957: Home Edition, 21.

Fox, Nellie. "Nellie Fox Reports: Sox Score on 2 of Only 3 Chances," **Chicago Sun-Times**, June 9, 1957: 84.

Maisel, Bob. "White Sox Blank Orioles, 2-0, on Pierce's 3-Hitter," **Baltimore Sun**, June 9, 1957: 1D-2D.

Munzel, Edgar. "Pierce Eyes Triple Crown of Hill — Wins, ERA, Whiffs," **The Sporting News**, June 5, 1957: 11.

Munzel, Edgar. "Sox Lead by 6, Jolt Orioles 2-0; Pierce Wins 10th on Mates' 2 Hits," **Chicago Sun-Times**, June 9, 1957: 84.

Vaughan, Irving. "Sox Win 2-0, on 2 Hits; Lead by 6 Games," **Chicago Sunday Tribune**, June 9, 1957: 2, 1-2.

"Hose 'Big Four' Could Win 95!" **Chicago American**, June 8, 1957: 10.

"White Sox Blank Baltimore 2 to 0," **Chicago Daily News**, June 8, 1957: 26.

THE BASE BALL PALACE OF THE WORLD

NOTES

1. Rob Neyer, "Billy Pierce," SABR Baseball Biography Project (sabr.org/bioproj/person/9e29afb8), accessed January 26, 2018.

2. Ibid.

3. Lou Hatter, "Oriole Pilot Hails Pierce," **Baltimore Sun**, June 9, 1957: 1D.

4. Jesse A. Linthicum, "Sunlight on Sports," **Baltimore Sun**, June 9, 1957: 2D.

5. Bill Nowlin, "Bill Wight," SABR Baseball Biography Project (sabr.org/bioproj.person/fc9fd79a), accessed January 31, 2018.

6. Edgar Munzel, "Pierce to Hurl With 3 Days' Rest," **Chicago Sun-Times**, June 8, 1957: 48.

7. David Condon, "Less Rest Helps Pierce's Control," **Chicago Sunday Tribune**, June 9, 1957: 2, 1.

8. Esposito was playing in place of All-Star Luis Aparicio, who had pulled a leg muscle in the last game of the previous series, against the Boston Red Sox. Warren Brown, "That Old Bad Habit Catches Up With Sox," **Chicago American**, June 8, 1957: 8.

9. The game was the shortest of the 1957 White Sox season, 1 hour and 49 minutes. As one Baltimore scribe noted, the game was so brief that a fan "hardly had time for two beers and a hot dog." Hugh Trader, "Red-Hot White Sox Nip Birds, 2-0," **Baltimore News American**, June 9, 1957: C-1.

10. "I Was Lucky This Time, Says Billy," **Chicago Sun-Times**, June 9, 1957: 84.

11. Ibid.

12. Edgar Munzel, "Hats Off … Billy Pierce," **The Sporting News**, June 19, 1957: 21.

13. Gene Kessler, "Lollar on Pitching," **Chicago Sun-Times**, June 9, 1957: 78.

KEEGAN USES NEW MOTION TO TOSS NO-HITTER

AUGUST 20, 1957
CHICAGO WHITE SOX 6, WASHINGTON SENATORS 0
(SECOND GAME OF DOUBLEHEADER)

By Gregory H. Wolf

"It was a new pitching motion that did it for me," explained Chicago White Sox right-hander Bob Keegan after tossing a no-hitter.[1] Finally heeding the advice of skipper Al Lopez and pitching coach Ray Berres to slow down his preliminary motion before throwing the ball, Keegan baffled the Washington Senators, disrupting their timing and keeping them off balance.

Keegan's gem was a much-needed salve to the second-place Pale Hose (69-47), who had lost 10 of their last 18 games heading into a Tuesday doubleheader to kick off a three-game series with the Senators. For most of the first three months of the season, the White Sox sat atop the AL, but their skid dropped them 7½ games behind the Yankees. The seventh-place Senators (45-72), heading to their 11th straight second-division finish, were playing their best ball of the season, having won 10 of their last 16 for skipper Cookie Lavagetto, who had replaced Chuck Dressen in early May.

A robust weekday crowd of 22,815 was on hand at Comiskey Park, located at the intersection of 35th and Shields on the South Side of the Windy City. In the first contest of the twin bill, the White Sox squandered an early 4-1 lead and lost it, 5-4, on Ed Fitz Gerald's solo home run to lead off the eighth. Sportswriter Edward Prell of the *Chicago Tribune* declared that the spectators and the ChiSox themselves were "shocked by the loss," leading to a hefty round of boos and catcalls.[2]

Tapped to stop the White Sox' slump was the 36-year-old Keegan, described by Prell as on the "rugged edge of big leagues when the season started."[3] After debuting with the White Sox in 1953, Keegan won 16 and earned an All-Star berth the next season, his first full one in the big leagues. However, chronic arm miseries had wiped out much of the next two campaigns, with a combined 7-12 slate. The White Sox had actively shopped him in the offseason, but found no takers for an ailing starter in his mid-30s. Assigned to the scrap heap of long relief as the season commenced, Keegan moved back into the starting rotation and entered this game with a 7-6 record (37-32 lifetime). Toeing the rubber for the Senators was veteran southpaw Chuck Stobbs, who had blanked the Boston Red Sox on five hits in his last start to improve his slate to 6-15 and 82-98 in parts of 11 seasons.

The ChiSox squandered a first-inning scoring opportunity after loading the bases with one out when Nellie Fox was plunked, Minnie Miñoso doubled, and Walt Dropo drew an intentional free pass. Stobbs fielded Larry Doby's soft dribbler and fired to catcher Lou Berberet to erase Fox at the plate, and then retired Sherm Lollar.

The "gloom started lifting" among the

Bob Keegan made his major-league debut with the White Sox as a 32-year-old in 1953. He posted a 40-36 record in six injury-plagued seasons, highlighted by his no-hitter in 1957. (Photo by Kidwiler Collection/Diamond Images/Getty Images)

Comiskey faithful, opined Prell, in the bottom of the third when the White Sox teed off on Stobbs.[4] Luis Aparicio and Fox led off with singles and raced home on Miñoso's two-bagger. Dropo's single accounted for another run, and then Doby cranked his 12th home run of the season, a two-run shot to make it 5-0.

The White Sox tacked on their sixth and final run in the fifth when Keegan singled, driving home Bubba Phillips, who had laced a one-out double.

Six runs were more than enough when Keegan flashed the game of his life. He set down the first 14 batters he faced. One of those outs was the only hard-hit ball of the game, a screeching liner by Herb Plews in the first inning. Center fielder Larry Doby raced and made a "back hand catch," an athletic, yet for the seven-time All-Star, routine play.[5] "I could tell then that the Senators didn't have any hits in them," Keegan said after the game.[6] He was also convinced that his new motion gave him better control, put less pressure on his right wing, and kept him from fatiguing so quickly.

Relying mainly on his sinking fastball and an occasional slider, Keegan mowed the Senators down. With two outs in the fifth, he surrendered his first baserunner when he walked Berberet on a 3-and-2 count. Keegan issued his second and final free pass of the game in the next inning, sending Faye Throneberry, pinch-hitting for Stobbs, to first on a 3-and-1 count. The next batter, Eddie Yost, hit a hit tapper back to the mound, which resulted in an inning-ending 1-4-3 twin killing.

Keegan began the eighth having faced just one batter over the minimum and six outs away from becoming the first White Sox hurler to author a no-hitter since Bill Dietrich held the St. Louis Browns hitless on June 1, 1937. The last no-hitter at Comiskey Park occurred on Opening Day 1940 when Bob Feller threw the first of his three career no-nos. The next no-hitter by a White Sox hurler was on September 9, 1967, by Joe Horlen.

"[Keegan] had great control, great stuff," gushed Lopez after the game, and that was readily apparent in the final two frames.[7] He needed just two pitches to record the first two outs in the eighth. After Bob Usher attempted to bunt, eliciting a hefty round of boos from the fans, Keegan's seventh pitch of the inning led to a weak grounder to short.

Lavagetto, a former four-time All-Star infielder with the Brooklyn Dodgers in his first season as a manager, was not about to make it easy on Keegan in the top of the ninth. He called on slugger Jim Lemon, who had missed the previous eight games, to pinch-hit for weak-hitting shortstop Rocky Bridges. Lemon grounded to short on the first pitch. Keegan then registered his first and only punchout of the game, fanning pinch-hitter Julio Becquer on four pitches. "Bob got Becquer on a slip pitch," revealed All-Star batterymate Sherm Lollar.[8] Keegan had picked up the pitch, sometimes called the palm ball or cosmic pitch by the club, from former skipper Paul Richards. On his second toss to Yost, Keegan induced a routine popup that first sacker Walt Dropo corralled in foul territory to preserve the no-hitter and conclude the game in 1 hour and 55 minutes.

The Comiskey crowd went wild and many stormed the field and mound. Keegan, mobbed by his teammates, as well, was finally escorted to the dugout and dressing room by police attempting to restore order.

Keegan was a model of efficiency, facing only 28 batters, and pitching to contact. "I'll bet he didn't throw more than 85 or 90 times," exclaimed Lollar.[9] The Senators pounded his sinkers and low sliders into the dirt all afternoon, resulting in 13 groundouts. The Pale House outfielders made just seven putouts in the game.

Keegan's perch at the top of the baseball world did not last long. In fact, he won only two more games in his career, one of which was his next start, a complete-game three-hitter against the Baltimore Orioles in the second game of a doubleheader five days later. He made only two starts in 1958 and was optioned to the Triple-A Indianapolis Indians of the American Association at the end of July. He never made it back to the majors, and finished with a 40-36 record.

The White Sox didn't catch the streaking 1957 Yankees, who captured their eighth pennant in nine seasons. Lopez's Go-Go Sox finally unseated the Bronx Bombers two years later, capturing the club's first pennant since the 1919 Black Sox.

SOURCES

In addition to the sources cited in the Notes, the author also accessed Retrosheet.org, Baseball-Reference.com, Newspapers.com, and SABR.org.

NOTES

1 Edward Prell, "Hurler Tells of Advice He Finally Took," **Chicago Tribune**, August 21, 1957: III, 1.

2 Edward Prell, "Bob Keegan Pitches No-Hit Gem, 6-0," **Chicago Tribune**, August 21, 1957: III, 1.

3 Ibid.

4 Ibid.

5 Ibid.

6 Gene Bludeau, United Press, "Bob Keegan Comes Up With 'Slow Motion Windup,'" **El Paso Herald-Post**, August 21, 1957: 16.

7 Prell, "Hurler Tells of Advice He Finally Took."

8 Ibid.

9 Ibid.

EARLY WYNN HOMERS LATE, WINS ONE-HITTER

MAY 1, 1959
CHICAGO WHITE SOX 1, BOSTON RED SOX 0

By Scott Ferkovich

In December 1957 the Chicago White Sox and the Cleveland Indians got together for a headline-making trade. Popular Cuban-born outfielder Minnie Miñoso was sent packing to the Tribe, along with utility infielder Fred Hatfield. For Miñoso, a five-time All-Star who had turned 32 just days before the deal, it was a homecoming of sorts; he had played a handful of games with the Indians to begin his big-league career. Chicago, meanwhile, landed a couple of All-Stars, one young, the other not so much. Twenty-nine-year-old Al Smith could play all three outfield positions as well as third base. Smith (who had played with the Cleveland Buckeyes of the Negro American League in 1946-48) would bring his solid bat and athleticism to the Windy City. Joining him was another big name, an anchor on one of the greatest pitching staffs the game had ever seen.

Early Wynn was a bulldog on the mound, a take-no-prisoners right-hander who did not hesitate to use the occasional brushback pitch if he felt it gave him an edge. Throughout his career, Wynn struggled with his control, which did not hurt his intimidation factor. He had been a promising, hard-throwing youngster with the lowly Washington Senators, but his fortunes changed when he was traded to the Indians after the 1948 season. In the early 1950s Cleveland abounded in great starting pitchers, but was a perennial bridesmaid to the powerhouse New York Yankees from 1951 to 1953. Finally, in 1954, under skipper Al Lopez, the Tribe won 111 games to capture the American League pennant by eight games over New York. Much of the success came on the strength of its five aces: Wynn (23 wins), Mike Garcia (19), Bob Lemon (23), Art Houtteman (15), and Bob Feller (13). But the Indians were swept by the New York Giants in the World Series.

Wynn won 20 or more games four times with Cleveland (1951, 1953, 1954, 1956). Nevertheless, at the time of his trade to the White Sox, he was fast approaching 38 years of age, coming off an unspectacular campaign in which he had won 14 and lost 17, with an unsightly 4.31 earned-run average. Despite his being reunited with Lopez, who was now skippering the White Sox, Wynn's first summer in Comiskey Park in 1958 was more of the same: 14 wins, 16 losses, and a 4.13 ERA, although he made his fifth All-Star Game appearance.

On the bright side, the 1959 White Sox looked like a team heading in the right direction. After half a decade of being the third-best squad in the AL after New York and Cleveland, Chicago had finished a distant second behind the Yanks each of the previous two seasons. Creating a buzz on Chicago's South Side was new owner Bill Veeck, an iconoclast known as much for his promotional genius as for his eye for talent. The White Sox did not have much offense. They featured solid pitching and fielding, however, and Lopez insisted to Veeck that the team was good enough to win. A lot hinged on what kind of contribution they could get from the geriatric Wynn.

Hoping for a comeback season, Wynn started 1959 well enough, with a complete-game victory against the Tigers in which he gave up only one earned run. He proceeded to get hit hard in his next three starts, including a dreadful game in Kansas City in which he gave up six earned runs in less than two innings to the doormat Athletics (but did not figure in the decision).

By May 1, Wynn's ERA was 6.14. He was scheduled to face the Red Sox that evening at Comiskey. Boston would be without the services of slugger Ted Williams, who was recovering from a stiff neck suffered in spring training. Although they were playing under .500, the Red Sox lineup still featured Pete Runnels, Vic Wertz, Jackie Jensen, and Frank Malzone. They were no pushovers. Chicago, in second place with a record of 10-6, was only a game behind the Indians.

With one out in the top of the first inning, Wynn stepped off the mound and gestured toward his shortstop, Luis Aparicio. Only two days removed from his 23rd birthday, Aparicio was a slick-fielding Venezuelan, an All-Star in 1958, and one of the rising stars in the game. Apparently, Wynn wanted Aparicio to take a few steps to his right. The positioning struck Aparicio as odd, given that the left-handed-hitting Runnels was due up. A classic singles hitter, Runnels had a great eye at the plate. A two-time .300 hitter, he was also riding a hot bat.

Aparicio, against his better judgment, moved slightly to his right. Moments later, Runnels hit a sharp grounder that eluded Aparicio's outstretched glove just to the left of the second-base bag. As the ball bounded into center field, Aparicio was convinced that had he not listened to Wynn, he would have gobbled up the ball and thrown Runnels out easily.

To the fans still shuffling in, it was just an innocuous-looking base knock. Wynn struck out the next batter, and White Sox catcher Sherm Lollar gunned down Runnels trying to steal second. Runnels' seeing-eye single, however,

At the age of 39, Early Wynn won an AL-best 22 games in 1959, helping the Go Go Sox to the pennant, and won the AL Cy Young Award. The Hall of Famer went 300-244 in parts of 23 big-league seasons. (Photo by Mark Rucker/Transcendental Graphics, Getty Images)

proved more significant as the game progressed.

Wynn was not at his best. Six times, he walked either the first or the second man in an inning (the second, third, fifth, sixth, and seventh). In the fifth, he issued back-to-back free passes after the first out. Through guile, however, along with a dizzying assortment of sliders, curves, and the occasional knuckleball, Wynn kept the Red Sox off-balance, fending off further trouble.

Wynn's mound opponent, veteran righty Tom Brewer, was pitching a very strong game. At age 27, the South Carolinian was, like Wynn, looking for a bounce-back year. An All-Star in 1956 when he won 19 games, Brewer was coming off a lackluster 12-12 campaign. Both pitchers exchanged zeros, but the Red Sox threatened in the top of the eighth. Don Buddin worked a leadoff walk, advancing to second on a wild pitch. After a fly to deep right, Buddin scampered to third. Wynn settled down, however, striking out the next two batters.

In the bottom of the eighth, Wynn was scheduled to bat leadoff. One of the better-hitting pitchers throughout his career, he had already collected a double in the game. He took two quick balls, then a strike, before lifting a high drive to left field. It was deep, but playable, for Bill Renna. At the base of the wall, Renna timed his leap, reached … and the ball bounced off his glove into the waiting hands of one Bobby Sura, a 16-year-old from the nearby town of Argo.[1] Wynn's home run, his first of the season and the 15th of his career, put Chicago up, 1-0.

Wynn set the Red Sox down in order in the ninth, including a game-ending strikeout of Renna. That gave Wynn 14 K's in the game (a career high), increasing his lifetime total to 1,849, the most among all active pitchers. After the first-inning hit by Runnels, Wynn did not allow another (although he walked seven). It was the second and final one-hitter of his career, the closest he ever came to a no-hitter. Later, in the clubhouse, Wynn admitted that he should never have directed Aparicio to reposition himself. "If I hadn't, he would have fielded it easily," he said. "After the game, Looey told me he'd never listen to me again."[2]

Brewer, the Boston pitcher, was equally parsimonious, surrendering only five hits and one walk in going the distance. He wound up with a 10-12 record in 1959, coupled with a 3.76 ERA. Shoulder problems ultimately forced him from the game at 29.

The victory was the 252nd of Wynn's career. Only Warren Spahn had tossed more shutouts among active moundsmen (45 to 38). Wynn would finish out his Hall of Fame career in 1963 with an even 300 victories.

The 13,000-plus in attendance savored the early-season highlight, a rousing start to the Veeck Era. The game helped kick-start a fantastic season for Wynn, who led the majors in wins (22), and the AL in starts (37) and innings pitched (255⅔). He also topped all of baseball in walks (119) for the second time. Wynn won the Cy Young Award in a landslide, back at a time when it was given to the single best pitcher in the major leagues.[3] The White Sox, meanwhile, soon earned the nickname [4]"The Hitless Wonders," riding their strong pitching and fielding all the way to the 1959 World Series, only to fall to the Los Angeles Dodgers in six games.

SOURCES

In addition to the sources mentioned in the notes, the author consulted Baseball-Reference.com and Retrosheet.org.

NOTES

1 Richard Dozer, "Wynn Wins 1-Hitter, 1-0, on Own Homer," *Chicago Tribune*, May 2, 1959.

2 Munzel, "Hats Off…!" *Sporting News*, May 13, 1959.

3 So who got the better of the trade? Wynn went 28-29 for Chicago over the next three seasons before being released, his career win total stuck at 299. He returned to Cleveland to pick up his 300th victory. Al Smith batted .276 in his five seasons in Chicago, including an All-Star Game appearance in 1960. He is most famous for the photograph taken of him in the 1959 World Series: Standing with his back to the Comiskey Park wall on a Charlie Neal home run, Smith is doused on the head when an excited fan accidentally spills a cup of beer on him. Fred Hatfield collected only one hit in his Indians career, and while Minnie Miñoso had two fine seasons in Cleveland, his stay was short-lived, as the Tribe dealt him back to the White Sox after the 1959 campaign.

4 The sobriquet was first applied to the 1906 White Sox, who won the AL pennant despite a team batting average of only .230, then captured the World Series from the crosstown Cubs, whose .763 season winning percentage still stands as the best in the majors.

WHITE SOX CLOBBER DODGERS IN FALL CLASSIC KICKOFF

OCTOBER 1, 1959
CHICAGO WHITE SOX 11, LOS ANGELES DODGERS 0
GAME ONE OF THE WORLD SERIES

By Russ Lake

After a 40-year drought, the Chicago White Sox clinched the American League pennant on September 22, 1959, with a 4-2 victory in Cleveland. Sirens were activated in Chicago to announce the significant baseball happening. The long-wailing scream pierced the night and frightened many sleepy residents who thought the city was under nuclear attack. Mayor Richard Daley dismissed questions of a federal probe for the unintended commotion by explaining that the city council had authorized the sirens. Daly added joyfully, "This is a great night in the history of Chicago."[1] An energetic fandom topping 25,000 apparently agreed with the mayor as they assembled at Midway Airport for the 2:05 A.M. arrival of the team plane. One homemade sign proclaimed that White Sox manager Al Lopez should be considered for president of the USA.[2]

The traditional midweek start of the World Series would have to wait an extra day because the Milwaukee Braves and the Los Angeles Dodgers were engaged in a best-of-three playoff to determine the winner of the National League pennant. The Dodgers swept the series, two games to none. They used eight pitchers during the pair of one-run triumphs, so manager Walter Alston had to sort out his staff before naming a Game One starter.

With a complement of rested hurlers, Lopez enjoyed some luxury as he chose veteran right-hander Early Wynn, who at 39 had led the AL with 22 victories, to start for the White Sox. Alston selected righty Roger Craig, who sported a 5-0 record during the dramatic pennant drive beginning on August 30. The 29-year-old Craig had a World Series record of 1-1 from Dodgers postseasons in 1955 and 1956 when the team represented Brooklyn. Pitching for the Cleveland Indians, Wynn started and lost the second game of the 1954 World Series.

On Thursday, October 1, some White Sox ushers found that their morning coffee routine might bar them from getting to their assigned gates since the entry access was locked to control crowds.[3] Ticket scalpers were plentiful, and one man carrying equipment and dressed in work clothes was turned away as a "gate-crasher" with a phony story that he needed to get to the office of team President Bill Veeck to repair an electrical circuit.[4] Four Chicago policewomen were on duty to watch for female pickpockets in the ballpark.[5]

Outside the ballpark, restaurants and cart suppliers "made a killing" by raising their prices for food and beverages. However, all merchandise costs inside the ballpark remained the same except for the game program which sold for a half-dollar instead of 15 cents.[6] Ever the showman, Veeck had 20,000 red roses handed

THE BASE BALL PALACE OF THE WORLD

In December 1958 Bill Veeck was the head of a group that purchased controlling interest in the Chicago White Sox. In 1959 skipper Al Lopez led the Pale Hose to their first pennant in 40 years. (Photo by Mark Rucker/Transcendental Graphics, Getty Images)

out to the women in the crowd. The White Sox explained the absence of traditional postseason bunting in the ballpark by saying they wanted the fans to see the interior just as it was during the season. Veeck also decided to have his players wear white stockings with black stripes for the first time in years and added that this had been suggested "by at least 500 letter writers this season."[7] A crowd of 48,013 moved toward their seats to get settled for baseball on a crisp and cool day. Vendors were ordered to peddle their wares without blocking the patrons' view of the game.[8] Singer-actor Tony Martin sang the National Anthem while the crowd gazed upon an American Flag that had stuck at half-staff because of a pulley problem on the hoist.[9]

The White Sox took the field as the fans roared to encourage their team. The starting battery of Wynn and Sherm Lollar waited while an honorary first pitch was delivered by 1917 White Sox world champion heroes Urban "Red" Faber and Ray Schalk. Dodgers switch-hitter Junior Gilliam stepped into the left-hand batter's box for the symbolic delivery.[10] Faber's "spitter" to Schalk was clearly outside, but plate umpire Bill Summers emphatically signaled a strike.[11] The game begun, Gilliam grounded a 1-and-2 pitch to shortstop Luis Aparicio who fielded the sphere cleanly and fired to first baseman Ted Kluszewski for the out. Charlie Neal knocked a one-out single off the glove of third baseman Billy Goodman. Neal stole second and Duke Snider walked. Wynn escaped the jam when Norm Larker lined out to right fielder Jim Rivera.[12]

Craig started out with a curve for a called strike before Aparicio popped up to shortstop Maury Wills. Nellie Fox walked and took a large lead from first base. During the regular season, the "Go-Go Sox" were tops in the American League in stolen bases. Dodgers catcher Johnny Roseboro called for a pitchout and Fox dived safely back to the bag.[13] Fox raced to third on a single to right-center by Jim Landis. No stranger to the National League and having had great past success versus Craig, the left-handed-batting Kluszewski drilled a groundball single past the lunge of first baseman Gil Hodges. Second baseman Neal dived for the ball, but came up empty; Fox came home and Landis scampered to third. The White Sox tally was the first postseason run recorded by the franchise since October 9, 1919. Landis came across to make it 2-0 after Lollar swatted a long drive to right-center that Larker gloved on the run.[14] (The opening excitement was too much for 62-year-old George Thielmann of Cary, Illinois, who collapsed in his box seat of a heart attack and died.[15])

Both hurlers retired the side in order in the second. Wynn completed another 1-2-3 inning in the top of the third after Neal's long two-out blast to left field barely hooked foul. In the bottom half, Craig retired his fifth consecutive batter before Fox lined a double into the right-field corner. Landis followed with another safety and plated Fox for the White Sox' third run. Kluszewski kept the Chicago fans on their feet by lofting a slider to deep right. The ball, aided by a crosswind, had just enough air under it to drop into the first row of the stands for a two-run homer and increase the White Sox lead to 5-0.[16] Alston pulled Craig and brought in right-hander Chuck Churn.

Lollar followed with a routine fly ball to left-center. The din of the crowd kept left-fielder Wally Moon and Snider from hearing each other,[17] and the outfielders collided. The ball was jarred from Snider's grasp and Lollar slid safely into second.[18] Goodman singled Lollar home, and Al Smith doubled to left-center over Moon's outstretched glove. As Snider chased down the ball, Goodman held up at third, but then he raced home and Smith dashed to third on Snider's errant throw to second. Rivera hit a grounder to second baseman Neal, whose throw home glanced off Rivera's bat in front of the plate and past Roseboro for the Dodgers' third error of the inning.[19] Smith scored and Rivera moved to second. Pitcher Wynn doubled to left-center to drive in Rivera with the seventh run of the inning. The White Sox sent 11 hitters to the plate and turned the opener into a 9-0 laugher.

In the bottom of the fourth, Kluszewski boomed his second home run of the afternoon with Landis on first after his third single for an 11-0 advantage. "Big Klu" sent a hanging curve from Churn down the right-field line, where it hit the facade of the upper deck and dropped to the field.[20] Alston removed Churn for right-hander Clem Labine, and later employed southpaw Sandy Koufax and righty Johnny Klippstein, who all quieted the South Siders' bats and kept the large Chesterfield scoreboard from displaying additional Chicago tallies.

Lopez stayed with Wynn until Gilliam's eighth-inning single. Wynn said his right elbow was stiffening,[21] so right-hander Gerry Staley relieved him and induced Neal to ground into a twin killing. Staley allowed two hits in the ninth, but Kluszewski saved the shutout with a nifty stab of Roseboro's smash and throw to Aparicio for a force play and the second out.[22] Pinch-hitter Carl Furillo then flied out to left to end the game in 2:35. The White Sox had 11 runs, 11 hits, and no errors; for the Dodgers it was no runs, eight hits, and three errors.

The "Main Man" in the victorious clubhouse was Ted Kluszewski, who had three hits, five RBIs, and nine total bases. A sportswriter asked the native of nearby Argo, Illinois, "What's Argo?" Kluszewski laughed and said, "Throw that guy out of here!"[23] Dodgers manager Alston moaned, "We had the Chicago speed figured out, but nobody told us about all this power."[24]

Later in the evening, Broadway odds-makers made the White Sox 9-to-5 favorites to win the World Series.[25]

SOURCES

In addition to the sources cited in the Notes, the author also accessed Retrosheet.org, Baseball-Reference.com, Newspapers.com, SABR.org/bioproj, and **The Sporting News** archive via Paper of Record.

THE BASE BALL PALACE OF THE WORLD

NOTES

1. Edward Prell, "White Sox Win Pennant, Riotous Welcome; Sirens Scare City," **Chicago Tribune**, September 23, 1959: 1.

2. Ibid.

3. "A Tough Cop Guards Gate at Sox Park," **Chicago Tribune**, October 2, 1959: 3.

4. George Bliss, "World Series Usher in 1938 Hits Top in '59," **Chicago Tribune**, October 2, 1959: 2.

5. "A Tough Cop."

6. Ibid.

7. "Veeck Gets Even With Perini," **Chicago Tribune**, October 2, 1959: 55-56.

8. "A Tough Cop."

9. Dave Condon, **The Go Go Chicago White Sox** (New York: Coward-McCann, Inc., 1960), 185.

10. Condon, 182 (photo caption).

11. "Veeck Gets Even."

12. Condon, 185.

13. Video Production, **Baseball Classics, 1959 World Series** (Rare Sportsfilms, Inc., 2000).

14. Ibid.

15. "Executive, 62, Dies at Game as Sox Take Early Lead," **Chicago Tribune**, October 2, 1959: 2.

16. Condon, 187.

17. Richard Dozer, "Losers Await New Day; Winners Too," **Chicago Tribune**, October 2, 1959: 55.

18. Video, **Baseball Classics, 1959 World Series**.

19. Ibid.

20. "Sox Crush Dodgers in Opener, 11-0," **Chicago Tribune**, October 2, 1959: 55.

21. Robert Cromie, "Losers Await New Day; Winners Too," **Chicago Tribune**, October 2, 1959: 55.

22. Video, **Baseball Classics, 1959 World Series**.

23. "Two Homers Klu's Greatest Thrill," **Los Angeles Times**, October 2, 1959: 75.

24. "Losers Await": 57.

25. "Revised Odds Say Sox 9-5 Series Favorites," **Chicago Tribune**, October 2, 1959: 55.

DODGERS CLUTCH HOMERS SINK SOX

OCTOBER 2, 1959
LOS ANGELES DODGERS 4, CHICAGO WHITE SOX 3
GAME TWO OF THE WORLD SERIES

By Russ Lake

A swarm of excited White Sox fans converged on the South Side ballpark's neighborhood to wait overnight for the bleacher gate to open at 8 A.M. on Friday, October 2, 1959. Through an intermittent drizzle, they passed the time by watching television, ringing cowbells, and playing bridge.[1] A male foursome from Pearl City, Illinois, even asked for their names to be put in the newspaper, so their spouses would believe they had ventured to the city to attend Game Two of the World Series.[2]

Los Angeles manager Walter Alston had watched the Dodgers lose the Series' first game, 11-0, the day before, and he did not want to go down two games before jetting back to the West Coast. Alston tabbed left-hander Johnny Podres, the pitching hero of the 1955 world champions, to start Game Two. During the regular season, Podres posted a 14-9 mark with a 4.11 ERA. Podres, just turned 28, struggled at the Los Angeles Coliseum, but was 10-4 on the road. White Sox skipper Al Lopez selected 26-year-old Bob Shaw as his starter. The right-hander came of age in '59 with an 18-6 record and 2.69 ERA.

The White Sox slightly adjusted their lineup from Game One. Lefty-swinging third baseman Billy Goodman and right fielder Jim Rivera were replaced by right-handed hitters Bubba Phillips and rookie Jim McAnany, respectively. LA's starting lineup was unchanged.

With Senator John F. Kennedy a guest in Mayor Richard J. Daley's field box,[3] the crowd of 47,368 cheered loudly when the White Sox took the field. Earlier, a steeplejack scaled Comiskey Park's 100-foot center-field flagpole to figure out why the American flag reached only half-staff for Game One. She diagnosed the problem as a defective pulley and repaired it.[4] Nerves got the best of singer Nat King Cole when he erred on the words slightly at the end of the National Anthem. "I realized too late I had made a mistake and I couldn't go back," said Cole.[5]

Shaw retired the first two Dodgers before Wally Moon and Duke Snider stroked consecutive singles. Norm Larker stranded the pair when he lined out to McAnany in right. White Sox leadoff batter Luis Aparicio was kept off the bases the day before, but this time he bounced a double past first base and moved to third on a fly ball to right by Nellie Fox. Jim Landis walked, and rookie right-hander Larry Sherry got up to throw in the Dodgers' bullpen.[6] Ted Kluszewski strolled to the plate accompanied by deafening cheers from the White Sox faithful. He bounced a sure double-play grounder to the right side, but second baseman Charlie Neal bobbled the ball. Neal managed to throw Kluszewski out, but Aparicio sped home with the first run and Landis went to second. Lollar hit a spinning grounder that squibbed past Neal and allowed Landis to race home with another tally.[7] Al Smith smashed a hot shot to shortstop Maury Wills, who fumbled it for an error. Podres got Phillips to ground into an unassisted force out at third to escape the first frame down 2-0.

Both hurlers worked out of two-out trouble in the second inning. The third and fourth proved uneventful with Chicago still in front. The "goose egg" scoreboard indicators were way too familiar for Dodgers veterans. Dating back to October 1956, the proud franchise had zeros displayed in 40 of the past 41 World Series innings. With two down in the top of the fifth, "the worm finally turned" for Los Angeles, accompanied by a "surprise splash." Neal connected off Shaw for a long drive to left. Al Smith backed up against the nine-foot wall only to watch the ball sail into the lower stands for a home run, and ended up drenched in the face by a cup of beer that was inadvertently knocked off the ledge by a first-row fan.[8] The Dodgers now trailed 2-1.

Shaw maintained the slim White Sox advantage until the seventh. With two outs, Alston sent up Chuck Essegian, a former Stanford fullback, to pinch-hit for Podres. Essegian deposited Shaw's 3-and-1 pitch into the left-center-field upper deck to tie the score.[9] Then Shaw walked Jim Gilliam, and Charlie Neal smoked a one-strike pitch deep to center field that was caught by Billy Pierce. The trouble with the slick grab was that Pierce backhanded Neal's blast while warming up in the White Sox bullpen.[10] Neal's second homer of the game put Los Angeles on top for the first time in the Series, 4-2. Shaw was replaced by right-hander Turk Lown, who tamped down the Dodgers' sudden scoring momentum.

In the bottom of the seventh, Alston penciled reliever Sherry into Larker's lineup spot. Ron Fairly entered as the right fielder and would bat ninth, while Don Demeter replaced Duke Snider in center. Sherry retired the top of the lineup with no problem while Chicago's stunned spectators remained silent. Rivera was substituted for McAnany in right field in the eighth, and Lown dispatched the Dodgers in order. The 24-year-old Sherry, called up at midseason from Triple-A St. Paul, had initially been used as a starter. However, armed with a new-found slider, he won headlines as a valued relief specialist.[11]

In the bottom of the eighth, Sherry faced the heart of the White Sox order. Kluszewski started things with a bloop single to center, and Lollar reached when his hard bounder glanced off Gilliam's glove.[12] With a rally brewing, the crowd resurrected its vocal support and foot stomping. Earl Torgeson ran for Kluszewski at second and Lopez decided to play "small ball" to move both runners along. With orders to bunt, Smith fouled a pitch and took a strike before watching three pitches out of the zone.[13] Both runners were moving on the full count when Smith boomed a deep drive to left-center. Torgeson played it past halfway before he headed home after the ball sailed over Moon's head and one-hopped the wall. The slow-footed Lollar momentarily lost sight of Smith's drive and paused briefly at second base.[14]

After hesitating, Lollar ran for third, where coach Tony Cuccinello was waving frantically and yelling, 'Go! Go!' since he was sure Lollar could make it safely home to tie the game. Cuccinello gambled that center fielder Demeter would have to chase Smith's ball down, and that the Dodgers would throw to third to keep the potential winning run at second.[15] But Moon swiftly grabbed Smith's knock on its rebound from the wall, and wheeled to throw a strike to the cutoff man, Wills, in short left. Wills turned and cut loose a relay peg that catcher Johnny Roseboro caught chest-high with Lollar still over 10 feet from home plate. Lollar did not slide and tried to sidestep Roseboro, but the tag was made. Plate umpire Frank Dascoli had an easy call as he signaled the out.[16]

Smith advanced to third base on the throw home, but the Dodgers still held a 4-3 advantage. Goodman struck out as a pinch-batter, and Rivera popped foul to Roseboro to strand the tying run. Los Angeles left a runner on second in its ninth, and Sherry induced groundball outs from pinch-hitter Norm Cash, Aparicio, and Fox to even the series at a game apiece in 2:21.

Line-score numbers showed four runs, nine hits, and one error for the Dodgers and three runs, eight hits, and no errors for the White Sox. Podres was the winning pitcher and Shaw, after allowing three home runs, the loser. Sportswriters surrounded Neal and Essegian to ask about their home run prowess,[17] while Sherry sat relatively calm.[18] Podres said he felt San Francisco and Milwaukee were better teams than the White Sox.[19]

Lopez was slightly ruffled as he described the Dodgers' long-ball attack: "All the home runs came on bad pitches. Bob Shaw was a bit high all day."[20] Cuccinello was on the "hot seat" for sending Lollar home in the eighth, but Lopez backed his coach's decision, saying, "I can't criticize Cooch. It was the right play. It just didn't work."[21]

As he changed clothes, Alston showed reporters that he had mistakenly put on a pair of mismatched socks that morning before leaving for the game. Revealing a superstitious side, he laughed and said, "You can bet I'll wear the same mixed-up pair of socks tomorrow and the next day."[22]

On a sad note, and for the second successive day, a fan was fatally stricken at the ballpark. After complaining of chest pains, Herman Ruschel of Dubuque, Iowa, collapsed and was pronounced dead at Mercy Hospital.[23]

SOURCES

In addition to the sources cited in the Notes, the author accessed Retrosheet.org, Baseball-Reference.com, Newspapers.com, SABR.org/bioproj, and *The Sporting News* archive via Paper of Record.

NOTES

1 Robert Wiedrich, "Sleepy Fans Dance to Band in Bleachers," **Chicago Tribune**, October 3, 1959: 5.

2 Ibid.

3 Photo caption, **Chicago Tribune**, October 3, 1959: 74.

4 "Chicago Mom Climbs Pole to Free Flag at Half-Staff," **The Sporting News**, October 14, 1959: 19.

5 "Singer Flubs National Anthem," **The Sporting News**, October 14, 1959: 19.

6 Dave Condon, **The Go Chicago White Sox** (New York: Coward-McCann, Inc., 1960), 191.

7 Video Production, **Baseball Classics, 1959 World Series** (Rare Sportsfilms, Inc., 2000).

8 Ibid.

9 Ibid.

10 Ibid.

11 Ralph Berger, Larry Sherry biography, SABR BioProject, sabr.org/bioproj/person/8d3f9b7e.

12 "Neal's Pair of Homers Paces Dodgers to Comeback Win," **The Sporting News**, October 14, 1959: 19.

13 Ibid.

14 Video Production, **Baseball Classics, 1959 World Series**.

15 Robert Cromie, "Cuccinello Signaled Lollar, 'All the Way,'" **Chicago Tribune**, October 3, 1959: 1.

16 Video Production, **Baseball Classics**.

17 Frank Finch, "Team Returns After Tieing Series," **Los Angeles Times**, October 3, 1959: 1.

18 Photo caption, "Having a Ball," **Chicago Tribune**, October 3, 1959: 28.

19 "Podres Isn't Impressed by White Sox," **Chicago Tribune**, October 3, 1959: 28.

20 Dave Condon, "In the Wake of News," **Chicago Tribune**, October 3, 1959: 28.

21 **The Go Go Chicago White Sox**, 194.

22 **The Sporting News**, October 14, 1959: 19.

23 Ibid.

DODGERS WIN THEIR FIRST WORLD SERIES AS THE LOS ANGELES DODGERS

OCTOBER 8, 1959
LOS ANGELES DODGERS 9, CHICAGO WHITE SOX 3
GAME SIX OF THE WORLD SERIES

By Alan Cohen

"I guess maybe I was a little hasty, but I had complete confidence in Sherry."

— Walter Alston, October 8, 1959.[1]

"I told Joe Becker, our pitching coach, that I felt real good, ready to pitch four or five innings. I never dreamed, actually, that I'd have to go that long."

— Larry Sherry, October 8, 1959.[2]

In 1959 Chicago's Comiskey Park saw its first World Series since the ill-fated Black Sox of 1919. The Go-Go Sox faced the Los Angeles Dodgers, who were just two years earlier domiciled in Brooklyn. In their first year in Los Angeles, they had stumbled to a seventh-place finish. Now they were on the precipice of becoming the first team to finish as low as seventh place in one season and win the World Series the next year. The White Sox were built on speed and the Dodgers were a blend of the old power merchants from Ebbets Field and the new speedsters that would come to define the Los Angeles Dodgers. The Dodgers led, three wins to two, as the Series moved back to Comiskey Park for Game Six on October 8.

After three games in front of more than 92,000 fans in the Los Angeles Coliseum, Game Six was played in front of 47,653 spectators.

The field was drenched in sunshine as the game began. Johnny Podres, who had won the clincher in the Dodgers' first World Series win in 1955, was given the opportunity to bring the Dodgers another championship. Chicago's hopes of extending the Series were entrusted to veteran pitcher Early Wynn, pitching on two days' rest after being knocked out of the box in the third inning of Game Five.

"It was a fast ball away from me. As he always does (Early Wynn) was putting 'em in and out. (My swing) had that good feel to it. When you hit a ball real good, you don't feel the contact."

— Duke Snider, October 8, 1959.[3]

The Dodgers broke out on top in the third inning when after a two-out walk to Wally Moon, Duke Snider homered to left-center field. The Duke of Flatbush in two seasons at the spacious Coliseum had been shown to be a mortal insofar as his home-run production had been concerned, and he had acquired a new nickname — the Silver Fox. Nursing an ailing knee, he had not played in the three games in Los Angeles, and asked manager Alston to put him in the lineup for Game Six. After the game, Snider said, "I don't know why I did it, but I'm glad I did. And Walt said, 'okay.' So here I am."[4] Snider's blast in Game Six was his 11th in World

Hall of Fame second baseman Nellie Fox played 14 seasons with the White Sox, earned 15 All-Star berths, led the AL in hits four times, and was named AL MVP in 1959, helping the Go Go Sox to the pennant. (Photo Reproduction by Transcendental Graphics/Getty Images)

Series competition, tying him for second most all-time. The two RBIs put him atop all National League players in the World Series.

Podres kept the White Sox off the board and the Dodgers broke the game open with six runs in the fourth inning. Norm Larker opened the inning with a single and pinch-runner Don Demeter advanced to second on Johnny Roseboro's sacrifice. A single by Maury Wills and a double by Podres increased the lead to 4-0 and chased Wynn from the mound. Relief pitcher Dick Donovan was not the answer. A walk to Junior Gilliam and a two-run double by Charlie Neal were followed by a two-run homer into the right-field stands off the bat of Wally Moon. Neal's double was one of 10 hits in the series for the Los Angeles second baseman, tying the Dodgers' own World Series hit record. With the score 8-0 and only one out in the inning, Turk Lown came on for the White Sox and although he allowed Gil Hodges' infield hit, he prevented further scoring.

The speedy White Sox were not without power. Ted Kluszewski, whose bulging muscles had led to uniform modifications when he played for Cincinnati and Pittsburgh, was acquired by the White Sox in late August and had played in 31 games for Chicago. In this first World Series, the first baseman had singled and hit a pair of homers in his first three at-bats to lead Chicago to an 11-0 win in Game One.

In Game Six, trailing 8-0, the White Sox had six innings to salvage the game and force Game Seven. In their half of the fourth inning, Nellie Fox popped up to lead off and Podres appeared to have an aura of invincibility. But then he couldn't find home plate. He hit Jim Landis in the head with a pitch and walked Sherman Lollar. That brought up Kluszewski, who was 7-for-20 in the Series to that point. Big Klu's three-run homer put a modest dent in the Dodgers lead and, after Podres issued a walk to Al Smith, manager Walter Alston decided to bring on Larry Sherry.

Kluszewski's homer had set the record for RBIs in a six-game World Series. His three RBIs gave him 10 for the Series and broke the record of eight shared by Bob Meusel and Billy Martin. The runs would be the last scored by the White Sox in 1959.

Sherry, a native of Los Angeles, had not been on the Dodgers' Opening Day roster. After appearing in five games at the beginning of 1958 and posting an ERA of 12.46, he was sent back to Triple-A and rejoined the Dodgers on July 4, 1959. He went 7-2 with three saves. He had appeared in each of the Dodgers' three wins in the first five games of the Series, saving two and winning one. In seven innings, he had given up four hits and allowed only one run.

The right-hander, after allowing a single to Bubba Phillips that put runners at the corners, worked his way out of the inning, but not without an anxious moment or two. With runners on first and third, White Sox manager Al Lopez called upon Billy Goodman to pinch-hit for left fielder Jim McAnany. Sherry struck out Goodman for the second out of the inning and then Lown was removed for pinch-hitter Earl Torgeson. Sherry fell behind Torgeson and Dodgers coach Chuck Dressen took issue with the calls of home-plate umpire Frank Dascoli. First-base umpire Ed Hurley told Dressen to shut up, and Dressen came out of the dugout to discuss matters with Hurley. As Dressen said afterward, "I told him to shut up and he chased me." Dressen became the third man ever ejected from a World Series game.[5] Torgeson wound up walking to load the bases, but Sherry avoided further damage by getting Luis Aparicio to pop out on the first pitch for the stanza's final out.

Gerry Staley took the mound for the White Sox in the fifth inning and pitched three scoreless innings. However, the White Sox were unable to mount a serious threat against Sherry. Billy Pierce pitched a scoreless eighth for Chicago, stranding two runners after allowing singles by Sherry (who went 2-for-2 at the plate) and Neal. Left-hander Pierce had been used sparingly in the Series as manager Al Lopez elected to go with right-handed starters in each of the games.

The White Sox could have mounted a rally in the fifth inning, but Snider, playing on a bad knee, put an end to a budding rally. Nellie Fox led off with a double and Jim Landis stepped in. He sent a fly ball to short center field that Snider caught in full gallop.

The Dodgers tacked on one more run in the ninth inning. Snider was due up, but it was time to give his injured knee a rest. Chuck Essegian, batting for Snider, hit his second pinch-homer of the Series, becoming the first player to hit two pinch-hit homers in a World Series. It came off the fifth Chicago pitcher, Ray Moore, and made the final score 9-3. The Dodgers had banged out 13 hits in securing the win. In the bottom of the ninth, Snider's spot in the outfield was taken by rookie Ron Fairly.

In the bottom of the ninth inning, Sherry retired the side in order and when Dodgers left fielder Wally Moon corralled a fly ball off the bat of Aparicio, the Dodgers were the champions and Sherry had secured his status as the World Series MVP with two wins and two saves in four appearances.

Three thousand miles east of Los Angeles, there wasn't much enthusiasm for the Dodgers' win at their former home. Ebbets Field was empty, and the wrecking ball would soon be set in motion. Author Gay Talese said, "Ebbets Field, occasionally used for soccer, was surrounded by closed candy stores, rotting hot dog stands, and people who no longer care so much for the Dodgers."[6]

But Los Angeles was ecstatic. The large crowds at the Coliseum contributed to a record attendance for a World Series — 420,784. The record still stood in 2018. By 1963, when the Dodgers next played in the Series, they were in a new ballpark in Chavez Ravine, Dodger Stadium.

SOURCES

In addition to Baseball-Reference.com and the sources cited in the notes, the author used:

Associated Press. "Series Success Climaxes Uphill Fight for Sherry," **Hartford Courant**, October 9, 1959: 27.

Drebinger, John. "Dodgers Win World Series by Beating White Sox, 9-3, in the Sixth Contest," **New York Times**, October 9, 1959: 1, 33.

NOTES

1. Bill Lee, "Dodgers Rout Chisox to Win Series," **Hartford Courant**, October 9, 1959: 25.
2. Bill Lee, "With Malice Toward None," **Hartford Courant**, October 9, 1959: 25.
3. Associated Press, "'Old' Dodger Duke Snider ignored Bad Knee to Play," **Hartford Courant**, October 9, 1959: 27.
4. Ibid.
5. Lee, "Dodgers Rout Chisox to Win Series," **Hartford Courant**, October 9, 1959: 25.
6. Gay Talese, "Brooklyn Displays Little Enthusiasm as Dodgers Win," **New York Times**, October 9, 1959: 34.

EARLY WYNN GAINS 275TH CAREER VICTORY AS CHISOX ERUPT FOR 21 RUNS

JUNE 26, 1960
CHICAGO WHITE SOX 21, BOSTON RED SOX 7

By Mike Huber

A Sunday afternoon doubleheader at Comiskey Park pitted the hometown Chicago White Sox against the visiting Boston Red Sox. A crowd of 37,281 was on hand to watch the White Sox attempt a four-game sweep of last-place Boston. Just one week earlier (June 19), "the White Sox were encased in gloom"[1] after a four-game losing streak dropped them into fifth place in the American League, a half-game behind the Detroit Tigers. Coming into this doubleheader, though, they had won four of five, with two of the victories coming in walk-off fashion.

Chicago triumphed in the opener, 4-3, behind the five-hit, seven-strikeout pitching of Billy Pierce, who was also credited with two RBIs and a run scored despite going 0-for-3 in the game. In the second game, Boston rookie Tom Borland squared off against Chicago's Early Wynn. The southpaw Borland (0-2, 4.23 ERA) was making just the third start of his major-league career. Wynn (3-6, 4.22 ERA), on the other hand, was in his 20th major-league season, making his 545th start. Wynn was the reigning wins leader in the American League, having posted a 22-10 record in 1959.

Chicago plated two runs in the bottom of the first. After Borland walked Minnie Miñoso with two outs, Roy Sievers drove the ball deep beyond the center-field fence for a two-run home run, his eighth of the season. A wire-service article in the *Baltimore Sun* reported that "the White Sox started fast in the nightcap and kayoed Tom Borland in the second inning."[2] Gene Freese started that inning for the White Sox with a walk. Sherm Lollar singled, advancing Freese to second. Jim Landis hit an RBI single to left. After Wynn popped out to second, Luis Aparicio singled to load the bases and drive in Lollar. Pinky Higgins, Boston's third manager of the season, called to the bullpen and right-hander Jerry Casale relieved Borland. Nellie Fox grounded out to second with Landis scoring on the play. Miñoso doubled to right, driving in Aparicio, and the White Sox quickly led, 6-0.

Wynn had struck out five Boston batters in the first two innings, but in the third the Red Sox scored a run without getting a hit. Wynn walked both leadoff batter Casale and Willie Tasby. Pete Runnels hit a comebacker to Wynn, who turned and threw to second, forcing Tasby out, and Casale moved up a base to third. Vic Wertz hit a fly ball to center, bringing Casale home for Boston's first run of the game to make the score 6-1. Chicago got the run back in its half, when Wynn singled with the bases loaded, driving in Al Smith and making it a 7-1 game.

In the bottom of the fourth, 15 Chicago hitters battered three Boston pitchers, banging out 10 hits that led to 11 runs. It turned out to be Chicago's largest inning of the year.[3] At the time, this was just two runs short of the American League record for runs scored in the fourth inning of a game (set by the White Sox on September 26, 1943, against the Washington Senators, in the first game of a doubleheader). Miñoso led off by depositing his 10th homer deep beyond the fence in left. After Casale retired Sievers but allowed a single to Smith and a double to Freese, his mound duty ended. Dave Hillman came on in relief. He lasted just six hitters and retired only one as Chicago tagged the righty for four runs on four hits and a walk. Hillman retired only one batter, striking out his counterpart Wynn. With two outs in the inning and five runs in, Hillman walked Miñoso to load the bases and then gave way to Billy Muffett. Muffett walked in a run and then gave up two singles and a double, as Chicago scored six more times. At the end of four innings, "Early Wynn had an 18 to 1 no-hitter."[4] (The Red Sox run came on two walks, a grounder, and a sacrifice fly.)

Boston had a mini-rally in the fifth. Doubles by Tasby and Wertz, followed by a Frank Malzone home run well beyond the left-field fence, resulted in three runs. Yet the Red Sox still faced a huge deficit as they now trailed, 18-4.

Muffett stayed on the mound, pitching the final four innings against Chicago. The White Sox got to him for solo runs in the sixth, seventh, and eighth innings. Joe Hicks struck out to start the sixth, but Muffett's pitch went wide of the plate and Hicks scampered safely to first base. He went to third when Rivera singled and then scored on a sacrifice fly by Freese. Landis socked a home run to lead off the seventh (his fifth), and Freese tripled in the eighth, plating Rivera.

Wynn just kept throwing, not worrying about hits or walks. In the top of the eighth, Gary Geiger homered, his fourth of the season. After Bobby Thomson grounded out, Don Buddin hit his sixth round-tripper, making the score 20-6. Boston added its final run in the ninth. Pumpsie Green walked, Wynn's fifth base on balls of the game. Wertz singled. Malzone hit into a 1-4-3 double play, and Green moved to third. Russ Nixon stroked a single into right field, and Green trotted home. Geiger also singled, but when Wynn retired Thomson on a fly ball to right, the game ended, with the score 21-7 in favor of the home team.

In the four-game series against Boston, Chicago's Freese "clobbered Boston pitching for 11 hits in 16 trips, smashed five doubles, two triples, and drove in four runs."[5] He went 3-for-4 in this game, missing hitting for the cycle by a double. He raised his batting average 34 points. In the eight games against Boston to this point in the season, Freese was hammering at a .655 clip (19-for-29) with nine runs driven in.[6]

Each of the four Boston hurlers was tagged for at least four hits and four runs. They combined to strike out eight White Sox batters, while Wynn fanned nine Red Sox batters on his own. The 40-year-old Wynn improved his record for the season to 4-6, and this gave him 275 career wins. Despite allowing seven earned runs (his earned-run average rose to 4.50), Wynn coasted "on the White Sox' biggest splurge this season."[7] By scoring 21 runs, the Chicago batters surpassed their previous high of 13 runs, accomplished two weeks earlier (June 10), also against the last-place Red Sox. Wynn finished the season with 13 victories against 12 defeats. His production then went down; he won eight games in 1961 and only seven in 1962. The future Hall of Famer's 300th and final career win came on July 13, 1963, in a game played at Comiskey Park, and Wynn was pitching for the Cleveland Indians.[8]

For the 1960 season, Chicago definitely had Boston's number, winning 17 of 22 contests. With this sweep, Chicago brought its record to 36-30, good for fourth place in the American League, while Boston fell to 22-42, keeping the Red Sox last. The White Sox were 51-26 at home and a month after this game, they held first place for 10 days, but it wouldn't last, as they ended the season in third place. Boston, meanwhile, was 29-48 on the road for the season and a seven-game win streak at the All-Star break lifted them to seventh place, where they remained for the rest of the season, except for one day (on September 10 they climbed to sixth place).

SOURCES

In addition to the sources mentioned in the notes, the author consulted Baseball-Reference.com and Retrosheet.org.

NOTES

1. Edward Prell, "Pierce, Wynn Complete Sweep of Boston Series," **Chicago Tribune**, June 27, 1960: 55.

2. "Yanks and Indians Split; White Sox Win Twin Bill," **Baltimore Sun**, June 27, 1960: 15.

3. "White Sox Whip Red Sox, 21-7, After 4-to-3 Triumph in Opener," **New York Times**, June 27, 1960: 29.

4. Prell.

5. Ibid.

6. For the season, Freese played in 16 games against the Red Sox, batting .500 (32-for-64) and slugging .828 with an on-base percentage of .528 (giving an OPS of 1.356).

7. "White Sox 21, and BoSox 7!" **Detroit Free Press**, June 27, 1960: 35.

8. The White Sox released Wynn on November 20, 1962, with a career record of 299-242. He signed with the Cleveland Indians on June 21, 1963, and earned that milestone victory against the White Sox. Cleveland released him after the 1963 season and Wynn retired.

MONBO WAS UNHITTABLE

AUGUST 1, 1962
BOSTON RED SOX 1, CHICAGO WHITE SOX 0

By Gregory H. Wolf

It was an unlikely time for the best game in Bill Monbouquette's career. An emerging star and fan favorite, the Boston Red Sox' 25-year-old right-handed local boy from Medford, Massachusetts, entered the 1962 campaign with a 38-36 career slate but hit a rough patch in July after earning his second All-Star berth. "I've been lousy the last three or four times out," he said.[1] That was an understatement. In his last four starts, Monbo, as teammates and Hub sportswriters called him, had been shelled for 25 hits and 15 earned runs in just 10⅔ innings. Batterymate Jim Pagliaroni noted that he was "having trouble with his pitching rhythm,"[2] while the hurler himself blamed one of his signature pitches, "My curve ball has been getting me in trouble a lot this year."[3] To top it off, Ralph Houk, manager of the AL All-Star squad, dropped him from the season's second All-Star game, on July 30.[4] "I was so bad," quipped Monbo, "I wasn't sore."[5]

Skipper Pinky Higgins's eighth-place Red Sox (46-56) were reeling when they arrived in Chicago to resume play after the second All-Star break. They had lost 12 of their last 15 games, trailed the front-running New York Yankees by 16½ games, and looked to Monbo (8-10, 4.58 ERA) to break out of his slump. The Pale Hose were in unusual territory. They had strung together 11 winning seasons, the last five under current pilot Al Lopez; however, a recent 5-8 skid had dropped them under .500 (52-53) and into sixth place. Toeing the rubber for the White Sox was 42-year-old future Hall of Famer Early Wynn, in search of his 298th career victory. Just 5-7 (4.55) thus far in '62, Gus had fired a five-hit shutout in his last outing, on July 24 against the Senators in Washington, in what proved to be his 49th and final career whitewashing.

A robust crowd of 17,185 packed Comiskey Park on the South Side of the Windy City on a gorgeous Wednesday evening with mild temperatures in the low 70s. Just two days earlier, the city's North Side team, the Cubs, had hosted the All-Star game at Wrigley Field. While that game featured 20 combined hits and 13 runs in the AL's dominant 9-4 victory, this one unfolded as a pitchers' duel. After all six batters were retired in the opening frame, Wynn worked around a two-out single to Lou Clinton and a free pass to Frank Malzone in the second.

In the bottom of the second, Charlie Maxwell connected on a Monbouquette fastball, sending a careening liner to the right corner. Outfielder Clinton made what sportswriter Richard Dozer described as a leaping catch against the wall.[6] It proved to be the hardest-hit ball of the game and the "closest thing" to a hit.[7] Perhaps stunned by the blast, Monbouquette issued a two-out walk to the next batter, Al Smith. "He started to chase a curve on a 3-2 count and then held up," said Monbouquette.[8] If Monbo had a weakness, it was control. The previous season, he had walked 100 batters (3.8 per 9 innings). In this game, however, Monbo's control was outstanding. He reached a 3-and-2 count only one other time, when he fanned Jim Landis to end the fifth.

In a performance described by Boston sportswriter Bob Holbrook as "truly brilliant," Monbouquette overpowered the White Sox.[9] After walking Smith, he set down 22 consecutive batters. He had command of his entire arsenal from the game's outset and kept the White Sox off balance. "At the start I was throwing a lot of curves," said Monbo about the first few innings, "but at the end it was all just fastballs and sliders."[10] The White Sox hit only seven balls to the outfield all afternoon. In the sixth, second baseman Billy Gardner sprinted to the outfield grass in short right to snare Sherm Lollar's "fast-falling blooper" to keep the no-hitter intact.[11]

Monbouquette knew all too well that a scratch hit could derail not just a no-hitter, but also a game. On May 9, he had flirted with a no-hitter for the first time in his big-league career, holding the Yankees hitless for 6⅓ innings until Tom Tresh bunted for a single. After an error and walk loaded the bases, Elston Howard cleared them with a double and Moose Skowron added an RBI single to collar Monbouquette with the loss.

Monbo faced a different challenge in this game: the old-timer Wynn, who debuted in the majors in 1939. Through seven innings, Wynn had matched zeros with Monbouquette, yielding just five hits. He escaped a jam in the fifth after Monbouquette and Gardner led off the frame with singles. Gus seemed to dodge another potential jam in the eighth when Gary Geiger led off with a walk, but was caught stealing for the second out. After Pagliaroni singled to left, the Red Sox and Monbouquette caught a break. Pete Runnels, en route to winning his second AL batting crown in three seasons and fresh off a pinch-hit home run in the All-Star Game, hit a blooper to shallow left. According to the *Chicago Tribune*, perennial All-Star shortstop Luis Aparicio was "inches short of making catch."[12] Clinton's third single of the game plated Pagliaroni for the game's first and only run.

Monbouquette began the ninth just three outs away from becoming the second Red Sox hurler in '62 to author a no-hitter. (Teammate Earl Wilson had held the Los Angeles Angels hitless on June 26 at Fenway Park.) Monbo whiffed Sherm Lollar for the first out while the Comiskey crowd demonstrated its approval by loudly cheering for the visiting hurler, a fact Boston newspapers found astonishing. "Monbouquette was throwing so hard in the late innings," gushed sportswriter Bob Ginsburg of the *Boston Record American*, "that he finished his motion nearly a foot onto the grass beyond the front of the mound on every pitch."[13] With Wynn due to bat, Lopez sent in Nellie Fox to pinch-hit, the last player Monbo wanted to see. "The only guy I was concerned about was Fox — he always manages to get a piece of the ball."[14] One of the game's best contact hitters and among the most difficult to strike out, the former AL MVP was mired in a month-long slump (17-for-96) and grounded weakly to third baseman Frank Malzone. To the plate stepped Aparicio, whose speed (he was en route to leading the AL in stolen bases for the seventh of nine consecutive seasons) made him a threat to beat out any infield grounder. After fouling off the first two pitches, he took what Boston sportswriters thought was a swing, but home-plate umpire Bill McKinley ruled that he had held up. Monbo fired his 10th pitch of the inning, another fastball, and Little Louis swung and missed.[15] Pagliaroni threw off his catcher's mask and raced to Monbouquette on the mound, where they were immediately met by their teammates in a joyous celebration of the no-hitter.

"I've been in baseball since 1930 and I can't remember a better game than that," declared manager Higgins.[16] Monbouquette faced 28 batters, fanned seven, walked one, and did not surrender a semblance of a hit. "He had that easy motion and that good fastball and slider," gushed pitching coach Sal Maglie. "Early in the game he had a good curve and then he switched. ... [T]hey didn't know what to expect."[17] Unsurprised by his batterymate's gem, Pagliaroni attributed Monbouquette's success to perfect mechanics and delivery. "He wasn't falling off the mound like he has been," stated Pags. "He was silky smooth and he got the ball just where he wanted to."[18]

Clinton's clutch hit handed a tough-luck loss to Wynn, whose quest to become the 14th member of the 300-win club would have to wait. He reached a milestone, though, by fanning five to move past Hall of Famer Lefty Grove with 2,272 punchouts. "I had good or better stuff tonight than I've had all year," said Gus, "but he just pitched a better ballgame."[19] Wynn eventually won number 300, but had to wait almost a year to achieve the milestone, and retired after the 1963 campaign with a 300-244 record.

In his next outing, Monbouquette yielded just two runs in eight strong innings against the Washington Senators at Fenway Park, but lost 2-0. His no-hitter helped turn his season around, and he finished with a 15-13 slate. The next season he won 20 games for the first and only time in his career and earned his third and final All-Star berth, but never again flirted with a no-hitter in his major-league career. He posted a 114-112 record and a 3.68 ERA in parts of 11 seasons, retiring after the 1968 campaign.

SOURCES

In addition to the sources mentioned in the Notes, the author consulted Baseball-Reference.com, MLB.com, and Retrosheet.org.

NOTES

1. Bill Liston, "I Never Quit on Myself –Monbo," **Boston Traveler**, August 2, 1962: 34.

2. Bill Liston, "Monbo's Bonus: $1000," **Boston Traveler**, August 2, 1962: 34.

3. Liston, "I Never Quit on Myself — Monbo."

4. From 1959 to 1962, two All-Star Games were played each season.

5. Liston, "I Never Quit on Myself — Monbo."

6. Richard Dozer, "Monbouquette Pitches No-Hit Game," **Chicago Tribune**, August 2, 1932: 73.

7. Ibid.

8. "Clinton's Third Hit Gives Red Sox 1-0 Victory," **Boston Herald**, August 2, 1962: 34.

9. Bob Holbrook, "Fast Ball, Slider Monbo's Big Pitches in No-Hitter," **Boston Globe**, August 2, 1962: 1.

10. Dozer.

11. Ibid.

12. Ibid.

13. Bob Ginsburg, "Going to Bust My Back in 9th — Monbo," **Boston Record American**, August 2, 1962: 38.

14. Henry McKenna, "Monbo Feared Fox in the 9th. Knew He Had No-Hit Game, Reward $1,000," **Boston Herald**, August 2, 1962: 33.

15. Pitch count in 9th inning from Joe Cashman, "Monbo Unfolds No-Hitter, Faces 28 ChiSox in 1-0 Win," **Boston Record American**, August 2, 1962: 16.

16. McKenna.

17. Ibid.

18. Bill Liston, "Monbo's Bonus: $1000."

19. Dozer.

CHISOX TALLY SIX IN ELECTRIFYING GAME-ENDING RALLY

SEPTEMBER 21, 1962
CHICAGO WHITE SOX 7, NEW YORK YANKEES 6

By Richard Riis

Only 825 spectators, the smallest crowd of the season at Comiskey Park, had turned out the night before to see the White Sox score two runs in the eighth and beat Boston, 6-4, but tonight would be different. Tonight the New York Yankees were in town.

The Yankees of 1962 were not the fence-busting juggernaut of 1961 — Roger Maris would launch little more than half the home runs he'd hit while breaking Babe Ruth's record, and Mickey Mantle would miss 39 games with injuries[1] — but they were still the biggest gate attraction in baseball and sitting atop the standings on their way to their 12th AL pennant in 14 seasons. At best, the fourth-place White Sox were hoping to overtake the surprising Los Angeles Angels for the consolation of finishing third. A crowd of 32,711 clicked through the turnstiles at Comiskey Park to watch the Yankees' left-handed ace, Whitey Ford, with a 16-8 won-lost record, take on the White Sox and left-hander Juan Pizarro (12-13).

The weather was cool and damp as the game got underway beneath the lights. Both pitchers were sharp from the start, but a faltering Yankees defense handed Chicago the game's first run when third baseman Clete Boyer booted a grounder,[2] allowing Al Smith to reach first, and Maris let a single by Mike Hershberger go through his legs in right field for a two-base error. Maris subsequently left the game with a strained muscle in his right shoulder[3] and was replaced by Hector Lopez.

Pizarro, meanwhile, retired the first eight Yankees and didn't surrender a base hit until the fourth inning, when Tom Tresh stroked a one-out single to center field. Tresh, on his way to winning AL Rookie of the Year honors, had begun the season as a fill-in while shortstop Tony Kubek was away on military duty and wound up making the All-Star team. Shifted to left field when Kubek returned in August, the switch-hitting Tresh had helped the defending World Series champions remain on top.

Pizarro sent Mantle sprawling with an inside pitch that catcher Cam Carreon thought nicked the batter,[4] allowing Tresh to scramble all the way to third on what was ruled a wild pitch. Mantle dusted himself off to bounce a single up the middle, sending Tresh home with the Yankees' first run.

With Lopez at bat, Mantle broke for second, but Carreon fired a bullet to second baseman Nellie Fox, and Mantle beat a hasty retreat. Fox's peg to Joe Cunningham at first plunked the slugger on the back of the head as he dived safely back to the bag.[5] Mantle, still wearing his batting helmet,[6] was dazed but not seriously hurt, and after a quick inspection by Yankees first base coach Wally Moses,[7] remained in the game. (Fox, entering the game with 64 straight games without an error, extended his streak to 71 before fumbling in the final game of the season to fall short of Bobby Doerr's then-AL

From 1956 through 1962, the dynamic duo of shortstop Luis Aparicio and second sacker Nellie Fox anchored the White Sox infield. The Pale Hose led the AL in fielding percentage in six of those seven seasons. (Photo Reproduction by Transcendental Graphics/Getty Images)

record of 73.[8])

Lopez struck out, Yankees catcher Elston Howard walked, and first baseman Moose Skowron tapped a slow roller past Smith at third for a base hit, scoring Mantle. Howard scored when Boyer lofted a fly to shallow center field that popped out of the glove of a sprinting Jim Landis. Ford flied out to right to end the inning with the score 3-1 Yankees.

The White Sox got back-to-back singles by Landis and Hershberger in the bottom of the fourth, but Ford coaxed fly outs from Fox and Carreon to halt any further threat.

Phil Linz, starting in place of Kubek, on the bench with a virus,[9] singled to open the fifth for New York, then was caught stealing. Tresh bunted to third for a base hit before Pizarro, too, put the Yankees away with no damage done.

Lopez walked to start the sixth, and the skies opened. When play resumed after a 63-minute delay, Skowron deposited a fastball by Pizarro in the left-field deck for his 22nd home run, increasing the Yankees' lead to 5-1.

Ford pitched to two batters in the bottom of the sixth but couldn't get his arm loose after the lengthy delay, and Yankees manager Ralph Houk brought in left-hander Bud Daley, who retired the White Sox.

Pizarro pitched a perfect seventh but was lifted by manager Al Lopez for a pinch-hitter in the bottom of the inning, and John Buzhardt assumed pitching duties for Chicago in the eighth.

Neither team scored in the eighth inning.

In the top of the ninth, Linz singled to center field, stole second, and scored on Tresh's ground-rule double, his third hit of the game, scoring Linz. Mantle drew a walk, and Jack Reed, nicknamed "Mantle's Legs," went in to run for him. Lopez grounded to third, but Smith's throw was wild, loading the bases. Buzhardt induced Howard to end the inning with a fly ball to Landis.

Trailing 6-1 going into the bottom of the ninth, the White Sox "quit playing dead."[10] Fox led off with a single past Linz at short. Carreon followed with a single to left, and Bob Roselli, a utility catcher who'd gotten in only 65 games in five seasons with the Braves and White Sox and was hitting a scant .180, was sent to the plate to bat for Buzhardt. Roselli lined a double to right-center, scoring Fox, but the White Sox, playing cautiously, held Carreon up at third.[11] Ken Berry went in to run for Roselli. Houk brought in another left-hander, Marshall Bridges, who walked Luis Aparicio to load the bases. Cunningham then stroked a double to left, clearing the bases and lifting the surging White Sox to within one run of the Yankees.

After Bridges walked left fielder Floyd Robinson, Houk again went to his bullpen, bringing in right-hander Jim Coates to face the right-handed Al Smith. Smith tried twice to bunt, fouling both to boos from the pumped-up crowd,[12] before lining a double inside the left-field line, scoring Cunningham. The game stood tied, 6-6, with runners on second and third for Chicago.

Grover "Deacon" Jones had been sent to the on-deck circle to hit for Landis, but was called back,[13] and Landis stepped to the plate to accept an intentional walk. Jones then returned to bat for Hershberger. Added to the roster on September 8 after hitting .319 with 26 home runs for Class A Savannah, Jones was nonetheless no raw recruit; at 28, he'd played in the minors since 1955 and set a Midwest League record in 1956 by hitting .409 at Dubuque. Over a drawn-in Yankee outfield,[14] Jones drove a pitch to deep left-center, and Robinson jogged home with the winning run.

The stunning comeback gave Buzhardt, "who apparently leads a charmed life against these Yankees,"[15] his third victory in as many games against New York, and improved his won-lost record to 8-12; Bridges (8-4), who faced three batters in the ninth and failed to get any out, was the loser. Despite winning for the 10th time in their last 12 games, the White Sox stumbled in the final week of the season to finish in fifth place.

"Did you ever see an inning like that?" a reporter asked Houk after the game. "No," the manager said, "and I never hope to see another one like it."[16]

SOURCES

In addition to the sources listed in the notes, the author also consulted:

Chicago Tribune.

Joplin (Missouri) Globe.

Minneapolis Star.

Allentown (Pennsylvania) Morning Call.

Newsday (Garden City, New York).

New York Times.

The Sporting News.

Tampa Tribune.

NOTES

1. Despite playing in only 123 games, Mantle was still voted the American League MVP.

2. Joe Trimble, "Chisox' 6-Run Ninth Beats Yankees, 7-6; Magic No. 3," New York Daily News, September 22, 1962: 26.

3. Ibid.

4. "Sox Rally Beats Yanks in 9th, 7 to 6," Chicago Tribune, September 22, 1962: 70.

5. "Yankee Tough Nut," Chicago Tribune, September 22, 1962: 69.

6. "Sox Yarns," Chicago Tribune, September 22, 1962: 70.

7. Richard Dozer, "Garner 7 to 6 Triumph on 6-Run Rally," Chicago Tribune, September 22, 1962: 69.

8. "Sox Rout Yanks 8-4; Finish in Fifth Place," Chicago Tribune, October 1, 1962: 62.

9. "Sox Rally Beats Yanks in 9th, 7 to 6," Chicago Tribune, September 22, 1962: 70.

10. Dozer.

11. Ibid.

12. Ibid.

13. "Sox Rally Beats Yanks in 9th, 7 to 6."

14. Trimble.

15. Dozer.

16. Trimble.

PATIENT GARY PETERS REGISTERS NEAR-PERFECT GAME

JULY 15, 1963
CHICAGO WHITE SOX 4, BALTIMORE ORIOLES 0

By Richard Cuicchi

It took five major-league seasons for Gary Peters to have a breakout year in his career; but when he finally did, he made the most of it by winning Rookie of the Year honors in the American League. One of the first games that propelled him into the spotlight was a 13-strikeout one-hitter, a near-perfect game, against the Baltimore Orioles on July 15, 1963.

Peters was originally signed by the White Sox organization as a 19-year-old outfielder in 1956. By 1959 he made his major-league debut as a pitcher with the White Sox. He pitched well enough in the minors to earn a late-season call-up to the big-league club for the next two seasons, before he was able to land a spot on the major-league roster coming out of spring training in 1962. He didn't stick with the White Sox that time, pitching in only five games before being sent back to Triple-A Indianapolis for the rest of the season.

The 26-year-old left-hander started the 1963 campaign with the White Sox in a relief role and finally got his first start of the season in an emergency situation on May 6. He was still making relief appearances between sporadic starts. A month later, though, Chicago manager Al Lopez had Peters taking regular turns in the starting rotation. He had a 6-5 record and 2.59 ERA before the game on July 15.

The White Sox, Minnesota Twins, Baltimore Orioles, and Boston Red Sox were locked in a tight race for second place behind the New York Yankees. Only three games in the loss column separated the four teams.

Orioles manager Billy Hitchcock started veteran Robin Roberts, the 36-year-old right-hander with 244 career wins under his belt before the 1963 season. Despite winning four consecutive decisions in May, Roberts had only a 6-8 record coming into the game.

In a night game before 17,764 spectators in Comiskey Park, both teams initially had trouble getting runners on base. Peters yielded a single to Roberts in the bottom of the third, while Roberts gave up three hits through four innings.

It wasn't until the bottom of the fifth inning that any runs were put on the board. The White Sox scored twice on a walk to Ron Hansen followed by a home run into the lower right-field seats by J.C. Martin.

Going into the sixth inning, Peters was locked in on the mound, having struck out seven and yielded just Roberts' hit. The score remained 2-0 until the bottom of the eighth inning, when rookie Tom McCraw hit his third homer of the season, into the right-center-field stands with rookie Pete Ward on base. McCraw had been brought up to the team about five weeks before to replace injured first baseman Joe Cunningham. Hansen and Martin singled, but George Brunet, who relieved Roberts, retired the side by getting Peters to fly out, leaving the score 4-0.

Peters continued to maintain his control and struck out two more Orioles in the ninth to claim the victory. He faced only one batter above the minimum, and struck out 13. He had a three-ball count on only three batters: Bob Johnson in the first inning, Al Smith in the seventh, and John Orsino in the eighth. Only two fly outs were made by White Sox outfielders.[1]

Roberts took his ninth loss of the season, giving up four earned runs on 10 hits and two walks in 7⅔ innings pitched. He pitched three more seasons before retiring in 1966 with 286 career wins and a 3.41 ERA. He was elected to the National Baseball Hall of Fame in 1976.

After the game, Peters remarked about Roberts' hit, which came on a high fastball smacked up the middle that ruined his work of art. "I knew he was a good hitter. … I was trying to get ahead of him, but got the ball too high. Had I succeeded, I would have come in with breaking stuff," Peters said.[2] White Sox second baseman Nellie Fox joked with his teammate in the clubhouse, "I fouled up your no-hitter. I wasn't playing Roberts right."[3]

Lopez commented, "The kid hasn't pitched a bad game all year. As I recall, he lost two of his five games in relief. What makes him good? His fastball tails off. He's got a good slider. Ten of those 13 strikeouts were against right-handers.

Rival manager Hitchcock praised Peters' performance as "terrific, the best-pitched game against us all season." This compliment came after his team had previously defeated left-handed pitchers 20 times during the season.[4]

Roberts' hit prevented Peters from becoming only the ninth pitcher in history to hurl a perfect game. The last perfect game by a White Sox pitcher was thrown by Charlie Robertson on April 30, 1922, against Detroit. The last no-hitter by a White Sox pitcher was by Bob Keegan on August 20, 1957; the next was on September 10, 1967, by Joe Horlen.

Peters had prior experience in the minors with low-hit games. On July 24, 1959, he pitched a no-hitter for Triple-A Indianapolis against Minneapolis, and threw a one-hitter for Indianapolis against Louisville in 1962.[5]

From July 11 to August 29, Peters had a streak of 11 consecutive winning decisions during which he posted an ERA of 1.15 and his opponents had a slash line of .181/.234/.228. He finished the season with a 19-8 record and a league-leading 2.23 ERA. In a retrospective application of advanced metrics, Peters led the league with 150 ERA+ and 2.34 Fielding Independent Pitching (FIP). Peters was voted the AL Rookie of the Year over teammate Pete Ward, who also had a fine season with 22 home runs, 84 RBIs, and a .295 batting average.

Peters' 11-game winning streak set a new rookie record for AL pitchers. It broke the record set in 1926 by Philadelphia A's pitcher Joe Pate and tied by Whitey Ford of the New York Yankees in 1950. The modern major-league record of 12 games was set by George "Hooks" Wiltse of the 1904 New York Giants.[6]

Peters' outstanding pitching in the second half of the season helped the White Sox get separation in the AL standings from the Twins, Orioles, and Red Sox, but they still finished in second place behind the Yankees by 10½ games.

SOURCES

In addition to the sources mentioned in the Notes, the author also consulted:

Armour, Mark. "Gary Peters," SABR BioProject, sabr.org/bioproj/person/28c24b41.

Baseball-Reference.com.

Holtzman, Jerome. "Wrinkled Pale Hose Boast One Smoothie: Gary Peters," The Sporting News, September 7, 1963: 10.

"Peters Proves the Value of Patience," The Sporting News, September 14, 1963: 12.

NOTES

1. Edward Prell, "Lefty Faces Only 28; Roberts Gets Hit," Chicago Tribune, July 16, 1963: 3, 1.
2. Ibid.
3. Douglas Brown, "Hitchcock Calls Mound Job by Peters Best vs. Birds," Baltimore Evening Sun, July 16, 1963: B8.
4. Ibid.
5. Prell.
6. "Peters Breaks Rookie Record," The Sporting News, September 14, 1963: 27.

PITCHING PROPELS WHITE SOX INTO FIRST PLACE

SEPTEMBER 6, 1964
CHICAGO WHITE SOX 3, CLEVELAND INDIANS 2
(13 INNINGS, SECOND GAME OF DOUBLEHEADER)

BY RICHARD RIIS

"There's more of a feeling on this club that we're going to win than there was even in '59," said veteran Jim Landis. "That '59 club had plenty of confidence, don't get me wrong, but this club has better pitching."[1]

Landis, the last member of the 1959 pennant-winning White Sox still with the team, was speaking to reporters on September 5 after Chicago beat Cleveland 8-2 on a six-hit, 10-strikeout performance by Joel Horlen that broke a first-place tie with the Baltimore Orioles, who had fallen to the Los Angeles Angels.

The eight runs were an achievement for the White Sox, and not just because the Indians had arrived in Chicago with victories in 11 of their last 12 games. Seventh in the league in runs scored, the White Sox' punchless lineup featured only one 20-home-run hitter, third baseman Pete Ward, and but one hitter within shouting distance of .300, right fielder Floyd Robinson at .294. At the very bottom of the official AL batting list were a trio of White Sox regulars — left fielder Dave Nicholson at .204, center fielder Landis at .199, and catcher J.C. Martin at .197. The acquisition on July 13 of first baseman Bill Skowron from Washington for first baseman Joe Cunningham and pitcher Frank Kreutzer had helped buoy the lineup. The veteran's timely hitting, steady glove, and experience gained playing for eight pennant winners in New York and Los Angeles contributed to keeping the scrappy White Sox at or near the top of the standings in the heat of a blistering pennant race.

But the White Sox' singular strength was pitching. Horlen, with an 11-8 won-lost record and an ERA of 2.18 after his outing against the Indians, was one of the AL's best trio of starters along with 1963 AL Rookie of the Year Gary Peters, 16-7, 2.43, and Juan Pizarro, 17-7, 2.11. A strong bullpen was anchored by the ageless Hoyt Wilhelm, at 42 and in his 13th season, still one of the game's premier relievers.

The first game of the September 6 twin bill with Cleveland demonstrated the White Sox' all-or-nothing reliance on pitching and pluck and little else. While Chicago hitters struggled to come up with four hits off the Indians' Jack Kralick, Peters had pitched perfect ball through 6⅓ innings only to lose 2-0 on a pair of runs in the ninth.

The second game pitted White Sox right-hander John Buzhardt (10-8) against Indians veteran Dick Donovan (7-7), who had spent six seasons (1955-60) with the White Sox. With Landis out with a leg injury made worse by a collision with an outfield wall two days before, Gene Stephens was inserted at center field, and utilityman Tommy McCraw in left gave Nicholson a rest.

With better baserunning, the Indians might

have won the game in the second inning. After a double to right by slugging left fielder Leon Wagner, catcher Joe Azcue hit a grounder to the mound that caught Wagner between second and third. As Azcue chugged around first, Wagner was chased back to second by Ward, who flipped to second baseman Don Buford. As Buford tagged Wagner on one side of the bag, Azcue slid safely into the other. The next batter, Vic Davalillo, also bounced one to the mound. This time it was Azcue who was trapped off second, thrown out by Buzhardt on a fielder's choice. Billy Moran followed with a double to center field, but Stephens' peg to Martin caught Davalillo at the plate to end the inning. The Indians managed to score in the third, when Woodie Held and Tito Francona hit a pair of doubles to give Cleveland a 1-0 lead.

Floyd Robinson opened the White Sox' half of the fourth with a single to right but was erased on Ward's bouncer to Donovan, who tossed to Dick Howser at short to start a 1-6-3 double play. Skowron drove a pitch over the right-field wall for his 17th home run of the season, tying the game, 1-1.

The Indians struck back in the top of the fifth with a leadoff double by Held, who drew a wild pickoff throw from Martin that allowed him to take third. After a walk to Donovan, Francona flied to right field. Held tagged up and scored to put the Indians ahead, 2-1.

Buzhardt having been lifted for pinch-hitter Jeoff Long in the bottom of the fifth, White Sox skipper Al Lopez sent right-hander Eddie Fisher to the mound for Chicago in the sixth. Fisher pitched two scoreless innings before he, too, was removed for a pinch-hitter. Pitcher Gary Peters, a solid batsman with a .300 average and one homer in pinch-hitting duty, flied out to center field.

With the White Sox still behind a run, 41-year-old knuckleballer Hoyt Wilhelm, who had warmed up by striking out the final Cleveland batter in the opener, came in to pitch in the eighth, retiring the Indians in order.

It was the flying feet of Tommy McCraw that tied the game in the bottom of the eighth for Chicago. McCraw, collecting his third hit of the game, singled to right, stole second, and scored one out later on Robinson's single to center. Robinson was gunned down by Azcue trying to steal second, and the White Sox and Indians entered the ninth inning tied, 2-2. With both Wilhelm and Donovan pitching a scoreless frame, the game proceeded into extra innings.

The Indians threatened in the 10th with a leadoff single to left by Moran, but Wilhelm got Held to hit into a 5-4-3 double play. Wilhelm walked Donovan, then threw a knuckler that catcher Martin couldn't handle, allowing Donovan to advance to second. Francona grounded out to Buford to squelch the threat.

The Indians threatened again in the 11th, Dick Howser taking first on a base on balls, then dashing to second on Fred Whitfield's sacrifice bunt to the mound. Martin let another knuckler from Wilhelm slip through his grasp, and Howser sprinted to third. Wagner, though, flied out to center and Wilhelm got Azcue swinging to allow the White Sox to escape the inning with the score still knotted.

Buford led off the bottom of the 11th with a single, Al Weis coming in to run for Buford. Weis stole second, only to be caught flat-footed when the next batter, Robinson, lined to Whitfield at first. Whitfield fired the ball to Howser, who tagged Weis for the double play.

Weis took Buford's position at second as Wilhelm retired the Indians in order in the top of the 12th. In the bottom of the inning, Skowron led off with his fourth hit of the game before being pulled for a pinch-runner, Mike Hershberger. Stephens' sacrifice bunt to the mound advanced Hershberger to second. Donovan issued his first pass of the game, intentionally, to Ron Hansen, but Martin struck out and Wilhelm flied out to center.

When the White Sox took the field for the 13th inning, Hershberger took Robinson's place in right field, Robinson shifted to left, and McCraw moved in from left field to play first in place of Skowron. In the inning, Cleveland manager

THE BASE BALL PALACE OF THE WORLD

Birdie Tebbetts opted to stick with Donovan, allowing the pitcher to remain in the game. Wilhelm struck out Donovan looking, retiring the Tribe in order once again.

As Chicago came to bat in the bottom of the 13th, the Indians shuffled the team on the field. Max Alvis came in the play third, Held was shifted to left field in place of Wagner, and Chico Salmon took Francona's spot in right. McCraw led off the inning, bunting safely for his fourth hit of the game. With Weis at the plate, McCraw again stole second, then advanced to third when Weis, too, beat out a bunt for a hit. Donovan intentionally walked Robinson to load the bases, bringing Ward to the plate. Ward, "in an aggressive mood"[2] for having endured nine trips to the plate that afternoon without a hit, smacked Donovan's second pitch deep into center field. As the ball settled into Davalillo's glove, McCraw raced home with the winning run.

Wilhelm took the victory for the Sox. His six-inning stint in relief was his longest of the season. In holding the Indians scoreless, Wilhelm was touched for only two hits while striking out three. Donovan went the distance for Cleveland, hurling 12⅓ innings while yielding 16 hits, 15 of them singles, and only two walks, both intentional. Although the White Sox hit safely in every inning but two, Donovan, with the benefit of five double plays behind him, was seldom in serious trouble.

White Sox manager Al Lopez was content with his team's effort that day. "Winning doubleheaders is one of the toughest things in baseball," he remarked after the game. "Sure, we're happy over the split. We're still in first place."[3]

Earlier that day, the Baltimore Orioles had defeated the Los Angeles Angels to tie Chicago again for first place. By pulling out the win in the overtime nightcap, however, the White Sox slipped just ahead of the Orioles, a half-game and one thin percentage point ahead in the standings.

SOURCES

In addition to the sources listed in the notes, the author also consulted:

Akron Beacon Journal.

Cleveland Plain Dealer.

Dallas Morning News.

Des Moines Tribune.

Mansfield (Ohio) News-Journal.

New York Times.

The Sporting News.

Tampa Times.

NOTES

1   Richard Dozer, "'Confident' Says Landis," **Chicago Tribune**, September 6, 1964: 3-1.

2   Richard Dozer, "Kralick of Indians Outduels Peters, 2-0; Wilhelm Victor in 13," **Chicago Tribune**, September 7, 1964: 3-1.

3   "Schedule Now Aids Al's Three Big Pitchers," **Indianapolis News**, September 7, 1964: 15.

EXTRA-INNING, WALK-OFF HOME RUNS TIMES TWO

AUGUST 28, 1966
CHICAGO WHITE SOX 4; MINNESOTA TWINS 3
(15 INNINGS, GAME ONE)

CHICAGO WHITE SOX 7 MINNESOTA TWINS 6
(11 INNINGS, GAME TWO)

By Alan Cohen

As August 1966 was about to turn into September, the chase for the American League pennant had deteriorated into a race for second place behind the Baltimore Orioles. The White Sox hosted the Minnesota Twins in a Sunday doubleheader at Comiskey Park on August 28 that was attended by 21,576 fans who got more innings than those for which they had bargained. At the end of play, the White Sox with a sweep, both wins in extra innings, had moved into fifth place, within 15½ games of the league lead and three games behind the second-place Tigers. The Twins, despite the losses, were in third place, two games behind Detroit.

The White Sox started the day in sixth place, largely for failing to win against the Twins during the season. Of the 13 contests between the two clubs, Minnesota had won 12.

In the first game, Bruce Howard of the White Sox pitched against Mudcat Grant of the Twins and the two engaged in a pitchers' duel. Chicago, after being held scoreless in the first two innings, got on the scoreboard in the third inning. A leadoff single by Pete Ward was followed by a triple down the left-field foul line by Al Weis, giving the home team a 1-0 lead. Weis tried to score on a grounder by Tommie Agee, but was thrown out by the Twins' shortstop, Zoilo Versailles. On the play, Twins catcher Earl Battey, making the tag, sustained a broken blood vessel in the thumb of his left hand. He came out of the game in the middle of the fourth inning and missed four games before returning to the lineup.

Chicago wasn't finished threatening in the third inning. After Agee stole his 34th base of the season and the White Sox loaded the bases on a walk to Don Buford and a single by Jerry Adair, the threat died when John Romano flied out to center field.

Howard was helped by a defensive gem in the fifth inning. With one out, Cesar Tovar singled to left field. With Jimmie Hall at the plate, pitcher Howard had Tovar picked off but threw the ball away and Tovar was safe at second. Then catcher Romano tried to pick Tovar off at second but threw the ball into center field. Tovar tried to score, but center fielder Agee gunned down him at the plate, and the score remained 1-0.

Howard preserved his shutout until the top of the sixth inning when, with one out, Harmon Killebrew of the Twins homered to tie the score. Howard's effectiveness diminished in that inning and the Twins loaded the bases with two out. Dennis Higgins came in to pitch for Chicago and retired Grant on a grounder. The score remained 1-1 as the game headed to the bottom of the seventh.

Grant showed no signs of letting down and kept Chicago from doing any further scoring through the 10th inning. He was in position to get his 11th win of the season when the Twins scored a pair of runs in the top of the 11th. By then Juan Pizarro, Chicago's fourth pitcher, was in the game. Pizarro retired the first two batters in the inning and then walked Zoilo Versalles. That brought up Grant. His slow grounder to third baseman Don Buford was mishandled, and Cesar Tovar walked to fill the bases. Rich Rollins pinch-hit for Jimmie Hall and singled in Grant and Versalles.

Grant was not able to hold the lead in the bottom of the 11th. With two out, Pete Ward beat out a bunt and pinch-hitter Wayne Causey singled to center field. The Twins then made a pitching change. Al Worthington entered the game. The first batter to face Worthington was the White Sox' 39-year-old pinch-hitter deluxe, Smoky Burgess. Burgess singled to center field for his 17th pinch-hit of the season. Ward scored from second and when the ball skipped through center fielder Ted Uhlaender's legs (his first error of the season), Causey scored the tying run. Worthington then worked around a single to Agee, getting Buford to hit a comebacker that ended the inning.

As part of a multiplayer switch with one out and one on in the top of the 12th inning, Joe Horlen came on to pitch for the White Sox and kept the score tied at 3-3. In the bottom of the 14th inning, the White Sox threatened as singles by Jerry Adair and Bill Skowron put runners on first and second with two outs, but Pete Cimino, the third Twins pitcher, struck out Tom McCraw to send the game to the 15th inning.

Horlen pitched a hitless 3⅔ innings, wrapping things up by retiring the side in order in the top of the 15th. In the bottom of the 15th, Chicago finally broke through against Twins reliever Cimino, who was in his third inning of relief. Once again, the White Sox scored with two outs. Causey walked and took off for second on a steal attempt. Cimino's pitch was wide of the plate and was beyond the reach of catcher Russ Nixon. Causey was credited with a stolen base, and the Twins elected to walk Burgess, who had gone behind the plate after entering the game as a pinch-hitter. Agee broke things up with a single to left field on the first pitch, scoring Causey with the winning run.

Horlen's win was his eighth of the season against 12 losses. Cimino's record went to 1-5.

In the second game, Twins manager Sam Mele intended to start Camilo Pascual, but Pascual asked out of the assignment, suffering from a sore arm. Pascual had been experiencing arm problems since May, and Mele had hoped to give his one-time ace an opportunity to get his first win since June 28. The Twins started Dwight Siebler. The White Sox countered with Jack Lamabe.

The Twins broke out on top as Harmon Killebrew hit his 30th homer of the season, a two-run shot in the first inning. Scoring ahead of Killebrew was Tony Oliva, who had singled with two outs. Chicago wasted no time in evening things up. Leadoff batter Wayne Causey walked and scored on a triple by Don Buford. Buford scored on Pete Ward's one-out sacrifice fly and the game was knotted after one inning. After a scoreless second, the Twins regained the lead in the third inning on a three-run homer off the bat of Oliva following hits by Cesar Tovar and Jimmie Hall. Once again, the White Sox countered quickly. Causey opened the bottom of the inning with a single and moved to third when Don Buford walked and Tommie Agee hit a fly ball to center field. With Pete Ward at bat, Buford stole second and Ward's fly ball to center field brought home Causey. A single by Tom McCraw scored Buford, making the score 5-4. Manager Mele replaced Siebler with Pascual at that point, as he was short on pitchers and had little in the way of alternatives. There was no further scoring in the inning.

An inning later, the Sox manufactured a run to tie the game. John Romano, who had four hits in the game, opened the bottom of the fourth with a single and went to third on a sacrifice bunt by Lamabe and a fly ball by Causey. First baseman Don Mincher mishandled a grounder by Buford, and Causey came home with the tying run. Lamabe and Pascual pitched a scoreless fifth inning, but the White Sox pushed across a run to take the lead in the sixth inning. Jerry Adair and John Romano singled to open the inning and moved up when Lamabe executed his second successful sacrifice bunt in as many at-bats. Causey's fly ball scored Romano and the White Sox had their first lead of the game.

Lamabe ran out of gas in the seventh inning. Hall singled to center field and was sacrificed to second by Oliva. Walks to Killebrew and Mincher filled the bases and veteran Hoyt Wilhelm came on in relief. Ted Uhlaender's fly ball, the fourth sacrifice fly of the game, scored Hall with the tying run. Wilhelm and Pascual kept the score tied through the ninth, and the game went into extra innings.

In the top of the 10th, Uhlaender was on third base with one out, but Zoilo Versalles struck out. Manager Mele said, "He was trying to hit the ball over the roof with that swing of his. All we needed was a fly ball."[1] Uhlaender was stranded at third when Rich Rollins flied out to center field. Al Worthington replaced Pascual in the bottom of the 10th and retired the White Sox in order.

In the top of the 11th, Wilhelm retired the Twins in order. The knuckleballer had allowed only two hits in 4⅔ innings. Although he had allowed an inherited runner to score in his first inning of work, he was in control thereafter, striking out three and walking none. He would not have to throw another pitch. Jerry Adair led off the bottom of the 11th with a homer off Worthington on a 1-and-1 pitch, and the White Sox had the sweep, winning both games in extra innings in their final at-bat. The run off Worthington was the first he allowed Chicago in five 1966 appearances, and the loss took his record for the season to 4-3. Wilhelm's win was his second of the season (he had not lost a game), and his ERA dropped to 1.41.

Killebrew's homers, one in each game, brought his career total to 327. By the time his career ended in 1975, he had 573 homers, the most (at the time) by a right-handed hitter in the American League. Of those, 27 were at Comiskey Park.

Pascual's 6⅓ innings represented his best performance since June 28. He had been experiencing arm problems since May, had sat out the month of July and had made only two appearances (totaling 3⅓ innings) in August. He was very much encouraged by his effort, saying, "This is my best game since I had arm trouble. I threw the ball past hitters with good fastballs several times. But I have thrown better on the sidelines in the past week. When you get in a game you try so hard sometimes you are just not right. I was getting my curve over, and my change of pace pitch."[2]

Pascual made only one more appearance in 1966, a start on September 5, in which he yielded four runs before leaving the game with one out in the seventh inning.

Versalles, whose strikeout in the 10th inning gave him 18 hitless at-bats since August 24, had seen his star diminish after winning the American league MVP Award the prior season. He was relegated to the bench. His 0-for-7 performance in the doubleheader with a caught-stealing did not help his status.

Wilhelm was on his way to establishing records for longevity. He pitched through 1972 and when he appeared in the final game of his career on July 10, 1972, he was 16 days shy of his 50th birthday, making him the third oldest pitcher in major-league history. He had appeared in 1,070 games as a pitcher, becoming the first pitcher in major league history to eclipse the 1,000-game plateau.

The win brought the White Sox record to 68-64. Chicago would split its last 30 games and finish the season in fourth place, 15 games behind the Orioles. The White Sox had last won a World Series in 1917 and would next win a championship (in 2005) long after all the players who played on August 28, 1966, were retired. Their 88 years of futility is the all-time record for an American League team.

The Twins went on a spurt after the double-loss, winning 20 of their last 30 games, but they were unable to make a serious dent in Baltimore's league lead. They finished in second place, nine games behind the eventual world champions.

SOURCES

In addition to Baseball-Reference.com and the sources cited in the notes, the author used:

Associated Press. "Sox Get Revenge from Twins, Win Two Extra-Inning Games," **Register Republic** (Rockville, Illinois), August 29, 1966: 35.

Associated Press Wirephoto. "If You Can't Get 'Em at Second," **Fremont** (Ohio) **News-Messenger**, August 29, 1966: 16.

Briere, Tom. "Twins Fall Twice Over 26 Innings," **Minneapolis Tribune**, August 29, 1966: 33, 36.

Dozer, Richard. "Sox Scramble to Win Pair in 26 Innings," **Chicago Tribune**, August 29, 1966: 3-1, 3-2.

Hartman, Sid. "Hartman's Roundup," **Minneapolis Tribune**, August 29, 1966: 34.

NOTES

1 Max Nichols, "Tovar to Replace Benched Versalles (0-for-18), **Minneapolis Star**, August 29, 1966: 10B.

2 Max Nichols, "Pascual: Can Do Even Better," **Minneapolis Star**, August 29, 1966: 12B.

WHITE SOX WALK-OFF CREATES FOUR-WAY TIE FOR FIRST PLACE

SEPTEMBER 6, 1967
CHICAGO WHITE SOX 3, CALIFORNIA ANGELS 2
(13 INNINGS)

By Russ Lake

The 1967 baseball season was winding down, with less than 25 games to go. On Wednesday, September 6, half of the 10 American League teams were in the thick of a tight pennant race.

The dark-horse California Angels (72-66) were in fifth place, trailing the league-leading Minnesota Twins (78-60) by six games. Sandwiched between those squads were the Boston Red Sox, Chicago White Sox, and Detroit Tigers. Boston (79-62) was a mere half-game behind Minnesota, with Chicago (77-61) a game back, and Detroit (77-62) 1½ off the pace.

Bill Rigney and the Angels came to Chicago for a one-game series knowing that each loss California endured would hinder their postseason aspirations. Rigney grumbled when he surveyed the condition of the ball field from the back of the batting cage. He said, "Look at that. Home plate's a marsh. A swamp."[1] Chicago skipper Eddie Stanky had White Sox Park tailored to benefit the strength of his roster. He had the grounds crew loosen the dirt and soak the home-plate area, and let the infield grass grow high enough to keep balls from scooting through for hits.[2] The manager bought a new suit for any of his starting pitchers who could get at least 20 groundball outs during a game.[3]

During an 11-year major-league playing career, Stanky enjoyed getting under the skin of his opponents. He carried this competitive personality into three-plus seasons as manager of the St. Louis Cardinals (1952-1955), and continued when the White Sox hired him after Al Lopez stepped down in 1965.[4] Nicknamed "The Brat," Stanky cleverly used the media to propel barbs at anyone who questioned the performance of his team. Stanky declared, "We're last in homers. We're last in hitting, last in double plays, and last in war and peace, but we're in first place in guts."[5] He later added, "Four clubs are going to spend $20,000 printing World Series tickets and won't use 'em. But the White Sox won't lose. We're down as the luckiest ballclub and the dullest — but you just wait."[6]

On September 6, a small gathering of 12,103 during a pennant drive showed glaringly that the team enjoyed only lukewarm backing from its fans. Joe Horlen (15-6, 2.40 ERA) would start for the White Sox against 32-year-old Angels left-hander George Brunet (11-17, 3.25). Since debuting in 1961, Horlen was having his best season, and this season would lead the league in ERA (2.06) and shutouts (6). The 30-year-old right-hander had taken to chewing on wadded tissues to settle his "mound-duty" nerves after tobacco and gum options did not work for him.[7]

The Angels went down in order to start the 8:05 P.M. contest. Tommy McCraw swatted a first-inning double, but he remained at second on fly-ball outs by Tommie Agee and Ken Boyer. Both teams were set down 1-2-3 during the second, and Horlen retired his ninth in a row in the top of the third. Hitting just .125, Horlen singled in the bottom half, and advanced to second on an error by center fielder Roger Repoz. Don Buford singled to left and Horlen moved to third. Stanky put on the team's first suicide squeeze of the season, but McCraw missed the bunt attempt. Horlen fell down about 12 feet from home and was tagged out by catcher Buck Rodgers.[8]

Aurelio Rodriguez singled to open the fourth, becoming the Angels' first baserunner. Jimmie Hall punched a one-out safety to center, and advanced to second when Agee's throw to third was not cut off. Former White Sox farmhand Don Mincher was intentionally passed, but first baseman McCraw forced Rodriguez at home on a grounder hit by Repoz. Horlen escaped the jam when Bubba Morton grounded out to leave the bases filled. In the top of the sixth with one out, the Angels' Hall raced to second on a groundball error by second baseman Buford. Mincher drilled a single to right, but Ken Berry's throw to backstop Duane Josephson nipped Hall at the plate.[9]

Tom Satriano batted for Brunet to lead off the eighth and walked. Paul Schaal ran for him. McCraw dashed in to field a bunt by Rodriguez and fired to shortstop Ron Hansen to force Schaal at second.[10] Horlen ended his night by getting Jim Fregosi and Hall on fly balls. Angels closer Minnie Rojas walked Buford to begin the bottom of the eighth, and McCraw sacrificed him to second. The speedy Buford was later caught in a 6-5-4 rundown on Agee's grounder.

Lefty Wilbur Wood, taking Boyer's lineup spot, was on the mound in the ninth to face left-handed swingers Mincher and Repoz. Wayne Causey moved to second base, and Buford took over at third. The 25-year-old Wood had a short night after he walked Mincher. Once Woodie Held was announced as a pinch-hitter, Stanky brought in right-handed reliever Don McMahon. Held bunted, and first sacker McCraw fired the ball to second for a force.[11] After a walk and a groundout, Angels runners were on second and third when McMahon fanned Bobby Knoop. In the bottom of the ninth, Rojas pitched around Berry's infield single to send the game into extra innings.

More changes dotted scorecards in the top of the 10th with Berry moving from right field to left and Buddy Bradford going to right while taking the batting spot of Pete Ward. McMahon retired pinch-hitter Rick Reichardt, Rodriguez, and Fregosi without a ball leaving the infield. Left-hander Curt Simmons came on for California and gave up a two-out single to McCraw. Rodgers took Simmons off the hook by throwing out McCraw at second on an attempted steal.

By now the out-of-town scoreboard showed that Luis Tiant and the Cleveland Indians had defeated the first-place Twins, 3-2, at Metropolitan Stadium. Also, Detroit was in the process of sweeping a twi-night doubleheader from the Kansas City Athletics at Tiger Stadium. Boston was idle, so these results put additional pressure on the Angels and White Sox.

In the Angels' 11th, Mincher poked a one-out double to left, and pitcher Clyde Wright ran for him. Held walked and Morton knocked an RBI single to right that plated Wright with the first run of the game as Held scampered to third. Right-hander Bob Locker replaced McMahon, and got the switch-hitting Rodgers to ground to Hansen at short. The only play was at first, and Held scored to make it 2-0.[12]

With the White Sox down two runs, Agee lined a leadoff double to right-center in the bottom of the 11th. Simmons was relieved by right-hander Jack Hamilton. The hard-throwing Hamilton had made national news when he beaned Boston's star right fielder, Tony Conigliaro, three weeks earlier in Fenway Park. Conigliaro suffered season-ending injuries. Pinch-hitter Rocky Colavito flied out, leaving Agee stalled at second. Forty-year-old Smoky Burgess, who was batting .120 and had not hit safely since July 25, sliced a double down the left-field line to score Agee.[13] Bill Voss ran for Burgess and

Hamilton walked Josephson. On came righty Bill Kelso, who walked Berry to load the bases. Right-hander Pete Cimino entered as the fourth Angels' hurler of the inning. Cimino's high and inside pitch to Hansen glanced off Rodgers' mitt for a passed ball and allowed Voss to come home with the tying run. Cimino struck out Hansen and walked Causey. Buford laced a liner to left-center, but Morton snagged it on the run just off the outfield grass.[14]

Back to scorecard markups in the top of the 12th as Colavito went to left field while Berry switched back to right. Rookie Chicago right-hander Fred Klages allowed a leadoff single to Rodriguez. After Fregosi's sacrifice, Klages retired Hall and Bill Skowron to keep the lead run on second. Cimino and Klages dispatched all of the hitters they faced during the bottom of the 12th and the top of the 13th.

After Cimino struck out pinch-hitter Marv Staehle to start the bottom of the 13th, Josephson followed with a single. Berry then boomed a long drive to left that Morton gloved on the first bounce. As Morton moved to his left, he slipped and fell, allowing Josephson plenty of time to score from first base[15] to win the 4-hour-43-minute marathon at 12:47 A.M.[16] The teams used 39 players, and California employed six pitchers to Chicago's five. Klages (4-3) was credited with the win, and Cimino (3-3) took the loss.

With the 3-2 walk-off victory, the White Sox tied the Twins for first-place at 78-61. The Red Sox and Tigers were a game behind with records of 79-62.[17] The Angels were in fifth place, 6 games from the leaders.

SOURCES

In addition to the sources cited in the Notes, the author accessed Retrosheet.org, Baseball-Reference.com, Newspapers.com, SABR.org/bioproj, and **The Sporting News** archive via Paper of Record.

NOTES

1. Jerome Holtzman, "Sox and Tigers Collide, Rub Chin, Back Off to Race Again," **The Sporting News**, September 23, 1967: 5.
2. Ibid.
3. "John Throttles BoSox, 4-0, Wins Suit from Stanky," **The Sporting News**, September 16, 1967: 33.
4. Holtzman, "Lopez to Help Pick Successor as Sox Pilot," **The Sporting News**, November 20, 1965: 7.
5. Holtzman, "The Brat Sees Red over 'Dull White Sox' Tag," **The Sporting News**, September 9, 1967: 15.
6. Ibid.
7. "Horlen Prefers Tissue," **The Sporting News**, June 17, 1967: 27.
8. Edward Prell, "Four A.L. Teams Deadlocked for First," **Chicago Tribune**, September 7, 1967: 83-84.
9. Ibid.
10. Ibid.
11. Ibid.
12. Ibid.
13. Ibid.
14. Ibid.
15. Ibid.
16. According to Baseball-Reference.com, this contest was the White Sox' third longest game in 1967. On June 12, they lost 6-5 in 22 innings (6:38) to the Washington Senators at D.C. Stadium. On July 25, the White Sox won 6-5 in 16 innings (4:47) in the second game of a doubleheader vs. the Cleveland Indians at White Sox Park.
17. The White Sox went 11-12 the rest of the way to finish in fourth place at 89-73, three games behind the pennant-winning Red Sox.

JOE HORLEN'S NO-HITTER REKINDLES CHISOX' DREAMS OF PENNANT

SEPTEMBER 10, 1967
CHICAGO WHITE SOX 6, DETROIT TIGERS 0

By Gregory H. Wolf

Joe Horlen "turned the White Sox's darkest hour into a glittering personal triumph," gushed *Chicago Tribune* sportswriter Robert Markus after the right-hander's stunning no-hitter against the Detroit Tigers.[1] "[I]t was the biggest game, the toughest spot, the White Sox were in all season," opined sportswriter George Cantor in the *Detroit Free Press*.[2]

The 1967 American League pennant race was one of the most memorable in the history of the junior circuit. On September 6 there was an unprecedented late-season four-way tie for first place, with the Chicago White Sox, Detroit Tigers, Minnesota Twins, and Boston Red Sox each six games in front of the California Angels. The White Sox, who had held sole possession of the top spot for most of the summer, had a chance to make a statement when the Tigers invaded Comiskey Park for a four-game series beginning on September 8. However, skipper Mayo Smith's bunch derailed those plans, taking the first game, 4-1 and then inflicting a soul-crushing defeat by scoring seven runs in the ninth inning for a dramatic comeback victory, 7-3, in the second contest. "Our team was down Saturday night," said Horlen as he prepared for his start on Sunday. "That was the lowest I'd seen them all year."[3] Tightly wound Pale Hose pilot Eddie Stanky was on edge: "I didn't sleep a wink all night."[4] The loss (described by Joe Falls in the *Free Press* as a "suffocating setback") dropped the White Sox (78-63) two games behind the Tigers (81-62), who were tied with the Twins for first place; the Red Sox (81-63) were a half-game back.

Stanky counted on Horlen to resuscitate the White Sox' fading pennant hopes. The 29-year-old from Texas was one of the era's most effective and often overlooked hurlers. Over a five-year period (1964-68), Horlen led the AL in ERA (2.32). Entering the biggest game of his career, the seven-year veteran had a record of 70-57, including 15-6 with a 2.31 ERA thus far in '67, and had earned his first and only All-Star berth two months earlier. A nervous type, known to chew paper while on the mound, Horlen took a cerebral approach to the game, relying on movement instead of power for his success.[5]

A disappointing crowd of 23,625 showed up at Comiskey Park, on the South Side of the Windy City for the Sunday doubleheader, prompting Edward Prell of the *Chicago Tribune* to suggest that the team "had cause to wonder what's happened to their fans."[6] The hitherto biggest series of the season drew just over 60,000 spectators.

Horlen was coming off a strong performance in his last start, tossing eight scoreless innings against the Angels, but picked up a no-decision when his teammates failed to score for him. The tables turned against the Tigers after Horlen breezed through the first. In what seemed like an annual refrain, the White Sox were a poor-hitting (.225 batting average) and low-scoring (second fewest runs in the AL) team, but they came out swinging against 25-year-old right-hander Joe Sparma, who was enjoying a breakout season (14-8). Tommie Agee led off with a single to extend his hitting streak to 13 games, and then swiped his 26th bag of the campaign. Bill Voss hit a routine, one-out grounder to first baseman Norm Cash, who fielded the ball cleanly, but Sparma fumbled his relay throw, permitting the speedy Agee to scamper home for the game's first run. Consecutive singles by Ken Boyer and Pete Ward plated the second run (also unearned). Wayne Causey followed with a line-drive triple, which according to the *Tribune*, rolled to the wall in left center, driving in two more.[7] Sparma, who had tossed a two-hit shutout in his last start, was relieved by former Los Angeles Dodgers All-Star Johnny Podres. He dispatched J.C. Martin then intentionally walked Ron Hansen to face Horlen, who ripped a single, scoring Hansen and giving the White Sox a 5-0 lead.

"We lost our momentum immediately," said a dejected Smith after the White Sox' unusual offensive outburst coupled with Sparma's crucial miscue.[8]

The game was mostly uneventful for the next seven innings. Only two Tigers reached base. The Tigers got a scare when their All-Star catcher Bill Freehan was hit on the right wrist in the third; he left the game in the sixth for precautionary reasons and did not play in the second game of the twin bill. The Tigers exacted retribution when Horlen was plunked in the fourth. Graybeard Eddie Mathews reached on Boyer's error in the fifth, but was immediately erased when Jim Northrup hit into a 1-6-3 twin killing. The Tigers pounded Horlen's sinkers into the ground all afternoon, hitting only two balls into the outfield the entire game. "My control and a fastball that was sinking," responded Horlen when asked about the reasons for his success. "I threw some curves early, but they weren't getting over so I concentrated on the fastball."[9]

A trio of Tigers relievers (Podres, Dave Wickersham, and Pat Dobson) matched Horlen's zeros, yielding only two hits over 7⅓ innings until the bottom of the eighth. Causey connected for a two-out single off rookie Mike Marshall and moved to second on a passed ball charged to Freehan's replacement, Bill Heath. Martin followed with a single, driving in Causey for the White Sox' sixth and final run.

Horlen took the mound in the ninth just three outs away from his first no-hitter. He admitted after the game that he was thinking about the only other time he entered the ninth with a no-no intact. On July 29, 1963, Chuck Hinton of the Washington Senators crashed Horlen's party at D.C. Stadium with a one-out single. Two batters later, Don Lock walloped a walk-off, two-run homer for a dramatic 2-1 victory.

Up to this point in today's game, Horlen had given up nothing that resembled a hit. "[M]y legs were a little rubbery going out there in the ninth," he candidly revealed later. "He didn't seem excited, but I knew he was," said his batterymate Martin, who made two trips to the mound in the last frame. "I just told him not to throw anything down the middle."[10]

The Tigers' first batter, Jerry Lumpe, hit what seemed to be a seeing-eye single over second base. Keystone sacker Wayne Causey moved quickly to his right and made, according to sportswriter George Cantor, a sensational grab and an "off balance throw" to first base.[11]

As if divining such a play, Stanky had replaced Boyer at first to start the inning with 6-foot-6 Cotton Nash, whose "extra reach was vital," suggested Edward Prell.[12] When first-base umpire John Stevens immediately and emphatically called Lumpe out on a bang-bang play, Mayo Smith burst from the dugout and argued the call, as did Lumpe, but to no avail.

"We always shade [Lumpe] up the middle," said Horlen about the defensive gem. "As soon as Wayne got there, I was just hoping it would get there in time. I knew it had a chance because Lumpe is not a fast runner."[13]

Heath followed with a tricky, short-hop bounder to third baseman Don Buford, who fielded it on the run and then rifled a bullet to Nash for out two. Horlen retired Dick McAuliffe on an easy grounder to short to end the game and complete the only no-hitter in his career in 2 hours and 17 minutes. He threw his glove into the air as his teammates rushed from the field and dugout to congratulate him.

Horlen faced 28 batters, fanned four and walked none, but more importantly gave the White Sox a morale boost. It was the 12th no-hitter in the history of the White Sox, a charter member of the AL in 1901, and the first since Bob Keegan's no-hitter against Washington on August 20, 1957. The Tigers suffered their second no-hitter of the season. However, they won the first, on April 30 in Baltimore, when three walks, a wild pitch, and an error led to two runs in the ninth, saddling Steve Barber (8⅔ innings) with an unusual loss (Fred Gladding recording the final out in that game).

In the second game of the doubleheader, White Sox rookie starter Cisco Carlos tossed six scoreless innings to pick up his first big-league win, 4-0, combining with relievers Hoyt Wilhelm and Bob Locker on a five-hit shutout. The White Sox "don't propose to abdicate from the sizzling four-club American League race," wrote Prell euphorically in the *Tribune*.[14]

Horlen continued his hot pitching, posting a microscopic 1.17 ERA in his final five starts, including two more shutouts. He finished the season with a career-best 19 wins (seven losses) and led the AL in ERA (2.06), tied five other pitchers for the lead in shutouts with six. He also placed second in the Cy Young Award voting and fourth in MVP voting.

Unlike Horlen, the White Sox faltered down the stretch, winning just nine of their final 19 games to finish in fourth place (89-73). The Red Sox defeated the Twins, 5-3, on the last day of the regular season to complete the "Impossible Dream" and snag the pennant.

SOURCES

In addition to the sources cited in the Notes, the author also accessed Retrosheet.org, Baseball-Reference.com, the SABR Minor Leagues Database, accessed online at Baseball-Reference.com, SABR.org, and **The Sporting News** archive via Paper of Record.

NOTES

1. Robert Markus, "Joe's Gem Gives Sox New Sparkle," **Chicago Tribune**, September 11, 1967: C1.
2. George Cantor, "No-Hitter Fires White Sox to Sweep — Tigers 4th Now," **Detroit Free Press**, September 11, 1967: 1D.
3. Joe Falls, "Horlen Gets Sox Go-Going," **Detroit Free Press**, September 11, 1967: 1D.
4. Ibid.
5. Gregory H. Wolf, "Joe Horlen," **SABR Biography Project**, sabr.org/bioproj/person/968eb078.
6. Edward Prell, "Horlen Hurls No-Hitter; Sox Take 2," **Chicago Tribune**, September 11, 1967: C1
7. "First Game," **Chicago Tribune**, September 11, 1967: C2.
8. Cantor.
9. Markus.
10. Ibid.
11. Cantor.
12. Prell.
13. Markus.
14. Prell.

JOE HORLEN TOSSES EXTRA-INNING SHUTOUT

MAY 17, 1968
CHICAGO WHITE SOX 1, OAKLAND ATHLETICS 0
(10 INNINGS)

By John Gabcik

The 1968 Chicago White Sox opened the season with 10 straight losses; they then followed up the disastrous start by winning 11 of their next 17 games. An astute fan might not have been surprised by either set of events.[1]

The previous season's team had finished in fourth place, three games behind the league-leading Boston Red Sox, and had been in first place for two months straight (June 11 – August 12), finally faltering over the last 10 games of the season. This ill-fated attempt at success was achieved with great pitching, derring-do speed on the bases, capable fielding, and very little offensive prowess. While the '67 competition — the Red Sox, Tigers, and Twins — featured blasters like Carl Yastrzemski, Al Kaline, and Harmon Killebrew, the White Sox had to make do with a lineup that topped out with Don Buford and Ken Berry hitting .241, and with little power.[2]

Despite the excitement of the season, the White Sox attendance had been below a million for the second year in a row (after having surpassed that level in 14 of the 15 previous seasons). On October 30, 1967, White Sox owner Arthur Allyn had announced that the franchise would play nine of its "home" games in Milwaukee, facing each American League opponent once, Allyn professing "to develop the Milwaukee market for our enterprises."[3] Manager Eddie Stanky and the players expressed indifference: "We're professional; we'll play in Alaska if we have to," Stanky said.[4] But this, along with the change of television outlets from WGN to a UHF station, reception-challenged WFLD, had not done much to please White Sox fans, or win their support.[5] In nine dates at Comiskey Park, the White Sox had exceeded 10,000 in attendance only once.

The White Sox rotation mainstays — Joe Horlen, Gary Peters, Tommy John — and an accomplished bullpen — were used to winning with little support, and thus far in 1968 that was about all they'd got. On Friday, May 17, the White Sox had returned from their first game in Milwaukee, against the California Angels,[6] to face the Oakland Athletics in Comiskey Park. The White Sox were in last place in the American League but poised for a climb.

Horlen's season so far was an image of the team's results: He'd lost his first five decisions (getting zero run support in two of them, along with shaky defense),[7] followed by two straight wins. His last start was 6⅔ shutout innings against the Athletics on May 11, a win for Horlen with relief help from Wilbur Wood.

In 1967 Horlen had led the American League with a WHIP of 0.953, a 2.06 ERA, and six shutouts; he'd come in fourth in the Most Valuable

Player Award voting with the most votes of any pitcher. His year-to-date ERA of 2.70, though not as stingy, should have produced more success than Horlen was having. But this wasn't new for Horlen; he had been second in the American League in ERA in 1964 with a 1.88 average, and second again to teammate Gary Peters in 1966, with a 2.43 average. Despite this consistency of excellence, the 30-year-old right-hander entered this game with a modest 76-63 lifetime won-lost record over eight seasons. The White Sox offense tended to take the day off when he was the starter.

Horlen's opponent was Jim Nash, a 23-year-old right hander. Nash, a 6-foot-5, 215-pound power pitcher, had faced the White Sox only once in his young career: On July 23, 1967, Nash had pitched a nine-inning one-run, three-hit complete game, but the (then Kansas City) Athletics had been shut out by Gary Peters, 1-0. Nash had accomplished a career high of 12 strikeouts in the defeat. So tonight's game, with 8,407 on hand, portended to be another low-scoring duel.

And that's what it was. After 6⅔ innings, Nash had fanned seven and the White Sox were hitless, their only baserunner being Bill Voss, who walked with one out in the first. The Athletics had two hits, a fourth-inning single by Reggie Jackson, who was immediately erased when Sal Bando grounded into a double play, and another single in the sixth by Jim Gosger. Other than the two hits, only one other Horlen offering had left the infield.

As Voss and Pete Ward were striking out to lead off the White Sox seventh, bombastic A's owner Charlie Finley was in the press box announcing that Nash would receive a $2,500 bonus for throwing a no-hitter, and that catcher Jim Pagliaroni would get $500.[8] A moment later, White Sox first baseman Tom McCraw boomed a triple to deep center to end the drought; McCraw was stranded when Russ Snyder grounded out to short.

Nash gave up his second walk to lead off the bottom of the eighth, putting White Sox third baseman Bill Melton aboard. Optimistically, Eddie Stanky brought in fleet-footed Sandy Alomar to pinch-run. Alomar stayed at first as the next three batters went out quietly, then took Melton's place at third base.

As Horlen continued to plug away, the Athletics managed singles by Bert Campaneris in the ninth and Sal Bando in the 10th. A sacrifice put Bando on second with one out but neither Floyd Robinson nor John Donaldson could move him along; the game remained scoreless.

Tom McCraw led off the White Sox 10th with another long triple. McCraw was on a power-hitting tear, having homered in his last at-bat against the Angels on Wednesday.[9] McCraw was an excellent runner for a first baseman, stealing 20 or more bases in each of the last two years. A fast man with the winning run on third and no outs sent Athletics manager Bob Kennedy's thinking into a pickle. Kennedy had to have an out, so he chose to have Nash pitch to Russ Snyder — and it worked; Snyder looked at a called strike three for the first out. Kennedy then had Nash intentionally walk Alomar and Wayne Causey, loading the bases, enhancing the possibility for a force out at home or an inning-ending double play.

Alomar was a bit surprised at the strategy, having had only three at-bats to date during the season. "I was surprised he walked me, especially after they had pitched to Snyder," he said.[10] But Kennedy apparently was much more concerned about the White Sox' small-ball skills than their ability to drive in the run. Tommy Davis, a former two-time National League batting champion, was next up, hitting for catcher Jerry McNertney. Davis had missed the last nine games with a pulled right hamstring, the same leg that had cost him almost all of the 1965 season.[11] No problem for Nash, or Kennedy's small-ball concerns; Davis took strike three, looking. This was Nash's 13th strikeout of the game, another career high set against the White Sox, and the most he would achieve in his major-league career.

With two out, it was Horlen's turn to bat. Joe had always been a good all-around athlete, often used by the White Sox as a pinch-runner. But Horlen had never been much of a batter,[12] a factor that depressed his won-lost record despite his tremendous skills as a moundsman. So Stanky pinch-hit for Horlen, sending catcher Duane Josephson to the plate; unless Josephson came through, Horlen would get an unpalatable no-decision for his efforts.

Nash fed Josephson nothing but fastballs, sending Josephson into a 1-and-2 count. The stocky catcher drove the next pitch, another fastball, deep into center field, over the head of shallow-playing Gosger. The White Sox had their shutout victory, and for Horlen, a third straight win.[13] "I had better stuff in the first two victories" he told the *Chicago Tribune*, which the next day at last could proclaim that the White Sox were no longer in last place.[14]

The White Sox went on to sweep the four-game series from Oakland; that Sunday night they were in sixth place with a 15-17 record. This would be the high point in the White Sox season. The team began to lose steadily, and two months later Stanky was out the door, replaced by Les Moss, and later in the year by franchise hero Al Lopez. The White Sox would end up in eighth place, tied with the Angels at 67-95, 36 games behind the champion Detroit Tigers; it was Chicago's first season out of the AL first division in 18 years. The White Sox drew 803,775 in attendance, but almost a third of the total, 265,452, came from the nine dates in Milwaukee.

SOURCES

In addition to sources cited in the Notes, I used the Baseball-Reference.com and Retrosheet.org websites for the box score and play-by-play of this game, player and team pages, and game logs.

NOTES

1 The Baseball Writers Association of America poll had predicted in **The Sporting News** (April 13, 1968: 7) that the White Sox would come in third, trailing the Minnesota Twins and Detroit Tigers. **Street and Smith's Official 1968 Baseball Yearbook** (42-43) had the White Sox second (behind the Twins) with "the best pitching in either league — actually one of the best of all time." But both publications stressed that the White Sox' hitting needed to improve.

2 Over the winter, the White Sox had attempted to beef up their position players, trading away speed and youth (Tommy Agee, Don Buford) for leadership, fielding (Luis Aparicio), and a potent bat (Tommy Davis).

3 **The Sporting News**, November 11, 1967: 38.

4 **The Sporting News**, June 1, 1968: 16.

5 John Snyder, **White Sox Journal** (Cincinnati: Cleresy Press, 2009), 386.

6 The White Sox lost 4-2. A crowd of 23,510 came out to County Stadium despite tornado warnings and a 90 percent chance of rain.

7 On May 3, against the Yankees, skillful fielder Tom McCraw tied a major-league record for errors by a first baseman in one inning, three; the errors led to three unearned runs for Horlen in the 3-2 loss. **The Sporting News**, May 18, 1968: 4.

8 **Chicago Tribune**, May, 18, 1968: 21.

9 McCraw had been using Tommy Davis's 34-ounce bat for both games. **Chicago Tribune**, May 18, 1968.

10 **Chicago Tribune**, May 18, 1968: 22.

11 Davis had come to the Sox with three other New York Mets in exchange for Tommy Agee and Al Weis on December 15, 1967. A year later, the White Sox let Davis go to the Seattle Pilots as part of the expansion draft.

12 In 694 major-league plate appearances, Horlen had a .136 batting average.

13 Horlen would earn two more shutout victories in 1969 for a career total of 18.

14 **Chicago Tribune**, May, 18, 1968: 21.

NYMAN SHUTS OUT YANKEES IN FIRST CAREER START — IN THE SHADOWS OF CONVENTION TURMOIL

AUGUST 28, 1968
CHICAGO WHITE SOX 3, NEW YORK YANKEES 0

By Doug Feldmann

White Sox fan Dennis Zweifel decided to leave Comiskey Park early on the night of August 28, 1968, looking to pop into one of the taverns lining Halsted Street on Chicago's Near South Side. The ballgame crowd, cheering on the performance of rookie pitcher Gerald "Jerry" Nyman, ultimately faded from Zweifel's ears with every step he took farther from the stadium.

As he turned left down Halsted from 35th Street, however, Zweifel noticed the growing murmur of a second crowd — as if he had shut down a lawnmower, only to discover that he had stumbled upon a buzzing bees' nest in the next instant.

The rumbling of the new throng grew more intense. Squinting down the dark asphalt, Zweifel could make out its origins. The commotion was emanating from the gate of the International Amphitheatre at 42nd Street, a nondescript structure built in 1934 as an exhibition venue for the adjacent Union Stockyards and now the home of the two-year-old Chicago Bulls basketball team. But instead of a collection of happy, entertained sports followers, the group toward which Zweifel now carefully slithered was a mob filled with anger and hostility.

At the corner of 42nd and Halsted, activists were denouncing those inside the Amphitheatre, the participants in the Democratic National Convention. Some of the protesters had marched five miles to the location from their main downtown rendezvous point, the entrance to the Conrad Hilton Hotel, the conventioneers' place of lodging, across the street from Grant Park. The scene outside the hotel turned ugly with each passing hour, with those already in front of the Amphitheatre at the time of Nyman's first pitch having eluded a war zone that escalated throughout the night. "The principal clash of the police and a portion of the 5,000 demonstrators still around the hotel area came around 8:00 p.m.," the *Chicago Tribune* reported, "when demonstrators blocked Michigan Avenue at Balbo Drive."[1]

Zweifel had been one of just over 10,000 attendees at Comiskey Park largely unaware of the events taking place throughout the city while the White Sox were hosting the New York Yankees. The Yankees entered the night with an even 65-65 record and the unusual standing — for them — of sixth place in the American League. The White Sox, meanwhile at 27 games back, were struggling to stay out of the cellar at 55-77, just four games ahead of the last-place Washington Senators.

Pressure was being heaped on Yankees manager Ralph Houk to make a late-season charge. The team had spent three straight seasons in the second division, a nearly unprecedented performance that included a last-place finish in 1967– the first time the franchise found itself at the very bottom since 1912.

That night the Yankees' frustration would only continue.

"Understandably fatigued after playing nine games in five days," wrote Leonard Koppett in the *New York Times*, "the Yankees had thoroughly as unsuccessful a time in Chicago tonight as the peace-plank doves inside the Democratic convention and the chanting yippies in Grant Park."[2]

A week earlier, Nyman had been elevated from the minors to take the roster spot of Joe Horlen, who was sidelined with a bad back. Nyman, a Mormon and one of eight children of a Utah chicken farmer, had been "only a fringe member of the Brigham Young University baseball team," the *Tribune* disclosed, "and recalled that he had to constantly check the list to see if he'd been cut from the squad in 1963 and 1964."[3] At a Dodgers tryout in the summer of 1964, he was told to "forget about baseball."[4] Nonetheless, he refused to give up; and before returning to Utah, he attended one more audition in California with the White Sox and was signed. "I got a small bonus, but I'd have taken anything," Nyman said.[5]

Nyman had made his major-league debut four days earlier against the Twins, pitching two-thirds if an inning of relief in the second game of a doubleheader at Comiskey in which he allowed a double and a walk with one strikeout in a 9-1 Minnesota romp. He had been summoned from Honolulu in the Pacific Coast League, where he beat the crosstown Cubs' Tacoma team for his seventh win of the summer before leaving or Chicago with a 3.09 ERA. "Nyman is small as pitchers go," *Tribune* sportswriter Richard Dozer informed his readers of the new arrival. "He's 5-10, weighs only 163, and says he needs a lot of milkshakes to keep his weight even that high."[6]

With a team batting average of .212 heading into the game against Nyman, the Yankees — characteristic of many clubs that season — had been kept afloat by their pitching staff. One of the leaders was the evening's starter, Mel Stottlemyre, going after win number 18 and entering the game with a 2.49 ERA after two straight complete-game wins against the Twins and the Detroit Tigers.

Striding to the hill, Nyman was almost overcome with jitters after seeing Mickey Mantle in the visitors' dugout, with the star toiling in his final major-league season. "The young lefthander candidly admitted that he undertook last night's emergency project with fear in his heart," Dozer wrote, "and was completely awed by facing Mantle and company — a team which he revealed had been the longtime favorite of his dad."[7]

Horace Clarke opened the game with an infield hit, and Nyman nervously walked Mantle two batters later. Next was the Yankees' leading hitter, Roy White, but Nyman got him to tap a soft grounder back to the mound. Suddenly feeling as though he really belonged in the majors, Nyman pounced on the ball and sent Mantle back to the dugout by firing a strike to Luis Aparicio at second who relayed to first baseman Tommy McCraw to complete the double play.

The game remained scoreless into the bottom of the third, when Nyman led off in his first big league at-bat. He jumped on a Stottlemyre pitch and rocketed a single off the glove of the Yankees' 27-year-old rookie third baseman Bobby Cox.

Luis Aparicio bunted Nyman to second, then the inexperienced baserunner stopped at third when Sandy Alomar looped a single to center field that could have scored him. But Tommy Davis then lined a hit to center, allowing the rookie pitcher to trot home with the game's first run. McCraw and Walt Williams followed with hits as well, and the White Sox had staked Nyman to a 3-0 lead.

It was more than the novice hurler would need.

By the time Mantle led off the ninth, the 3-0 score held up as only two Yankees had reached second base. Nyman was jolted when Mantle started the ninth by pulling a sharp single to left; but White followed by skidding a double-play ball once again, this time to Alomar at second. And when Andy Kosco bounced a ball to Pete Ward at third, Nyman had shut out one of baseball's legendary franchises in his first start, in a game that lasted 1 hour and 55 minutes.

Producing 18 outs on grounders, Nyman credited catcher Jerry McNertney with calling a terrific game behind the plate — while the backstop affirmed that Nyman had shaken him off only once during the evening. "I had a better fastball in the last three or four innings," Nyman said. "It had zip on it."[8]

Around the time the White Sox were converging on the pitcher's mound to congratulate Nyman, Hubert H. Humphrey was receiving the Democratic nomination for president of the United States on the delegates' first vote inside the Amphitheatre.

Nyman would rarely again soar to such heights. He won only once in five starts in September, struggled to stay in the rotation in 1969 (despite a one-hit shutout in his first start that season), and was out of the majors after a brief stint with the San Diego Padres in 1970 before embarking on a long career in coaching. Even so, his grand entrance onto the big-league stage would always be coupled with one of the more historic — yet infamous — nights in Chicago history.

SOURCES

In addition to the sources cited in the Notes, the author also consulted the following: Baseball-Reference.com, Retrosheet.org, and SABR.org.

NOTES

1. "Scores Hurt in Battle on Michigan Av.," **Chicago Tribune**, August 29, 1968: 1, 1.

2. Leonard Koppett, "White Sox Down Yanks, 3-0," **New York Times**, August 29, 1968: 47.

3. "Gerry Got to Majors Hard Way," **Chicago Tribune**, August 29, 1968: 3, 8.

4. Ibid.

5. Ibid.

6. Richard Dozer, "Nyman Wins 1st Start in Majors, 3-0," **Chicago Tribune**, August 29, 1968: 3, 8.

7. Ibid.

8. Ibid.

BILL MELTON BECOMES THE FIRST WHITE SOX PLAYER TO LEAD THE LEAGUE IN HOMERS

SEPTEMBER 30, 1971
CHICAGO WHITE SOX 2, MILWAUKEE BREWERS 1

By Joe Schuster

Over their first 70 seasons, Chicago White Sox fans saw some historic moments. Early on, they won two World Series, in 1906 and 1917. Two years after the latter, they suffered the most infamous Series loss ever, in 1919, when eight of their players took money to throw the Series to Cincinnati. The team's fans had also seen some all-time greats: Joe Jackson, whose participation in the 1919 scandal has kept him out of the Hall of Fame; Luke Appling, a two-time batting champion who is in the Hall of Fame; pitcher Ed Walsh, who is also in the Hall of Fame and is one of only two post-nineteenth-century pitchers to win 40 games in a season.

One thing the White Sox fans did not see in those years was a home-run title for the home team.

For that, they had to wait until 1971, when Bill Melton snatched the crown from Reggie Jackson and Norm Cash on the final day of the season. To win it, Melton had to pull himself out of a nearly monthlong slump and slug three round-trippers over the final two days to claim the title by a single homer, 33 to 32.

Melton, who turned 26, was in his third full season with the White Sox. The previous year he'd become the first player in franchise history to hit 30 home runs when he slugged 33, sixth best in the league. (Frank Howard was tops with 44.)

Despite that, 1970 had sometimes been a struggle for him.

In his first two dozen games as White Sox third baseman, he committed 12 errors, six of them in a stretch of four games. On the last, he misjudged a popup that broke his nose.[1] In late June manager Don Gutteridge shifted him to right field. Melton publicly expressed unhappiness: "I just don't like it. ... Besides, I think it's affecting my hitting, and I lose my concentration out there. You don't feel like you're in the ballgame."[2]

His stats bear this out. When Gutteridge moved him, Melton was hitting .295 with an .825 OPS. After the move to right, he hit only .239 over his next 71 games although his OPS was a nearly identical .822. He also tied two ignominious records: In July, he tied a major-league mark that still stood in 2018 when he struck out seven times in a doubleheader. He also tied the American League record for fanning in 11 consecutive at-bats between July 23 and July 28.

Coming into 1971, however, Melton and others expected a better year. One difference: The White Sox had fired Gutteridge the previous September and new manager Chuck Tanner had shifted Melton back to third, after giving him a few tips he thought would help his fielding. (They apparently did. At third in 1970,

THE BASE BALL PALACE OF THE WORLD

In 1971 Bill Melton belted 33 home runs to become the first White Sox hitter to lead the AL in round-trippers. (Photo by 1972 SPX/Diamond Images via Getty Images)

his fielding average, .926, ranked lowest of any player with at least 50 games at the position. In 1971, it was .968, tied for fourth best. In addition, he led AL third basemen in range factor.) *The Sporting News* said that with Melton back in the infield, the team was stronger than it was without him there.[3] One Chicago sportswriter went so far as to predict that Melton would win the AL home-run crown.[4]

Early on, it did not seem Melton would fulfill that forecast. While he homered in the White Sox' first two games (an April 7 doubleheader), he didn't hit his third until May 15. By May 31 he had only six. Meanwhile, Jackson had 10 and Cash 11.

In June, however, Melton got hot, slugging a dozen home runs, and ended that month tied for the league lead with Tony Oliva at 18. His performance earned him his only career All-Star selection. While he cooled off, hitting only nine home runs combined in July and August, as September began his 27 total round-trippers tied him for the league lead with Cash and Reggie Smith.

But if Melton was cool in August, he was cold for nearly the entire final month. From September 1 to 28, he hit only .204 with three home runs. However, his competitors for the crown had suffered their own power outages. While Jackson hit 15 home runs combined in August and September, he hit only one in July. From August 8 to September 24, Cash hit only five. (Smith hit only three for all of September, ending the year with 30.)

As play ended on September 28, both Jackson and Cash had 32 home runs while Melton had 30. The next day Tanner sought to boost what was perhaps an outside chance for Melton to win the crown by shifting him to leadoff from his customary number-four spot to give him an additional at-bat.[5] Melton responded by slugging two round-trippers in a 2-1 White Sox win over Milwaukee. When neither Cash nor Jackson homered that day, Melton was assured of at least a tie for the crown, since both of their seasons were over.

After the game, Melton said that his two long balls were due to several factors: "I spread myself out more in the batter's box, moved closer to the plate, choked two inches on the bat and was using a heavier bat. ... I was going for the home run. I have been for three weeks."[6]

This set up the season finale and Melton's last shot for sole claim on the title.

The game itself meant nothing in the standings. At 78-83, the Sox had clinched third in the division while their opponent, Milwaukee, 69-91, had clinched last.

The Brewers sent rookie right-hander Bill Parsons (13-16) to the mound while the White Sox countered with southpaw Jim Magnuson (1-1) who, although in his second season, was still officially a rookie since he'd thrown only 44⅔ innings in 1970. For 1971, he'd been up and down between Chicago and Triple-A Tucson.

In his first at-bat, Melton grounded to short in a scoreless first inning. Magnuson set down the Brewers in order in the first two innings, while the White Sox went up 1-0 in the bottom of the second when Tony Muser tripled and Chuck

Brinkman singled.

Melton batted again leading off the third. Because it was the only significant event of the contest, the *Tribune* devoted the lede in its game account to Melton's swing on a 2-and-2 count:

"Bill Melton drove his bat into a fastball and the scene in Comiskey Park … froze as if waiting for a picture to be snapped.

"The ball soared in a low, screaming arc toward the left center field lower deck. As it gathered momentum … the freeze was shattered by the sudden realization that the . . . third-base star had made the final day … one of the most memorable in the 71-year existence of the club.

"When the ball landed in the third row of the lower deck, Melton became the White Sox' first American League home run champion."[7]

Melton, not surprisingly, was ecstatic, saying, "I didn't know how to touch the bases, I was so excited. … The thing that amazes me is that I was trying to hit home runs the last two days and I hit 'em."[8]

As he reached the dugout after rounding the bases, giving the White Sox a 2-0 lead, he tossed his helmet into the crowd, who kept cheering, bringing him back to acknowledge their ovation.

In the top of the fourth, Melton went out to third, but after the first pitch Tanner replaced him with Walt Williams so Melton could have another ovation as he left the field.[9] Later, the fan who caught the home-run ball gave it to Melton, who reportedly paid him $50.[10]

The White Sox held their 2-0 lead through eight innings, as Tanner sent a series of rookies to the mound for two innings each (after Magnuson came Rich Hinton, Don Eddy, and Denny O'Toole) until Stan Perzanowski finished in the ninth. He allowed the Brewers their only run. Jose Cardenal singled and John Briggs and Dave May reached on White Sox errors on successive plays, loading the bases. After fanning Andy Kosco, Perzanowski walked Darrell Porter, forcing in a run, before closing out the 2-1 victory. Hinton (3-4) got the win, while Parsons (13-17) took the loss. Perzanowski earned his first career save.

That year was the high point of Melton's career. In November he fell off a ladder, hurting his back. By late June 1972, the pain was so bad that he had season-ending surgery, and finished with just 7 home runs. That season, too, Dick Allen eclipsed Melton's short-lived White Sox home-run record when he led the league with 37.

Melton played three more seasons in Chicago, averaging only 18.4 home runs a year. In 1975, when he hit .240 with 15 home runs, the fans who'd celebrated him four years earlier were booing him and he asked for a trade.[11] The White Sox obliged, sending him to the Angels. After a season with California and one in Cleveland, he retired.

SOURCES

Retrosheet.org/boxesetc/1971/B09300CHA1971.htm.

Baseball-Reference.com/boxes/CHA/CHA197109300.shtml.

NOTES

1 Jerome Holtzman, "Agony of Errors … Ordeal of Chisox' Melton," **The Sporting News**, May 23, 1970: 5.

2 George Langford, "White Sox's Melton Is Unhappy; Prefers Third Base to Outfield," **Chicago Tribune**, June 30, 1970: 32.

3 C.C. Johnson Spink, "Spink's Forecast: Orioles and Dodgers to Win," **The Sporting News**, April 10, 1971: 5.

4 "Repeat of 1970? That's What Poll Says," **Chicago Daily Herald**, April 5, 1971: 2-3.

5 George Langford, "Melton A.L. Home Run King," **Chicago Tribune**, October 1, 1971: 63.

6 Ibid.

7 Langford, "Melton A.L. Home Run King."

8 Ibid.

9 Ibid.

10 Ibid.

11 Jerome Holtzman, "Boos Stir Melton to Hope for Trade," **The Sporting News**, November 1, 1975: 23.

WILBUR WOOD TOSSES THREE-HIT SHUTOUT IN FIRST CHICAGO NIGHT OPENER

APRIL 18, 1972
CHICAGO WHITE SOX 14, TEXAS RANGERS 0

By Bob Wood

The Chicago White Sox were scheduled to open their season on Thursday, April 6, 1972, in Comiskey Park, hosting the Oakland Athletics. Midway Airport reported winds ranging from 9 to 23 mph that day, with some traces of fog, a bit of rain (0.02"), and some thunder, following the 5:25 A.M. sunrise.[1] Not that it mattered. The park would remain empty all day long — and all week long, as the Major League Players Association went on strike, canceling games until a settlement was reached on April 13.

It was estimated that the strike cost the 24 major-league owners $5 million, and denied the players $1 million in salaries. The strike forced the cancellation of 86 games, which were never played, resulting in unbalanced schedules.[2]

During the offseason, Chicago had traded 13-game winner Tommy John and infielder Steve Huntz to the Los Angeles Dodgers to acquire Dick Allen, hoping to improve upon their third-place finish in the American League West Division. Allen had held out, finally signing a $135,000 contract, before making his debut with the White Sox, and was expected to be the linchpin for an improved offense.[3] Allen already had 508 extra-base hits in his nine-year career, and would provide the White Sox with one of the best offensive seasons in Comiskey Park, winning the American League Most Valuable Player Award while leading the league in home runs (37), RBIs (113), walks (99), on-base percentage (.420), and slugging percentage (.603), while hitting .308. Manager Chuck Tanner hoped the addition of Allen would give the White Sox the offensive punch they needed to improve upon their 79-83 record of the year before.

The Texas Rangers had made even more dramatic changes, packing their bags, relocating from Washington to the Dallas-Fort Worth area and changing their name from the Senators to the Rangers. Texas had been scheduled to begin its new venture in Arlington, Texas, on April 6, opening the season against the Kansas City Royals. The strike canceled all of those games, as well as a White Sox series in Minnesota and a Rangers series in Oakland.

The White Sox finally were able to open their season on Saturday, April 15, in Kansas City, suffering a 2-1 loss in 11 innings to the Royals. Their hard luck continued as they dropped both ends of a Sunday doubleheader in Kansas City, 2-1 in the opener, and 4-3 in 10 innings in the nightcap.

The Rangers, managed by Hall of Famer Ted Williams, finally got to make their debut, with their new name and new uniforms, in California on April 15, dropping a 1-0 decision to the Angels and Andy Messersmith, a 20-game winner in 1971, who had finished fifth in the Cy

Young Award voting. Texas rebounded with a 5-1 victory the next day. Both the White Sox and Rangers had travel days scheduled for Monday, April 17, allowing them to prepare for their Tuesday evening matchup to open the Comiskey Park season. This would be the first night-game opener in Chicago.[4]

Chicago called upon knuckleballer Wilbur Wood to make his second start of the season. Wood had won 22 games in 1971, finishing third in the Cy Young Award voting and ninth in the Most Valuable Player Award poll, while compiling a 1.91 ERA in 334 innings, after making 282 relief appearances and 10 spot starts in his first four seasons with the White Sox. The converted reliever would be facing Bill Gogolewski of the Rangers. Gogolewski was making his first appearance of the season, after a 6-5 campaign in 1971, and was beginning his third season in the big leagues. Wood, a 30-year-old left-hander who had debuted as a teenager for the Boston Red Sox in 1961, was in his 11th major-league season, and had done well, pitching the opener in Kansas City, shutting out the Royals until Bob Oliver hit a game-tying two-out, solo home run in the bottom of the ninth inning, resulting in a no-decision for Wood.

The game began with 20,943 fans in the stands. "The crowd, a noisy and sometimes unruly group, set the tempo, lavishing long ovations on Allen, Bill Melton and the others as they were introduced," reported the *Chicago Tribune*. "Obviously, neither the players' strike nor Allen's long holdout had dulled their enthusiasm for their favorites."[5]

Wood fanned the leadoff man, Lenny Randle, then got two groundouts to retire the side.

Chicago wasted no time at the plate. Pat Kelly tripled leading off. Jorge Orta singled Kelly home, opening the scoring. Dick Allen drew a base on balls and Bill Melton singled to drive home Orta. Carlos May capped the rally with a three-run home run. It would be quite a day for May, who added two singles, a double, and a base on balls before the game ended, knocking in six runs. Although Gogolewski struck out the

Over a five-year stretch (1971-1975), knuckleballer Wilbur Wood won 106 games while averaging 336 innings, 45 starts, and 20 complete games per season. (Photo by Focus on Sport/Getty Images)

next three hitters, the game was already out of hand, as the White Sox had scored five runs before an out was recorded.

The White Sox chased Gogolewski with a four-run fourth inning, then added five more against reliever Jim Panther in the fifth inning.

Wood was in top form, allowing a second-inning single to Tom Grieve and a third-inning walk to Toby Harrah before retiring 11 hitters in a row. Dave Nelson led off the Rangers seventh inning with a single, but was erased from the basepaths when Frank Howard grounded into a 5-4-3 double play. Randle was the last hitter to reach base for the Rangers when he doubled with two outs in the top of the ninth inning.

In all, Wood faced just 29 batters, tossing a shutout for his first victory, and the first victory for the White Sox, in 1972. By season's end Wood had 24 wins, 17 losses, and eight shutouts. Wood started an amazing 49 games for the White Sox, the most by any pitcher since Ed Walsh made 49 starts for the White Sox in 1908 and Jack Chesbro started 51 times for the Yankees in 1904. Wood finished second to Gaylord Perry in the

Cy Young Award voting by just six votes (64-58), and pitched 376⅔ innings, the most since Pete Alexander threw 388 innings in 1917.

The final score of 14-0 was the biggest victory of the White Sox season. They didn't score more than 10 runs in a game until more than a year later, when they defeated the Royals in Kansas City, 16-2 on April 20, 1973. While Allen had a tremendous season personally, team production dropped significantly, from .250/.325/.372 in 1971 to .238/.310/.346 in 1972, resulting in a second-place finish behind Oakland in the American League West Division.

SOURCES

In addition to the sources mentioned in the Notes, the author consulted Baseball-Reference.com and Retrosheet.org.

Baseball-Reference.com/boxes/CHA/CHA197204180.shtml.

Retrosheet.org/boxesetc/1972/B04180CHA1972.htm.

NOTES

1 wunderground.com/history/airport/KORD/1972/4/6.

2 Stan Isle, "Clubs' Losses in Strike to Run Into Millions," **The Sporting News**, April 29, 1972: 6.

3 George Langford, "Sox Rout Texas 14-0 in Home Opener," **Chicago Tribune**, April 19, 1972: 3, 1.

4 Ibid.

5 Ibid.

A TWO-DAY MARATHON

MAY 26, 1973
CHICAGO WHITE SOX 6, CLEVELAND INDIANS 3
(21 INNINGS)

By Joseph Wancho

The Chicago White Sox entered a Memorial Day weekend series having just swept the California Angels in a three-game series at Comiskey Park. As a result, Chicago increased its lead in the American League West to 3½ games. There was a logjam of three teams in second place: the Angels, Minnesota, and Oakland. In the finale, on May 24, the setting was a classic pitching duel between the Angels' Nolan Ryan and the White Sox' Wilbur Wood. Ryan, who had just pitched his first career no-hitter, against the Royals on May 15, struck out 12, walking one. But he surrendered four earned runs. Wood, the knuckleballing savant, struck out six and led the Chisox to a 4-1 victory.

The White Sox' opponent for the weekend was the Cleveland Indians. As the Indians made their way to the Windy City, they were in sixth place in the AL East, but just three games behind front-runner Detroit. The Tribe owned a modest two-game winning streak and was looking to gain further momentum.

In the opener, on May 25, the Indians did just that as they extended their winning streak to three games. Home runs by Chris Chambliss, Oscar Gamble, Charlie Spikes, and Dave Duncan accounted for six of the eight runs in the 8-3 win. The loss eclipsed Chicago's three-game win streak.

The pitching matchup for the game on May 26 was the Indians' Gaylord Perry (6-5, 2.75 ERA) going against Stan Bahnsen (6-3, 2.92 ERA). Perry was the reigning Cy Young Award winner in the AL. He had shared the league lead in wins (24) with Wood in 1972. Bahnsen also had a good year in 1972 with a career-high 21 wins for the White Sox.

The Indians opened as though they were going to dent the scoreboard. Buddy Bell led off the game with a triple to right field. But Bahnsen struck out John Lowenstein for the first out. Chambliss and Spikes followed with groundouts, and Bahnsen escaped without giving up a run.

Perry kept the White Sox off the scoreboard until the bottom of the fifth inning. With one out, Jorge Orta bunted safely to the third-base side, and went to second on a throwing error by Indians third baseman Buddy Bell. Eddie Leon followed with a single to right field to score Orta. Although it appeared that right fielder John Lowenstein might have nailed Orta with his one-hop throw to the plate, Orta avoided Duncan's tag and was ruled safe. Leon went to second base on the throw home. Perhaps Perry was rattled, as he heaved a wild pitch and Leon advanced to third. The White Sox loaded the bases when Pat Kelly and Bill Sharp walked. But Perry got out of it when Dick Allen bounced into a 6-4-3 double play to end the inning.

Cleveland tied it in the top of the seventh inning. Lowenstein led off with a double to right field and came home on a single to right by Duncan. The Indians took the lead at 2-1 in the top of the eighth. Tom Ragland singled to left field

THE BASE BALL PALACE OF THE WORLD

In his first season with the White Sox, mercurial Dick Allen led the AL with 37 home runs and 113 RBIs, and was named the league's MVP in 1972. (Photo by Focus on Sport/Getty Images)

and scored when Frank Duffy doubled to left. Bill Melton evened matters in the bottom of the frame, smashing a one-out home run to the left-field pavilion. It was Melton's ninth home run of the year, and knotted the score at 2-2.

For the next five innings, Perry and Bahnsen pitched goose-eggs. Neither team mounted a serious threat. Both hurlers proved their mettle and each went 13 innings. Perry surrendered 10 hits, walked five and struck out eight. Bahnsen gave up nine hits, walking three and whiffing four.

Cleveland summoned Jerry Johnson from the bullpen in the top of the 14th inning. The White Sox followed suit by turning to Terry Forster in the bottom of the frame. Johnson, a right-hander and lefty Forster continued what their predecessors started. Although both squads put men on base, both hurlers threw three innings of scoreless baseball. As if the game did not take long enough, there was a 17-minute rain delay in the 14th inning.

As the clock approached 1 A.M., the American League's curfew deadline, play on the diamond was suspended. Thus far, the game was 4 hours and 29 minutes long. It was to be resumed before the regularly scheduled game the next afternoon. But that Sunday game was rained out. So Saturday's contest would be resumed on Monday, May 28, before the regularly scheduled game.

When play resumed on May 28, Wood replaced Forster in the top of the 17th inning. Wood was also scheduled to pitch the regularly scheduled game. Milt Wilcox took the mound for the visitors in the bottom of the 17th.

The White Sox threatened in the 17th inning, when Wilcox walked two and added two wild pitches for good measure. But the threat was snuffed out when Rick Reichardt grounded out with runners on second and third base. Cleveland broke through for an unearned run in the top of the 21st inning. Spikes walked with two out and moved to second when shortstop Leon booted Duncan's grounder. Walt Williams singled to center field to plate Spikes. Wood whiffed George Hendrick to ensure that there would be no further damage.

Chicago took little time in coming back in the home half of the inning. Tony Muser led off with a double and advanced to third when Chuck Brinkman sacrificed. Leon atoned for his error in the top of the inning and singled over Ragland's head into right field to send Muser home with the tying run. Cleveland skipper Ken Aspromonte trudged to the mound and replaced Wilcox with Tom Hilgendorf. The southpaw could not do the job as Pat Kelly singled, moving Leon to second. Aspromonte again made a pitching change and called in Ed Farmer. Chicago's Johnny Jeter sent a groundball to Duffy at shortstop. A double play seemed to be in order, but the Tribe was only able to get the force out of Kelly at second base. Dick Allen stepped to the plate and unloaded his 10th home run of the year into the right-field pavilion. The final score was Chicago 6, Cleveland 3. Wood won his 12th game of the year against three losses. Wilcox took the loss and his record slipped to 3-1. It was the most innings played by a Cleveland team in the Indians' history. For Chicago, it tied the longest. The White Sox had lost to Detroit, 6-5, in a 21-inning affair on May 24, 1929.

For an encore, Wood pitched a nine-inning complete game in the nightcap, beating the Indians 4-0. Wood's record improved to 13-3, with a 1.71 ERA. "I call him Wilbur Wonderful," said White Sox manager Chuck Tanner.[1] Wood was off the mound 22 minutes between games. "It was just like a long inning between trips to the mound," he said.[2]

Wilbur Wood's record in 1973 was 24-20 with a 3.46 ERA. He led the AL for the second consecutive year in innings pitched with 359⅓ after pitching 376⅔ innings in 1972. Cleveland finished the year in last place in the AL East with a record of 71-91. Chicago, at 77-85, ended up in fifth place in the West.

SOURCES

In addition to the sources cited in the Notes, the author also accessed Retrosheet.org, Baseball-Reference.com, SABR.org, and **The Sporting News** archive via Paper of Record.

NOTES

1   Richard Dozer, "Wood Beats Indians Twice," **Chicago Tribune**, May 29, 1973: 3-1.

2   Ibid.

KITTY KAAT MOWS 'EM DOWN

SEPTEMBER 4, 1973
CHICAGO WHITE SOX 14, TEXAS RANGERS 0

By Joe Schuster

Both Jim Kaat and the Chicago White Sox came into 1973 with high expectations.

As the year opened, Kaat was in his 15th major-league season. The active leader in victories by left-handers with 179, he'd spent his entire career with the same franchise, starting with the Washington Senators in 1959 before moving with the team to Minnesota in 1961, becoming the Twins. Over those years, he'd been an All-Star twice. In 1966, if there had been a Cy Young Award in each league instead of one for both leagues, he would have been a likely candidate in the American League when he led the AL with 25 wins and 19 complete games, finished second in strikeouts (205), and ranked sixth in ERA (2.75). As it was, the sole Cy Young Award winner that year was Sandy Koufax, who led the majors with 27 wins, a 1.73 ERA and 317 strikeouts.

In 1972 Kaat got off to a start that suggested he might have his best season ever. By early July he was 10-2 and his 2.06 ERA ranked fourth in the league. He was talking openly about what it would mean to make a third All-Star team.[1] But on July 2 Kaat broke a bone in his pitching hand when he dived into second base to break up a double play. He didn't throw another pitch in a game for the rest of the year.

Coming into 1973, Kaat felt healthy and was so confident that he initially refused to sign the contract the Twins offered him, saying he was holding out for a three-year deal with a substantial raise, from $45,000 to $60,000.[2] (Some stories suggested that if he did not sign, he would be a free agent at the end of year and that was part of his plan.[3]) The Twins and Kaat eventually settled on a deal that gave him the salary he was looking for but gave him only one year.[4]

That season, however, did not go the way Kaat expected. While he won his first three starts, he was inconsistent after that and when he had six successive bad outings from late July into August, giving up 28 runs on 40 hits, the Twins waived him with his record at 11-12 with a 4.41 ERA. Three teams claimed him — the Yankees, the Royals, and the White Sox. Twins owner Clark Griffith reportedly tried to work out a deal with the Royals, who offered him 20-year-old George Brett in exchange.[5] Because the White Sox had the worst record of the three teams, they had first rights on Kaat and offered only the minimum waiver price of $20,000.[6]

Although Kaat, as a player with at least 10 years of major-league service, could have vetoed the deal, he accepted it happily, for two reasons. One, Chicago agreed to a contract for 1974 with a substantial raise to $70,000; two, Johnny Sain was the White Sox pitching coach and Kaat wanted to work with him since Sain had been the Twins' coach during Kaat's 1966 season.[7] (Kaat felt so strongly about Sain that when the Twins fired him after 1966, he wrote an angry letter to Griffith saying that the Twins' dumping Sain was like "the Green Bay Packers firing Vince Lombardi."[8])

The team Kaat joined was having a season just as disappointing as his. Before Opening Day, several pundits had picked them to contend

Jim Kaat won 21 games in 1974 and 20 in 1975 in his only two full seasons with the White Sox. In his 25-year big-league career (1969-1983), Kitty won 283 games and 16 Gold Glove Awards as the finest-fielding pitcher of his generation. (Photo by Ron Kuntz Collection/Diamond Images/Getty Images)

for the American League West title. *The Sporting News* said, "The Athletics and the White Sox should run a beautiful race in the A.L. West."[9] Meanwhile, broadcaster Howard Cosell said the White Sox would not only win the division but meet the Pirates in the World Series."[10]

Initially, it seemed the predictions would bear out: The White Sox and the Oakland Athletics were neck-and-neck the first three months of the season and the White Sox actually held first place for all of May and much of June. However, when they went 20-33 from July 1 to August 15, they found themselves in fourth place, a dozen games back.

Kaat's joining the White Sox coincided with a resurgence. He won his first start with them, a three-hit, 4-1 victory over Detroit on August 26, beginning a 13-1 run for Chicago. (While the team also won Kaat's second start, on September 1, he did not pitch well: Chicago gave him a 4-1 lead over the California Angels by the fourth inning but he surrendered it in a poor fifth when he faced four batters without recording an out before being pulled with the game tied 4-4; the White Sox eventually won 7-5.)

On September 4, the White Sox' opponent was the Texas Rangers, who came in with the worst record in the AL, 47-90, 32½ games back.

For the Tuesday night game, which drew 5,502 to Comiskey Park, Kaat and Sain decided he should experiment with a no-windup delivery. Kaat said, "I was getting lazy with my arm and wrist so we decided to try the no-windup delivery to quicken it up a little bit.[11]

The experiment worked: Kaat was strong from the first pitch. He fanned the first two batters, Dave Nelson and Toby Harrah, on his way to setting down the first eight he faced. The Rangers' ninth hitter, Ken Suarez, broke the string when he managed a third-inning infield single, and Kaat gave up a second hit that inning to Nelson before retiring Harrah on a groundball.

Meanwhile, the White Sox got to Rangers starter Jim Bibby almost immediately, thanks in good part to Bibby's wildness. After he retired White Sox leadoff man Pat Kelly, he walked the next three and then, with Carlos May batting, unleashed two wild pitches that each brought in a run. After May grounded out, Jorge Orta tripled to left, driving in the third run of the inning.

The first inning was a microcosm of the entire game for Rangers pitching and White Sox hitting. A walk to Kelly and Tony Muser's double added a run in the second. In the third, May hit a one-out single but was cut down trying to turn it into a double; then Bibby walked the next two, and his night was finished. Jackie Brown came on in relief.

The Rangers bullpen was no better. By the end of the fourth, it was 7-0. In the sixth, the White Sox exploded for six runs on five hits, a walk, and a hit batter. The big blow was a two-run homer by May, which set up a small moment of drama an inning later.

With no outs in the seventh and a runner on, Lloyd Allen, the fourth Rangers hurler of the game, hit May with a pitch. After May went to first, White Sox manager Chuck Tanner lifted him for a pinch-runner and on his way back to the dugout, May deliberately walked across the mound. Umpire John Rice rushed from behind the plate to prevent a fight but May simply asked Allen if he'd hit him on purpose. Allen said, "Naw. I know better than that."[12]

Meanwhile, Kaat continued to be sharp. He set the Rangers down in order in the fourth, fifth, and sixth innings, then retired the first two in the seventh before Jim Fregosi singled. But Fregosi was stranded at first when Kaat retired Dick Billings on a fly to center.

Kaat finally ran into a small spot of trouble in the eighth. With one out, Elliott Maddox singled and then, with two outs, Dave Nelson also singled, sending Maddox to third. Nelson stole second, putting two Texas runners in scoring position for the first time that night. But Kaat got Harrah to ground out and the threat was over. When he retired the side in order in the ninth, he had his complete-game shutout. His line: five hits, no runs, no walks, five strikeouts.

The win gave the White Sox their sixth consecutive victory and their 10th in 11 games.

While Kaat had a couple of rough outings from then through the end of the season, he ended up going 4-1 with a 4.22 ERA in his stint that year with the White Sox. Chicago did not sustain the level of play they realized just after Kaat joined them. While the White Sox won their next two games, pushing their win streak to eight, they went 6-14 through the rest of the season, finishing fifth, 17 games behind the Oakland A's.

Kaat spent two more seasons with Chicago and while the team did not finish above .500 in either of those years, Kaat pitched well, winning at least 20 games each year, going a combined 41-27 with a 3.02 ERA. He finally managed to make his third All-Star team, in 1975, but after that season the White Sox traded him to the Philadelphia Phillies.

SOURCES

In addition to the sources cited in the Notes, the author also accessed Retrosheet.org, Baseball-Reference.com, and SABR.org.

NOTES

1   Tom Briere, "Kaat Gets 10th Victory; Twins, Chicago Divide," **Minneapolis Star Tribune**, July 3, 1972: 17.

2   Bob Fowler, "Kaat Sticks to Guns, Playing without Pact," **The Sporting News**, March 31, 1973: 44.

3   Sid Hartman, "Kaat Still Waiting," **Minneapolis Tribune**, March 10, 1973: 18.

4   Sid Hartman, "Kaat Signs," **Minneapolis Tribune**, April 6, 1973: 36.

5   Sid Hartman, "Sid Hartman," **Minneapolis Tribune**, August 15, 1973: 24.

6   Sid Hartman, "Sid Hartman," **Minneapolis Tribune**, August 17, 1973: 36.

7   Jerome Holtzman, "Kaat Gives Chisox Head Start for 74," **The Sporting News**, September 1, 1973: 16.

8   Bill Hengen, "Kaat Gets 'Take Off' Sign," **Minneapolis Star**, August 16, 1973: 45.

9   C.C. Johnson Spink, "Spink Picks Red Sox in Closest Division Race," **The Sporting News**, April 14, 1973: 4.

10 Aaron Gold, "Tower Ticker," **Chicago Tribune**, April 6, 1973: 40.

11 George Langford, "Sox Romp 14-0," **Chicago Tribune**, September 5, 1973: 71.

12 Ibid.

THE RYAN EXPRESS FANS 18 AND WALKS 9 IN 185-PITCH EFFORT

SEPTEMBER 10, 1976
CALIFORNIA ANGELS 3, CHICAGO WHITE SOX 2

By Gregory H. Wolf

"Any time they cut into your arm, you're going to worry, but I think I've proved I'm all right," said Nolan Ryan, the California Angels' flamethrower, after fanning 18 Chicago White Sox.[1] The White Sox' Ralph Garr, a former batting champ with the Atlanta Braves, agreed, gushing that Ryan "threw better than anyone I've seen for a long time."[2]

Ryan began the 1976 season with major question marks. Three years earlier, he recorded the most punchouts (383) in big-league history as part of a three-year stretch (1972-1974) leading the majors in strikeouts. Seemingly on his way to his fourth straight campaign of at least 300 whiffs in '75, Ryan came down with elbow pain and eventually underwent season-ending surgery to remove four bone chips from his right elbow. Many wondered if the "Ryan Express" could bounce back in 1976; few expected the 29-year-old to regain his mantle as the hardest thrower in baseball history.

"I knew I was okay in January when I started throwing again," Ryan said confidently.[3] He was right. He yielded a sole hit and struck out seven, but also walked six in seven innings in his season debut and lost. Two starts later, he tossed a three-hit shutout, fanning 12 Baltimore Orioles. Ryan demonstrated that he still possessed his world-class heater and knee-buckling curveball, but there was no disguise for his offensively challenged teammates, the AL's lowest-scoring team.

The Angels (63-77) were in fifth place in the AL West as they prepared for the first game of a four-game series against the White Sox (59-80), the West Division's cellar dweller. The teams were going in opposite directions. Since Norm Sherry replaced skipper Dick Williams in late July, the Angels were on a 24-20 roll; the Pale Hose, piloted by 67-year-old Paul Richards, were in a free-fall, having lost 32 of their last 48.

Ryan entered the game with a lackluster 12-17 record and a high 3.84 ERA in 232⅓ innings, while leading the majors in strikeouts (260) and walks (144). He had whiffed at least 10 batters in nine of 33 starts, including 17 in 10 innings in a 5-4 victory against the Detroit Tigers on August 18. Toeing the rubber for the White Sox was Bart Johnson, who missed the entire 1975 season because of a herniated disc and underwent an experimental procedure to revive his once promising career. "It's a new treatment they're using for disc and back problems," he explained. "They give you two or three injections of papaya juice right into the disc area and supposedly that strengthens the disc."[4] Johnson's 9-13 slate pushed his career mark to 39-42 in parts of seven seasons.

On a pleasant Friday evening, a modest crowd of 6,575 was at Comiskey Park, on the South Side of the Windy City. That was about 5,000 less than the season average (which ranked 10th of 12 AL teams) despite the announcement earlier that day that the White Sox had activated Minnie Miñoso, the 50-year-old coach and former White Sox All-Star. It was yet another publicity stunt by the master showman, club owner Bill Veeck, who thought the one time "Cuban Comet," who had retired in 1964, could serve as a DH. Veeck ultimately decided to push back Miñoso's debut one day so he did not have to face Ryan.

After Johnson worked around a two-out double by Mike Easler in the first inning, Ryan had a close call in the bottom of the frame. He issued a two-out walk to Jim Spencer, then tossed Jorge Orta's tapper to the mound over first baseman Tony Solaita's head and into right field. According to the *Tribune*, the White Sox might have scored had Spencer not pulled up short at third on the error. Ryan fanned Sam Ewing (batting .174) to escape scoreless.

The Angels averaged a measly 3.4 runs per game and batted a paltry .235 in '76, so their two-run outburst in the second was music to Ryan's ears. Bruce Bochte belted his second home run of the season, a one-out solo shot to right field for the Halos' first run. Dave Chalk sliced a two-out single and then scored on Andy Etchebarren's double to right.

Through four innings, Ryan had fanned nine and walked three (two in the third) and had surrendered only a single to Alan Bannister. "My curve was really working in the early innings," he said, "but then I got tired and had to go to my fastball."[5] Ryan's fatigue resulted in a tough fifth when he battled his wildness which was as legendary, as were his walk totals (such as 202 in 1974, six off Bob Feller's record in 1938). His lack of control was the main reason the New York Mets gave up on him and shipped him along with Frank Estrada, Don Rose, and Leroy Stanton to the Angels for former All-Star shortstop Jim Fregosi after the 1971 season in what proved to be one of the most lopsided trades in big-league history. Ryan put runners on first and second via a walk and single sandwiched around two more punchouts, then surrendered a game-tying two-run double by Orta. Ryan seemed out of gas, but Norm Sherry, a former catcher with the Los Angeles Dodgers who experienced Sandy Koufax's periods of wildness and utter dominance, stuck with his big Texan. Ryan walked the next two hitters to load the bases, but the bullpen remained silent. Bannister popped up to right field to give Ryan a new lease on life.

The Angels wasted no time regaining the lead. Rusty Torres, who had pinch-run for Solaita in the third after he suffered an injury running out a single, tripled to center field with one out.[6] Two batters later, Bochte's double drove him in for a 3-2 Angels lead. Bochte's hit was the team's third to right field, landing in front of Garr, whom skipper Richards had criticized for failing to snag them. "[T]he sod out there in right is loose," quipped the defensively challenged Garr, in his first season with the ChiSox. "You can't start on it."[7]

Ryan settled into a groove after a rocky fifth. He worked around a leadoff walk to Bucky Dent in the sixth, the only inning in which he did not register a strikeout. He fanned two more in the seventh, then had another lapse of control in the eighth. He walked his eighth and ninth batters, interrupted by Dent reaching base on third baseman Bill Melton's error. With the bases jammed and just one out, the Express punched out Garr and Bill Stein to escape unscathed. "I don't think strikeouts," quipped Ryan, "but in the eighth inning when they had the bases full, I was."[8]

Strikeouts are "the ultimate proof that he's still throwing as hard as ever," declared the *Los Angeles Times* about Ryan's overpowering performance against the White Sox.[9] At no time was the Express more unhittable than when he fanned the side to complete the 3-2 victory in 2 hours and 29 minutes.

A fast worker who seemed to have an infinite number of pitches in his right wing, Ryan flung the orb 185 times and recorded 18 strikeouts, one off the major-league record he shared with Tom Seaver and Steve Carlton, and he himself accomplished three times, for a nine-inning game. He shrugged off his nine free passes, declaring, "I wasn't really that wild although the box score looks it. I was around the plate on most pitches."[10] White Sox pilot Paul Richards admitted that Ryan had a tough curve and powerful heater, but claimed his club would have won "if we don't [sic] swing at so many bad balls."[11]

Notoriously modest and self-effacing, Ryan took a sober approach to his 13th win. "I guess that would be the highlight of my season," he said. "I haven't really accomplished much. I've struggled with my rhythm all year. But at least I found out my arm was all right."[12] It was more than all right. Ryan concluded the '76 season on fire. From August 31 to the end of the season, he went 7-1 in 8 starts, yielded just 30 hits in 70 innings with a 1.41 ERA, fanned 86, and walked 48. His final line (17-18, 3.36) with a major-league-most 327 strikeouts, as well as 183 walks while allowing a big-league fewest 6.1 hits per 9 innings proved that the Express was not yet ready to slow down.

SOURCES

In addition to the sources cited in the Notes, the author also accessed Retrosheet.org, Baseball-Reference.com, and SABR.org.

NOTES

1. Associated Press, "Ryan Fans 18 Sox," **Dixon (Illinois) Evening Telegraph**, September 11, 1976: 9.
2. Richard Dozer, "Ryan Strikes Out 18 Sox in 3-hiter," **Chicago Tribune**, September 11, 1976: section 2, 1.
3. AP, "Ryan Fans 18 Sox,"
4. Bill Maddon, United Press International, "Bart's Back," **Daily Herald** (Chicago), March 23, 1976: 6.
5. "Ryan Fans 18; Angels Win, 3-2," **Los Angeles Times**, September 11, 1976: 49.
6. Dozer.
7. Ibid.
8. UPI, "Nolan Ryan Fans 18 in Win Over ChiSox," **Redlands (California) Daily Facts**, September 11, 1976: 7
9. "Ryan Fans 18; Angels Win, 3-2."
10. Dozer.
11. Ibid.
12. Ibid.

JIM SPENCER KNOCKS IN EIGHT IN CHISOX ROUT

MAY 14, 1977
CHICAGO WHITE SOX 18, CLEVELAND INDIANS 2

By Don Zminda

The 1977 Chicago White Sox — known ever after as the "Southside Hitmen" — may have been the most celebrated third-place club in major-league history. From Opening Day until season's end, the Hitmen were never dull, either in victory or defeat. But Bill Veeck's players really outdid themselves on the morning (and early afternoon) of May 14, as the White Sox took on the Cleveland Indians.

Did I say "morning"? Indeed; the White Sox-Indians game that day began a little after 10:30 A.M. Although this was the only game of club President Bill Veeck's second White Sox tenure (1976-80 seasons) that was scheduled to begin prior to noon,[1] such contests were part of Veeck's long tradition. While running the minor-league Milwaukee Brewers during World War II, Veeck staged several "Rosie the Riveter" contests, with fans receiving bottles of milk and breakfast fare upon entering the park.[2] The 1977 White Sox morning game may not have included many riveters, but the Saturday contest did draw a crowd of 13,923 (including the author and a friend), with the attendees given coupons for a free breakfast.[3] In all honesty, that was fairly modest attendance for the 1977 White Sox, who entered the May 14 game in second place in the American League West with a 19-11 record, only a half-game behind the division-leading Minnesota Twins. Indeed, of the eight Saturday day games the White Sox played in 1977 (doubleheaders not included), only the April 16 contest against the expansion Toronto Blue Jays drew lower attendance.

Sparse crowd or not, those who attended the May 14 game saw plenty of action — much of it provided by first baseman Jim Spencer. One of the few members of the Southside Hitmen known for his fielding prowess, Spencer would win two Gold Gloves at first base during his major-league career, including one in 1977 (the first was in 1970). On offense Spencer could hardly be considered a slugger, but he reached double figures in home runs eight times during his 15-year major-league career, with a career total of 146 homers. (He would reach his single-season high in 1979 with 23.) In 1976 the left-handed-hitting Spencer had actually tied Jorge Orta for the White Sox team lead with the modest total of 14 homers, and his 18 home runs in 1977 would be tied for the second-highest total of his career. However, he entered the May 14 contest with only three homers and 13 RBIs for the season (in 30 games played). Spencer was so modestly regarded that he was not even listed on the 1977 American League All-Star Game ballot.[4]

Spencer's big day began in the bottom of the second inning, with the game still scoreless. After Richie Zisk led off the inning with a triple to center field, Spencer followed with a home run off Indians starter Jim Bibby. After Bibby retired Oscar Gamble, the White Sox responded with three more hits, prompting Cleveland manager Frank Robinson to replace Bibby with left-hander Sid Monge. The rally continued, and when Zisk came up for the second time in the inning with two outs and runners on first and third, Robinson made the somewhat unorthodox move of ordering an intentional walk, setting up a lefty-against-lefty matchup against Spencer but moving Alan Bannister to second to load the bases. "Can't figure that one out," one of the White Sox coaches told *Chicago Tribune* writer Richard Dozer about the move.[5] The strategy backfired when Spencer singled to right for two more runs, giving the White Sox seven runs in the inning, with four RBIs credited to Spencer.

It was still 7-0, White Sox, when Spencer next came to the plate, in the bottom of the fourth inning. He was facing Cleveland's third pitcher, right-hander Pat Dobson, and once more the bases were loaded, with two out. Spencer responded with the first grand-slam of his major-league career, making the score 11-0 and giving Spencer eight RBIs on two home runs and a single in only four innings of play.

The eight RBIs matched the White Sox team record for runs batted in a game held by Carl Reynolds (July 2, 1930) and Tommy McCraw (May 24, 1967). (At the time the White Sox reported that Joe Jackson had also driven in eight runs in a game in 1920, but that was later corrected.) More importantly, Spencer figured to have at least a couple more plate appearances to challenge the major-league record for RBIs in a game (12 by the Cardinals' Jim Bottomley on September 16, 1924; later equaled by the Cards' Mark Whiten in 1993) or the American League single-game record of 11 RBIs (the Yankees' Tony Lazzeri on May 24, 1936).

But Spencer never got the opportunity; with the White Sox holding an 11-0 lead, manager Bob Lemon took Spencer out of the game, replacing him with Lamar Johnson after the completion of the fourth inning. It's a tantalizing "what might have been," as the White Sox continued to pound away at Cleveland pitching, ultimately winning the game 18-2. It was the most runs scored by the White Sox in a single game since an 18-8 defeat of the Twins on June 20, 1971.

All other things being equal, Lemon's decision to remove Spencer from the game would have drawn no controversy. The Sox and Indians had played a 7:30 P.M. game on Friday night[6] (a 5-3 White Sox victory), and since the game had lasted 2:42, the teams were taking the field on May 14 a little over 12 hours after the previous night's game had concluded. Lemon had removed right fielder Richie Zisk (replacing him with Wayne Nordhagen) after the third inning, when the score was 7-0, and he removed left fielder Ralph Garr (replacing him with Jerry Hairston) after the fourth inning along with Spencer. Cleveland manager Frank Robinson also removed two of his starting position players after the third inning. Spencer's replacement, Lamar Johnson, wound up batting twice, coming up with a runner on third with one out in the sixth inning and then leading off the inning in the eighth. "I didn't have any idea that he had a shot at setting a record, but if I did, I'd have asked him if he wanted to stay in," Lemon said after the game. "Next time he drives in eight, I'll remind him," he quipped.[7]

Lemon was joking, but he didn't have to wait long to see Jim Spencer have another eight-RBI game. Facing the Minnesota Twins at Comiskey Park on July 2, Spencer drove in eight runs once more; again his big game included a grand-slam (off left-hander Bill Butler) in the fourth inning, along with an RBI single in the sixth and a three-run homer in his final trip to the plate in the eighth inning of a 13-8 White Sox victory. Two eight-RBI games in a single year: not bad for a fellow who was primarily noted for his glove!

SOURCES

In addition to the sources cited in the Notes, the author also accessed Retrosheet.org, Baseball-Reference.com, and SABR.org.

NOTES

1. Verified by a review of the league schedules (which included start times) in the **American League Red Books** from 1976-80.

2. Sam Levy, "Prexy Bill's Side-Splitting Sideshows Putting Merry Click in Milwaukee Gate," **The Sporting News**, August 5, 1943.

3. Richard Dozer, "Spencer Drives in 8 Runs as Sox Whip Indians 18-2," **Chicago Tribune**, May 15, 1977.

4. Richard Dozer, "Spencer Answers All-Star Snub With RBI Show for White Sox," **The Sporting News**, June 4, 1977.

5. Dozer, "Spencer Drives in 8 Runs."

6. "Sports Log," **Chicago Tribune**, May 13, 1977.

7. Dozer, "Spencer Answers All-Star Snub."

JIM SPENCER DRIVES IN EIGHT RUNS FOR SECOND TIME IN TWO MONTHS

JULY 2, 1977
CHICAGO WHITE SOX 13, MINNESOTA TWINS 8

By Michael Marsh

Chicago White Sox owner Bill Veeck faced a dilemma after the 1976 season. The White Sox had finished that campaign, their fourth consecutive losing season, with a 64-97 record. Only 914,945 fans attended games at Comiskey Park. The team needed stars to improve the record and increase attendance. The start of free agency, however, boosted salaries for star players. Veeck, in his second stint as owner of the team, lacked the financial resources to compete for them.[1]

Veeck and general manager Roland Hemond thought outside the box in order to stock the team. The White Sox traded pitchers Rich Gossage and Terry Forster to the Pittsburgh Pirates for outfielder Richie Zisk and Silvio Martinez. They sent shortstop Bucky Dent, who had started for the three previous seasons in Chicago, to the New York Yankees for outfielder Oscar Gamble, minor leaguer Robert Polinsky, future Cy Young Award winner LaMarr Hoyt, and $200,000.[2] Both Zisk and Gamble were essentially one-year rentals expected to seek long-term deals after the season. The team signed former Minnesota Twins third baseman Eric Soderholm, who sat out the 1976 season while he recovered from knee surgery. To bolster the pitching staff, Veeck took another chance and signed Steve Stone. Stone had recovered from a rotator-cuff injury during the previous season. Zisk, Gamble, Soderholm, and Stone joined key holdovers first baseman Jim Spencer, outfielder Chet Lemon, and outfielder Ralph Garr.

Veeck also hired Bob Lemon, a pitcher elected to the Hall of Fame the previous year and a former manager (Kansas City Royals, 1970-1972) with a cool head, to manage the team.

Two other additions enhanced the fans' experience at games. Team announcer Harry Caray led fans in singing "Take Me Out to the Ball Game" over the public-address system during the seventh-inning stretch. Late in July 1977, organist Nancy Faust started to play "Na Na Hey Hey Kiss Him Goodbye," a classic rock tune by the group Steam, when White Sox bats knocked opposing pitchers out of the game.[3] The additions, along with the scoreboard that shot fireworks after White Sox home runs, helped create a raucous atmosphere at the park.

Veeck's efforts paid off. The 1977 White Sox defied limited expectations and emerged as a contender, finishing June 1977 with a 40-32 record. The scoreboard frequently exploded after home runs. Players took curtain calls after their round-trippers before adoring fans. Over time, they became known as the South Side Hitmen. The White Sox battled the Kansas City Royals, Minnesota Twins, and Texas Rangers for the American League West crown and brought excitement back to Comiskey Park.

Spencer, a 6-foot-2, 195-pound veteran who threw and batted left-handed, had emerged as a fan favorite. A Gold Glove winner for the 1970 California Angels, he had continued his fancy fielding for the White Sox. Spencer also sparked the Team with his bat. Fans began hanging a banner that read: "C'MON SPENCE, OVER THE FENCE."[4] On May 14, 1977, he hit two home runs and drove in eight runs as Chicago beat the visiting Cleveland Indians, 18-2.

On Saturday, July 2, 1977, Spencer repeated the feat in a crucial game before 35,271 fans at Comiskey Park. He hit two home runs and drove in eight runs as the White Sox beat the Minnesota Twins, 13-8. He became the first White Sox player to drive in eight runs in a game twice in a season.

Minnesota had traveled to Chicago for a midseason series that doubled as an early showdown in the American League West. The Twins, with a 42-33 record, were tied with the White Sox for first place after the opening game of a four-game series. Minnesota's Rod Carew and Larry Hisle helped carry the team's offense. Carew entered the game with a .411 batting average and a 12-game hitting streak.

Minnesota drew first blood against Chicago starter Jack Kucek, making his season debut, in the top of the second inning. Mike Cubbage hit an RBI single. Rob Wilfong drove in another run with a groundout for a 2-0 lead.

Twins starter Bill Butler (0-1) retired the first nine White Sox batters. Wildness in the bottom of the fourth, however, cost him. He walked Alan Bannister and Jorge Orta. Butler retired Zisk and Lamar Johnson on fly balls. He walked Lemon to load the bases. Spencer then got Chicago's first hit of the game: a grand slam. That gave the White Sox a 4-2 lead.

The game turned into a seesaw battle for the next few innings. In the top of the fifth inning, Hisle hit a two-run double that knocked Kucek out of the game and forged a tie. Kucek's replacement, Bart Johnson, gave up a sacrifice fly to Dan Ford that gave the Twins a 5-4 lead.

The Twins switched Butler for Tom Burgmeier for the bottom of the fifth. Burgmeier didn't hold the lead. He gave up a two-out double to Bannister. Orta's single drove home Bannister and tied the game. Afterward, Zisk singled off Burgmeier. The Twins lifted Butler for Tom Johnson (9-3), who struck out Lamar Johnson to end the inning.

Spencer delivered another clutch hit in the bottom of the sixth. Lemon led off with a triple off Johnson. Spencer's single drove in Lemon and gave the White Sox a 6-5 lead.

Minnesota reclaimed the lead in the top of the eighth inning. Butch Wynegar hit a two-out single off Bart Johnson that drove in Cubbage and Wilfong, who had both singled. The Twins took a 7-6 lead. Johnson left the game, and Lerrin LaGrow replaced him. LaGrow struck out Hisle to end the inning.

The White Sox fought back again. During a wild rally, they scored seven unearned runs in the bottom of the eighth. With one out, Garr grounded to first baseman Carew. Carew tossed the ball to Johnson, who missed the base.[5] The next batter, Jim Essian, hit a grounder to shortstop Roy Smalley. Smalley attempted to backhand the ball, but it bounced off his glove. Essian was credited with a single. Bannister hit a routine fly to right field. Ford, who was not wearing sunglasses, lost the ball in the sun. He dropped to his knees in a last-ditch attempt to locate the ball, but it fell for a hit.[6] Orta hit a line-drive single to right that drove in Essian and Garr. Zisk drove in Bannister with a sacrifice fly. Tom Johnson, the eventual losing pitcher, departed the game after a wild pitch. Dave Johnson replaced him. Lamar Johnson drove in Orta with a single. Lemon also singled. Spencer hit a three-run homer into the right-field stands to give the White Sox a commanding 13-7 lead.

LaGrow (4-1), the eventual winner, gave up one run in the top of the ninth inning. The Twins' Glenn Adams doubled and advanced to third on a wild pitch. Adams scored on Ford's groundout.

After the loss, an angry Twins manager Gene Mauch held a closed-door meeting with his players and discussed their sloppy play during the White Sox' seven-run rally. He later gave a tongue-in-cheek comment to a reporter. Mauch said: "I neglected to check all our players when they took the field in the eighth inning to see that they were all wearing shoes, gloves, and glasses."[7]

Meanwhile, White Sox fans exulted over the win. *Chicago Sun-Times* columnist Bill Gleason captured their jubilation. Gleason wrote: "When it finally ended at 4:17 P.M., the 35,271 spectators went home with the joyful conviction that they had witnessed one of the wildest, weirdest, most hysterical games ever played."[8]

Spencer told the *Chicago Tribune* that Zisk's advice had boosted his performance. "Saturday's my day. But Zisk helped me. He handed me a heavier bat — about 34 ½ ounces — and told me to use it because I'd been pulling a lot of pitches foul. It's about two ounces heavier than the bat I've been using."[9]

Spencer finished the season with 18 home runs and 69 RBIs and won his final Gold Glove. He played a key role as the White Sox notched a 90-72 record and took third in the division. Despite his achievements, however, Veeck used Spencer as trade bait. Veeck traded Spencer, Polinsky, and Tommy Cruz to the New York Yankees for minor leaguer Ed Ricks, Stan Thomas, and cash in December 1977.[10]

SOURCES

In addition to the sources cited in the Notes, the author also used the Baseball-Reference.com, Baseball-Almanac.com, and Retrosheet.org websites for box-score, player, team, and season pages, pitching and batting game logs, and other pertinent material.

NOTES

1. Veeck had owned the White Sox between 1959 and 1961.
2. Mark Gonzales, **The Good, the Bad & the Ugly: Heart-Pounding, Jaw-Dropping, and Gut-Wrenching Moments from Chicago White Sox History** (Chicago: Triumph Books, 2009), 199.
3. Phil Rosenthal, "White Sox's Summer of 1977 Gave Us Two Great Sports Musical Traditions," **Chicago Tribune**, August 5, 2017. Retrieved May 16, 2018.
4. Dan Helpingstine, **South Side Hitmen: The Story of the 1977 Chicago White Sox** (Chicago: Arcadia Publishing, 2005), 74.
5. Joe Goddard, "Spencer Is the Difference," **Chicago Sun-Times**, July 3, 1977: 95.
6. Ibid.
7. Tom Briere, "Sox Slap Twins 13-8," **Minneapolis Star Tribune**, July 3, 1977: 1C.
8. Bill Gleason, "Just Another Saturday Afternoon at Old Ballpark," **Chicago Sun-Times**, July 3, 1977: 99
9. Bill Jauss, "Spencer Has Twins Behind the 8 Ball," **Chicago Tribune**, July 3, 1977: B1.
10. Helpingstine, 116.

CHICAGO'S "DISCO DEMOLITION NIGHT" DOUBLEHEADER RESULTS IN LOSS AND FORFEIT

JULY 12, 1979
DETROIT TIGERS 4, CHICAGO WHITE SOX 1 (GAME ONE)

DETROIT TIGERS WIN BY FORFEIT (GAME TWO)

By Mike Huber

Five days before the 1979 All-Star Game, two fifth-place teams in the American League had a twi-night doubleheader scheduled, as the Detroit Tigers visited the Chicago White Sox. Mike Veeck, son of White Sox owner Bill Veeck, was the director of promotions for the White Sox. He had conspired with Steve Dahl, a Chicago disc jockey, for a one-of-a-kind promotion, in order to attract crowds and improve the abysmal White Sox attendance. Chicago was riding a four-game win streak and had won seven of eight, but the team was still drawing small home crowds. The Tigers, meanwhile, had lost four of their last five games.

Dahl had been fired by Chicago radio station WDAI-FM on Christmas Eve 1978[1] when the station transitioned to an all-disco format; popular movies like *Saturday Night Fever*, released in 1977, vaulted disco music to rule the airwaves. Dahl was hired by rock station WLUP-FM and began a crusade against disco music. The popular morning radio personality was going to literally use fireworks to blow up hundreds of disco records between the two games of the doubleheader.

An electric crowd of 47,795 fans, more than 3,000 over Comiskey Park's capacity of 44,492, packed the ballpark, eager to see the show.[2] Veeck and the WLUP staff were hoping for 20,000 attendees, and security had been hired for 35,000, but some estimates put the crowd as high as 60,000.[3] The stands were filled with fans who each could gain entry to the ballpark for just 98 cents (the radio frequency of WLUP, known as 98 Rock, was 97.9), "if they brought a record to be destroyed."[4] Those in attendance and in the dugouts watched as the playing field was ultimately destroyed.

The first game was set to begin at 6:00 P.M. The first pitch was thrown out by Lorelei, a "blonde rock 'n' roll siren"[5] who worked for WLUP's advertising group. Chicago manager Don Kessinger sent Fred Howard (1-3) to the mound, opposed by Detroit's Pat Underwood (3-0).

The Tigers scored a run in the opening frame. With one out, Lou Whitaker walked and moved to third when Rusty Staub singled into right field. With Jason Thompson batting, Staub attempted to steal second base. Chicago backstop Mike Colbern threw the ball away and Whitaker scampered home. Detroit added a run in the second. Jerry Morales reached on an error charged to third baseman Jim Morrison.

He then stole second and scored as Tom Brookens drove a one-out triple into left field. The first two innings resulted in two unearned runs for the Tigers.

In the home half of the second, Rusty Torres singled to left field after Wayne Nordhagen had grounded out. Morrison struck out, but Greg Pryor lined a run-producing double to left, cutting the Detroit lead to 2-1. Chicago's Howard continued to labor in the third. Staub drew a one-out walk and two batters later, Champ Summers singled to the right side to send Staub to second base. Morales followed with a single into right field, plating Staub. The Tigers had sent 16 batters to the plate in the first three innings. Howard settled down a bit, retiring the Tigers in order in the fourth and fifth. Meanwhile, after allowing the run in the second inning, Underwood retired 12 in a row until the bottom of the sixth, when he gave up a single to Chet Lemon and a walk to Lamar Johnson, but both runners were stranded. Underwood continued his dominance of the Chicago hitters, pitching 7⅔ innings. He allowed one earned run on five hits and two walks, and he struck out three.

Summers led off the top of the sixth with a single off Howard. He stole second, the third swipe off the Howard/Colbern battery. Morales grounded out and Summers remained at second. Lance Parrish stroked an RBI single to center, and the Tigers had a 4-1 advantage. Parrish's base knock brought Kessinger to the mound, and Howard was done for the day. Journeyman Ed Farmer came on in relief. Chicago was the right-hander's seventh team in seven years in the big leagues.[6] Farmer finished the game for the White Sox, shutting out the Tigers on three hits.

Chicago had a mini-rally in the bottom of the eighth, with two men on and two outs, on a double from Junior Moore and a walk to Lemon. Aurelio Lopez trotted in from the bullpen and induced Johnson to hit into a force out. Lopez pitched a perfect ninth, getting Jorge Orta to foul out and then striking out pinch-hitter Claudell Washington and Morrison to end the game. Detroit won, 4-1.

Then the show began. Dahl blew up a crate of records in the outfield and a riot ensued. According to NPR, "[A]n estimated 7,000 people slid down the foul poles, lit things on fire and literally stole the bases."[7] With the security forces outside the stadium, attempting to keep thousands of people from crashing the gates, spectators already in Comiskey Park stormed the field with little resistance. When Dahl set off the explosives, Detroit pitcher Jack Morris said, "[A]ll hell broke loose. They charged the field and started tearing up the pitching rubber and the dirt. They took the bases. They started digging out home plate."[8] White Sox announcer Harry Caray took to the public-address system, urging fans to calm down, to no avail. The batting cage was knocked over. Fans who had brought records but not turned them in started "flinging records like Frisbees."[9] Chicago police arrived and arrested 37 people.

Former AL umpire Nestor Chylak, now a supervisor of umpires, was present at Comiskey. After the riot on the field, Chylak met with the umpire crew (headed by crew chief Dave Phillips), Bill Veeck, and Tigers manager Sparky Anderson. Detroit television commentator Al Kaline (elected into the Hall of Fame in 1980) was also in attendance at the meeting. According to Kaline, the participants at the meeting were "afraid of somebody getting hurt, and also, the fact that home plate was uprooted from the ground and it has not been measured, it has not been properly put back in."[10] The only option for the White Sox was to forfeit the second game of the doubleheader. Phillips called American League President Lee MacPhail, who ordered the second game postponed until Sunday. Anderson was not satisfied and cited the rule book, insisting that the White Sox were responsible for the field conditions, which did not merit a postponement but a forfeit instead. The next day, MacPhail informed his longtime friend Bill Veeck "that his struggling White Sox had lost a game by forfeit."[11]

Chicago pitcher Rich Wortham, a Texan who preferred the sounds of country crooners Willie

Nelson and Waylon Jennings over disco, told the *Chicago Tribune* that "this wouldn't have happened if they had country and western night."[12] Thirty years after the event, the *New York Times* reported, "Few sports promotions ever went so awry; few are remembered as well."[13] Roland Hemond was the general manager of the White Sox and he claimed that it was a "great promotion."[14] Many folks blamed either Dahl or Mike Veeck for the riot. Sportscaster Howard Cosell instead blamed Caray, saying that Caray "contributed to a 'carnival' atmosphere."[15] The younger Veeck had been on the field when Dahl started his pyrotechnics. He reflected on the event almost 40 years later, saying, "I never left second base. … I was just standing there thinking about what my next job would be, because I knew that my life as I knew it right then was over."[16]

There was a precedent for the forfeit, though. On April 26, 1925, the Cleveland Indians defeated the White Sox 7-2 in a not-quite-nine-inning game at Comiskey Park that was called with two outs in the ninth, after the crowd thought the game was over. It was shortened "because, the history books say, 'the fans stormed the field.'"[17]

SOURCES

In addition to the sources mentioned in the notes, the author consulted Baseball-Reference.com and Retrosheet.org.

NOTES

1. Andy Behrens, "Disco Demolition: Bell-bottoms be gone!" ESPN.com, July 12, 2009, found online at espn.com/chicago/columns/story?page=disco/090712. Accessed September 2017.

2. **Sporting News Baseball Guide** (St. Louis: The Sporting News Company, 1979), 11.

3. Joe LaPointe, "The Night Disco Went Up in Smoke," **New York Times**, July 4, 2009, found online at nytimes.com/2009/07/05/sports/baseball/05disco.html. Accessed September 2017. The **Chicago Tribune** reported that the attendance was closer to 59,000, still more than 10,000 higher than the "official" mark of 47,795.

4. Ibid.

5. George Bova, "Disco Demolition's Lorelei," found online at whitesoxinteractive.com/rwas/index.php?category=11&id=2300. Accessed September 2017.

6. Farmer was traded to the Yankees in March 1974 but was sent to Philadelphia a week later, so he could claim eight teams from 1971 to 1979. He did not pitch in the majors in either 1975 or 1976, and pitched in only four games in 1977 and 1978.

7. John Derek, "July 12, 1979: 'The Night Disco Died' — Or Didn't," National Public Radio, July 16, 2016, found online at npr.org/2016.07.16/485873750/july-12-the-night-disco-died-or-didnt. Accessed September 2017.

8. LaPointe.

9. Phil Vettel, "Steve Dahl's Disco Demolition at Comiskey Park," **Chicago Tribune**, 2017, found online at chicagotribune.com/news/nationworld/politics/chi-chicagodays-disco-story-story.html. Accessed September 2017.

10. LaPointe.

11. Richard Dozer, "Veeck Protests Sox Forfeit, but Accepts Responsibility," **Chicago Tribune**, July 14, 1979: 21.

12. David Israel, "When Fans Wanted to Rock, the Baseball Stopped," **Chicago Tribune**, July 13, 1979: 62.

13. LaPointe.

14. Ibid.

15. Vettel.

16. Paul Sullivan, "'Disco Demolition' Night Fondly, and Not-So-Fondly, Remembered," **Chicago Tribune**, August 4, 2017, found online at chicagotribune.com/sports/columnists/ct-chicago-disco-demolition-white-sox-spt-0806-20170805-column.html. Accessed September 2017.

17. Richard Dozer, "Tigers Ask for Forfeit of 2d Game," **Chicago Tribune**, July 13, 1979: 60.

IRISH NIGHT BRINGS LUCK TO CLAUDELL WASHINGTON, RAINING DOWN THREE HOMERS TO DANCING FANS

JULY 14, 1979
CHICAGO WHITE SOX 12, DETROIT TIGERS 4

By Mark Mullane

The 1979 White Sox were accustomed to excitement in Comiskey under the ownership of the promotional Bill Veeck, but it wasn't usually from the ballgame. That changed on July 14, when outfielder Claudell Washington slammed three home runs against the Detroit Tigers. A strong player who made it onto the American League All-Star team in 1975 at the age of 20 while playing for the Oakland Athletics, his performance wasn't that of a slugger with only 10 home runs in that season. White Sox manager saw potential in Washington, stating that "He has unlimited ability, and all he needs is day-to-day consistency."[1]

Washington's performance couldn't have come at a better time for the struggling White Sox. The team had a 40-49 record going into the game, and had dropped the first three games in the series, including a forfeited second game of a doubleheader after the ill-fated Disco Demolition Night ended with members of the crowd of 50,000 storming the field, having to be chased off by Chicago riot police. That didn't stop Veeck from continuing promotions, however, and Washington's home-run feat was witnessed by an Irish Night crowd of almost 24,000, "who danced gleefully in the aisles" despite the 95 percent humidity of a classic Chicago summer.[2]

The Tigers had lost four out of the last five against the Minnesota Twins and Milwaukee Brewers, putting them at 41-44 going into the series against the White Sox.

On the mound for the White Sox was left-handed Ross Baumgarten, a 20th-round draft pick by the White Sox in 1977 who was having a breakout season with an 8-5 record going into the game. Baumgarten opened strong, retiring Ron LeFlore and Lou Whitaker on grounders. A walk put Jerry Morales on base, but a fly ball from Lance Parrish ended the inning.

Steve Baker had a shakier start to his first full season with the Tigers than Baumgarten. After a 2-4 season in 1978, Baker was looking far worse; he had racked up five losses to one win by July 14. After striking out leadoff hitter Alan Bannister, he yielded a double to center field by Ralph Garr, who scored on a single by Jorge Orta.

The Tigers responded quickly. Baumgarten walked Rusty Staub with one out in the second. Staub went to third on a single by Lynn Jones and he scored on a fielder's choice grounder to shortstop by Tom Brookens. (Jones was out at third.) Alan Trammell's double to deep left field plated Brookens and gave the Tigers a 2-1 lead.

Washington struck in the bottom of the third, smacking a pitch by Baker into the right-field stands, tying the score.

The Tigers picked up another run in the fourth when Milt May walked, was sacrificed to second by Jim Morrison, and was driven home by a single from player-manager Don Kessinger. Leading 3-2, the White Sox never looked back.

Baker was relieved in the fifth by Milt Wilcox, a veteran righty who was normally a starter. The White Sox jumped on Wilcox in the sixth. Morrison singled, was sacrificed to second by Kessinger, and was driven home by Alan Bannister's triple. Ralph Garr homered to right for two more runs. Wilcox struck out Orta and Lamar Johnson, but the White Sox had expanded their lead to 6-2.

Despite the heat and humidity, Baumgarten kept cool by ducking into the air-conditioned clubhouse while his team was batting. "I'd just wait until there were two outs and go back to the bench," said Baumgarten. "No problem, especially when they give you all those runs to work with."[3]

Wilcox faltered again in the seventh. Washington homered to right and Torres followed with another. The struggling Wilcox gave way to closer Dave Tobik. He got May on a fly out but Morrison followed with a round-tripper to left, making the score 9-2.

The Tigers showed signs of life in the ninth. Jerry Morales and John Wockenfuss homered, making the score 9-4. Staub singled and Baumgarten was relieved by Ed Farmer, a recent arrival via trade from the Texas Rangers in mid-June. After a wild pitch to Lynn Jones that let Staub take second, Farmer finished the inning with two groundouts.

In the bottom of the eighth, Tobik allowed a single by Moore and walked Orta. After Mike Squires struck out, Washington stepped to the plate and smacked homer number three, this time to left, and the White Sox led 12-4. "I felt tired and drained by then and I really didn't think the ball would carry that far," Washington said after the game. "I hit one better than that last night and it didn't carry, even though the air was a lot heavier this time."[4]

The Tigers offense couldn't muster a run in the top of the ninth, ending the game at 12-4. The White Sox had bashed six homers, the second most the club had ever managed in a game, behind the seven slugged in a 29-6 rout of the Kansas City Athletics in 1955.

"This is a night I'll cherish," said Washington.

"Nothing like it has ever happened to me."[5] While it may have been the first, it wasn't the last. Traded to the New York Mets the next season, Washington smacked three balls out of the park on June 22 to secure a 9-6 win over the Los Angeles Dodgers. Washington is one of only a handful of players who have hit three home runs in a game in both leagues.

As for the 1979 game, the Tigers returned the favor the next day, taking the White Sox down 14-5, a feat the Tigers accomplished without a single home run. The Tigers had a strong second half of the season, finishing at 85-76, good enough for fifth place in a strong AL East.

The one-time performance wasn't enough to turn the tide of the beleaguered White Sox, who were plagued with injuries and roster changes. "How do you sing 'Take Me Out to the Ball Game' when your team is losing 14-3?" wondered the *Chicago Tribune* after the Tigers routed them in the Sunday game.[6] Washington remained hopeful though: "It's only a matter of time until I really show Chicago fans what I can do," he said after his three-homer performance. Despite the optimism, the White Sox failed to match their 12 runs scored for the rest of the season, and ended with a record of 73-87, coincidentally finishing fifth in the AL West.

SOURCES

In addition to the sources cited in the Notes, the author also accessed Retrosheet.org, Baseball-Reference.com, and SABR.org.

NOTES

1   Bob Logan, "Washington's 3 HRs Lead White Sox Explosion," **Chicago Tribune**, July 15, 1979: C1.

2   Ibid.

3   Ibid.

4   Ibid.

5   Ibid.

6   Rick Talley, "Sox Fans Getting Very Cheap Thrills," **Chicago Tribune**, July 16, 1979: E1.

WHITE SOX OVERCOME SEVEN-RUN DEFICIT IN LAST TWO INNINGS TO WIN SEASON FINALE

OCTOBER 4, 1981
CHICAGO WHITE SOX 13, MINNESOTA TWINS 12

By Thomas J. Brown Jr.

The Chicago White Sox had played well in the first half of the 1981 season. When a strike by the players brought a halt to the season on June 12, the White Sox had a 31-22 record. The strike ended on July 31. After games resumed on August 9, the White Sox struggled in the second half of the strike-shortened season and would finish the second half with a 23-30 record.

On October 3, the White Sox beat the Minnesota Twins 5-4 to raise their record to 53-52. They wanted to win their final game of the season, the next day, in order to finish with a winning record for the first time since 1977.

The Minnesota Twins had won just 17 games before the strike. They had improved their play after the strike, and their second-half record was 24-28 entering this last day of the season.

Chicago sent Richard Dotson to the mound. He had a 9-8 record and had lost his last outing, 5-1 to the California Angels. The Minnesota starter was Albert Williams. He had lost his previous two starts and his record was 6-10. He was hoping to finish a disappointing year on a positive note.

The White Sox jumped out to the lead in the bottom of the first inning. Leo Sutherland singled, stole second base and ended up on third on a wild pitch. He came home when Jerry Hairston hit a sacrifice fly to center field.

Dotson maintained a shutout through the first four innings, allowing the Twins just three hits, two doubles by Kent Hrbek and another by Tim Corcoran. Meanwhile, the White Sox continued to score runs and build their lead. Jay Loviglio led off the third with a walk and moved to second on a sacrifice. He moved to third on Tony Bernazard's grounder to first and scored the White Sox' second run when Hairston hit a sharp groundball to the second baseman, Rob Wilfong, who couldn't handle the ball.

The White Sox continued to hit Williams, scoring two more runs in the fourth inning. Carlton Fisk walked to lead off the inning, and went to third when Mike Squires singled to right field. Greg Pryor hit another single, scoring Fisk and moving Squires to third. Loviglio hit a ground ball up the middle. The Twins' only play was to second and they got a double play. But Squires scored and the White Sox now led 4-0.

Dotson fell apart in the fifth inning after getting the first out. Rick Sofield and Wilfong hit consecutive doubles. After Dave Engle singled and sent Wilfong home for the second Twins run, Tony La Russa replaced Dotson with left-hander Kevin Hickey. Twins manager Billy Gardner sent switch-hitter Roy Smalley to the plate to face him.

Smalley hit a sharp groundball that the shortstop couldn't handle, leaving runners on first and second. Chuck Baker then tripled and the Twins had tied the game. Hickey hit Hrbek, putting runners on first and third. La Russa pulled Hickey and replaced him with Lynn McGlothen. Gary Ward grounded out but Baker scored and the Twins had grabbed the lead, 5-4.

Although the Twins had given Williams some offensive help, he continued to struggle. After getting Bernazard to ground out, he walked Hairston and Greg Luzinski in the bottom of the fifth, Wayne Nordhagen doubled to score Hairston and tie the game. Gardner finally replaced Williams with right-hander Don Cooper, who walked Fisk but got the final out by getting Squires to ground into a double play.

The game would not stay tied for long. In the top of the sixth, McGlothen gave up a double to Ron Washington and a single by Sofield to start the inning. La Russa replaced McGlothen with Ed Farmer, who did no better. After Wilfong reached on an error that allowed Washington to score, Engle singled to score another run. Glenn Adams pinch-hit and singled for the third Twins run of the inning. After Farmer struck out Baker for the first out of the inning, he gave up another hit, a single to Hrbek. It was Hrbek's third hit of the game and it scored Engle. The Twins regained the lead, 9-5.

Harry Caray led the crowd in singing "Take Me Out to the Ball Game" during the seventh-inning stretch. He had started singing for the fans in 1976 after Bill Veeck heard him humming the song in the announcers' booth. Although Caray resisted, he finally agreed after Veeck told him that he had already taped him singing and would play that instead. The song quickly became a big deal and White Sox fans came expecting to hear him sing.[1] Today would be the final time that he would entertain the crowd at Comiskey. He would move to their crosstown rivals, the Chicago Cubs, after the season.

The Twins extended their lead in top of the eighth inning. Reggie Patterson replaced Farmer for the White Sox. After getting the first out, he walked Baker and gave up a single to Hrbek, his fourth hit of the game. Gary Ward tripled to score both runners. Ward scored when Tim Laudner hit a groundball that gave the shortstop just one option, getting the runner out at first. But now the White Sox were facing a daunting comeback with the Twins leading 12-5.

They scratched away at the Twins' lead in the bottom of the eighth. Squires led off with a single. After Pryor struck out, Loviglio singled. When Sutherland hit a groundball that third baseman Chuck Baker dropped for an error, the bases were loaded for Hairston, who hit a grand slam. The Twins' lead was cut to three runs. Gardner replaced Cooper with John Verhoeven, who struck out Luzinski to end the inning.

Verhoeven was still on the mound when the White Sox came to bat in the ninth losing 12-9. It was their last chance to score and things looked bleak. The situation became dire when Nordhagen fouled out to first and Marc Hill lined out to shortstop. With two outs, Squires singled. La Russa sent left-handed batter Bob Molinaro to pinch-hit against the right-handed Verhoeven. Molinaro singled and Squires reached third on the play. Doug Corbett replaced Verhoeven on the mound. La Russa now pinch-hit Jerry Turner for Loviglio. He hit the White Sox' third consecutive single. Squires scored and the White Sox were down just two runs. Corbett then walked Sutherland, loading the bases. Bernarzard hit the White Sox' fourth single of the inning. Molinaro and Turner scored, and the game was tied.

Hairston then singled to right and Sutherland scored for the White Sox win, cementing their winning season. It was Hairston's sixth RBI of the game. His walk-off single climaxed the White Sox' improbable comeback as they scored eight runs in the final two innings.

As Sutherland scored, Bill Veeck's exploding scoreboard went off. The "lights, sirens, a 'Soxogram' message board and multicolored pinwheels"[2] had been delighting fans since 1960. Although the explosions were usually reserved for White Sox home runs, one can imagine the excitement that the almost 8,000 fans must have felt when it went off on this October afternoon.

Harry Caray shouted, "Holy Cow!" one final time for White Sox fans when Hairston singled to score Sutherland. After 11 seasons, the veteran broadcaster was heading across town to Wrigley Field.

SOURCES

In addition to the sources cited in the Notes, the author also used the Baseball-Reference.com, Baseball-Almanac.com, and Retrosheet.org websites for box-score, player, team, and season pages, pitching and batting game logs, and other pertinent material.

NOTES

1. Wayne Drehs, "Thank Caray, Chicago for Popularity of 'Take Me Out to the Ballgame,'" ESPN.com, July 8, 2008.

2. Tim Bannon, "The Story Behind Bill Veeck's Exploding Scoreboard," **Chicago Tribune**, April 3, 2015.

BAINES BELTS THREE

JULY 7, 1982
CHICAGO WHITE SOX 7, DETROIT TIGERS 0

BY KATIE DICKSON
WITH GREGORY H. WOLF

The Chicago White Sox exploded, according to sportswriter Robert Markus of the *Chicago Tribune*, "like so many 4th of July skyrockets" on Wednesday, July 7th, knocking off the Detroit Tigers, 7-0.[1] This game signaled the emergence of a new offensive threat, 23-year-old Harold Baines. The third-year player walloped three consecutive home runs, one of which was a grand slam. Brian Bragg of the *Detroit Free Press* acknowledged the achievement by writing, "Baines single-handedly destroyed the Tigers Wednesday with the most fantastic night of his career."[2]

The White Sox and Tigers owned identical 41-36 records, but were both reeling as they arrived at Comiskey Park to play the first of a two-game set.[3] Skipper Tony La Russa's Pale Hose had lost eight of 11 contests to fall four games behind the Kansas City Royals and were tied with the Seattle Mariners for third place in the Central Division. The Tigers were "positively floundering," according to Bragg.[4] Occupying first place in the East about four weeks earlier, manager Sparky Anderson's squad had won just five of its last 23 games to fall 3½ games behind the Milwaukee Brewers in the East.

"The Baseball Palace of the World," as some people called Comiskey, gradually filled with 24,018 spectators on a clear night. Temperatures had settled in the low 80s at the 6:30 start time as White Sox right-hander Dennis Lamp took the mound. Sporting a 40-50 record in parts of six seasons (including 5-3 thus far in '82), Lamp looked sharp from the outset, breezing through the first five innings and yielding only three hits. The Tigers' right-hander Jerry Ujdur was even more impressive. Called up to the big club just a month earlier from the Triple-A Evansville Triplets of the American Association, Ujdur held the White Sox hitless through four frames, belying his dismal 1-4 won-loss record.

Baines broke up the no-hitter in the bottom of the fifth with a line-drive home run, his seventh of the season, which "barely cleared the right-field wall," according to Bragg, and landed in the front row of the bleacher seats.[5] "I was looking for a curve," said Baines, "and he threw me a fastball."[6] After Lamp set down Detroit in order in the top of the sixth, Tony Bernazard led off the seventh with a double. Ujdur escaped a jam when he intentionally walked clean-up hitter Greg Luzinski with one out and gave up a screeching liner to. Tom Paciorek that third baseman Tom Brookens snared and doubled Bernazard off second.

It was *deja vu* all over again when Baines led off the Chicago half of the seventh against Ujdur, who was working on a two-hitter. This time, however, the left-handed line-drive hitter, who had slugged just 23 home runs in his first two seasons in the big leagues, smashed one deep to right-center. The ball traveled an estimated 420 feet and landed in the bullpen to put the White Sox up 2-0. According to the *Tribune*, the modest

THE BASE BALL PALACE OF THE WORLD

Hall of Famer Harold Baines began, ended, and played in parts of 14 seasons of his 22-year big-league career with the White Sox. A model of consistency, the six-time All-Star collected 2,866 hits and drove in 1,628 runs. (Photo by Ronald C. Modra/Sports Imagery/Getty Images)

Baines reluctantly acknowledged the partisan crowd's standing ovation by waving his glove.[7]

The game was tight until the fateful eighth inning when the White Sox blew it open. Ujdur was replaced by southpaw reliever Dave Rucker, making his first appearance of the season, and just the third of his career, since his promotion from Evansville. With one out, Rucker caught the speedy Bernazard napping at first, but his throw sailed over first baseman Richie Hebner's head for a two-base error. The next batter, Steve Kemp, singled to drive in Bernazard, opening the flood gates and sending Rucker to the showers. After Kemp greeted veteran rubber-armed reliever Elias Sosa by stealing second, the slow-footed Luzinski was treated to an intentional walk in hopes of a twin killing. The plan backfired when Sosa hit Pacoriek to load the bases.

With the White Sox up 3-0, "the best was yet to come," Markus wrote.[8] Baines stepped to the plate as many in the stadium no doubt held their breath. With the count 3-2, Baines hit a flyball that according to the *Tribune*, Tigers center fielder Chet Lemon almost caught in a miraculous attempt.[9] The ball landed just over the wall for a grand slam, extending the White Sox lead to 7-0. "All I was looking for was something to hit hard, any place," said Baines after the game. "I would have been happy to hit even a sacrifice fly for another run. This time I'm looking for the fastball, not the curve, because it's 3 and 2."[10] Baines remained cool and collected as he circled the bases and crossed home plate without cracking a smile. His teammates even had to push him back onto the field to again acknowledge the cheering crowd. "I've never hit three home runs in a game" he explained after the game. "It felt good inside, but I didn't jump up for joy."[11]

With the game out of reach, the only question was whether Lamp would record his first shutout since blanking the Los Angeles Dodgers on May 23, 1980 at Wrigley Field during his days with the Chicago Cubs. Hebner led off the ninth with a single, but was erased on a 6-4-3 double play. Lamp added his exclamation point to the victory by punching out Lance Parrish to end the game in two hours and 16 minutes.

"The way Lamp was pitching," gushed the Tigers Sparky Anderson, "we weren't going to score a run. He pitched outstanding tonight."[12] In fashioning his sixth career shutout, the California native yielded only five hits, did not issue a walk, and fanned seven. Normally a fastball pitcher, Lamp credited pitching coach Ron Schueler for his success and his change in approach. "Ron told me to throw a lot of breaking balls. He finally convinced me," revealed Lamp. "I showed them the breaking ball early. When you establish that, they can't sit on the fast ball. I've never had a breaking ball this good for nine innings."[13]

Despite Lamp's strong performance, the White Sox' true hero was Baines, whose "magnificent night," noted the *Chicago Tribune*, overshadowed all other stories. In a closely fought contest until the bottom of the eighth, Baines proved to be the difference maker. Ujdur, a tough-luck loser, yielded only three hits in seven strong innings, but two of those were solo shots hit by Baines. The outfielder's third round-tripper, the first of 13 eventual grand slams in his career, gave him six RBIs, a new career-high. "I'm an aggressive hitter," Baines said, "but I still have to learn to stay aggressive at times. This time, I'm concentrating just to get a hit."[14]

Baines' feat marked the third and last time in the history of pitcher-friendly Comiskey Park, that a White Sox player would hit three home runs there in one game. Gus Zernial did it first, on Oct 1, 1950, in a loss to the St. Louis Browns. Claudell Washington did it against the Tigers, on July 14, 1979.

Baines enjoyed a breakout season in 1982, ending up with 25 home runs and 105 RBIs. He belted three home runs in a game two other times in his career but never developed the reputation as a slugger.[15] Over the course of 22 campaigns, he hit at least 20 homers 11 times, reaching a career high of 29 in 1984, and finishing with 384.

SOURCES

In addition to the notes above, the author consulted Baseball-Reference.com, Retrosheet.org, and SABR.org.

http://www.Baseball-Reference.com/boxes/CHA/CHA198207070.shtml

http://www.Retrosheet.org/boxesetc/1982/B07070CHA1982.htm

NOTES

1. Robert Markus, "Sox and La Russa Both Explode,"*Chicago Tribune*, July 8, 1982: E1.

2. Brian Bragg, "Tigers' bane: Home run Baines," *Detroit Free Press*, July 8, 1982: D1.

3. According to Retrosheet, Detroit entered the game with a 40-36 record. The discrepancy in records lies with how BaseballReference and Retrosheet calculate tie games. BaseballReference bases it on the date the game was originally scheduled and Retrosheet on when it is finished.

4. Ibid.

5. Ibid.

6. Joseph Durso, "How to get three Homers: Try for Hits," *New York Times*, July 9, 1982: A14.

7. Markus, "Sox and La Russa Both Explode."

8. Ibid.

9. Ibid.

10. Durso.

11. Markus, "Sox and La Russa Both Explode,"

12. Bragg.

13. Robert Markus, "Lamp puts in plug for shaky Schueler," *Chicago Tribune*, July 8, 1982: e1.

14. Durso.

15. In addition to the game in 1982, Baines belted three home runs in a 7-3 victory over the Minnesota Twins on September 17, 1984 at Metrodome; and also as a member of the Oakland A's, defeating the Baltimore Orioles, 11-3, on May 7, 1991 at the Oakland Coliseum.

ATMOSPHERE AT THE 1983 ALL-STAR GAME

By Alan Reifman

With nearly 37 years' perspective, one can see how all the forces lined up to make the 1983 All-Star Game at old Comiskey Park — played on July 6, exactly 50 years after the first major-league All-Star Game, also played at Comiskey — the spectacular success many consider it to have been.[1]

Chicago's sports teams were almost uniformly in the doldrums at the time, making a festive, celebratory occasion stand out even more. The city's last major championships had been won by the 1963 Bears (pre-Super Bowl era) and the 1961 Blackhawks. As of 1983, the Bulls' drafting of Michael Jordan was a year away and the Bears' "Super Bowl Shuffle" championship, two years off.

Fittingly, the one Windy City team showing promise as the 1983 All-Star Game approached was the host White Sox, whose last appearance in the postseason was in the 1959 World Series. After a 16-24 start (through May 26), the '83 White Sox had gone 24-13 to pull within 3½ games of the American League West Division-leading Texas Rangers on the eve of the All-Star Game.[2]

Finally, it had been 33 years since the last All-Star Game played at Comiskey (1950), and for those who followed such things, the National League had won 11 straight midsummer classics (and 19 of the last 20) heading into 1983. Thus, for White Sox fans who also identified with the American League, the '83 All-Star Game provided a rare in-person chance to see the junior circuit reverse its fortunes.

The present essay focuses on the atmosphere at the 1983 All-Star Game. I share my recollections from attending the game (refreshed 35 years later by viewing a full-length video of the NBC broadcast of it on YouTube).[3] A separate entry in this book reviews what took place on the field between the teams.

One of my favorite parts of an all-star game is the introduction of the players and associated personnel. The Comiskey crowd was certainly revved up at this point, giving outfielder Ron Kittle, the only member of the host White Sox to be selected for the game, a nearly 40-second ovation when he was introduced.

The fans appeared to show some degree of partisanship toward the American League, for example, giving a more sustained and raucous ovation to one legend making his final All-Star appearance — Carl Yastrzemski of the AL's Boston Red Sox — when he came up to bat, than to another legend in the same situation — Johnny Bench of the National League's Cincinnati Reds. However, Chicago ties seemed to override someone's league, as the fans gave former Cubs great and NL honorary captain Ernie Banks an "Ernie! Ernie!" chant during the introductions.

An oddity in the festivities was comedian and actor George Burns, then a youthful 87 years old (he lived until age 100[4]), coming onto the field, telling a few jokes, and leading the crowd in singing "Take Me Out to the Ball Game" — before the home-half of the *fifth* inning.

As a native Chicagoan who had grown up elsewhere, I had been fascinated by the spirit of the mid-late 1970s' White Sox — the softball-type navy blue uniforms, including one variation that included short pants; the 1977 White Sox squad that came out of nowhere to win 90 games after capturing just 64 victories the year before;[5] the "Na-Na-Na-Na, Hey-Hey-Hey" song;[6] and even the ill-fated 1979 Disco Demolition Night.[7] These developments occurred during Bill Veeck's second stint as owner of the team, which ended after the 1980 season.[8] One aspect of that era that survived Veeck's departure was Nancy Faust's perch at the Comiskey Park organ, where she led the "Na-Na, Hey-Hey" song and played numerous other popular songs.[9] I must have seen on a televised game at some point that Faust played in a publicly accessible booth. So, in my one and only game ever at the old Comiskey Park — the 1983 All-Star Game — I decided that I had to get Nancy Faust's autograph!

With the American League well on its way to ending its long losing streak to the National League by the third inning, leading 9-1 en route to a 13-3 victory, the crowd's enthusiasm and energy continued unabated. It was a night to soak in the modern history of baseball (with Banks, Yastrzemski, and Bench), cheer for the AL and the Chicago participants, and satisfy any "Bucket List" wishes one had.

NOTES

1. Bob Verdi, "Take a Bow, Sox, for a Stellar Show," **Chicago Tribune**, July 8, 1983. Verdi cites then-Commissioner Bowie Kuhn and American League All-Star Rod Carew, praising how the game and associated festivities were handled.

2. Historical standings by day and year were obtained at: shrpsports.com/mlb/stand.htm.

3. youtube.com/watch?v=bfJDfhI5KKI.

4. en.wikipedia.org/wiki/George_Burns.

5. Baseball-Reference.com/teams/CHW/.

6. The song is known either as "Kiss Him Goodbye" or "Na Na Hey Hey Kiss Him Goodbye," and was released in 1969 by a group that called itself "Steam." en.wikipedia.org/wiki/Na_Na_Hey_Hey_Kiss_Him_Goodbye.

7. chicagomag.com/Chicago-Magazine/July-2016/The-Night-Disco-Died/.

8. Veeck spent his final years sitting in the bleachers at Wrigley Field, home of the White Sox' intracity rival the Cubs, as he never hit it off with new White Sox owners Jerry Reinsdorf and Eddie Einhorn (Michael Shapiro, "Happy in the Bleachers," **New York Times**, June 21, 1982. nytimes.com/1982/06/21/sports/happy-in-the-bleachers.html). Nevertheless, Veeck attended the 1983 All-Star Game at Comiskey ("Veeck shows up for the players" [Notes], **Chicago Tribune**, July 7, 1983).

9. The Baseball Reliquary, a website devoted to cultural contributions to the sport, named Faust to the "Shrine of the Eternals" in 2018. The Reliquary's tribute referred to her as "without question, the most famous ballpark organist of the past half-century, during which time she entertained the faithful on Chicago's South Side between 1970 and 2010" (Terry Cannon, "Shrine of the Eternals Class of 2018," May 6, 2018. baseballreliquary.org/2018/05/shrine-of-the-eternals-class-of-2018/).

IN A GOLDEN ALL-STAR ANNIVERSARY, THE AMERICAN LEAGUE GRAND SLAMS NATIONAL LEAGUE DOMINANCE SHUT

JULY 6, 1983
AMERICAN LEAGUE 13, NATIONAL LEAGUE 3
ALL-STAR GAME

By Brian Wright

July 6, 1933: the first All-Star Game at Comiskey Park and, in the third inning, the first home run — quite appropriately off the bat of Babe Ruth as part of a 4-2 American League victory.

Fast forward exactly 50 years at the same venue, and another long-ball feat was achieved: The first grand slam in midsummer-classic annals and, to this day, the only one. California Angels outfielder Fred Lynn did it and in the process put the AL's decade-plus drought to rest.

At a time when the All-Star Game was regarded more as competition than exhibition, there was little in the way of parity. The National League had reigned supreme, experiencing defeat just once since 1963 and having won each game since 1972. Many of the last 11 were close. Yet each ended with the junior circuit being regarded as the lesser of the two leagues.

But in '83, annual cries of American League inferiority dissipated beneath the reverberation of an incessant power display. Both the 13 runs in the game and the 7 in the third inning set All-Star records, while seven extra-base hits tied another.

The brilliance of the AL offense was preceded by an error-filled opening unbecoming a contest featuring baseball's premier talent.

Los Angeles Dodgers second baseman Steve Sax led off against Toronto Blue Jays hurler Dave Stieb (10-7), and bounced one to the right side. Stieb, normally a fine fielding pitcher, caught it on the bounce near the first-base line and fired wildly over Rod Carew's head.

After Sax stole second, Stieb got a much easier chance on a meek grounder to the mound. His throw was accurate, but Carew lost the ball in the setting sun piercing through the Comiskey Park stands. Raines scooted all the way to third as Sax slid into the plate ahead of the tag of catcher Ted Simmons.

Stieb, with 112 strikeouts so far, settled down and limited the damage, impressively fanning Andre Dawson, Dale Murphy, and Mike Schmidt in succession, and went on to spin three hitless frames.

The AL responded against the Cincinnati Reds' Mario Soto (9-7, 124 K's). Taking advantage of the NL's own infield miscues, a pair of sacrifice flies by future Hall of Famers George Brett and Robin Yount put the Americans up 2-1 after two — a small sampling of what was to come in the third.

Atlee Hammaker, a nine-game winner who had allowed only two home runs over the first half of '83 with the San Francisco Giants, was the unsuspecting casualty of the long-awaited AL vengeance.

The left-hander quickly surrendered a homer to Red Sox slugger Jim Rice. Brett followed with a triple. New York Yankee Dave Winfield singled to pad the advantage. Manny Trillo of the Cleveland Indians followed with a base hit that pushed Winfield into scoring position. With two outs, batting wizard Carew worked his magic wooden wand to generate an RBI single, prolonging the inning and Hammaker's misery. Trillo advanced to third and Carew moved to second on the throw home.

First base was unoccupied as Yount stepped in. National League manager Whitey Herzog elected to give a free pass to the 1982 AL MVP in favor of a lefty-on-lefty matchup with Lynn. It was rare strategy to employ in an All-Star environment and justifiably raised the ire the of nine-time participant.

"I was pissed they walked Robin Yount intentionally to pitch to me," said Chicago native Lynn. "That kind of stuff gets me riled up and I'm able to focus all my attention on that particular pitcher."[1]

Hammaker got ahead in the count at 1-and-2 before throwing a pitch that might have caught the outside corner, except in the sight and mind of home-plate umpire George Maloney.

On the next offering, there was zero doubt. Lynn parked it into the lower stands beyond the right-field fence and raised his right hand as he rounded first base.

Fred had been an All-Star in each of his big-league seasons with the Red Sox and Angels, but never on a winning side. So to him, the reaction to the grand slam was less a moment of personal satisfaction than of team triumph.

"I never showed emotion like that," he said. "It had more to do with knowing that we were finally going to win one of these things. We had them on the ropes a few times before and we were long tired of hearing how the National League had the upper hand. It was nice that we didn't have to hear it again that year."[2]

While Lynn entered his name into the history books resoundingly, Hammaker did so dubiously. His six hits and seven runs allowed in a single inning remain (as of 2019) All-Star worsts.

"To put it bluntly, it's probably the worst exhibition of pitching you'll ever see," Hammaker said in a moment of personal reflection. "And I couldn't have picked a worse spot for it, either — my first All-Star Game in front of all those people."[3]

"If you don't make the pitches against this kind of competition, you're going to get hurt. I was getting ahead of the hitters the way I wanted to, but I couldn't put them away."[4]

The destruction of the third inning put the NL down 9-1 and in the unfamiliar spot of inevitable defeat. There was little that could be done, but the team did manage to scratch for runs on RBIs by Murphy in the fourth and Sax in the fifth. That was pretty much be the extent of the NL offense.

Over the final four innings, an American League bullpen triumvirate of Bob Stanley, Matt Young, and Dan Quisenberry allowed no NL runner past first base.

The AL bats, on the other hand, still had some retribution to unload.

Lou Whitaker's seventh-inning triple produced a run and Willie Wilson's double four batters later added another. More damage was inflicted in the eighth when Brett scored on a muffed fly ball by the Los Angeles Dodgers' Pedro Guerrero. Milwaukee's Cecil Cooper made the record 13th tally when he crossed the plate on Rickey Henderson's groundout.

But there was more than runs for fans to marvel at. In the midst of the late scoring spurt, the Comiskey crowd got a chance to cheer for its own. White Sox outfielder Ron Kittle, a rare rookie-turned-All-Star, beat out an infield hit in the seventh. (He was 1-for-2.)

The evening was a first for Kittle and a last for two Cooperstown shoo-ins. Johnny Bench and Carl Yastrzemski, who each would retire at season's end, were greeted with rousing ovations during the pregame introductions and their at-bats.

Those moments of individual recognition were the last pieces of significance in a contest sapped of drama once Lynn hit the grand slam. To no one's surprise, he was unanimously voted the game's MVP.

When the White Sox hosted the All-Star Game again in 2003, the tables had completely turned. The American League won — prolonging an unbeaten streak that eventually reached 15.

SOURCES

In addition to the sources cited in the Notes, the author also consulted Baseball-Reference.com, Retrosheet.org, and Ultimatemets.com

NOTES

1   Author interview with Fred Lynn, February 26, 2015.

2   Ibid.

3   "Slam by Lynn Snaps a Jinx." **Chicago Tribune**. July 7, 1983: 8.

4   "Seven Runs Later, Hammaker Still Can't Believe It." **Chicago Tribune**. July 7, 1983: 3.

THREE WALKS AND A FLY BALL — WHITE SOX CLINCH DIVISION WITH WALK-OFF

SEPTEMBER 17, 1983
CHICAGO WHITE SOX 4, SEATTLE MARINERS 3

By Mike Huber

The Chicago White Sox were headed to the playoffs! Needing either a win or a loss by the Kansas City Royals, Chicago was on the verge of playing for the American League crown. The mid-September game itself had somewhat symbolically been delayed, held up for 38 minutes because of a heavy rainstorm. Even after the rain stopped, throughout the game "a constant roar of thunder accompanied by bolts of lightning crackled overhead, as if in tribute and anticipation."[1] However, "there was no way the enthusiasm of Chicago baseball fans could have been dampened."[2] The last time the White Sox won the American League pennant was in 1959 (in the National League, the Cubs' last pennant was in 1945), and so the title drought for a Chicago baseball team finally ended after 24 years, and the Chicago faithful went wild. It had even been 11 years since the White Sox finished as high as second in the AL West Division.

Chicago had won five previous pennants, "but their famine for any title was the second longest in the American League."[3] They had gone 2-2 in World Series play. They captured their first pennant when they topped the American League in its inaugural season (1901), before the era of the World Series. In 1983 the White Sox had a slow start to the campaign. They lost the first three games of the season. They finished April with a mark of 8-10 and May with a record of 12-15.

On June 1, the White Sox were in fifth place. On June 22, they beat the Seattle Mariners to even their record at 33-33, putting them in fourth place. Four weeks later, on July 18, they grabbed first place in the West Division and were there to stay. Further, with their success, the White Sox became the first baseball team in Chicago to draw more than 2 million fans, a mark they surpassed with this game's attendance of 45,646. The victory in this game "climaxed an amazing turnaround."[4] Manager Tony La Russa summed up the season by saying, "The object was to get so far ahead that the manager couldn't screw it up."[5]

With the champagne chilling in the clubhouse, La Russa called on veteran Jerry Koosman. The 40-year-old lefty started the season as a relief pitcher for the White Sox, but on May 24, he started against the Boston Red Sox and picked up the win. He became a member of the starting rotation, and he now was seeking his 10th win of the season and 201st career win. Chicago had won 10 of 11 coming into this game, and four of those games (including the sole loss) ended via the walk-off. Seattle countered with right-hander Jim Beattie, who had dropped eight of his last nine decisions for the last-place Mariners, losers of their previous five games.

Maybe it was the delay, maybe it was nerves, but the White Sox were a bit unsteady in the first inning. Koosman issued a one-out walk to Phil Bradley and a single to Tony Bernazard. Al Cowens hit a grounder to White Sox shortstop Scott Fletcher, who threw to second baseman Jose Cruz, forcing Bernazard. But Cruz made an errant throw to first trying for the double play. Bradley scored and Cowens advanced to second. Koosman struck out Steve Henderson to retire the side.

Beattie was also a bit wild through the first three innings, issuing a free pass in each frame. He managed to escape the first two innings without yielding a run, but in the third, Cruz led off with a walk. After Rudy Law flied out, Carlton Fisk singled and Cruz motored to third. Harold Baines grounded to second baseman Bernazard, whose only play was at first. Baines was retired but got an RBI as Cruz crossed the plate on the play.

Chicago took the lead in the bottom of the fourth when Tom Paciorek, who had doubled to right field to start the inning, scampered to third on Ron Kittle's a slow grounder to the pitcher for the first out. Paciorek then scored on a suicide squeeze bunt by Vance Law, a move that caught everyone by surprise. Fletcher followed by drawing a walk. With Cruz batting, Fletcher took off for second. Mariners catcher Orlando Mercado threw the ball away, allowing Fletcher to get to third, but he was stranded there when Cruz hit a comebacker to the mound for the third out.

And the score remained 2-1 Chicago. With each Seattle out, the atmosphere became more tense. Baines led off the bottom of the eighth inning by bashing a solo home run that gave the White Sox an all-important insurance run. His 18th home run of the season was also his third round-tripper in the last three games.[6]

Koosman had gone eight innings, facing the minimum from the fifth inning through the eighth. He had allowed one earned run on six hits and a walk. He struck out five Mariners and left the game in the ninth with a 3-1 lead after yielding a leadoff single to Bernazard. Koosman had pitched well enough to win, but reliever Dennis Lamp couldn't save the game. Lamp's first batter was Cowens, who reached on an infield single. Steve Henderson grounded a ball to short and was retired, but both runners moved up a base. Ricky Nelson pinch-hit for Dave Henderson, and he greeted Lamp by stroking a double into center field. Bernazard and Cowens both scored, tying the game. Lamp then intentionally walked Ron Roenicke. Darnell Coles grounded out and Lamp struck out Mercado with runners on second and third. This turn of events definitely "fueled the drama."[7] According to the *Los Angeles Times*, "the partisan fans had some anxious moments,"[8] but none of them left the ballpark.

Now it was Chicago's turn to bat. Seattle skipper Del Crandall made a call to the bullpen, bringing in righty Bill Caudill to pitch for Beattie. The day before, Caudill had been roughed up for five runs (all earned) on three hits and two walks, all in the same inning. With this game tied, Caudill was again wild. Leadoff batter Jerry Hairston lined out to Caudill. Then Caudill walked Cruz, Rudy Law, and Fisk in succession. Fisk had a full count and as Caudill delivered the pitch, Cruz took off for third. Home-plate umpire Al Clark barked ball four. The Mariners "beefed, contending Fisk had swung and missed the pitch for strike three."[9] Fisk didn't help matters by standing in the batter's box instead of trotting down to first. Seattle's appeal to first-base ump Jim Evans was denied. Fisk took first and the bases were loaded. Caudill was sent to the showers, and in came southpaw Ed Vande Berg to face the left-handed-batting Baines.

All Baines had to do was hit the ball out of the infield. When he swung the bat at Vande Berg's first pitch, the ball traveled 380 feet for an out. But that was only out number two, and it was deep enough for a sacrifice fly. Cruz tagged third and raced home with the game-winner. So did third-base coach Jim Leyland, almost beating Cruz to the plate. The White Sox had won another game in walk-off fashion. Fans stormed the field. Vande Berg had faced one batter, had thrown only one pitch, and had gotten that batter out, yet the Mariners lost the game. After the game, standing far from the excitement all around him on the field, Baines said, "Deep down inside, I'm feeling good. But I don't like being over-emotional."[10] He had driven in three of Chicago's runs.

The front page of the *Chicago Tribune* celebrated the end of the postseason drought with the headline "Sox Are Champs!"[11] The second-place Kansas City Royals also won their game, but they could no longer catch the White Sox; they were down by 16 games with 15 to play. In the clubhouse, the players celebrated, showering each other with that chilled champagne. Cruz "was working on a magnum and talking. 'I want to thank [general manager] Roland Hemond for thinking about me, for considering me as a player who could help his team. I'm at the top of my career thanks to these guys.'"[12] Not far away, Hemond "was acting like a kid with an unlimited expense account in a sweet shop." He told reporters, "This is absolutely precious."[13]

La Russa was ecstatic, gushing, "Think about it. Just think about it. We are the champions. Not New York. Not Los Angeles. Chicago."[14]

SOURCES

In addition to the sources mentioned in the Notes, the author consulted Baseball-Reference.com and Retrosheet.org.

Baseball-Reference.com/boxes/CHA/CHA198309170.shtml.

Retrosheet.org/boxesetc/1983/B09170CHA1983.htm.

NOTES

1. Jerome Holtzman, "Hail to the Champs!" **Chicago Tribune**, September 18, 1983: 45-46.

2. "It's Party Time in Chicago: The White Sox Clinch," **Los Angeles Times**, September 18, 1983: 74.

3. **Chicago Tribune**, "Sox Are Champs!" September 18, 1983: 1, continued on 13. The Cleveland Indians were the only other AL team with a longer wait, having won the American League pennant in 1954.

4. **Los Angeles Times**.

5. Ibid.

6. Baines hit a home run the next night as well, giving him four consecutive games with a round-tripper.

7. Holtzman.

8. **Los Angeles Times**.

9. Holtzman.

10. Mike Kiley and Linda Kay, "'Think About It: We Are Champions,'" **Chicago Tribune**, September 18, 1983: 45.

11. "Sox Are Champs!"

12. Steve Daley, "Moment Has Magic for Sox Players," **Chicago Tribune**, September 18, 1983: 45.

13. Bob Verdi, "Golden Gate Opens for Sox, Hemond," **Chicago Tribune**, September 18, 1983: 47.

14. Kiley and Kay.

CHISOX ROUTED IN FIRST PLAYOFF GAME ON SOUTH SIDE IN 24 YEARS

OCTOBER 7, 1983
BALTIMORE ORIOLES 11, CHICAGO WHITE SOX 1
GAME THREE OF THE ALCS

By Brian P. Wood

Baseball fever found its way to Comiskey Park on October 7, 1983, for the first time since the final game of the 1959 World Series. The White Sox hosted the Baltimore Orioles in Game Three of the American League Championship Series. Both teams ranked in the top three in their league in runs scored, home runs, and ERA.

Chicago's 99 wins were one shy of the club record posted by the 1917 World Series champions and helped in setting its attendance mark (2 million fans).[1] The team finished the season at a .758 clip (50-16).

Texas Rangers manager Doug Rader commented, "They're not playing that well. They're winning ugly." The team and fans rallied around the moniker and called their unique red, white, and blue uniforms with "SOX" emblazoned on the front "Winning Ugly" uniforms.[2]

Manager Tony La Russa, in his first postseason, and fellow future Hall of Famer Carlton Fisk (26 HR/86 RBIs) led the White Sox, complemented by sluggers Ron Kittle (35 HR/100 RBIs/1983 AL Rookie of the Year), Greg Luzinski (32 HR/95 RBIs), and Harold Baines (20 HR/99 RBIs). Chicago sported two 20-game winners, Cy Young Award winner LaMarr Hoyt (24) and Game Three starter Rich Dotson (22).

Baltimore's duo of Cal Ripken Jr. (1½ seasons into his 2,632-consecutive-game streak) and Eddie Murray finished 1-2 in the American League MVP voting.

Dotson struck out leadoff man Al Bumbry before a crowd of 46,635 chanting "Let's Go, Sox! Let's Go, Sox!"[3] However, things quickly turned sour. Jim Dwyer's double to right field[4] and Ripken's single preceded Murray blasting a fastball[5] into the upper deck in right-center field high above the 374-foot sign.[6]

In the second, Bumbry's slicing double to left scored Rick Dempsey (walk) for a 4-0 lead.[7] In the bottom half, Kittle doubled to left and scored on an infield hit by Vance Law.

In the fourth, starter Mike Flanagan's[8] breaking ball hit Kittle in the left kneecap,[9] clearing both benches.[10] Beer had been thrown at Kittle in Game Two,[11] so tensions were already high.[12] Kittle tried to go after Flanagan but umpire Nick Bremigan intervened. While no fisticuffs occurred, a heated exchange developed between White Sox infielder Julio Cruz and Orioles pitching coach Ray Miller.[13] Kittle departed in the sixth and did not play in Game Four, arriving in a wheelchair due to the injury.[14]

Dotson hit Ripken on a 1-and-0[15] two-out pitch in the fifth.[16] Ripken walked to first and did not say anything to the White Sox pitcher. No warnings were issued to the teams.[17] The next pitch was inside to Murray, precipitating a second "bench clearing" event.[18] Bremigan again acted as peacemaker, stepping between Murray and Dotson. Orioles bullpen coach Elrod Hendricks heatedly barked at La Russa, "You know better than that." La Russa replied, "Rod, it's part of the game." Hendricks answered, "Play baseball!"

La Russa declared after the game, "I am here to tell you that Ripken was not hit intentionally." However, Dotson contradicted his skipper, saying, "I kind of got the message: 'Get the first two guys out of the way and hit the third guy,'"[19] and that, perhaps, he had thrown at Murray. Kittle noted, "The Orioles hit only seven guys all year, and in two days, they've already thrown at three of us."[20]

Dotson seemed to be undone by the events and walked Murray before giving up a two-run double to right field by John Lowenstein[21] for a 6-1 lead.

In the top of the eighth, Murray walked and eventually scored on Todd Cruz's single to left.

In the ninth, 40-year-old Jerry Koosman gave up a Ripken double to right field[22] and two walks (John Shelby and Murray), loading the bases. Reliever Dennis Lamp walked pinch-hitter Gary Roenicke, bringing in the seventh Oriole run. Left fielder Jerry Hairston muffed pinch-hitter[23] Joe Nolan's fly ball, allowing Ripken and Murray to score. Dauer banged a fly ball to right field, scoring Roenicke for an 11-1 lead. The remaining crowd showered their "'Winning Ugly' darlings with boos."[24]

Flanagan and Sammy Stewart (four innings) combined for a six-hitter, allowing just one run. That run, scored by Kittle in the second, turned out to be the last of only three in the four-game series for Chicago.[25]

Ripken (2-for-4, three runs/double) and Murray (1-for-2, four runs, three RBIs, three walks, and a home run) led the O's. The 10-run margin of victory tied an ALCS record.[26] Nine walks led to six Orioles runs. Bob Maisel of the *Baltimore Sun* commented that Chicago tried to change momentum through a beanball war and it backfired. "They roared like lions and played like lambs the rest of the way," he wrote.[27]

The *Chicago Tribune's* Bob Verdi noted, "To borrow from Rodney Dangerfield, 46,635 people went to a baseball game at Comiskey Park Friday night and a hockey game broke out."[28] The consensus was that Chicago overreacted to Flanagan hitting Kittle. "If a savvy pitcher like Flanagan intentionally plunked a batter on a full-count offering, the man to go after Flanagan wouldn't be Kittle. It would be Baltimore manager Joe Altobelli. … If all else fails, La Russa can … pick up and throw third base just to show the White Sox where it is."[29]

Asked if Chicago was humiliated in the 11-1 loss, Kittle responded, "Humiliated? What kind of question is that? We'll just try to get as much sleep as we can and come back swinging."[30]

Unfortunately for Kittle, neither he nor the South Siders did much swinging in the remainder of the series.

SOURCES

In addition to the sources mentioned in the Notes, the author consulted Baseball-Reference.com, MLB.com, Retrosheet.org, and SABR.org.

NOTES

1 By 475,000 fans.

2 Sean Evans, "The 25 Greatest Moments in White Sox History," Complex.com. Complex Media. Retrieved September 5, 2017.

3 Jerome Holtzman, "Orioles Brush Off Sox, Tempers Flare in 11-1 Loss," Chicago Tribune, October 8, 1983: 2, 1.

4 Associated Press, "Orioles' Murray Blows the Lid Off White Sox," Sioux Falls (South Dakota) Argus-Leader, October 8, 1983: 1C.

5 Bill Free, "Tip from Coach Helps Murray," Baltimore Sun, October 8, 1983: B2.

6 This ended a 0-for-29 postseason skid for Murray dating back to the 1979 World Series.

7 Kent Baker, "Murray's 3-Run HR Launches 11-1 Oriole Rout of Chisox," Baltimore Sun, October 8, 1983: B1-2.

8 Flanagan was 12-4 in 20 games. In the first game of a doubleheader against Chicago on May 17, 1983, at Baltimore's

THE BASE BALL PALACE OF THE WORLD

Memorial Stadium, Flanagan attempted to field a comebacker from Tony Bernazard when he caught his spikes in the dirt on the mound. His knee popped out and back in again, causing him to leave the game after just two batters. Bernazard was credited with a single. Flanagan spent 2½ months on the disabled list. Susan Ramirez [Reimer], "Flanagan's Injury Has Affected Orioles From Top to Bottom," **Baltimore Sun** (via **Asbury Park** [New Jersey] **Press**), June 12, 1983: B14.

9 Bill Glauber, "'Yes, I Threw at Ripken,' Says Dotson," **Baltimore Sun**, October 8, 1983: B2.

10 AP, **Sioux Falls Argus-Leader**.

11 The perpetrator was charged with "throwing a missile and resisting arrest." "Sox Notebook, Burns Hopes He's a Mystery to Orioles," **Chicago Tribune**, October 8, 1983: 2, 4.

12 Bob Verdi, "Secret's Out: They Dislike Each Other," **Chicago Tribune**, October 8, 1983: 19.

13 Bill Free, "Dauer's Willing to Forgive Dotson," **Baltimore Sun**, October 8, 1983: B2.

14 Dave Nightingale, "Little Guys Big Heroes for Orioles," **The Sporting News**, October 17, 1983: 15.

15 Kent Baker, "Orioles Romp, 11-1, Lead Playoff 2-1; Flanagan, Stewart Stymie White Sox," **Baltimore Sun**, October 8, 1983: B1.

16 Where the ball hit Ripken is anyone's guess. Depending on the source, Ripken was hit on the hip (Free, **Baltimore Sun**), arm (Maisel, **Baltimore Sun**), leg (Verdi, **Chicago Tribune**) and/or ribs (Nightingale, **The Sporting News**).

17 Verdi.

18 AP, **Sioux Falls Argus-Leader**.

19 AP, **Sioux Falls Argus-Leader**.

20 Glauber. Baltimore starter Mike Boddicker hit White Sox first baseman Tom Paciorek in the second inning and DH Greg Luzinski in the ninth inning of Game Two. These were not only his first two hit batsmen in 1983, but also in his career.

21 Bob Maisel, "This Time, Chisox Play Ugly, Lose Even Uglier," **Baltimore Sun**, October 8, 1983: B2.

22 AP, **Sioux Falls Argus-Leader**.

23 Palmer had pinch-run for DH Singleton in the eighth. Both Koosman (Mets) and Palmer (Orioles), both on the rosters for this series, also played key roles on their 1969 teams that faced each other in the World Series.

24 Holtzman.

25 The three runs by a team is the fewest in a League Championship Series. The 1970 Pirates also scored three, in three games.

26 The New York Yankees downed the Oakland Athletics in Game Two of the 1981 ALCS, 13-3, as part of a three-game sweep. As of the end of the 2017 season, the largest run differential was 12: The Boston Red Sox defeated the Yankees 13-1 in Game Three of the 1999 ALCS, their only victory in a five-game series.

27 Maisel.

28 Verdi.

29 Verdi. Earlier in the season, La Russa had, in fact, picked up third base and thrown it in a game against the Orioles.

30 Glauber.

WHITE SOX CLOSE COMISKEY POSTSEASON HISTORY

OCTOBER 8, 1983
BALTIMORE ORIOLES 3, CHICAGO WHITE SOX 0
GAME FOUR OF THE ALCS

By Doug Feldmann

For the Chicago White Sox and their fans, the zany summer of 1983 was unlike any in the team's history. Their home ballpark, Comiskey Park hosted the All-Star Game on July 6 and the opening date of the much-anticipated "Synchronicity" tour of the band Police three weeks later. While the White Sox still hovered around the .500 mark during that sultry month, an unrelenting assault by Tony La Russa's team would soon take place in the second half of the schedule — coupled with the rallying cry "winning ugly" as coined by Texas Rangers manager Doug Rader. After Sting, Andy Summers, and Stewart Copeland packed up their instruments on July 23, the White Sox posted a blistering 51-18 record on their way to the team's first American League Western Division championship

Six years removed from the similar bashing by the "South Side Hit Men" team of 1977, the 1983 White Sox also relied upon an overpowering offense to throttle opponents. With Greg Luzinski (32 home runs), Rookie of the Year Ron Kittle (35), Carlton Fisk (26), Harold Baines (20), and others depositing the ball in different corners around Comiskey, speedsters Rudy Law and Julio Cruz (the latter a midseason acquisition from the Seattle Mariners) tore up the basepaths on the South Side. The major-league-leading 800 runs the team scored were more than enough for starting pitchers LaMarr Hoyt (the Cy Young Award winner with a 24-10 record), Rich Dotson (22-7), and left-hander Floyd Bannister (193 strikeouts) as the team clinched the West with two weeks to spare on September 17. Enjoying the ride were members of the team who had never tasted the fruits of the postseason, including Mike Squires, Jerry Hairston, and Britt Burns.

Once the headliner of a bevy of young White Sox pitching prospects from the late 1970s, Burns — whose ill-fitting cap would sometimes fall off in the course of his delivery on the mound —authored a one-hitter, a two-hitter, and a three-hitter after making a delayed 1983 debut on May 9. Now Burns was being given the ball by La Russa in a do-or-die contest in the American League Championship Series against the Baltimore Orioles, who had jumped out to a 2-games-to-1 lead in the best-of-five slate.

With the Orioles on the brink of a pennant, manager Joe Altobelli (in his inaugural season at the helm after taking over for the legendary Earl Weaver) countered with 21-year-old George "Storm" Davis. Having advanced rapidly through the Orioles' system after being drafted out of a Jacksonville high school in 1979, Davis had appeared in 29 games for Baltimore in 1982 — mostly out of the bullpen — before becoming a regular in Altobelli's starting rotation in 1983. Davis had been hit hard in his last regular-season start, against the New York Yankees on September 30 in Memorial Stadium in Baltimore, allowing six runs in just over four innings after the Orioles had already wrapped up the AL East title.

With a large banner reading "TRUE BRITT" hanging from the left-field stands, Burns and Davis went to work and were masterful, keeping the other side scoreless into the bottom of the seventh. At that juncture, Altobelli decided to lift Storm Davis and hand the task to his left-handed ace out of the bullpen, Felix "Tippy" Martinez — against whom the White Sox muffed a golden opportunity to seize control.

After first baseman Greg Walker singled, Squires entered as a pinch-runner and advanced to second on Vance Law's hit. Jerry Dybzinski followed and bounced a bunt on home plate, which catcher Rick Dempsey was able to pounce upon and fire to third to get the lead runner. Things looked to return to Chicago's favor when Cruz drove a single to left; but while third-base coach Jim Leyland was holding up Law at third, Dybzinski overran the second-base bag and was caught in no-man's land. He tried to keep himself in a rundown to give Law time to score, but second baseman Rich Dauer slung a strike to Dempsey, who squared up against the runner and held his ground as Law failed in his attempt to bowl him over. Martinez balked Dybzinski to third and Cruz to second, but the threat ended when Rudy Law flied out to left.

Dybzinski redeemed himself in the ninth by singling with one out and moving to third on another Cruz base hit. But Martinez was able to retire Rudy Law once again, this time looking at strike three –the ninth and tenth runners stranded by the Sox in the game. The efficient Burns was permitted by La Russa to continue into the Orioles 10th, getting a called third strike on John Shelby for the first out.

Next was Tito Landrum, in the lineup for injured right fielder Dan Ford. Landrum had batted only 47 times during the regular season, and homered only once, on September 4 when as his fly ball to the warning track in left field bounced off Mickey Hatcher's glove and into the stands at the Metrodome.

On his 150th pitch of the afternoon, Burns paid for his fatigue. Landrum caught hold of an offering on the outer half of the plate, and sent a line drive soaring toward the facade of the upper deck in left for a 1-0 Orioles lead. The attack continued as Burns left the game for reliever Salome Barojas, who enabled the Baltimore advantage to climb to 3-0.

As the desperate White Sox mounted their last charge in the bottom of the 10th, Martinez returned for his fourth inning of work. With two outs and two strikes on Tom Paciorek, he induced the batter to swing at a ball in the dirt as most of the 45,477 in attendance moaned in anticipation of the inevitable. The pitched caromed off Dempsey, but the hard-nosed catcher scooped it up and threw to first baseman Eddie Murray as the Orioles stormed out of the visitors' dugout, ready to make their first return trip to the World Series in four years.

The White Sox' usually powerful bats had produced only three runs in the four playoff games (absent from the Chicago lineup on this day was Kittle, who was hit in the knee with a pitch in Game Three). Their lone batting stars were the speedy second baseman Cruz, 3-for-3 with two stolen bases, and Baines with two singles. Landrum's home run was the only extra-base hit of the game. "I wasn't going to give their good hitters anything good to hit," Burns said afterward. "If I was going to get beat, it was going to be by the bottom or the top of their order."[1]

The businesslike manner of the Orioles impressed the Chicago side. "It wasn't the first time Baltimore has killed somebody else's dream with a Tito Landrum of its own," wrote the *Chicago Tribune*'s Bob Verdi, referring to the organization's run of success, which now included six pennants in 17 years. "The Orioles are long on role players but short on egos."[2] Watching the celebration was their proud owner, Edward Bennett Williams. "That was the greatest thing I've seen since the elevator door opened the other night," said Williams — who was stuck for 28 minutes inside the shaft of Memorial Stadium after his team dropped the series opener.[3]

Landrum, who joined the Orioles from the St. Louis Cardinals on August 31, the last day for a player to be eligible for the postseason, played in three games in the team's 1983 World Series triumph over the Philadelphia Phillies but did not make a single plate appearance.

His home run against the White Sox was not his final postseason heroics. A relatively obscure figure over his nine-year major-league career, Landrum returned to the Cardinals in 1984. In 1985 he replaced an injured Vince Coleman in the Cardinals' outfield for their cross-Missouri World Series battle vs. the Kansas City Royals. In the midst of the "Don Denkinger Debacle" in Game Six and the Joaquin Andujar meltdown in Game Seven, Landrum would likely have been named the World Series MVP if the Cardinals had pulled out either contest — he batted a team-leading .360 during the Series, while the rest of the Cardinals managed a mere .185

Even so, October 8, 1983, was perhaps Landrum's most memorable day on the field.

It was also the last postseason game Comiskey Park would ever see.

As the Orioles arrived at the airport back in Baltimore, a local disc jockey had overtaken the sound system in the terminal and played the song, "The Night Chicago Died" for travelers and fans to enjoy.

SOURCES

In addition to the sources listed below, the author also consulted the following: Baseball-Reference.com, Retrosheet.org and SABR.org.

NOTES

1   Jerome Holtzman, "Sox Lack Power to Help Out Burns," **Chicago Tribune**, October 9, 1983.

2   Bob Verdi, "Sox Have a Classy Example to Follow," **Chicago Tribune**, October 9, 1983.

3   Bill Free, "HR Blast Rockets Landrum to Stardom," **Baltimore Sun**, October 9, 1983.

JACK MORRIS THROWS A NO-HITTER

APRIL 7, 1984
DETROIT TIGERS 4, CHICAGO WHITE SOX 0

By Nathan Bierma

No-hitters are often remembered for dramatic defensive plays that preserved them. Plays outside the pitcher's control nonetheless define the paramount pitching achievement. The later it comes in the game, the more dramatic the defensive play is; sometimes it's even the 27th out.[1] But other times it's the very first out, when no one could imagine what is at stake.

Rudy Law of the Chicago White Sox led off the bottom of the first against the Detroit Tigers on April 7, 1984, and launched a blast to right field. The home crowd cheered, thinking extra bases or maybe a round-tripper. But Kirk Gibson raced back and made the catch at the wall. Gibson had been stymied by swirling winds the day before on a deep double that scored a run, but today he made the play. "When … the ball [left] the bat I didn't think Gibson was going to catch up with it," said commentator Lorn Brown on the White Sox radio broadcast. "He played it perfectly."[2] That was the first out. Jack Morris then struck out Carlton Fisk and Harold Baines to end the inning.

It was a chilly Saturday afternoon at Comiskey Park. The season was less than a week old. The game marked the season debut of NBC's *Game of the Week*, with Vin Scully and Joe Garagiola starting their second year together in the booth. NBC chose the game in order to feature the American League debut of new White Sox pitcher Tom Seaver, but a rainout earlier in the week bumped Seaver's start back and spoiled their storyline.[3] It was too early to draw any conclusions, but the Tigers were 3-0 after beating Tony La Russa's defending AL West champion White Sox 3-2 the day before and looking to finish out a perfect first week.

In the top of the second, Lance Parrish drew a leadoff walk off White Sox starter Floyd Bannister, and Chet Lemon– who played for the White Sox for seven seasons before being traded to Detroit — homered to give the Tigers a 2-0 lead.

Morris retired the White Sox in order his first time through the lineup. But in the bottom of the fourth, Morris seemed to go from dominant to derailed. Law led off and worked the count to 2-and-0. Then Morris licked his hand and homeplate umpire Durwood Merrill charged Morris a ball for going to his mouth on the mound. Morris went ballistic, walking toward the plate and waving his arms, but the count was 3-and-0. The rattled Morris walked Law, then walked Fisk, and walked Baines. The bases were loaded with nobody out. It was still too early to think about a no-hitter; now Morris was just looking for a way out of the inning.

But the next batter, Greg Luzinski, checked his swing and bounced back to the mound. Morris fired to Parrish for the force out at home and Parrish relayed to first to retire Luzinski. Suddenly there were two outs and still no runs across. Morris later called it "the turning point of the game."[4] Then Morris struck out Ron Kittle to end the inning and leave the White Sox not only without a run, but still without a hit.

Lemon led off the fifth inning with a double,

and Gibson followed with another double to bring him home. After moving to third on a sacrifice bunt by Tom Brookens, Gibson headed home on a grounder to second by Lou Whitaker. Julio Cruz threw to home plate but Gibson beat the tag. The Tigers led 4-0.

Morris gave up a walk but nothing else in the fifth. That's when he, the crowd, and a national TV audience started thinking seriously about a no-hitter. "I knew I had it going in the fifth inning," he said. "Usually by the fifth inning I don't have a no-hitter going. I looked up at the board and saw zero."[5]

Morris would need more defensive help to keep it that way. Dave Bergman came in as a defensive replacement at first base in the seventh inning and immediately made his mark.

"That's got to be tough, in the cold, coming off the bench to play defense in a no-hitter," Scully said on NBC.[6] As soon as Scully said it, Tom Paciorek hit a hard line shot toward first. Bergman reached and made the backhand stab.[7]

After the seventh inning, everyone in the Tigers dugout seemed tense except Morris. A couple of hecklers next to the dugout were loudly reminding Morris what was at stake — the only ones in the vicinity who dared to bring it up. But Morris turned to the hecklers and stated, "I know I've got a no-hitter, and you just sit back and watch the next two innings because I'm going to get it." Tigers pitching coach Roger Craig, who was in the Brooklyn Dodgers dugout for Don Larsen's perfect game in the 1956 World Series, said, "That shocked the superstitious types in our dugout, but also broke the tension."[8]

"I'm not superstitious," said Morris, whose only career one-hitter so far, in 1980, featured a first-inning single and thus no suspense. "I told Roger, 'Hey, I've come this far, I've got to do it.' Sure, I'm cocky, but I have to be."[9]

Morris was known for his ego and his volatile temperament, which could alienate umpires, the media, and at times even teammates. Sometimes it seemed to be his undoing, as it was when he walked the bases loaded in the fourth after being penalized. And yet his fiery drive could also push him to beat the odds, as he did in escaping that inning unscathed. Now it may have given him an edge as the tension mounted.

But if Morris was staying loose, the rest of the Tigers were nursing nerves. They remembered what happened at Comiskey Park not quite one year earlier. On April 15, 1983, Detroit's Milt Wilcox took a perfect game into the ninth inning and had two outs. Then pinch-hitter Jerry Hairston came up for Chicago and singled to center. Wilcox got the next batter to groundout to finish one hit short of perfection.

"Because of what Milt went through, I wanted this one double for Morris," said Tigers shortstop Alan Trammell.[10]

Improbably, in the eighth inning — in the same park and nearly the same date and situation — Jerry Hairston came in to pinch-hit for the White Sox. Sure enough, he hit a hard groundball down the first-base line. But Bergman shone again. He slid to his knees and snared the ball, and threw to Morris at first for the out. After two more groundouts, Morris was three outs away.

Morris started the bottom of the ninth by getting Fisk to pop out to Bergman at first. "I wanted to get the first hitter out. I threw Fisk a good forkball and got him," he said. "Then I got gung ho about the no-hitter."[11]

Next up was Baines. Morris considered him the toughest out in the White Sox lineup.[12] But Baines bounced back to the mound, and Morris was one out away.

Luzinski, the cleanup hitter, stepped in. "How about the loneliness of a man on a mound one out away from a no-hitter?" said Scully.[13] With the count 2-and-2, one strike away, pouring everything he had into the pitch, Morris fell off the mound in his delivery and bounced the ball to the plate. Then, with a full count, Morris fired a beauty that just missed the outside corner. Parrish rose out of his crouch to celebrate but stalled when he didn't hear the call. The Comiskey crowd, on its feet and hoping to see history, booed Merrill, the umpire.

Morris slapped his hip in disbelief but kept his cool. He saw Dave Stegman come into the game to run for Luzinski. Stegman played for the Tigers when Morris broke into the big leagues and roomed with him on the road. "Relax, roomie," Morris called over to Stegman. "You're not going anywhere."[14]

Kittle was up next. He had struck out to end that nearly calamitous fourth inning. Morris got ahead of him in the count, 1-and-2, and then unfurled his signature pitch, the forkball. Kittle waved at the pitch as it tailed away for strike three.

The crowd cheered, the dugout emptied. Parrish rushed toward the mound, and he and Morris collided in an embrace.

"I'm so excited I can hardly talk," Morris said afterward. "I've had better stuff before, but anytime you throw a no-hitter or even a shutout, you have to have luck."[15]

"It wasn't a Picasso, but it might have been a Rockwell," said Merrill.[16]

Few fans had been watching as nervously as Carol Morris, in Birmingham, Michigan. She had two televisions and a radio all tuned to the game, but couldn't bear to idle near any of them as her husband collected hitless innings. "I was so nervous, I cleaned my whole house," she said.[17] After waxing the kitchen floor, she finally settled in front of the TV to watch the last three innings. "It seemed like an eternity. I got more nervous with each inning, each out, each pitch."

Morris became the fourth Tiger to throw a no-hitter, the first since Jim Bunning in 1958.[18] He also tied the mark for the earliest date of a no-hitter; Ken Forsch threw one for the Astros on the same date in 1979.[19] (Bob Feller pitched a no-hitter on Opening Day in 1940, but that happened on April 16.)

Columnist Joe Falls said the no-hitter showed how much Morris had grown.

"Something always seemed to be going wrong with this scowling right-hander," Falls wrote. "He seemed to be fuming all the time. … Now, at the age of 28, the man has matured. … More than mastering the best team in the American League West, he has learned to master himself."[20]

The timing was right for the Tigers, who improved to 4-0 and would quickly take control of the AL East. Morris's no-hitter provided a hint that a historic April might be in store for the 1984 Tigers — as well as a memorable October.

SOURCES

In addition to the sources mentioned in the Notes, the author consulted Baseball-Reference.com and Retrosheet.org:

Retrosheet: B04070CHA1984.

Baseball-Reference: Baseball-Reference.com/boxes/CHA/CHA198404070.shtml.

http://www.Baseball-Reference.com/boxes/CHA/CHA198404070.shtml

http://www.Retrosheet.org/boxesetc/1984/B04070CHA1984.htm

NOTES

1 A recent example is Steven Souza Jr.'s diving catch to complete Jordan Zimmermann's no-hitter on the final day of the 2014 season.

2 Detroit Tigers at Chicago White Sox. WMAQ, Chicago, April 7, 1984. Accessed at youtube.com/watch?v=UBu9a0Jyi4I.

3 "Garagiola, Scully Take 'Giant Egos' Into 2d Year," **Detroit Free Press**, April 7, 1984: 32.

4 Joe Mooshil, "Morris No-hits the White Sox," **Spokane (Washington) Spokesman-Review**, April 8, 1984: 45.

5 Ibid.

6 Jerry Green, "Scully, TV Cameras Capture Drama Perfectly," **Detroit News**, April 8, 1984: 1C.

7 Roger Craig noted that Bergman was playing off the bag with a runner on first only because the slow-footed Luzinski (who had walked) wasn't a threat to steal. "Sparky admitted later that he would have had Bergman holding almost any other runner on first, which would have allowed Paciorek's line drive to reach right field for a base hit." See Roger Craig and Vern Plagenhoef, **Inside Pitch: Roger Craig's '84 Tiger Journal** (Grand Rapids, Michigan: Wm. B. Eerdmans Publishing Company, 1984), 15.

8 Craig, 16.

9 Bill McGraw, "The Right Stuff," **Detroit Free Press**, April 8, 1984: 33.

10 Tom Gage, "Morris' Masterpiece Silences White Sox," **The Sporting News**, April 16, 1984: 25.

11 Mooshil, "Morris No-hits the White Sox."

12 McGraw, "The Right Stuff."

13 Joe Lapointe, "NBC Covers All Bases on Morris' No-hitter," **Detroit Free Press**, April 8, 1984: 42.

14 Gage, "Morris' Masterpiece."

15 "Tigers' Morris Hurls No-Hitter," **Detroit Free Press**, April 8, 1984: 1.

16 McGraw, "The Right Stuff."

17 Anne Tobik, "Carol Morris Worried Along With Her Husband," **Detroit Free Press**, April 8, 1984: 42.

18 The other two were Virgil Trucks, who threw two no-hitters in 1952, and George Mullin in 1912. As of 2017, Justin Verlander has since thrown two no-hitters for Detroit (in 2007 and 2011), while Armando Galarraga was robbed of a perfect game in 2010 on a bad call on what would have been the final out.

19 Mooshil, "Morris No-hits the White Sox."

20 Joe Falls, "Maturity 1st, Greatness 2nd for Morris," **Detroit News**, April 8, 1984: 1C.

THE LONGEST GAME IN MAJOR LEAGUE HISTORY

MAY 8-9, 1984
CHICAGO WHITE SOX 7, MILWAUKEE BREWERS 6
(25 INNINGS)

By Ken Carrano

George Bernard Shaw once wrote, "Baseball has the great advantage over cricket of being sooner ended."[1] On May 8 and 9, 1984, the Chicago White Sox and Milwaukee Brewers challenged that notion, playing the longest major-league game by time at 8 hours and 6 minutes.[2] Along the way to the White Sox' 7-6 win over the Brewers in 25 innings, the 14,754 spectators at Comiskey Park were treated to 13 runs, 43 hits, 4 errors (almost all of them costly), and sleep deprivation. "That was the most unbelievable game I've ever seen," Brewers catcher Jim Sundberg said. "Guys dropping balls. Bad baserunning. A coach grabbing a guy. It was amazing."[3]

Neither team entered this game playing well. The Brewers, although having outscored their opponents by 18 runs in 26 games sat at .500, 9½ games behind the surging Detroit Tigers in the AL East.[4] The defending AL West champions were worse off in fifth place at 12-15, 3½ games behind the California Angels. Taking the mound this day would be future Hall of Famer Don Sutton for the Brewers and Bob Fallon, making his third career start for the White Sox. Sutton's baseball journey ended in Cooperstown. Fallon's major-league season did not survive the game; he was sent to the White Sox' Triple-A affiliate in Denver after the game.[5]

Despite the contrast in careers, Fallon was Sutton's equal on this chilly May night. Fallon faced the minimum through six innings, surrendering a single in the third and walks in the first and fourth innings, all eliminated by double plays. (The Brewers pulled off six in all.) Sutton was not quite as efficient as Fallon, walking two in the first inning, and allowing two singles in the third, but with no damage to the scoreboard. The Brewers gifted the White Sox a run in the sixth. Greg Walker singled with one out and stole his first base of the season after Greg Luzinski fouled out. Walker should have been stranded on second, but Brewers third baseman Randy Ready dropped Harold Baines' foul popup. Baines walked, and the White Sox' Tom Paciorek singled in the first run of the game. Ready redeemed himself by scoring the tying run in the seventh, getting a leadoff walk and making it 1-1 on singles by Sundberg and Robin Yount. The Brewers lost their chance to take the lead when Sundberg was caught trying to score from third on Ted Simmons's grounder to third baseman Vance Law. It wasn't Sundberg's day on the basepaths; in the 11th inning he was thrown out after taking too large a turn at first on his single.

The Brewers took a 3-1 lead in the top of the ninth off White Sox left-hander Britt Burns, who had temporarily lost his spot in the rotation to Fallon. Yount led off with a double to left, and with one out stole third and scored on catcher

The White Sox acquired 39-year-old Tom Seaver prior to the 1984 campaign. Tom was terrific, winning 15 and then 16 in 1985, including his 300th game, on August 4, 1985, at Yankee Stadium. (Photo by Jonathan Daniel/Getty Images)

Carlton Fisk's throwing error. Simmons singled, moved to second on a wild pitch, and scored on Ben Oglivie's single to center. Pitcher Rollie Fingers came in seeking his fifth save of the year, but more sloppy fielding by the Brewers took that chance away. Right fielder Charlie Moore dropped Paciorek's fly, allowing him to get to second. "I screwed it up. What can I say?" Moore said after the game. "I got there in plenty of time. I closed my glove too fast."[6] Fingers retired the next two batters, but Julio Cruz's double over Oglivie's head scored Paciorek, and Rudy Law's single plated Cruz with the tying run and saddled Fingers with his first blown save in nearly two years. That ended the scoring for the day, but not the baseball.

Extra innings were becoming common for the Brewers — this game would be their fifth extra-inning game of their last eight. The White Sox had played only two so far in 1984, both 10-inning walk-off wins. The Brewers had runners on in every inning from the 10th to the 13th, but Sundberg's baserunning error in the 11th and pitcher Al Jones's pickoff of Jim Gantner at second base in the 13th killed rallies. White Sox bats were quiet until the 13th, when they had runners at first and second with two out after a double by Baines off Tom Tellmann and an intentional walk to Paciorek, but could not bring the winning run home. The White Sox had the bases loaded in the 14th with one out after three singles, but Rick Waits struck out pinch hitter Marc Hill, and Dave Stegman popped up to end the threat.

This was becoming a late night. The fans were treated to a second helping of "Take Me Out to the Ball Game" in the middle of the 14th, and around midnight, the scoreboard operator played the ever-popular game "Can you remember tonight's attendance?"[7] The 15th through 17th innings went by without incident, and when Baines grounded out to second to end the 17th on the 506th pitch of the game, it was 1:03 A.M. and AL rules called for the game to be suspended.[8] "When it's 1 A.M., it's time for little kids and ballplayers to be in bed," said Tom

Seaver.[9] "We should have won the game in nine," moaned Brewers manager Rene Lachemann. "We didn't play very good defense, and we didn't have baserunning."

The game would resume quickly — in 17 hours, at 6:30 P.M. before the teams' next game. Lachemann had slated Chuck Porter to start that day's game, but with the Brewers having gone through five pitchers already, Porter started the 18th, replacing Watts. "If the first game didn't go too long then I would start the second game. Then they were going to bring in Bob McClure in when I got tired," Porter said.[10] Juan Agosto, who had thrown four innings for the White Sox when the game was suspended, got the ball back as it resumed, throwing three more. Ron Reed took over for the White Sox in the 21stst, and after retiring the first two hitters gave up a single to Cecil Cooper, a walk to Simmons, and a three-run home run to Oglivie. Normally that might be enough for the Brewers, but normal had left this game 12 innings earlier. Rudy Law hit a groundball to third that Ready threw into the grandstand and the White Sox were in business. Fisk's single scored Law from second, and after a single by Hill, Paciorek's single to center scored Fisk and White Sox starter Richard Dotson, running for Hill, and the game was tied again, 6-6. There appears to be no record of the playing of "Take Me Out to the Ball Game" for the 21st-inning stretch.

The White Sox nearly ended the game in the 23rd when Stegman singled to lead off the inning, and after a fly out Paciorek got his fifth hit of the game. Unfortunately for Stegman, he couldn't hit the brakes rounding third and ran into the arms of third-base coach Jim Leyland, or barely touched him, depending on your dugout. Lachemann claimed interference, and first-base umpire Ted Hendry agreed, calling Stegman out. White Sox manager Tony La Russa played the remainder of the game under protest. "I interpret the ruling to mean that the coach has to physically assist the runner," said La Russa. "I don't think Leyland did that."[11] Leyland for his part claimed innocence. Gesturing toward the manager's office, Leyland joked "You have to talk to my lawyer." (La Russa has a law degree.)[12] Vance Law's single after the incident would have scored Stegman.

The White Sox brought in their scheduled Wednesday starter, Seaver, to pitch the top of the 25th. The future Hall of Famer had not pitched in a relief role since 1976, but the White Sox were just about out of warm bodies. Their only player to have not appeared in the game once Seaver came in was LaMarr Hoyt, who had started the game before the marathon. "I didn't feel comfortable coming in in relief," said Seaver,[13] but after giving up a leadoff single to Bill Schroeder, he got Yount to ground into his third double play of the game and retired Cecil Cooper on a fly ball to left, setting up the fateful bottom of the 25th. Dave Stegman struck out when he bunted foul with two strikes. (He had five K's in the game.) Not to worry. Baines stepped up, drove a 420-foot blast to center,[14] and the longest game in the major leagues ended, making a winner of Seaver. "I think I found myself out at the plate before the ball went over the wall," exclaimed La Russa.[15] "I wish it would have went a little longer," said Porter, who took the loss.[16] The White Sox scoreboard operator spoke for everyone else, putting up "Thanks Harold!" on the center-field scoreboard at 9:12 P.M., 25 hours and 42 minutes after the game started.[17]

As scheduled, Seaver started the scheduled game. He pitched 8⅓ innings and won, 5-4. The game lasted 2 hours and 9 minutes.

SOURCES

In addition to the sources cited in the notes, the author accessed Retrosheet.org, Baseball-Reference.com, SABR's BioProject via SABR.org, The Sporting News archive via Paper of Record, and the Chicago Tribune via newspapers.com.

Baseball-Reference.com/boxes/CHA/CHA198405080.shtml.

Retrosheet.org/boxesetc/1984/B05080CHA1984.htm.

NOTES

1 brainyquote.com.

2 "About L-O-N-G Games;" **The Sporting News**, May 21, 1984: 4. The previous longest game by time (7 hours and 23 minutes) was played between the San Francisco Giants and New York Mets on May 31, 1964. It was game two of a doubleheader: Baseball-Reference.com/boxes/NYN/NYN196405312.shtml. In all, the Mets and Giants played 9 hours and 52 minutes that day.

3 Tom Flaherty, "Longest day Is Longest for Brewers," **Milwaukee Journal**, May 10, 1984: Sports 1.

4 The Tigers won their first nine games in 1984, and were 23-4 on May 8. They went wire-to-wire to win the AL East, and lost only one postseason game on their way to winning the World Series.

5 Mike Kiley, "25 + 9 = Sox sweep," **Chicago Tribune**, May 10, 1984: 72. Fallon returned to the major leagues with the White Sox in 1985, making 10 appearances in relief.

6 Tom Flaherty, "Any Lead Is Unsafe as Brewers Play 17," **Milwaukee Journal**, May 9, 1984: Sports 1.

7 Mike Kiley, "Sox Battle Brewers — Endlessly," **Chicago Tribune**, May 9, 1984: 81.

8 Randy Minkoff, "Tom Seaver Likes AL's Curfew Rule," UPI Archives, August 18, 1984. At the time, the American League had a rule that no inning could start after 12:59 A.M. local time.

9 Ibid.

10 Tom Flaherty, "Baseball's Longest Day Is Longest for Brewers," **Milwaukee Journal**, May 10, 1984: Sports 3

11 Mike Kiley, "Sox," **Chicago Tribune**, May 10, 1984: 81.

12 Michael Bauman, "Hey, It's No Big Deal to Seaver," **Milwaukee Journal**, May 10, 1984: Sports 3.

13 Mike Kiley, "Sox."

14 "About L-O-N-G Games," **The Sporting News**, May 21, 1984: 4. The 25th was the latest inning in which a major-league home run had been hit.

15 Joe Goddard, "25 Innings Later, Chisox Were Winners," **The Sporting News**, May 21, 1984: 4.

16 Tom Flaherty, "Baseball's Longest Day Is Longest for Brewers," **Milwaukee Journal**, May 10, 1984: Sports 3

17 Ibid.

CARLTON FISK HITS FOR THE CYCLE WITH ONLY TRIPLE OF THE SEASON

MAY 16, 1984
KANSAS CITY ROYALS 7, CHICAGO WHITE SOX 6

By Mike Huber

At Comiskey Park in mid-May 1984, there was a chance for "a miraculous happening,"[1] an opportunity for something that had not happened since between July 1 and August 6 of 1977, when both Chicago teams were in first place for more than a month.

Six weeks into the season, as May 16 arrived, the Cubs were a half-game behind the New York Mets in the National League East, with the White Sox in a similar position, a half-game behind the California Angels in the American League West.

Over in the NL, the Cubs did their part. They beat the Cincinnati Reds 10-4, while the Mets lost to the San Francisco Giants 4-3, vaulting the Wrigley Field team into first place.

The White Sox, meanwhile, had defeated the Kansas City Royals in the first two games of a three-game series, and a victory in the finale could sweep the Pale Hose to the top of the division. The Baltimore Orioles already had shut out the Angels 5-0, making the miracle possible.

In a close ballgame, the White Sox scored in each of the first four innings against Kansas City but could not hold the lead, falling 7-6 before a crowd of 21,669. The Royals' comeback overshadowed the effort of Chicago catcher Carlton Fisk, who went 4-for-5 at the plate and hit for the cycle.

White Sox manager Tony La Russa handed the ball to Floyd Bannister for the start, while Royals skipper Dick Howser called on Larry Gura. Bannister brought a 2-4 won-lost record and a 4.97 earned-run average into the contest. Gura, on the other hand, was 5-1 with a solid 2.72 ERA. Kansas City had allowed only 10 runs in its last five games as Chicago looked for a series sweep.

The Royals put across a run in the first without the aid of a hit. Willie Wilson, who was playing in his first game since returning from a suspension for drug possession,[2] walked to lead off the frame. With one out, he stole second. Bannister, in an attempted pickoff at second, threw the ball past second baseman Julio Cruz, and Wilson raced around the bases to score.

In Chicago's half of the first, Fisk doubled with one out and Tom Paciorek walked. Greg Luzinski flied out to right, allowing Fisk to tag and advance to third. Ron Kittle then singled, Fisk scored, and the game was tied, 1-1.

In the second, Dave Stegman led off with a solo home run to give Chicago a 2-1 lead. Vance Law followed with a single, moved up two bases on two groundouts, and scored on Fisk's RBI single. Stegman added a two-run homer off Gura in the third inning to stake Bannister to a 5-1 lead.

Bannister nearly gave up the lead in the fourth. Hal McRae singled to open the frame and scooted to second when Bannister threw a wild pitch with Steve Balboni at the plate. Leon Roberts doubled home McRae after Balboni struck out, John Wathan walked, and Greg

Pryor doubled to score Roberts. U.L. Washington drove in Wathan with a sacrifice fly to center field. Suddenly, it was 5-4.

Through three innings, Gura had faced 17 Chicago batters, yielding seven hits and a walk, with only one strikeout. Howser kept him in the dugout as the bottom of the fourth started and brought in Joe Beckwith. After two quick outs, Fisk came up for the third time in the game and belted a solo home run, extending Chicago's slim lead to 6-4.

However, Bannister ran out of gas in the sixth. He retired Roberts but gave up a single to Wathan, who scored when Pryor doubled. Left fielder Kittle made an error on the play, and Pryor continued to third base. La Russa called to the bullpen for Salome Rojas, ending Bannister's night. Washington greeted the new pitcher with a single and the score was tied, with all the runs charged to Bannister.

The seventh inning was highlighted by triples from both teams. Roberts's two-out shot plated Balboni with the go-ahead run for Kansas City. Fisk led off the bottom of the seventh with a three-bagger off new Royals pitcher Dan Quisenberry, but his Chicago teammates stranded him there, failing to drive him home on two groundouts and a strikeout. This was Fisk's first triple of the season (and would be his only one).

He had hit for the cycle, but his team was still losing. The White Sox had a final chance in the bottom of the ninth, with Fisk at the plate and Cruz on first. But Quisenberry's slider caused Fisk to ground into a double play, and the hopes for the first-place miracle vanished.

Fisk, coming off a 1983 season that ended with a third-place finish in the AL MVP voting, had been struggling at the plate for much of the season. He hit safely in only 12 of his first 26 games. In this game, he "busted out of his 0-for-18 slump with a strong display of hitting,"[3] becoming just the third White Sox player in history to hit for the cycle.[4] Speaking about the cycle, he told reporters, "I didn't know it until somebody told me."[5] Besides knocking in two runs and scoring twice, he raised his average 31 points, but still only to .198.

The loss broke Chicago's three-game winning streak and evened its record at 18-18. As Tony La Russa said, "It's a shame to do all the things we did in this game and not be able to celebrate."[6] The White Sox left five men on base, including two left on by Fisk. They also wasted Stegman's two homers. Chicago lost six of its next eight games, falling to fifth place. Kansas City won five of eight but remained in sixth place.

Fisk finished his 24-year career with 47 triples, but he hit one or none in 14 seasons. (Interestingly, Fisk led the AL with nine triples in 457 at-bats as a 24-year-old in 1972. The following season, he went to bat 508 times and did not triple.)

His cycle came 10 days after Baltimore's Cal Ripken Jr. accomplished the feat on May 6. Later in the season, Willie McGee of the St. Louis Cardinals (June 23) and Dwight Evans of the Boston Red Sox (June 28) enjoyed cycle games.

SOURCES

In addition to the sources mentioned in the Notes, the author consulted Baseball-Reference.com, MLB.com, and Retrosheet.org.

NOTES

1 Mike Kiley, "Sox Miss Shot at Top," *Chicago Tribune*, May 17, 1984: 63.

2 Wilson and Royals teammates Willie Aikens and Jerry Martin were suspended for one season by Commissioner Bowie Kuhn on December 15, 1983, for attempting to possess cocaine. After a grievance hearing on April 3, arbitrator Richard I. Bloch commuted Wilson's and Martin's suspensions to May 15. Kuhn commuted Aikens' sentence to May 15. *Los Angeles Times*, August 21, 1997.

3 Ibid.

4 The others before Fisk were Ray Schalk (June 27, 1922, against the Detroit Tigers) and Jack Brohamer (September 24, 1977, against the Seattle Mariners). Since Fisk's feat, two more White Sox have hit for the cycle: Chris Singleton (July 6, 1999) and José Valentin (April 27, 2000).

5 Kiley.

6 Ibid.

BASEBALL'S OLDEST DIAMOND MARKS ITS DIAMOND ANNIVERSARY

JULY 1, 1985
SEATTLE MARINERS 3, CHICAGO WHITE SOX 1

By Robert Kimball

The expression "wait 'til next year" permeates baseball. But for fans waiting for the White Sox to entertain the Seattle Mariners on July 1, 1985, the past was very much part of the program as Comiskey Park's message board noted: "CELEBRATING 75 YEARS THE PALACE OF BASEBALL."[1]

The oldest ballpark in the majors at the time, the facility on Chicago's South Side debuted as White Sox Park on July 1, 1910, under owner Charles Comiskey, the man nicknamed "The Old Roman" and who called his steel-and-concrete home the "Baseball Palace of the World."[2] And while baseball games were the main attraction, his Comiskey Park would be the site of numerous sports memories.[3]

The White Sox dropped the Comiskey opener, 2-0 to the St. Louis Browns, with future Hall of Famer Big Ed Walsh taking the loss. Fast-forward to the diamond anniversary, and the White Sox fell to the surging Mariners 3-1, suffering their sixth consecutive defeat and 10th in 11 games.[4]

But the setback aside, the 30,041 fans in attendance witnessed a pregame ceremony that featured 11 people who were at that first game at the corner of 35th and Shields. In fact, one of those honored fans, 92-year-old Bill Trow, even recalled Walsh pitching as far back as the 1906 World Series. "His attitude made Walsh the most popular player with Sox fans," Trow said.[5]

The White Sox also invited Art Wheeler, who at 95 remembered fondly rooting against the crosstown Cubs as a youngster — a tradition still alive on the South Side.[6] For Frank Bentivegna, his Comiskey Park memories included sneaking under the fence and sitting in the bleachers to watch outfielder Shoeless Joe Jackson. "The fans used to ask him, 'How many homers you gonna hit today, Joe?' And he would hold up two fingers."[7]

The Comiskey family was also in attendance, with Charles Comiskey's grandson Chuck tossing out the first ball and receiving a greeting from White Sox catcher Carlton Fisk.[8]

The White Sox featured three future Hall of Famers that night, including Fisk, who at 37 still caught 130 games in 1985. Cooperstown was also on deck for manager Tony La Russa, who was in his final full season on the South Side, and 40-year-old Tom Seaver, who was in his next-to-last big-league season. The right-hander, who played 2½ seasons for the White Sox, liked working at Comiskey, saying, "It's a joy to pitch here."[9]

There were postgame fireworks as part of the celebration, but the lack of runs on the field translated to zeros on the scoreboard as the clubs played scoreless baseball for seven innings. Seattle right-hander Frank Wills was having the best of it and at one time retired 11 consecutive Chicago hitters. His counterpart, Floyd Bannister, worked out of the stretch more often as he allowed runners in every inning he pitched.

In the fateful eighth, Bannister gave up a one-out single to Ivan Calderon and a walk to Gorman Thomas, setting the stage for Al Cowens, who homered for a 3-0 lead. On the game-deciding blast, Cowens said Bannister gave him just what he wanted: "I was hoping to get a fastball and I got it."[10]

Bannister faced one more batter, then departed after throwing 136 pitches — usually an unreachable total in the twenty-first century.[11] The left-hander fell to 5-7 and finished the year with four consecutive victories for a 10-14 record and a 4.87 ERA. Dan Spillner pitched the last 1⅓ innings for the White Sox.

Wills, in his third major-league season, worked 7⅔ innings and earned the victory. In the eighth he got the first two outs before walking pinch-hitter Jerry Hairston. Pinch-runner Julio Cruz stole second and Rudy Law hit an RBI single. Manager Chuck Cottier had seen enough and pulled Wills to end his longest big-league stint. He had allowed one run on four hits and three walks.

"I'm tired of bouncing around," said Wills, who had been was brought up from Triple-A Calgary on June 5 after spending the 1983 and '84 seasons in Kansas City. "I'm looking for consistency."[12] However, Wills' only consistency in 1985 was in the loss column: He went to 4-1 that night at Comiskey, but dropped 10 of his final 11 decisions for a 5-11 record and fat 6.00 ERA.

Ed Vande Berg and Edwin Nunez finished the five-hitter, with Nunez notching his 12th save against a listless Sox offense that had batted only .213 and averaged just 2.4 runs in its last 11 games. The offensive woes were certainly foremost in La Russa's mind. Before the game he said there were pros and cons to having extra hitting for slumping players. "Sometimes you hit too much. Sometimes you're better off taking less batting practice." La Russa also believed taking extra swings could be advantageous in two instances: Maintaining your stroke when you're hitting well and using batting practice to correct a "mechanical weakness."[13]

For the season, the Sox batted .253, eight points below the American League average (ranked 12th out of 14 AL teams), while they scored just under the league average of 4.6 runs a game.

But La Russa remained optimistic, saying "the worm will turn"[14] if the White Sox kept putting runners on base. Chicago had men on in each of the last four innings, but only Law's hit produced a run. La Russa never saw Cowens' homer or Law's RBI single from the dugout; plate umpire Ken Kaiser had ejected him for arguing balls and strikes in the top of the fourth.

"The umpires did not beat us," said La Russa. "Seattle has a good ballclub."[15]

The win, the Mariners' ninth in 10 games gave them a 37-37 record and let them slip into fourth place in the American League West, a half-game ahead of the White Sox, who dipped to 35-36. Asked if the M's were "for real," a stern-faced Cowens told the Associated Press, "We've always been for real."[16]

Cowens was certainly a big part of the Seattle surge, with three homers and 10 RBIs in his last seven games, all Mariners victories. Cottier cited his mound corps as a reason for the recent good play, saying, "We've been getting steady pitching from our starters."[17] Over the last 10 games, Seattle starters had a 3.30 ERA.

Despite the midseason run of good baseball, the Mariners finished 74-88 and 17 games off Kansas City's division-leading pace. The White Sox wound up six games behind the eventual World Series champion Royals at 85-77.

As the fans looked back that night on Comiskey Park's 75th anniversary, the man in charge looked ahead to a new breed of ballparks. Commissioner Peter Ueberroth, in town for the festivities, told the *Chicago Tribune*, "From now on, we're going to go backwards a bit. The trend will be toward nostalgia and intimacy in ballparks of the future."[18] Was Ueberroth somehow seeing past the sterile new Comiskey just six years away and envisioning the prototype retro stadium opening in 1992 at Baltimore's Camden Yards?

THE BASE BALL PALACE OF THE WORLD

SOURCES

In addition to the sources cited in the Notes, the author also accessed Retrosheet.org, Baseball-Reference.com, and SABR.org.

NOTES

1. Information from photos by Charles Cherney, Section 1, Page 1 and Section 4, Page 1, **Chicago Tribune**, July 2, 1985.

2. Michael Gershman, **Diamonds: The Evolution of the Ballpark** (New York: Houghton Mifflin Company, 1993), 92.

3. Notable happenings at Comiskey included Joe Louis winning the heavyweight boxing title in 1937, baseball's first All-Star Game in 1933, Cleveland's Larry Doby integrating the American League in 1947, the Chicago Cardinals beating the Philadelphia Eagles to capture the 1947 NFL title, and unruly fans rushing the field on Disco Demolition Night in 1979, forcing the White Sox to forfeit a game to the Detroit Tigers.

4. Associated Press, "White Sox Continue Fade," July 2, 1985.

5. Bob Logan, "A Comiskey Hurrah — But Is It the Last?" **Chicago Tribune**, July 2, 1985.

6. Logan, "It's Still a Palace," **Chicago Tribune**, June 30, 1985.

7. Logan, "A Comiskey hurrah."

8. Cherney photo, Section 1, Page 1; **Chicago Tribune**; Associated Press, "White Sox Continue Fade."

9. Logan, "A Comiskey Hurrah."

10. Bill Jauss, "Punchless Sox Can't Cool Off Hot Mariners," **Chicago Tribune**, July 2, 1985.

11. Ibid.

12. Associated Press, "White Sox Continue Fade."

13. Jauss, notes column, **Chicago Tribune**, July 2, 1985.

14. Jauss, "Punchless Sox."

15. Ibid.

16. Associated Press, "White Sox Continue Fade."

17. Ibid.

18. Logan, "A Comiskey Hurrah."

BREWERS RUN PERFECT SEASON STREAK TO 13

APRIL 20, 1987
MILWAUKEE BREWERS 5, CHICAGO WHITE SOX 4

By Steven C. Weiner

As they made their way down I-94 to Comiskey Park for this Monday night game, the 12-0 Milwaukee Brewers and their fans were in a celebratory mood after their dramatic win on Sunday against the Texas Rangers at Milwaukee County Stadium. Yes, they were still one game shy of tying the major-league record set by the 1982 Atlanta Braves for the most consecutive wins at the beginning of a season. But the manner of that victory ensured its place forever in Brewer history to be called merely "Easter Sunday 1987."[1]

Was the 11-game winning streak doomed as the Brewers batted in the bottom of the ninth inning trailing 4-1? No. With one out and two runners on base, Rob Deer hit his second home run of the game to tie the score at 4-4. But that wasn't enough drama. With two outs, Jim Gantner walked and Dale Sveum hit a walk-off home run off Greg Harris to secure the improbable 6-4 win and ensure that the winning streak was going to Chicago.

There was another reason for Brewers fans to celebrate. In 1948, George Webb, a baseball fan, opened a lunch counter in Milwaukee and predicted that the American Association's Milwaukee Brewers would win 17 straight games. When the Boston Braves moved to Milwaukee in 1953, George Webb Restaurants predicted a 12-game winning streak at some time in the future without ever actually promising a celebratory gesture when the feat was accomplished. When it finally happened, on Easter Sunday 1987, the chain of 42 restaurants delivered on its "promise" by handing out 168,194 free hamburgers across Wisconsin on April 22, despite miserable weather in Milwaukee.[2]

The Brewers brought their 12-0 record into Comiskey Park for this Easter Monday night game. Five years earlier, Comiskey Park witnessed a more modest season-opening winning streak of eight games by the home team in their sweep of the Yankees, Red Sox, and Orioles to start the season. Recent success as Comiskey Park visitors also came with the Brewers. The White Sox had last won a series against the visiting Brewers in 1984, and their record against Milwaukee at home stood at 5-13 in the past three years.

The game also got the attention of the media around the country, including Atlanta, Los Angeles, Detroit, Baltimore, New York, and elsewhere. The *Chicago Tribune* reported that the White Sox had received 97 additional requests for media credentials on Monday morning, creating a World Series-like atmosphere.[3] Comiskey Park hadn't seen this intensity level since the 1983 playoffs when the Baltimore Orioles beat the White Sox in the ALCS.[4]

As 24,019 fans settled in for the game, it was evident that Comiskey Park, home for the Chicago White Sox since 1910, was showing its wear.[5] The lower deck in right field remained closed while repairs were in progress on the underside of the upper deck.⁶ In the second inning of the White Sox home opener against the Detroit Tigers on April 10, a chunk of concrete had fallen from the upper deck into Section 103 of the lower stands.⁷ A second piece of concrete fell later in that game and sections remained closed to fans until repairs were completed.

Pitching-wise, the White Sox seemed well prepared for the Brewers. In two starts, Jose DeLeon had already accounted for two of the four White Sox victories in the young season. In fact, he yielded no runs and only four hits in 14⅓ innings of work in road victories at Kansas City and Toronto. He was matched against Juan Nieves. In his previous start, on April 15, Nieves no-hit the Baltimore Orioles 7-0, despite, by his own admission, a "mediocre fastball and an awful slider"⁸ in the early going. His strong finish would have gone for naught except for Robin Yount's diving catch of a line drive to right-center field off the bat of Eddie Murray with two outs in the bottom of the ninth inning.

The Brewers got off to a quick 2-0 start in the first inning against Jose DeLeon with Greg Brock's home run scoring Paul Molitor, who had doubled. In the White Sox first, any notion that Nieves would duplicate Johnny Vander Meer's feat of consecutive no-hitters in 1938 was quickly dispelled. Gary Redus lined a single to left field on Nieves' first pitch in the bottom of the first and eventually scored on Carlton Fisk's single to center field to cut the Brewers early lead to 2-1.

The Brewers added a run in the second inning when Dale Sveum's two-out double to right field scored Bill Schroeder, who had also doubled to right. Nieves struggled in the bottom of the second and didn't help his own cause in the field. After one-out singles by Fred Manrique and Ozzie Guillen, Nieves threw a sure double-play grounder into center field, allowing Manrique to score. A single by Redus scored Guillen and the score was tied at 3-3.

Nieves settled down a bit, but couldn't get out of the fifth inning by his own undoing. Ivan Calderon doubled to center field and scored on consecutive groundouts by Fisk and Greg Walker for a 4-3 White Sox lead. A double by Tim Hulett, an intentional walk to Manrique, and another error by Nieves loaded the bases and ended his night, replaced by Chuck Crim, who struck out Ron Karkovice. Crim not only got the Brewers out of that jam, he gave up only a harmless single to Jerry Hairston in another three innings of work.

Meanwhile, the Brewers rallied for two runs in the seventh inning to take a 5-4 lead. DeLeon walked Bill Schroeder. When Paul Molitor's double scored pinch-runner B.J. Surhoff to tie the game, White Sox manager Jim Fregosi called on relief pitcher Bobby Thigpen. But Robin Yount's single to right scored Molitor and the Brewers had the lead for good, 5-4. Brewers southpaw closer Dan Plesac gave up a leadoff single to Jerry Royster in the ninth inning. But two strikeouts and a flyball secured his fifth save of the young season and the Brewers were 13-0 to start the season, just like the 1982 Atlanta Braves. Sometime after the game, the Brewers manager, Tom Trebelhorn, was asked how he could bring in a lefty to face three right-handed hitters. His answer was simple: "I told them that if a guy can throw 94 mph, as Danny can, then it really doesn't matter which arm he uses."⁹

What Comiskey Park gave the Brewers on this night, it took away on the very next night. Joel Davis pitched for the White Sox while Mark Ciardi started for the Brewers. Davis got the call because of an injury to starting pitcher Neil Allen.¹⁰ Ciardi in his rookie season had won the eighth game of the winning streak by going five innings and beating Baltimore, 7-4. Ciardi didn't make it out of the third inning as the White Sox took a 5-0 lead that included a first-inning home run by Donnie Hill. After a not-so-impressive first start of the season, Davis held the Brewers to four hits and no runs in 5⅓ innings of work to record the win in the 7-1 White Sox victory.

The record-tying winning streak was over! The Brewers bounced back in the next week to win four games in a row for a 17-1 record, but their early-season lead in the American League's East Division was only 3½ games over the 14-5 second place Yankees on April 27. That season-opening start enabled the Brewers to beat the 16-1 getaway of the 1984 Detroit Tigers, who won 35 of their first 40 games en route to a World Series win.

The Brewers lost their grip on first place on May 14 amid a 12-game losing streak and finished the season in third place in the American League's East Division with a 91-71 record, seven games behind the Detroit Tigers. Recapturing the glory of five years earlier in winning the 1982 American League title was not to be. Nonetheless, the importance of the 13-0 streak was not to be lost on the players. Their sentiment was best expressed by their 23-year-old shortstop and future manager, Dale Sveum: "Those were the funnest 13 days of my life."[11]

SOURCES

In addition to the references cited in the Notes, the author also accessed Baseball-Reference.com and Retrosheet.org.

Baseball-Reference.com/boxes/CHA/CHA198704200.shtml.

Retrosheet.org/boxesetc/1987/B04200CHA1987.htm.

NOTES

1. Bill Schroeder with Drew Olson, *If These Walls Could Talk: Stories from the Milwaukee Brewers Dugout, Locker Room, and Press Box* (Chicago: Triumph Books, 2016).

2. "A blast from Brewers History: Easter Sunday '87," OnMilwaukee.com, April 8, 2007, accessed September 24, 2017, onmilwaukee.com/sports/articles/brewerseaster87.html. Note: The rainy weather in the Midwest was enough to cause the postponement of the third game in the White Sox-Brewers series at Comiskey Park on that day.

3. Ed Sherman, "White Sox Fall as Milwaukee Runs Streak to 13," *Chicago Tribune*, April 21, 1987: 47.

4. Sherman: 45.

5. The author settled into his seat in Section 118 without the fear that crumbling concrete might distract from the enjoyment of this record-matching game.

6. Sherman: 47.

7. Jack Houston, "Fear Not, Sox, Cubs Fans: Comiskey Park Repairs Completed," *Chicago Tribune*, May 18, 1987.

8. "Brewers' Nieves Hurls No-Hitter," *New York Times*, April 16, 1987.

9. Dave Nightingale, "Funnest Days for Brewers, Milwaukee's Streakers Warm Up to Spring," *The Sporting News*, May 4, 1987: 18.

10. Sherman, 47.

11. Nightingale.

HAROLD BAINES SETS WHITE SOX FRANCHISE HOME RUN RECORD

JULY 22, 1987
BALTIMORE ORIOLES 10, CHICAGO WHITE SOX 5

By Brandon Lee

Harold Baines first attracted the attention of the Chicago White Sox as a 12-year-old, when then-team owner Bill Veeck saw him hit a 400-foot home run in a little league game.[1] Six years later, in 1977, the White Sox made Baines, a high-school senior in St. Michael's, Maryland, the number-one overall pick in the June amateur free-agent draft.

Baines made his major-league debut in the White Sox season opener in 1980. By 1987 he had established himself as a cornerstone player in the franchise and one of the better players in the major leagues, indicated by his three consecutive All-Star Game appearances (1985-87) and a handful of down-ballot MVP votes including a ninth-place finish in 1985. By July 1987, the 28-year-old Baines was approaching a team milestone: the White Sox home-run record.

Bill Melton held the record, set during his tenure on the South Side between 1968 and 1975. Before the White Sox traded him to the California Angels, Melton hit 153 home runs, enough to eclipse Minnie Miñoso, the franchise's previous home-run leader.

Baines started off the 1987 season with the team record in sight, but suffered two separate issues with his right knee early on. First, he missed half of spring training in 1987 while recovering from right-knee surgery the previous October.[2] The outfielder suffered an unrelated injury on Opening Day against Kansas City and underwent arthroscopic surgery on the same knee, which resulted in a trip to the disabled list[3] and caused him to miss a month of action.

Baines did not miss a beat in the batter's box upon his return to the lineup in May, though he spent time almost exclusively at designated hitter rather than his customary right field. Baines hit well enough in the first half, even with the missed time, to represent the White Sox in the All-Star Game. By the time the Orioles came to town in July, Baines had 13 home runs and a .311 batting average.

Baines tied Melton's franchise record at home on July 21 with a home run to right-center field off Orioles pitcher Ken Dixon.[4] "A win would have made it better," said Baines after the game, which the White Sox dropped to the Orioles, 11-6.[5]

The next night, Wednesday, July 22, Baines would have the opportunity to claim first place all for himself in front of the hometown crowd at Comiskey Park. José DeLeón would take the mound for the 37-54 White Sox looking to avoid the series sweep against starting pitcher Mike Boddicker and the 41-53 Baltimore Orioles, who had won seven straight.

Batting third and starting as the designated hitter, Baines struck out but reached base on a throwing error by Orioles catcher Terry Kennedy in his first plate appearance. Baines ended up being forced at second to end the inning.

After two uneventful frames, the Orioles got the scoring started with a three-run third inning.

Mike Young and Ken Gerhart reached on singles. After Alan Wiggins sacrificed, Billy Ripken walked, bringing up the heart of Baltimore's order. Cal Ripken Jr. went down on strikes for the second out of the inning, but Eddie Murray kept it going by drawing a walk, forcing Young home. Larry Sheets followed Murray with another single that plated two runs. Ray Knight struck out looking to end the inning with the Orioles up 3-0.

The White Sox answered in the bottom of the third inning. Ken Williams hit his fifth home run of the year, a solo shot off the starter Boddicker. Shortstop Ozzie Guillén, batting leadoff for the game, singled to right field, stole second, and reached third base on Donnie Hill's groundout. This brought Baines to the plate for his second plate appearance of the evening.

On a tailing fastball[6] from Boddicker, Baines made White Sox history, hitting the pitch 416 feet into the center-field bullpen[7] for his 155th home run, setting the franchise record and tying the game at 3-3.

As he rounded the bases, Baines "reacted with uncharacteristic emotion" and clapped his hands while rounding first base, according to Ed Sherman of the *Chicago Tribune*.[8] Baines received a standing ovation and a curtain call from the 12,780 White Sox faithful,[9] and eventually emerged from the dugout to tip his cap in appreciation.

"Curtain calls go along with the job," Baines said after the game. "But I don't like to do that."[10]

"In a way it shows up the pitcher, but I think you should go out when you get a standing ovation," said Baines.[11]

Boddicker said he didn't intend to pitch to Baines at all, and that home-run ball off Baines's bat "wasn't in the strike zone."[12]

"That's a good case for the rabbit ball," Boddicker said of the Baines home run,[13] alluding to the speculation that Major League Baseball had done something to make the ball livelier in the 1987 season, leading to more hitter-friendly conditions, including an increase in home runs.[14]

Iván Calderon followed Baines with a solo home run of his own to put the White Sox ahead. Greg Walker singled and Carlton Fisk walked, bringing up Daryl Boston, who singled home Walker to give the White Sox a 5-3 lead. John Habyan came on to replace Boddicker and gave up a single to Steve Lyons but got out of the jam without further damage.

The Orioles retook the lead in the top of the fourth and did not look back from there. Mike Young's single and stolen base were followed by Ozzie Guillén's error allowing Alan Wiggins to reach first. With runners on second and third and two outs, Billy Ripken drove in Young with a single off DeLeón to bring the Orioles to within one run. Baltimore tied the game on back-to-back walks to Cal Ripken Jr. and Eddie Murray, which chased DeLeón from the game. Scott Nielsen came in from the bullpen and gave up singles to Larry Sheets and Ray Knight, accounting for three more runs, before Terry Kennedy flied out. The Orioles batted around in the inning and led, 8-5. All five runs they scored were charged to DeLeón and were unearned because of Guillén's error, which would have ended the inning had he made the play cleanly.

After putting out the fire in the bottom of the third, Habyan was perfect against the White Sox the rest of the game, not allowing a baserunner from the fourth inning on. Baltimore capped off its scoring with two solo home runs off the bat of center fielder Ken Gerhart, one in the fifth inning off Nielsen, and one in the ninth off Bob James. The final score was 10-5 Baltimore, with the win going to Habyan in relief and DeLeón taking the loss.

The Orioles' win completed their series sweep of the White Sox at Comiskey Park. It was Baltimore's eighth win in a row and seventh consecutive road win, completing their best road trip in more than 22 years.[15]

"Breaking the record was fine, but I rather would have won the game," said Baines, echoing his quote from the night before. "I'm happy to be a part of a record. Maybe after the season it will sink in."[16]

The White Sox finished the 1987 season with

a 77-85 record. The Orioles ended at 67-95, despite running off an 11-game winning streak that included the sweep of the White Sox. Baines wrapped up 1987 with a .293 batting average, a .352 on-base percentage, a .479 slugging average and 20 home runs; the sixth consecutive season he reached 20-homer mark. Never again would Baines be a regular outfielder, and he spent the rest of his career as a designated hitter because of his early-season injuries in 1987.

Baines spent 14 of his 22 major-league seasons with the White Sox. In 1989 they traded him to the Texas Rangers for Wilson Alvarez, Scott Fletcher, and Sammy Sosa. Baines returned to the White Sox as a free agent before the 1996 season, then was traded again at the trade deadline in 1997, to the Orioles. The White Sox reacquired Baines from the Orioles one final time at the trade deadline in 2000 and he helped Chicago win a division title. Baines finished his career after the 2001 season with 384 home runs, including 221 with the White Sox.

SOURCES

In addition to the sources listed, the author also consulted Baseball-Reference.com.

NOTES

1. Jim Kaplan, "Hard-headed About Hitting," **Sports Illustrated**, August 27, 1984, si.com/vault/1984/08/27/620202/hard-headed-about-hitting.

2. "AL West Notebook," **The Sporting News**, April 20, 1987: 17, 20.

3. Ibid.

4. Ed Sherman, "No Frosting on Baines' Record-Tying Cake," **Chicago Tribune**, July 22, 1987.

5. Ibid.

6. Tim Kurkjian, "Habyan, Big Hits Run Orioles' Streak to 8 with 10-5 Win," **Baltimore Sun**, July 23, 1987.

7. Joe Goddard, "Baines' 155th Homer Sets Sox Record in Loss," **Chicago Sun-Times**, July 23, 1987.

8. Ed Sherman, "Curtain Call for Baines in Sox Turkey: Slugger Sets Club Home Run Mark," **Chicago Tribune**, July 23, 1987.

9. Goddard.

10. Sherman.

11. Goddard.

12. Richard Justice, "Habyan Joins Fun as Orioles Attain 8th in Row, 10-5; Boddicker Chased but Relief Is Airtight," **Washington Post**, July 23, 1987.

13. Kurkjian.

14. Frank Deford, "Rabbit Ball: Whodunit?" **Sports Illustrated**, July 27, 1987, si.com/vault/1987/07/27/115808/rabbit-ball-whodunit-when-the-baseball-seems-lively-rational-folks-go-haywire.

15. Justice.

16. Sherman.

FISK RECORDS 2,000TH HIT

JULY 17, 1989
CHICAGO WHITE SOX 7, NEW YORK YANKEES 3

By Paul Hofmann

On July 17, 1989, the New York Yankees and Chicago White Sox opened a scheduled three-game series at Comiskey Park.[1] The Yankees entered the game with a 46-45 record, six games behind the AL East-leading Baltimore Orioles. The White Sox had won four straight but were 36-56, buried deep in the AL West Division cellar, 18½ games behind the front-running California Angels. The game carried no greater implications than any of the other 161 games on the schedule. What made this game special was the milestone achievement of one of the game's greatest catchers, Carlton "Pudge" Fisk.

An announced crowd of 18,070 was on hand to watch the nondescript Monday evening pitching matchup that featured a pair of struggling left-handers. The Yankees started journeyman Dave LaPoint, who was pitching for the first time since June 29 because of tendinitis in his left shoulder.[2] LaPoint entered the game with a record of 6-6 and a 5.48 ERA. The White Sox countered with southpaw Steve Rosenberg, who was 2-5 with a 4.69 ERA. Rosenberg, who was making his 11th start of the season, had been inserted into the White Sox rotation after veterans Jerry Reuss and Shawn Hillegas struggled in starting roles.

The game-time temperature was a warm 81 degrees and there was little more than a hint of a breeze as Rosenberg delivered the first pitch at 7:37 P.M. Three pitches later, Steve Sax singled to left. Rosenberg then retired Luis Polonia, Don Mattingly, and Steve Balboni in order, all on fly balls to left fielder Dan Pasqua.

LaPoint also yielded a single to the first batter he faced. Dave Gallagher dropped a single into short right-center and advanced to third when second baseman Fred Manrique sent a liner down the left-field line that skipped into the seats for a ground-rule double. Harold Baines followed with a line-drive single to left-center, scoring Gallagher and Manrique. After Ivan Calderon flied out to center, Fisk came to the plate stuck on 1,999 career hits.

Despite missing more than six weeks with a broken right hand (the same hand he broke in 1988 that caused him to miss 10 weeks), the 41-year-old backstop was enjoying a solid year.[3] Entering the game, he was hitting .299 (his highest average since joining the White Sox in 1981) with 5 home runs and 25 RBIs. The right-handed hitting Fisk banged a two-hopper off the mound and through the infield as Baines advanced to third. Play was halted for a brief salute to the newest member of the 2,000-hit club as Fisk simultaneously acknowledged his family and fans.[4]

After the standing ovation, the game resumed with Carlos Martinez sending a line-drive single to short left field to score Baines. Fisk stopped at second base. Pasqua followed with an infield single to third to load the bases with one out, and for a moment it looked as though LaPoint might not make it through the first inning. However, first baseman Russ Morman ended the inning by grounding into a 6-4-3 double play. While the White Sox had scored three runs on six hits,

LaPoint and the Yankees were fortunate the damage was not worse.

Jesse Barfield trimmed the White Sox lead to 3-1 when he led off the top of the second with a home run to center field. In the bottom of the inning, LaPoint recovered from his shaky first and retired the White Sox in order.

The Yankees cut into the White Sox' lead again in the top of the third. With one out Luis Polonia doubled to left-center and scored when Calderon erred on Mattingly's liner to right-center. Balboni followed by hitting into a 5-4-3 inning-ending double play.

With the White Sox ahead 3-2, the two starting pitchers settled in a bit. LaPoint tossed perfect innings in the third, fourth, and fifth, as Rosenberg also kept the Yankees in check.

LaPoint retired the first two White Sox hitters to start the sixth, his 14th and 15th consecutive batters retired. Fisk ended the streak with a double to left-center. LaPoint intentionally walked Martinez to pitch to the left-handed-hitting Pasqua, who singled to right to plate Fisk with the White Sox' fourth run of the game. Martinez and Pasqua both advanced on the throw. After Morman was intentionally walked, Ozzie Guillen lined out to right to end the inning.

Right-hander Eric Plunk replaced LaPoint in the bottom of the seventh and immediately ran into trouble. Gallagher drew a leadoff walk and moved to second when Plunk balked. With one out and the right-handed-hitting Calderon on deck, Baines was intentionally walked to set up a force or possible double play. Calderon nixed the Yankees' plan when he hit a groundball single up the middle to score Gallagher. Next up was the man of the evening, Carlton Fisk. Fisk collected his third hit of the night when he singled to left to drive in Baines and increase the White Sox' lead to 6-2. An aggressive Calderon was thrown out trying to advance to third on the play. Martinez advanced Fisk to second with a single but Pasqua struck out looking to end the inning.

The Yankees mounted a threat in the eighth when Polonia singled with one out and advanced to third on a two-out single to left by Balboni.

Hall of Famer and 11-time All-Star Carlton Fisk played the final 13 seasons (1981-1993) of his 24-year career with the White Sox. In 1985 he set personal bests with 37 home runs and 107 RBIs. (Photo by Ron Vesely/MLB Photos via Getty Images)

With runners on first and third, White Sox manager Jeff Torborg lifted Rosenberg and called on Hillegas to face Barfield, who was 2-for-2 with a home run and walk off Rosenberg. Hillegas uncorked a wild pitch on his first offering to the Yankees' right fielder, and Polonia scored to cut the White Sox lead to 6-3. Barfield eventually walked but Hillegas retired Mel Hall, who was pinch-hitting for Tom Brookens, on a foul pop that White Sox third baseman Martinez squeezed for the final out of the inning.

Yankees manager Dallas Green summoned left-hander Dave Righetti from the bullpen to pitch the bottom of the eighth. Guillen reached on a one-out infield single, stole second, and advanced to third when catcher Don Slaught's throw sailed into center field. Guillen and Gallagher executed a squeeze play and Guillen scored. Hillegas worked a 1-2-3 ninth and the White Sox won, 7-3. Fisk finished his special night 3-for-4 with a double, one run scored and one RBI.

After the game Fisk described the pitch he hit for number 2,000. "He locked it right in there, right next to me," Fisk said of the pitch he hit off LaPoint, a former teammate in Chicago. "I'm just glad he didn't start laughing."[5]

At the time Fisk became the 173rd player and the 12th active player to reach 2,000 hits.[6] The single was his 1,878th hit as a catcher, the most ever.[7] Speaking to reporters, Fisk put his achievement into a broader context. "It wasn't the one hit," Fisk said. "It was the culmination of 17 years of hard work."[8] Jim Fregosi, who managed Fisk from 1986 to 1988, substantiated the catcher's approach to the game. "Pudge works harder than anyone I know because he sets goals for himself and then follows through. I think he's the ultimate professional," Fregosi said.[9]

Fisk played another four seasons, until the age of 45. He finished his 24-year Hall of Fame career, which spanned four decades, with 2,356 hits, 1,276 runs scored, 376 home runs, and 1,330 RBIs. At the time he retired, his 351 home runs as a catcher stood as a major-league record until it was broken by Mike Piazza in 2004.

NOTES

1. The teams played only two games. The Tuesday, July 18, game and the second game of the Wednesday, July 20, doubleheader were rained out. Because this was the Yankees' final trip to Comiskey Park in 1989, the game was not replayed and both teams played 161 games that season.

2. Michael Martinez, "Yankees Hit the Wall Again," **New York Times**, July 18, 1989, B7.

3. "Fisk Out for Weeks," **Bend (Oregon) Bulletin**, April 13, 1989, D2.

4. "NYY@CWS: Carlton Fisk reaches 2000th hits in Majors," youtube.com/watch?v=cla1bza43Ms.

5. Michael Martinez.

6. "American League Roundup: Fisk Gets 2,000th Hit as White Sox Win Again," **Los Angeles Times**, July 18, 1989, B4.

7. Ibid.

8. Ibid. Fisk's 2,000th hit actually came in his 20th major-league season and 23rd professional season.

9. "Carlton Fisk," baseballhall.org/hall-of-famers/fisk-carlton.

SOURCES

In addition to the sources cited in the Notes, the author also accessed Retrosheet.org, Baseball-Reference.com, and SABR.org.

Baseball-Reference.com/boxes/CHA/CHA198907170.shtml.

Retrosheet.org/boxesetc/1989/B07170CHA1989.htm.

WHITE SOX EKE OUT A WIN IN THE FINAL OPENING DAY AT COMISKEY

APRIL 9, 1990
CHICAGO WHITE SOX 2, MILWAUKEE BREWERS 1

By Nathan Bierma

The rising rafters of New Comiskey Park peered over the wall of the old ballpark across 35th Street, as though they, too, wanted one last look.[1]

It was the final Opening Day at Comiskey Park, kicking off the last of 81 seasons there. Sorrow for the storied park was somewhat tempered by the new one taking shape across the street. After the White Sox narrowly averted a move to Florida in 1988,[2] the shiny new ballpark ensured that the team was staying put at the corner of 35th and Shields.

Still, this would be a season for nostalgia at the oldest ballpark in the major leagues.

"There's a lot of tradition in this place," said White Sox manager Jeff Torborg the day before. "I'm kind of a romantic anyway. ... The guys here now may not be thinking of the history. They're thinking about whether we're going to win tomorrow. But it's nice to be a part of something. In some ways, it's sad. But in other ways, it's progress."[3]

Not all of the 40,008 fans in attendance on Opening Day were as even-handed. "The last true Sox opener," read a banner hanging from the left-field upper deck.[4]

Opening Day was set to be a rare double feature in Chicago. For the first time in modern major-league history, both Chicago teams would open their season at home on the same day.[5] The nightcap would come at Wrigley Field, its first evening opener since lights were installed less than two years ago.[6]

The White Sox were up first. Their game "matches two clubs in very different situations," wrote the *Chicago Tribune*.[7] After finishing at an even 81-81 the year before, the Milwaukee Brewers were aiming for an AL East crown in manager Tom Trebelhorn's fourth full season, re-signing reigning AL MVP Robin Yount and adding free-agent slugger Dave Parker.[8] Meanwhile, "the Sox were expected to mature more than contend in the tough AL West, and nothing happened in spring training to change that," the *Tribune* stated.[9] Torborg's young team tallied just 69 wins the year before, and a season of patience seemed to be in store.[10] Comiskey Park itself would be the star attraction this year.

Lacking a bona-fide ace, the White Sox would hand the ball to Melido Perez, coming off an uninspiring 1989 season in which he went 11-14 with an ERA of 5.01. The Brewers had their ace, Chris Bosio, who had the sixth best ERA in the American League in 1989 (2.95) and tied for fourth in both strikeouts (173) and complete games (eight).

After waiting over a half-hour for a drizzly rain to subside, the White Sox led off with a nod to history, sending out Chuck Comiskey to throw the ceremonial first pitch.[11] It was his grandfather Charles who built the ballpark, calling it "The Baseball Palace of the World."

The first pitch that counted would mark another milestone. When White Sox catcher

Carlton Fisk caught the opening pitch from Perez to Brewers leadoff batter Gary Sheffield, it marked the fourth decade in which Fisk had played in the major leagues. He became the 18th major leaguer to achieve that milestone, and the ball was removed to be displayed in the team's Hall of Fame in the new stadium.[12] Then, in his first at-bat of the season, in the second inning against Bosio, the ageless Fisk knocked a double down the left-field line.

But the Brewers scored first the following inning. Edgar Diaz singled, advanced on a bunt, and came home on a ground-rule double by B.J. Surhoff. The White Sox tied the game in the fifth inning when Ozzie Guillen led off with a triple down the right-field line and scored on a wild pitch by Bosio.

That was about it for offense for most of the afternoon. Perez cruised through six innings, collecting six strikeouts with just one walk and four hits. "Perez had the best tempo I've ever seen from him," said White Sox pitching coach Sammy Ellis.[13] But wanting to ease his starter into the new season, Torborg pulled him for Scott Radinsky, making his major-league debut, to start the seventh. After one batter and one out, Barry Jones came on to finish the inning.

The White Sox would take control of the game in the bottom of the seventh. After Robin Ventura drew a leadoff walk from Brewers reliever Tony Fossas, Sammy Sosa laid a bunt down the first-base line. First baseman Greg Brock charged and fired to second, but not in time to get Ventura.[14] Guillen came up and bunted, but Surhoff came out from behind the plate to field it and fire to third to force out Ventura. Then Lance Johnson loaded the bases with what the *Tribune* called "a 43-foot single that died barely along the third-base line."[15] Scott Fletcher hit a sacrifice fly to right field that sent Sosa home. The White Sox had scored a run on a walk, two bunts, a meek infield single, and a sacrifice fly, to take the lead, 2-1.

After five straight outs from Jones, Torborg brought in Wayne Edwards in the ninth to face Parker in a lefty-lefty matchup, and Edwards got him swinging. Then in came Bobby Thigpen, and he struck out Rob Deer and got Brock to fly out to Ivan Calderon in foul territory in left. The White Sox were victors on Opening Day.

"This is one 40,008 people will treasure long after old Comiskey Park is turned to memory and dust," wrote the *Tribune*.

So would Edwards, whose one retired batter was enough to make his mark on Comiskey Park history.

"I wanted to get in on Opening Day," Edwards said afterward. "It's nice to be a part of history."[16]

SOURCES

In addition to the sources cited in the Notes, the author also accessed Retrosheet.org, Baseball-Reference.com, and SABR.org.

NOTES

1 This description is based on a photo by Chris Walker on the front page of the **Chicago Tribune**. It appeared under Phil Hersh, "Opening Day Twice Blessed — and Doused," **Chicago Tribune**, April 10, 1990: 1.

2 The White Sox were poised to move to St. Petersburg before the Illinois legislature approved funding for a new stadium at midnight on June 30, 1988. Bob Verdi, "A most fantastic dream come true," **Chicago Tribune**, February 8, 1990: 49.

3 Alan Solomon, "Historic Opening for Sox," **Chicago Tribune**, April 9, 1990: 25.

4 "Opening Day twice blessed — and doused."

5 Ibid.

6 The rain would have other plans, washing out the Cubs game after two innings.

7 "Historic opening for Sox."

8 Ibid.

9 Ibid.

10 In reality, the Brewers would plunge to sixth in the East in 1990, at 74-88, while the surprising White Sox would surge to 94 wins and a strong second-place showing in the AL West behind the mighty Oakland A's, and Torborg would be named AL Manager of the Year.

11 "Opening Day twice blessed — and doused."

12 Bill Jauss, "With the Game's First Pitch, Fisk Makes It 4 Decades," **Chicago Tribune**, April 10, 1990: 53.

13 Bill Jauss, "Pitchers Give Sox 5 Reasons to Smile," **Chicago Tribune**, April 10, 1990: 46.

14 Alan Solomon, "White Sox, History Winners at Comiskey," **Chicago Tribune**, April 10, 1990: 43.

15 Ibid.

16 Ibid.

HAWKINS TOSSES NO-NO AND LOSES

JULY 1, 1990
CHICAGO WHITE SOX 4, NEW YORK YANKEES 0

By Stew Thornley

In 1906 the Chicago White Sox won the World Series with a team called the Hitless Wonders. On July 1, 1990, the White Sox truly were hitless but still victorious.

The 80th anniversary of Comiskey Park that day was also its last. Across the street to the north, a new Comiskey Park was rising and visible above the roof of the existing ballpark.

It was also Bat Day, an event that caused a delay in getting fans into the park. The gates were not opened until barely an hour before game time because the souvenir bats were late in arriving; the bats handed out to the kids were not the only ones slow in showing up.[1]

Andy Hawkins of the New York Yankees and Greg Hibbard of the White Sox combined to retire the first 29 batters in the game. Hibbard took a perfect game into the sixth before allowing a pair of one-out infield hits; he made it through seven innings without allowing a run but ended up as the forgotten man in the game.

Hawkins was making the most of a reprieve from a month before. With a won-lost record of 1-4 in early June, he was given the choice of a demotion to the minors or a release; he chose the latter. However, Mike Witt injured his elbow the next night, and Hawkins stayed with the Yankees. By the end of June, he was still winless over nearly the last two months although he had been pitching better, just without good fortune. His luck didn't improve with the coming of a new month.[2]

As Hibbard cruised through the opening innings, Hawkins put down the first 14 hitters he faced before walking a pair in the fifth. Sammy Sosa then crushed a ball to left that surely meant the end of the no-hitter and shutout — except that a stiff wind from the north kept the ball in and moved it toward the left-field line, and Jim Leyritz corralled it on the warning track to end the inning. The *USA Today* box score listed the game-time weather as 70 degrees with the wind at 16 miles per hour.[3] What this information didn't convey was how the wind swirled inside the ballpark, a challenge for fielders that would become a factor a few innings later.

The game was still scoreless, and the White Sox still hitless, with two out in the eighth when Sosa hit a grounder to third. Mike Blowers tried to backhand the ball, knocked it down, and then threw too late to get a sliding Sosa at first. A novice scoreboard operator jumped the gun and immediately flashed a hit on the board.[4] But official scorer Bob Rosenberg hadn't even had the chance to rule on the play; when he did, it was an error.

Many thought he had first called a hit and then changed it to an error, but Rosenberg said, "I called it [an error] right away. The Yankees in the dugout were giving me the finger," he said of what happened before the correct decision made it onto the scoreboard.[5]

Hawkins didn't remember any obscene gestures directed toward Rosenberg, but he did see waving and "commotion over there in the dugout." He thought his no-hitter was gone, but "the next thing I know I hear this cheer go up [an indication of the error finally being flashed on the scoreboard], so I went from, 'Oh, it's over' to 'I gotta get it back going again.'"[6]

The scoring decision finally set straight, the game continued. Sosa stole second, and Hawkins walked the next two hitters, causing stirring in the New York bullpen and a mound visit from manager Stump Merrill.

Hawkins got Robin Ventura to lift a fly to left. Leyritz followed the ball through the wind, found the range, and then had the ball hit off his glove and roll into the corner. Three runs scored as Ventura pulled into second. Suddenly Hawkins went from needing three outs for a no-hitter to just one out, since the error meant the White Sox would probably not be batting in the ninth.

It looked as if he had his out as Ivan Calderon hit an easy fly to right. But Jesse Barfield, battling the sun, had the ball pop in and out of his glove for another error as Ventura scored. After Hawkins retired Dan Pasqua on a pop fly to short, he walked off the mound with a no-hitter — albeit down by four runs — as the fans gave him an ovation. The game ended a few minutes later as the Yankees went down in the ninth.

Ironically, the two outfield butchers who cost Hawkins the game were also the two who made his no-hitter possible with fine catches to start the game. Leyritz charged and slid to make a shoestring catch of Lance Johnson's blooper leading off the bottom of the first. Barfield then ran and leaped to catch a shot hit by the next batter, Ventura.

The Sunday no-hitter by Hawkins was the third of the weekend in the majors. Two nights before, Dave Stewart of the Athletics and Fernando Valenzuela of the Dodgers had hitless outings, with different outcomes than Hawkins. "This is not even close to the way I envisioned a no-hitter would be," Hawkins told Michael Martinez of the *New York Times* after the game. "You dream of one, but you never think it's going to be a loss. You think of Stewart and Fernando, coming off the field in jubilation. Not this."[7]

Pitching a no-hitter and losing is a rare event. Ken Johnson had this happen to him in 1964.

Of Hawkins, Johnson said, "I'm sorry to hear he joined me. I was very happy being the only man to lose a no-hitter."[8]

However, Johnson had not been alone in this distinction. Baltimore pitchers Steve Barber and Stu Miller combined on a losing no-hitter for Baltimore on April 30, 1967, and there was one other game that resembled the one pitched by Hawkins. In the Players League in 1890 Charles "Silver" King of Chicago no-hit Brooklyn but lost 1-0, a result that meant that King, like Hawkins, pitched only eight innings because Brooklyn did not have to bat in the bottom of the ninth. (Since Hawkins, there have been two other of these eight-inning-type no-hitters.)

"If Comiskey II, currently under construction across 35th Street, lasts another 80 years, it will not house a stranger game," wrote Bill Jauss in the *Chicago Tribune*.[9]

Hawkins's struggles continued beyond the bizzaro in Comiskey I. He didn't win again until late July. Not only that, in the meantime, he was the losing pitcher in another no-hitter with the White Sox, this one by Chicago's Melido Perez although the game was called by rain in the top of the seventh on July 12.

Rain-shortened no-hitters such as these usually weren't considered as "real" no-hitters by sentiments of the time. But no-hitters in games played to their natural conclusion were treated with the lofty status of others, even if the pitcher went only eight innings.

However, the next year Hawkins's game was dropped from the list of "official" no-hitters by a committee fiat because he had pitched fewer than nine innings.

Regardless of the ruling of a committee, his great pitching and bad luck created far more of a buzz than just about any official no-hitter. The game story made the top of the front page (not just the front sports page) in *USA Today* with the headline "Yankee's no-hitter is no winner" and a jump to the sports section for more on this "Unbelievable game."[10] The game led sportscasts and also had prominence on regular news programs.

On the 25th anniversary of the game, Grant Brisbee in *SBNation* chronicled the event in words and video, making clear that this was a no-hitter like no other.[11]

NOTES

1 Memory of the author, who attended this game.

2 Michael Martinez, "Hawkins lucky to be around for this one," **New York Times**, July 2, 1990: 3E.

3 **USA Today**, July 2, 1990.

4 Bob Logan, "Scoreboard operator makes biggest error in White Sox' win," **Arlington** (Illinois) **Daily Herald**, July 2, 1990: section 4, page 8.

5 Telephone interview with Bob Rosenberg, August 1, 2015.

6 Author interview with Andy Hawkins, August 12, 2015. Until this interview, Hawkins was not aware that the errant decision on the scoreboard was the result of an incompetent operator and not the result of the official scorer first ruling a hit and then changing it to an error.

7 Michael Martinez, "Hawkins hurls no-hit gem, but Yanks blow it." **New York Times**, July 2, 1990: 1E.

8 "An asterisk for the books," **Minneapolis Star Tribune**, July 2, 1990: 1C.

9 Bill Jauss, "Sox's hitless victory a real wonder," **Chicago Tribune**, July 2, 1990: section 3, page 1.

10 Mel Antonen, "Yankee's no-hitter is no winner," **USA Today**, Monday, July 2, 1990: 1A.

11 Grant Brisbee, sbnation.com/2015/7/1/8841355/andy-hawkins-no-hitter-yankees-white-sox. Brisbee gets a few facts wrong (such as the claim of Hawkins striking out 17 in the game — it was 3 — and on the number of pitches it took for Hawkins to retire the first two batters in the bottom of the eighth), but his tone is appropriate for conveying the significance of this no-hitter. For the record, the author's scorebook shows that Hawkins retired the first two batters in the eighth on 10 pitches (not 14, as claimed by Brisbee), and the scorebook showing of 131 pitches in the game for Hawkins (including 37 in the eighth inning) is consistent with the total listed by **USA Today** in its box score the next day.

"FAREWELL, OLD BEAUTY"

SEPTEMBER 30, 1990
CHICAGO WHITE SOX 2, SEATTLE MARINERS 1

By John Bauer

After 80 years in the same home on the South Side of Chicago, the White Sox were moving. Two years before, the team was dangerously close to moving to St. Petersburg, Florida, until a last-minute, late-night deal in the Illinois Legislature ensured that the name Chicago, instead of Florida, would remain in front of the words White Sox. With their new home towering above their old home, the White Sox hosted one final game at the original Comiskey Park on September 30, 1990. Complete with the amenities and revenue streams associated with modern stadiums, White Sox owner Jerry Reinsdorf touted the financial advantages in moving across the street: "Now we can compete."[1] Perhaps those potential dollars would keep together a club experiencing a surprising 1990 season that would end in a worst-to-almost-first turnaround, as Chicago improved from 69 wins to 94 wins. Only the juggernaut Oakland Athletics denied the team the AL West Division title.

This contest was one where the game was secondary to the occasion. The occasion was such that there was a lottery to identify the person who would turn off the ballpark lights for good. Edith Alexsevitz won the honor. She did not enter the contest because she liked the White Sox, or even baseball for that matter; rather, she entered lotteries as a hobby.[2] As a result, Charles Comiskey's grandson, Chuck, was drafted to assist. Before the lights went off, the White Sox were to play the Seattle Mariners, and right-hander Jack McDowell strode to the mound seeking his 14th win of the campaign. Leading off, Seattle's Harold Reynolds struck out. Ken Griffey Sr. lined out to Lance Johnson in center field, before Ken Griffey Jr. singled over the head of second baseman Scott Fletcher. Shortstop Ozzie Guillen had to back up in order to get under cleanup hitter Alvin Davis's popup, and the catch ended the top of the first. In the home half of the inning, the White Sox stirred the crowd of 42,849 by getting the first two batters on base against Mariners rookie starter Rich DeLucia: Ivan Calderon through a walk and Johnson with a single to right. With runners at the corners, Chicago could not convert. Carlton Fisk and Frank Thomas hit successive pop flies to shortstop Omar Vizquel, and Dan Pasqua's fly ball to Griffey Jr. in center field ended the frame.

McDowell struck out Tino Martinez and Jay Buhner to start the second, but the Mariners got singles from Dave Valle and Vizquel. McDowell walked Jeff Schaefer to load the bases for Reynolds, but the latter's grounder to Fletcher ended the inning. Fletcher earned a two-out walk in the home half, but that proved the only blemish against DeLucia.

The game remained scoreless through five innings, with baserunning mistakes damaging possible run-scoring opportunities. Johnson's one-out single meant a baserunner for the White Sox in the third. After Fisk struck out, DeLucia's pickoff throw caught Johnson off the bag, and Martinez flipped to second baseman Reynolds to apply the inning-ending tag. With one out in the Seattle fourth, Buhner sliced a single between Guillen and third baseman Robin Ventura. After Valle flied to Johnson in short center field, Vizquel kept the inning alive with a bullet to right. Like Johnson in the previous inning, Vizquel was caught off base when McDowell threw to Thomas for the pickoff and Thomas fired to Guillen to catch Vizquel.

The Mariners broke the scoreless deadlock in the top of the sixth. Opening the inning, the 20-year-old Griffey Jr. worked a full count and then ripped a groundball to right for a triple. With Davis at the plate, McDowell's wild pitch allowed Griffey to streak home for the game's first run. Davis struck out swinging, and Martinez and Buhner flied out to Calderon in left field.

Johnson led off the bottom of the sixth and lofted DeLucia's first pitch toward right field. The wind did the rest. The ball carried away from Buhner and dropped into the corner. Johnson raced around the bases, stopping at third. Mariners manager Jim Lefebvre observed, "That was a fly ball that got caught up in the wind and kept blowing away."[3] Fisk tried desperately to bring Johnson home, but his seven-pitch at-bat ended with a big swinging strikeout. Caught up in the occasion, Pudge said later, "I tried so hard to get a hit. I was more nervous than I was in the World Series."[4] No matter. Thomas got the game-tying hit, ripping a line drive to center field for a run-scoring single. The hit extended Thomas's hitting streak to 13 games.[5] Pasqua worked the count full before hitting a screamer toward Griffey Sr. in left field. Instead of being fielded for a possible single, the ball, in Griffey's words, "was going one way and all of a sudden it went the other way about a foot and a half."[6] The ball rolled to the wall, allowing Thomas to score the go-ahead run from first and earning Pasqua his third triple of the season. Ventura and Sammy Sosa hit first-pitch grounders for routine defensive plays to close the sixth, but the White Sox now led, 2-1.

Having lost the lead, the Mariners came out aggressively in the top of the seventh. Valle drove a ball to right that went past Sosa to the wall. The Mariners catcher made it safely to second, but with Sosa bobbling the ball, third-base coach Bill Plummer waved Valle to third. Sosa threw to Fletcher, who rifled the ball to Ventura. The ball beat Valle to third with Ventura applying the tag. Plummer took the blame for the out, saying, "It was my fault."[7] The cost of his decision became apparent on the next play, when Vizquel singled to right-center with a ball that might have scored Valle. Schaefer launched McDowell's pitch into deep center field, but Johnson got under the ball for the second out. Although Reynolds lined a single into right to move Vizquel into scoring position, Griffey Sr.'s fly to Calderon ended the threat. After the stretch, the White Sox appeared poised to add to their lead. Fletcher led off with a single and Guillen bunted him to second. Calderon's single to center gave the White Sox runners at the corners with one out, but Johnson's grounder to second baseman Reynolds started a double play that ended the seventh.

Griffey Jr. opened the eighth with a long fly to Johnson, then Davis doubled to deep left to start a nascent Seattle rally. Greg Briley ran for Davis, but the move was wasted. Martinez struck out and Buhner lined out to Calderon to close the half-inning. Davis may have betrayed some frustration about the Mariners' inability to convert hits into runs. He said, "The story of the game was the 11 hits we got and one run that came on a wild pitch."[8] Fisk led off the home eighth with a popup easily gathered by first baseman Martinez in foul ground. The fans nonetheless paid tribute to the longtime White Sox catcher with a standing ovation; Fisk had to be coaxed from the dugout to acknowledge the crowd. As Andrew Bagnato wrote in the *Chicago Tribune*, "Only after Guillen jumped onto the steps to wave his cap did Fisk bound up the steps with the legs of a teenager to acknowledge the tribute."[9] Thomas singled, but Pasqua popped up and Ventura grounded out to close the inning.

As he had done many times during the season, White Sox manager Jeff Torborg handed the ball to Bobby Thigpen to close out the game. Thigpen had long since shattered the major-league season record for saves.[10] Hitting for Valle, Scott Bradley drove Thigpen's first pitch through the gap in the right side of the infield for a leadoff single. Vizquel attempted to bunt Bradley to second, but the White Sox forced Bradley at second. Pete O'Brien, batting in place of Schaefer, launched the ball into deep left-center, but Johnson made the catch for the second out. Harold Reynolds proved to be the last batter in the history of Comiskey Park when he pulled Thigpen's fastball to his second-base counterpart; Fletcher flipped the ball to Steve Lyons for the ballpark's final out at 4:23 P.M. Central time. Thigpen's 57 saves would stand as the American League and major-league record until Francisco Rodriguez achieved 62 for the Los Angeles Angels in 2008.

After the final out, the crowd sang along as organist Nancy Faust played "Na Na Na Na, Na Na Na Na, Hey Hey."[11] The players strolled through the outfield, about which Thigpen commented, "It was goose-bumpy."[12] Four hundred police officers and security personnel ringed the field to prevent souvenir hunters from tearing up the ground, and two paddy wagons were parked along the warning track as an additional deterrent.[13] The public-address announcer proclaimed, "See you across the street next April 18."[14] After the last fans left the ballpark, the players had one final moment with Comiskey Park. The *Chicago Tribune* wrote, "Farewell, old beauty. ... [I]n the way that baseball and its places abide and grow in loving American recollection, and its ghosts walk among us for one more turn on the fields where they played, you will always be there."[15]

SOURCES

In addition to the articles cited in the Notes, the author consulted Baseball-Reference.com and **The Sporting News**.

NOTES

1. Bob Verdi, "Dear Friend Will Be Missed, but Better Days Are Ahead," **Chicago Tribune**, October 1, 1990: 3, 1.

2. Andrew Bagnato, "Sox Turn Out Lights in Style," **Chicago Tribune**, September 30, 1990: 3, 13.

3. Jim Street, "Sox Rock Comiskey, M's for One Last Win," **Seattle Post-Intelligencer**, October 1, 1990: D1.

4. Bagnato, "One Last Sox Win for Old Comiskey," **Chicago Tribune**, October 1, 1990: 3, 1 and 10.

5. Ibid.

6. Street.

7. Ibid.

8. Ibid.

9. Bagnato, "One Last Sox Win": 10.

10. Dave Righetti had held the record with 46 saves for the New York Yankees in 1986.

11. Phil Hersh, "At Comiskey, Farewell to an Old Friend," **Chicago Tribune**, October 1, 1990: 1, 1.

12. Bagnato, "One Last Sox Win": 10.

13. John Gilardi, "Next Ball Tossed at Comiskey Will Be Iron." **Seattle Post-Intelligencer**, October 1, 1990: D8.

14. Hersh.

15. Editorial, "Comiskey Park Passes Into Memory," **Chicago Tribune**, October 1, 1990: 4, 2.

COMISKEY PARK BY THE NUMBERS

By Dan Fields

0-0

Score of a 16-inning tie between the White Sox and Philadelphia Athletics on August 4, 1910. Pitchers Ed Walsh of Chicago and Jack Coombs of Philadelphia pitched the entire game.

1ST

All-Star Game in major-league baseball, on July 6, 1933. Babe Ruth hit the first home run in an All-Star Game. The midsummer classic was also played at Comiskey Park in 1950 (when Ted Williams broke his elbow by crashing into a wall to make a catch and missed the rest of the season) and 1983 (50th anniversary game).

1ST

Major-league pitch faced by Sam Vico of the Detroit Tigers in which he hit a home run, on April 20, 1948.

1ST

Black player in White Sox history: Minnie Miñoso, on May 1, 1951, against the New York Yankees. He hit a home run in his first at-bat with the team, off Vic Raschi. In the same game, Mickey Mantle of the Yankees hit his first major-league home run, off Randy Gumpert.

1ST

Major-league hit by Wade Boggs of the Boston Red Sox, on April 26, 1982 (first game of doubleheader), off Rich Dotson of the White Sox.

1ST

Black player to appear in an American League game: Larry Doby of the Cleveland Indians on July 5, 1947.

1.74

ERA of the White Sox at Comiskey Park in 1917.

2

Games of a doubleheader that the White Sox won on walk-off home runs, on July 25, 1967, against the Indians.

2

Consecutive games in which Greg Luzinski of the White Sox hit a grand slam, on June 8 and 9, 1984.

2

Consecutive games in which switch-hitting Eddie Murray of the Orioles homered from both sides of the plate, on May 8 and 9, 1987.

4

World Series played at Comiskey Park, in 1917 (White Sox vs. New York Giants), 1918 (Chicago Cubs vs. Boston Red Sox), 1919 (White Sox vs. Cincinnati Reds), and 1959 (White Sox vs. Los Angeles Dodgers). The Black Sox Scandal of 1919, in which eight members of the White Sox were accused of intentionally losing the Series in exchange for money from a gambling syndicate, resulted in their permanent ban from professional baseball.

5.28

ERA of the White Sox at Comiskey Park in 1934.

8

Innings in which the White Sox scored on May 11, 1949, against the Red Sox (each inning). Chicago won 12-8.

9

No-hitters thrown at Comiskey Park, by Ed Walsh, White Sox, August 27, 1911; Joe Benz, White Sox, May 31, 1914; Vern Kennedy, August 31, 1935; Bill Dietrich, White Sox, June 1, 1937; Bob Feller, Indians, April 16, 1940 (on Opening Day); Bob Keegan, White Sox, August 20, 1957 (second game of doubleheader); Bill Monbouquette, Red Sox, August 1, 1962; Joe Horlen, White Sox, September 10, 1967 (first game of doubleheader); and Jack Morris, Tigers, April 7, 1984.

9

Players who hit for the cycle at Comiskey Park: Baby Doll Jacobson, St. Louis Browns, April 17, 1924; Roy Carlyle, Red Sox, July 21, 1925 (first game of doubleheader); Mickey Vernon, Washington Senators, May 19, 1946 (second game of doubleheader); Joe DiMaggio, Yankees, May 20, 1948; Elmer Valo, Philadelphia Athletics, August 2, 1950; Brooks Robinson, Orioles, July 15, 1960; Lyman Bostock, Minnesota Twins, July 24, 1976; Carlton Fisk, White Sox, May 16, 1984; and Robin Yount, Milwaukee Brewers, June 12, 1988.

10

Consecutive hits by Harry McCurdy of the White Sox, from September 6, 1926 (second game of doubleheader), to September 10, 1926, and by Rip Radcliff of the White Sox from August 3, 1938 (second game of doubleheader), to August 4, 1938 (second game of doubleheader).

17-4

Record of pitcher Eddie Cicotte at Comiskey Park in 1917.

17

Consecutive home wins by the White Sox from August 27 to September 18, 1983.

23

Consecutive games with a hit at Comiskey Park by Minnie Miñoso from July 20 to August 30, 1955. He had 36 hits in 92 at-bats (.391) during the streak.

COMISKEY PARK

25TH

Inning in which Harold Baines of the White Sox hit a walk-off home run, on May 9, 1984 (the game began on May 8). The White Sox beat the Brewers 7-6.

26

Consecutive batters retired by Billy Pierce of the White Sox on June 27, 1958, and Milt Wilcox of the Tigers on April 15, 1983, before giving up a hit to end a perfect-game bid. Pierce gave up a double to Ed Fitz Gerald of the Washington Senators, and Wilcox gave up a single to Jerry Hairston of the White Sox.

27-48

Record of the White Sox at home in 1948, for a winning percentage of .360.

28

East-West Games played at Comiskey Park, from 1933 to 1960. The East-West Game was the All-Star Game of the Negro Leagues.

40 AND 41

Age in years of starting pitcher Jerry Reuss and catcher Carlton Fisk, respectively, of the White Sox on July 24, 1989.

45

Home runs by Babe Ruth at Comiskey Park, the most by any player never on the White Sox.

47

Extra-base hits by Dick Allen at Comiskey Park in 1972. He hit 17 doubles, 3 triples, and 27 home runs. By comparison, he had 23 extra-base hits on the road: 11 doubles, 2 triples, and 10 home runs.

49 1/3

Consecutive scoreless innings pitched at Comiskey Park by Ray Herbert from April 18 to May 28, 1963.

50

Age in years of Minnie Miñoso of the White Sox when he got for his last major-league hit, in the first game of a doubleheader on September 12, 1976, against the California Angels. As designated hitter, he singled in three at-bats.

50TH

Save of the season by Bobby Thigpen of the White Sox, on September 15, 1990, against the Red Sox. He was the first major-league pitcher to reach this mark.

51

Batters faced by Hod Lisenbee of the Philadelphia Athletics, in eight innings, on September 11, 1936, against the White Sox. Chicago won the nine-inning game by a score of 17-2.

56-21

Record of the White Sox at home in 1917, for a winning percentage of .727.

THE BASE BALL PALACE OF THE WORLD

85

Batters faced by Ted Lyons of the White Sox, in 21 innings, on May 24, 1929, against the Tigers. He pitched the entire game, giving up six runs on 24 hits and two walks. Detroit won 6-5.

103

Home runs by the White Sox at Comiskey Park in 1984, the most in any year.

192

Total bases by Dick Allen at Comiskey Park in 1972. He had 113 total bases on the road.

.208

Batting average of the White Sox at Comiskey Park in 1967, the lowest of any full season. (The White Sox batted .207 in 51 games at Comiskey Park in 1910.)

.305

Batting average of the White Sox at Comiskey Park in 1927, the highest of any season.

519-461-6

Regular-season record as manager by Jimmy Dykes at Comiskey Park: 486-426-6 with the White Sox, 21-12 with the Philadelphia Athletics, 4-7 with the Orioles, 5-7 with the Tigers, and 3-9 with the Indians.

907TH

Career game (all ballparks) by Hoyt Wilhelm of the White Sox on July 24, 1968. Pitching the ninth inning in the first game of a doubleheader against the Oakland Athletics, Wilhelm broke Cy Young's longtime record for most games by a pitcher.

1,778

Total bases by Luke Appling at Comiskey Park, the most of any player.

3,326-2,889-32

Season record of the While Sox at Comiskey Park from July 1, 1910, to September 30, 1990.

5,445

Days between home runs as a batter at Comiskey Park by Early Wynn, from June 3, 1944, to May 1, 1959.

55,555

Attendance at a May 20, 1973, doubleheader between the White Sox and the Twins, a record for the ballpark.

2,136,988

Regular-season attendance at Comiskey Park in 1984, the most in any year.

COMISKEY PARK

CAREER LEADERS AT COMISKEY PARK

BATTING

GAMES

1224	Luke Appling
1071	Nellie Fox
893	Eddie Collins
877	Ray Schalk
796	Luis Aparicio

PLATE APPEARANCES

5092	Luke Appling
4679	Nellie Fox
3854	Eddie Collins
3359	Luis Aparicio
3065	Ray Schalk

AT-BATS

4393	Luke Appling
4145	Nellie Fox
3156	Eddie Collins
3042	Luis Aparicio
2582	Ray Schalk

RUNS

645	Luke Appling
577	Nellie Fox
567	Eddie Collins
460	Minnie Miñoso
426	Luis Aparicio

HITS

1380	Luke Appling
1190	Nellie Fox
1025	Eddie Collins
852	Luis Aparicio
790	Minnie Miñoso

DOUBLES

224	Luke Appling
149	Nellie Fox
145	Harold Baines
138	Minnie Miñoso
126	Luis Aparicio

TRIPLES

63	Eddie Collins
58	Nellie Fox
55	Shano Collins
54	Luke Appling
50	Shoeless Joe Jackson

HOME RUNS

94	Carlton Fisk
88	Harold Baines
88	Bill Melton
66	Ron Kittle
66	Sherm Lollar

RBIS

573	Luke Appling
428	Harold Baines
424	Eddie Collins
395	Minnie Miñoso
348	Carlton Fisk

WALKS

649	Luke Appling
502	Eddie Collins
375	Minnie Miñoso
364	Nellie Fox
346	Ray Schalk

THE BASE BALL PALACE OF THE WORLD

INTENTIONAL WALKS

42	Harold Baines
41	Sherm Lollar
38	Carlton Fisk
28	Carlos May
27	Minnie Miñoso

STRIKEOUTS

361	Harold Baines
355	Carlton Fisk
294	Ron Kittle
294	Bill Melton
258	Jim Landis

HIT BY PITCH

70	Minnie Miñoso
55	Nellie Fox
48	Sherm Lollar
37	Buck Weaver
36	Carlton Fisk

BATTING AVERAGE (MIN. 1,400 AT-BATS)

.325	Eddie Collins
.324	Bibb Falk
.316	Rip Radcliff
.314	Luke Appling
.312	Minnie Miñoso

ON-BASE PERCENTAGE (MIN. 1,400 AT-BATS)

.420	Eddie Collins
.412	Minnie Miñoso
.403	Luke Appling
.394	Earl Sheely
.386	Johnny Mostil

SLUGGING PERCENTAGE (MIN. 1,400 AT-BATS)

.482	Minnie Miñoso
.475	Harold Baines
.458	Bill Melton
.446	Jorge Orta
.446	Chet Lemon

OPS (MIN. 1,400 AT-BATS)

.894	Minnie Miñoso
.832	Eddie Collins
.825	Harold Baines
.811	Bibb Falk
.809	Chet Lemon
.809	Johnny Mostil

STOLEN BASES

181	Eddie Collins
178	Luis Aparicio
99	Minnie Miñoso
93	Ray Schalk
91	Buck Weaver

COMISKEY PARK

PITCHING

ERA (MIN. 500 INNINGS)

0.65	Ed Walsh
1.58	Jim Scott
1.82	Joe Benz
1.96	Eddie Cicotte
2.19	Reb Russell

ERA data for Walsh, Scott, Benz, and Cicotte may be incomplete because ERA was not an official statistic in the AL until 1913.

WINS

139	Red Faber
131	Ted Lyons
98	Billy Pierce
88	Eddie Cicotte
84	Wilbur Wood

LOSSES

106	Ted Lyons
93	Red Faber
74	Wilbur Wood
71	Billy Pierce
53	Richard Dotson

WINNING PERCENTAGE (MIN. 60 DECISIONS)

.734	LaMarr Hoyt
.714	Jim Kaat
.698	Eddie Cicotte
.650	Lefty Williams
.627	Reb Russell

GAMES PITCHED

337	Red Faber
288	Wilbur Wood
287	Ted Lyons
225	Billy Pierce
184	Hoyt Wilhelm

GAMES STARTED

242	Red Faber
234	Ted Lyons
194	Billy Pierce
146	Wilbur Wood
134	Joe Horlen

COMPLETE GAMES

176	Ted Lyons
136	Red Faber
101	Billy Pierce
90	Eddie Cicotte
72	Thornton Lee

SHUTOUTS

23	Billy Pierce
20	Eddie Cicotte
18	Red Faber
14	Tommy John
14	Reb Russell

SAVES

75	Bobby Thigpen
48	Hoyt Wilhelm
39	Terry Forster
29	Clint Brown
28	Bob James

THE BASE BALL PALACE OF THE WORLD

INNINGS PITCHED

2089⅓	Red Faber
2068⅔	Ted Lyons
1511⅔	Billy Pierce
1277	Wilbur Wood
1159⅓	Eddie Cicotte

WALKS

575	Red Faber
539	Ted Lyons
513	Billy Pierce
345	Early Wynn
335	Richard Dotson

INTENTIONAL WALKS

36	Joe Horlen
33	Tommy John
33	Thornton Lee
28	Billy Pierce
23	Wilbur Wood

STRIKEOUTS

945	Billy Pierce
781	Red Faber
661	Wilbur Wood
590	Ted Lyons
524	Joe Horlen

HOME RUNS ALLOWED

108	Billy Pierce
102	Ted Lyons
89	Wilbur Wood
84	Richard Dotson
64	Joe Horlen

HIT BY PITCH

47	Red Faber
31	Wilbur Wood
29	Joe Horlen
25	Tommy John
23	Lefty Williams

HIT BY PITCH

47	Red Faber
31	Wilbur Wood
29	Joe Horlen
25	Tommy John
23	Lefty Williams

COMISKEY PARK

SINGLE-SEASON LEADERS AT COMISKEY PARK

BATTING

Games: 82 by Ken Henderson, 1974

Plate appearances: 370 by Ernie Johnson, 1921

At-bats: 338 by Ernie Johnson, 1921

Runs: 65 by Nellie Fox, 1957

Hits: 116 by Luke Appling, 1936

Doubles: 27 by Harold Baines, 1988

Triples: 14 by Carl Reynolds, 1930

Home runs: 27 by Dick Allen, 1972

RBIs: 82 by Dick Allen, 1972

Walks: 62 by Luke Appling, 1949

Intentional walks: 11 by Ed Herrmann, 1972; Jim Spencer, 1976

Strikeouts: 72 by Ron Kittle, 1983; Sam Sosa, 1990

Hit by pitch: 11 by Minnie Miñoso, 1952; Minnie Miñoso, 1953

Batting average: .397 by Luke Appling, 1936

On-base percentage: .470 by Luke Appling, 1936

Slugging percentage: .730 by Dick Allen, 1972

OPS: 1.161 by Dick Allen, 1972

Stolen bases: 38 by Rudy Law, 1983

PITCHING

ERA: 1.24 by Eddie Cicotte, 1917 (Note: the years 1910 through 1912 were excluded because ERA did not become an official statistic in the AL until 1913.)

Wins: 17 by Eddie Cicotte, 1917

Losses: 14 by Stan Bahnsen, 1973

Games pitched: 42 by Eddie Fisher, 1965

Games started: 25 by Wilbur Wood, 1972

Complete games: 16 by Eddie Cicotte, 1917

Shutouts: 6 by Ray Herbert, 1963

Saves: 27 by Bobby Thigpen, 1990

Innings pitched: 200⅓ by Wilbur Wood, 1972

Walks: 75 by Vern Kennedy, 1936

Intentional walks: 12 by Tommy John, 1970

Strikeouts: 143 by Ed Walsh, 1912

Home runs allowed: 19 by LaMarr Hoyt, 1984

Hit by pitch: 10 by Mike Cvengros, 1923

Wild pitches: 11 by Rich Wortham, 1979

THE BASE BALL PALACE OF THE WORLD

SINGLE-GAME BATTING LEADERS AT COMISKEY PARK

(* = extra-inning game)

Runs: 5 by Rollie Zeider, White Sox, October 8, 1911; Earl Sheely, White Sox, September 9, 1921; George Sisler, St. Louis Browns, May 30, 1921 (first game of doubleheader); Lou Gehrig, Yankees, June 12, 1928; Earle Combs, Yankees, September 19, 1930; Rudy York, Tigers, May 24, 1942 (second game of doubleheader); George Metkovich, Red Sox, September 30, 1944; Bobby Murcer, Yankees, June 3, 1972*

Hits: 6 by Doc Cramer, Philadelphia Athletics, June 20, 1932; Hank Steinbacher, White Sox, June 22, 1938

Doubles: 4 by Marv Owen, White Sox, April 23, 1939

Triples: 3 by Gus Williams, St. Louis Browns, April 24, 1913; Joe Kuhel, Washington Senators, May 13, 1937

Home runs: 3 by Lou Gehrig, Yankees, May 4, 1929; Merv Connors, White Sox, September 17, 1938 (second game of doubleheader); Charlie Keller, Yankees, July 28, 1940 (first game of doubleheader); Gus Zernial, White Sox, October 1, 1950 (second game of doubleheader); Ted Williams, Red Sox, May 8, 1957; Mike Epstein, Washington Senators, May 16, 1969; Paul Blair, Orioles, April 29, 1970; Claudell Washington, White Sox, July 14, 1979; Harold Baines, White Sox, July 7, 1982

RBIs: 8 by Jim Spencer, White Sox, May 14, 1977; Jim Spencer, White Sox, July 2, 1977

Walks: 5 by Lou Gehrig, Yankees, August 27, 1935 (second game of doubleheader); Minnie Miñoso, White Sox, May 27, 1956 (first game of doubleheader)*; Bobby Grich, Orioles, August 9, 1975

Intentional walks: 3 by Joe Kuhel, White Sox, May 3, 1941*; Jim Spencer, White Sox, May 19, 1976

Strikeouts: 5 by Rick Manning, Indians, May 15, 1977; Dave Stegman, White Sox, May 8, 1984*; Rob Deer, Brewers, August 8, 1987 (first game of doubleheader)

Stolen bases: 4 by Hal Chase, New York Highlanders, August 2, 1912; Oris Hockett, White Sox, August 6, 1945 (second game of doubleheader); Tommy Harper, Seattle Pilots, June 18, 1969 (second game of doubleheader)*; Ron LeFlore, Tigers, May 1, 1976

SINGLE-GAME PITCHING LEADERS AT COMISKEY PARK

(* = extra-inning game)

Innings pitched: 21 by Ted Lyons, White Sox, May 24, 1929*

Runs allowed: 20 by Bob Groom, Washington Senators, May 11, 1911

Hits allowed: 26 by Hod Lisenbee, Philadelphia Athletics, September 11, 1936

Walks: 13 by Dick Welk, Washington Senators, September 1, 1949

Intentional walks: 7 by Herb Pennock, Yankees, August 21, 1933*

Strikeouts: 18 by Jack Coombs, Philadelphia Athletics, August 4, 1910*; Nolan Ryan, California Angels, September 10, 1976

Home runs allowed: 4 by Ted Lyons, White Sox, July 25, 1937 (first game of doubleheader); Johnny Marcum, Red Sox, September 2, 1937 (first game of doubleheader); Ted Lyons, White Sox, July 28, 1940 (first game of doubleheader); Bill Dietrich, White Sox, July 4, 1942 (second game of doubleheader)*; Billy Pierce, White Sox, April 27, 1956; Dick Donovan, White Sox, July 7, 1956; Jim Wilson, White Sox, June 28, 1958; Russ Kemmerer, Washington Senators, September 14, 1958 (second game of doubleheader); Wilbur Wood, White Sox, September 21, 1975; Steve Stone, White Sox, June 5, 1977; Jesse Jefferson, Blue Jays, April 11, 1978; Dave Lemanczyk, Blue Jays, April 12, 1978; Doug Bird, Red Sox, May 24, 1983; Floyd Bannister, White Sox, June 23, 1983; Buddy Black, Royals, May 31, 1985

Hit by pitch: 4 by Tommy John, White Sox, June 15, 1968

Wild pitches: 4 by Walter Johnson, Washington Senators, September 21, 1914*; George Turbeville, Philadelphia Athletics, June 7, 1937; Les Cain, Tigers, May 1, 1970

SOURCES

Society for American Baseball Research. **The SABR Baseball List and Record Book** (New York: Scribner, 2007).

Solomon, Bert Randolph, ed. **The Baseball Maniac's Almanac** (fourth edition) (New York: Skyhorse Publishing, 2016).

Baseball-Reference.com.

NationalPastime.com.

Retrosheet.org/boxesetc/C/PK_CHI10.htm.

COMISKEY PARK: A ROSTER OF ALL-STAR CONTRIBUTORS

Frank Amoroso, Esq. is a writer of historical fiction. Most recently, he has written a three-volume novel about Babe Ruth entitled *Wopper: How Babe Lost His Father and Won the 1918 World Series Against the Cubs*. Volume 1, *Pigtown*, chronicles the early life of the Babe in Baltimore and his days at St. Mary's Industrial School. Volume 2, *The Show*, recounts his debut as a professional baseball player and his ascent to stardom with the Boston Red Sox. Volume 3, *The Series*, is the trilogy's explosive conclusion and deals with how the Babe handles the death of his father and the pressure of playing in the World Series in Chicago, a city torn by wartime hysteria.

John Bauer resides with his wife and two children in Parkville, Missouri, just outside of Kansas City. By day, he is an attorney specializing in insurance regulatory law and corporate law. By night, he spends many spring and summer evenings cheering for the San Francisco Giants and many fall and winter evenings reading history. He is a past and ongoing contributor to other SABR projects.

The first two major-league ballparks **Nathan Bierma** set foot in as a kid were Tiger Stadium and Wrigley Field, and they forged a lifelong love of baseball and historic ballparks. Nathan is a SABR member and SABR Games Project contributor, and curates @SABRGames and @TigersHistory on Twitter. He grew up and currently lives in Grand Rapids, Michigan, but lived in Chicago during the Cubs' fateful 2003 season. Nathan's writing has appeared in the *Chicago Tribune, Chicago Tribune Magazine, Chicago Sports Review, Detroit Free Press*, and DetroitAthletic.com. He is the author of *The Eclectic Encyclopedia of English: Language At Its Most Enigmatic, Ephemeral, and Egregious*. His website is www.nbierma.com. Nathan roots for the Tigers and the Cubs, and won't feel conflicted about that until they meet in the World Series for a fifth time someday.

Stephen D. Boren, MD, MBA, FACEP, is an emergency-medicine physician and assistant professor of emergency medicine at the University of Illinois College of Medicine. He did his emergency medicine residency at Milwaukee County Hospital and frequently was a guest on Milwaukee's WTMJ radio answering baseball trivia questions. His articles have appeared on multiple occasions in the *Baseball Research Journal, The National Pastime*, and *Baseball Digest*.

Thomas J. Brown Jr. is a lifelong Mets fan who became a Durham Bulls fan after moving to North Carolina in the early 1980s. Tom joined SABR in 1995 when he learned about the organization during a visit to Cooperstown on his honeymoon. He has been active in the organization since his retirement after teaching high-school science for 34 years, and has written numerous biographies and game stories, mostly about the New York Mets.

Surrounded by Cubs fans in the northern suburbs of Chicago, **Ken Carrano** works as a chief financial officer for a large landscaping firm and as a soccer referee. Ken and his Brewers' fan wife, Ann, share two children, two golden retrievers, and a mutual distain for the blue side of Chicago.

Matthew M. Clifford is a freelance writer from the suburbs of Chicago. He joined SABR in 2011 with intentions to enhance his research abilities and literary talents to help preserve the accurate facts of baseball history. Clifford has a background in law enforcement and is certified in a variety of investigative techniques, all of which currently aid him with historical research and data collection. He has discovered and reported several baseball-card errors and inaccuracies of player history to SABR, BaseballAlmanac.com, Baseball-Reference.com, and the research department of the National Baseball Hall of Fame. His literary contributions have been added to the SABR Biography Project.

Alan Cohen serves as vice president-treasurer of the Connecticut Smoky Joe Wood Chapter, and is datacaster for the Hartford Yard Goats, the Double-A affiliate of the Rockies. He also works as a volunteer with Children's Reading Partners, working with at-risk elementary-school students. He has written 50 biographies for SABR's BioProject, and has expanded his research into the Hearst Sandlot Classic (1946-1965), which launched the careers of 88 major-league players. He has four children and six grandchildren and resides in Connecticut with wife Frances and their cat, Morty.

Richard Cuicchi joined SABR in 1983 and is an active member of the Schott-Pelican Chapter. After retiring as an information-technology executive, Richard authored *Family Ties: A Comprehensive Collection of Facts and Trivia about Baseball's Relatives.* He has contributed to numerous SABR BioProject and Games publications. He does freelance writing and blogging about a variety of baseball topics on his website, TheTenthInning.com. Richard lives in New Orleans with his wife, Mary.

Katie Dickson grew up in Elmhurst, Illinois and saw her first game at the new Comiskey Park in the early 2000s. Her contribution to this book was originally published by SABR in 2017 as a part of her senior seminar course at North Central College in Naperville, IL, on baseball's impact on American society. She currently teaches freshmen and seniors at St. Charles North High School as a part of the Social Studies department.

Greg Erion died in December 2017 after a brief illness. He retired from the railroad industry and taught history part time at Skyline Community College in San Bruno, California. He wrote several biographies and game articles for SABR. Greg was one of the leaders of SABR's Baseball Games Project. With his wife, Barbara, he was a resident of South San Francisco, California.

Doug Feldmann is a professor in the College of Education at Northern Kentucky University and a former part-time scout for the San Diego Padres, Seattle Mariners, and Cincinnati Reds. He is the author of 12 books, more information on which is available at dougfeldmannbooks.com.

Scott Ferkovich was the lead editor of the SABR book *Tigers by the Tale: Great Games at Michigan and Trumbull.* He is the author of *Motor City Champs: Mickey Cochrane and the 1934-1935 Detroit Tigers.* His first game at Wrigley Field was in 1984. He also attended the first "official" night game, on August 9, 1988.

Dan Fields is a senior manuscript editor at the *New England Journal of Medicine.* He loves baseball trivia, and he enjoys attending Boston Red Sox and Pawtucket Red Sox games with his teenage son. Dan lives in Framingham, Massachusetts, and can be reached at dfields820@gmail.com.

Brian Frank is passionate about documenting the history of major- and minor-league baseball. He is the creator of the website The Herd Chronicles (herdchronicles.com), which is dedicated to preserving the history of the Buffalo Bisons. His articles can also be read on the official website of the Bisons. He was a contributor to and assistant editor of the book *Seasons of Buffalo Baseball, 1857-2018*, and he's a frequent contributor to SABR publications. Brian and his wife, Jenny, enjoy traveling around the country in their camper to major- and minor-league ballparks and taking an annual trip to Europe. Brian was a history major at Canisius College, where he earned a bachelor of arts. He also received a juris doctor from the University at Buffalo School of Law.

John Gabcik passed away in August of 2019. He was born and raised in Chicago, and followed the White sox since 1952. He wrote biographies and game stories for SABR, concentrating on under-appreciated White Sox pitchers and other personalities. He also helped Retrosheet develop game play-by-play recreations.

Gordon J. Gattie serves as a human-systems integration engineer for the US Navy. His baseball research interests involve ballparks, historical records, and statistical analysis. A SABR member since 1998, Gordon earned his Ph.D. from SUNY Buffalo, where he used baseball to investigate judgment/decision-making performance in complex dynamic environments. Originally from Buffalo, Gordon learned early the hardships associated with rooting for Buffalo sports teams. Ever the optimist, he also cheers for the Cleveland Indians and Washington Nationals. Lisa, his lovely bride, who also enjoys baseball, continues to challenge him by supporting the Yankees. Gordon has contributed to multiple SABR publications.

Paul Hofmann, a SABR member since 2002, is the associate vice president for international affairs at Sacramento State University and a frequent contributor to SABR publications. Paul is a native of Detroit and a lifelong Tigers fan. He currently resides in Folsom, California.

Mike Huber is professor of mathematics at Muhlenberg College in Allentown, Pennsylvania, where he teaches a course titled *Reasoning With Sabermetrics*. He has been rooting for the same American League team for over 50 years and enjoys contributing to SABR's BioProject and Games Project.

Robert Kimball grew up an all-alone Red Sox fan within site of the Empire State Building in northern New Jersey in the late 1950s and early 1960s, and watched Ted Williams play in his final series at Yankee Stadium. Listened to Curt Gowdy broadcast games on Boston TV and radio when visiting his grandparents as a youngster before working as Gowdy's personal assistant from 1978 through 1980. He also had a production stint at the nation's first all-sports radio network, Enterprise Radio, followed by tenures writing sports scripts for Associated Press Broadcast and producing web and print sports at *USA Today*. He lives in Central Massachusetts less than 10 miles from where Lee Richmond pitched baseball's first perfect game in 1880.

A prolific contributor to SABR's BioProject and its various publications, **Norm King** died in 2018. Through his writing and research we met many of the heroes of his youth, including Warren Cromartie, Steve Rogers, Bill Lee, and Hall of Fame Expos broadcaster Dave Van Horne. In 2016 SABR published *Au jeu/Play Ball: The 50 Greatest Games in the History of the Montreal Expos*, for which Norm served as senior editor and main writer. It was SABR's top-selling book of the year.

Adam Klinker is a writer, Lutheran seminarian, and Pittsburgh Pirates fan living in Omaha, Nebraska, with his wife, JoDee, and children, William, Henry, and Mary.

Russ Lake lives in Champaign, Illinois, and is a college professor emeritus. The 1964 St. Louis Cardinals remain his favorite team, and he was distressed to see Sportsman's Park (aka

Busch Stadium I) being demolished not long after he had attended the last game there on May 8, 1966. His wife, Carol, deserves an MVP award for watching all of a 13-inning ballgame in Cincinnati with Russ in 1971 – during their honeymoon. In 1994 he was an editor for David Halberstam's baseball book, *October 1964*.

For over 20 years, **Kevin Larkin** patrolled the highways and byways of the roads in his hometown of Great Barrington, Massachusetts. When not at work keeping the citizens of his hometown safe, inevitably Larkin was listening to a baseball game on the radio. He has been going to baseball games since he was 5 years old. His baseball life is the only thing he loves more than his children and grandchildren. One day while browsing through the local bookstore, the owner of the bookstore asked him if he was interested in writing a book about baseball. Larkin's first effort was *Baseball in the Bay State: A History of Baseball in Massachusetts*. He then took quite an interest in the history of the game, authoring a book on one of his heroes, Lou Gehrig called, *Gehrig: Game by Game*, a look at every game the Iron Horse played during his major-league career. He has since published three more books on the sport and there were two more on the way. He also writes and fact-checks for SABR, an experience he considers the best decision he has ever made. According to Larkin, writing about baseball is a great way to keep the memory of the sport alive and he will continue to delve into sports history with more to come.

Bob LeMoine is a high-school librarian and adjunct professor in New Hampshire. He has contributed to several SABR book projects since joining in 2013, including co-editing with Bill Nowlin on 2016's *Boston's First Nine: The 1871-75 Boston Red Stockings*. Having baseball history on the brain, Bob is never far from jumping into yet another project.

Brandon Lee is a lifelong Cubs fan, born and raised in the Uptown neighborhood of Chicago. He was excited for his first SABR contribution to be about a game involving Harold Baines, who once signed an autograph for him at Taste of Chicago. You can find more of Brandon's work at the website Banished to the Pen, and keep up with him on Twitter at @bleeinternets. He spends his days organizing for immigrant rights and racial equity with Asian Americans Advancing Justice | Chicago, and still lives in Uptown with his wife, Carla, and his dog, Gus.

Len Levin, a retired newspaper editor, has been the copy editor for almost all of SABR's recent books. He lives in Providence and is the grammarian and editor for the Rhode Island Supreme Court.

SABR member and Massachusetts native **Mike Lynch** is the founder of Seamheads.com and author of five books, including *Harry Frazee, Ban Johnson and the Feud That Nearly Destroyed the American League*, which was named a finalist for the 2009 Larry Ritter Award and nominated for a Seymour Medal. His most recent work includes a three-book series called *Baseball's Untold History* and several articles that have appeared in SABR books and on The National Pastime Museum's website. He lives in Roslindale, Massachusetts, with the love of his life and their cats, Jiggs and Pepper.

Michael Marsh is a freelance writer based in Chicago. A former staff writer for the *Chicago Reader*, he also covered high-school sports for the *Chicago Sun-Times* and *Chicago Tribune*.

Mark Mullane was born in Joliet, Illinois, and is the son of two South Side natives and lifelong White Sox fans. A graduate student at North Central College in Naperville, Illinois, he works in the college's office of marketing and communications. He has contributed to SABR's Games project, and has previously written on the intersection of religion and sport.

Bill Nowlin lived on the South Side of Chicago while a graduate student in the late 1960s. He only made it to Comiskey one time, and never trekked north to Wrigley. We all have regrets. Disco Demolition Night might have been fun, but that was a decade later. By that time, he'd been helping run Rounder Records for many years. In addition to being a Rounder Founder, he has authored or edited a few dozen books, mostly about baseball and mostly for SABR. He lives in Cambridge, Massachusetts, and has been to something approaching 1,000 games at Fenway Park.

Will Osgood is a former *Bleacher Report*, Fansided and Cover32 writer, covering the New Orleans Saints, NFL draft, and MLB. He is a graduate of the School of Communication at San Diego State University, where he also minored in religious studies. He is also working on his master of divinity degree and plans to pursue a Ph.D. in sociology. Will has written chapters for SABR books on Arlington Stadium in a work about the 1972 Texas Rangers as well as the biography of Ed Steele for a work on the 1948 Birmingham Black Barons. He is a co-host of the podcast The NOLA Rundown and runs #HistoryMattersToday, a podcast, blog, and vlog. He is a passionate Saints and Chicago Cubs fan.

Bill Pearch is a lifelong Chicago Cubs fan in spite of pressure from his hard-core extended White Sox family. He is now happily married to a Milwaukee Brewers fan. He is a marketing communication manager with experience working for park districts, philanthropic organizations and civil-engineering firms. He has attended at least one game in 40 different major-league ballparks and writes about his travels on his blog at billpearch.com. This is his first contribution to a SABR publication.

Tom Pardo is retired as the information services manager for Amoco/BP worldwide. He is the author/editor of several works concerning archives and manuscript collections and most recently served as editor of *The Federal League … vs. The National League: Guide to the Digital Archive* and as a contributor to *Cincinnati's Crosley Field: A Gem in the Queen City*, both SABR publications. His essays are dedicated to his son, Jeff, who is *the* all-time great fan of the Cubs and Wrigley Field.

Jacob Pomrenke is SABR's director of editorial content. He is also the editor of *Scandal on the South Side: The 1919 Chicago White Sox* and chairman of SABR's Black Sox Scandal Research Committee. He lives in Scottsdale, Arizona, with his wife, Tracy Greer, and their cats, Nixey Callahan and Bones Ely.

Chicago native **Alan Reifman** is professor of human development and family studies at Texas Tech University and holds a Ph.D. from the University of Michigan. Within SABR, Alan's interests include ballparks and their surrounding neighborhoods, and statistics. He has contributed to the SABR books on Wrigley Field, the Houston Astrodome, and the 1984 Detroit Tigers.

Richard Riis is a writer, researcher, and genealogist with an abiding interest in baseball since he beheld his first baseball card in 1964. In addition to contributing to the SABR BioProject and ten SABR books, he has been a contributing editor for a popular music magazine and is presently working with a former television and movie actress on her memoirs. He lives in South Setauket, New York.

Paul Rogers is president of the Ernie Banks-Bobby Bragan (Dallas-Fort Worth) SABR Chapter and the co-author of four baseball books, including *The Whiz Kids and the 1950 Pennant*, written with his boyhood hero Robin Roberts, and *Lucky Me: My 65 Years in Baseball*, authored with Eddie Robinson. He is also co-editor of recent SABR team histories of the 1951 New York Giants and the 1950 Philadelphia Phillies as well as a frequent contributor to the SABR BioProject. His real job is as a law professor at Southern Methodist University, where he was dean of the law school for nine years and has served as the university's faculty athletic representative for 32 years.

Joe Schuster is the author of a novel, *The Might Have Been*, a finalist for the 2013 CASEY Award for the best book about baseball. He has also written two titles for the Gemma Open Door series of books for adult literacy programs, *One Season in the Sun*, about ballplayers who had major-league careers lasting a few weeks or less, and *Jackie Robinson*, published in the fall of 2018. A regular contributor to the official publications of the St. Louis Cardinals, he has also written for a number of SABR books, including *Cincinnati's Crosley Field*, *20-Game Losers*, *Sportsman's Park in St. Louis*, and *Sweet '60: The 1960 Pittsburgh Pirates*, among others. He lives outside St. Louis, is married, and is the father of five rabid Redbird fans.

Lyle Spatz has written and edited several books on baseball history and has edited two record books. He has been a member of SABR since 1973.

Mark S. Sternman made his Wrigley Field debut on August 1, 1990, when Greg Maddux hurled a five-hit shutout to lead the Cubs to a 5-0 win over the Pirates. A graduate of Dartmouth College like Kyle Hendricks, Sternman has profiled Glenn Beckert for the BioProject. He wishes he could go to more games at Wrigley and eat more food at Milt's Barbecue for the Perplexed.

Stew Thornley has been a SABR member since 1979. He is an official scorer for Major League Baseball, for Minnesota Twins home games, and is a member of the MLB Official Scoring Advisory Committee.

Joe Wancho joined SABR in 2005. He contributes to various research committees as time allows. His only visit to Comiskey Park occurred on June 29, 1990, a 1-0 victory by the White Sox over New York. The memory has faded, but he does remember Robin Ventura getting doused with a cup of beer trying to catch a foul pop just past the third-base dugout.

Bob Webster grew up in northwest Indiana and has been a Cubs fan since 1963. Now living in Portland, Oregon, Bob spends his time working on baseball research and writing and has contributed to quite a few SABR projects, as well as working as a stats stringer on the MLB Gameday app for three years. Bob is a member of the Northwest Chapter of SABR and on the board of directors of the Old-Timers Baseball Association of Portland.

Steven C. Weiner is a retired chemical engineer and a lifelong baseball fan starting with the Brooklyn Dodgers of the 1950s. During his undergraduate years at Rutgers University, Steven worked in the sports information office and broadcast baseball and basketball play-by-play on WRSU Radio. Steven obtained his doctorate in engineering and applied science from Yale University and has been a contributor to the technical literature on hydrogen and fuel cell safety. Steven currently serves as assignments editor for the SABR Games Project with essay contributions in two other SABR books, *Moments of Joy and Heartbreak* and *Met-rospectives*. He volunteers as an in-classroom tutor at a local middle school and serves as a fundraising volunteer for the Washington Nationals Dream Foundation. You can often find him at Nationals Park for a ballgame.

Gregory H. Wolf was born in Pittsburgh, but now resides in the Chicagoland area with his wife, Margaret, and daughter, Gabriela. A professor of German studies and holder of the Dennis and Jean Bauman Endowed Chair in the Humanities at North Central College in Naperville, Illinois, he has edited 10 books for SABR. He is currently working on projects about Griffith Stadium in Washington, Shibe Park in Philadelphia, and the

1982 Milwaukee Brewers. Since January 2017 he has been co-director of SABR's BioProject, which you can follow on Facebook and Twitter.

Bob Wood is a native Buckeye, growing up following the Cincinnati Reds, but has lived in the Chicago suburbs, with his wife, Jean, since 1977, rooting for the Sox and Cubs. An avid APBA re-player, Bob has contributed to the SABR Games Project and Oral History project while continuing to umpire Little League and Babe Ruth baseball, following retirement from careers in computer programming and sales.

Brian P. Wood (Woodie) is a longtime San Francisco Giants fan and resides in Pacific Grove, California, with his wife, Terrise. They have three sons, Daniel, Jack, and Nathan, and a dog, Bochy. A retired US Navy commander and F-14 Tomcat naval flight officer, Woodie is a research associate on the faculty at the Naval Postgraduate School in Monterey, California, specializing in field experimentation of new technologies before they are sent to military forces.

Brian Wright is the author of *Mets in 10s: Best and Worst of an Amazin' History*, which was released by Arcadia Publishing and The History Press in April 2018. Brian has been featured in *Bleacher Report* and the *Washington Examiner* and on NESN.com, SB Nation and The Cauldron. For three years, he was the lead MLB writer for *Sports Daily*. From 2014 through 2017, he hosted his own sports history podcast, "Profiles in Sports," featuring in-depth interviews with such notables as Mario Andretti, Jack Ham, Ken Burns, and Tony Perez. He has also contributed to SABR books on the greatest games in the history of the Mets and San Diego Padres, and in the tenure of old Comiskey Park. He currently resides in Washington, DC.

Don Zminda has been a White Sox fan since attending his first game at Old Comiskey in August of 1954. As director of publications for STATS, Inc. (now STATS LLC) from 1988-2000, he co-authored or edited a dozen annual sports publications. His book *The Legendary Harry Caray: Baseball's Greatest Salesman* was published by Rowman & Littlefield in April 2019. A SABR member since 1979, he is retired and has lived in Los Angeles with his wife, Sharon, since 2000.

Friends of SABR

You can become a Friend of SABR by giving as little as $10 per month or by making a one-time gift of $1,000 or more. When you do so, you will be inducted into a community of passionate baseball fans dedicated to supporting SABR's work.

Friends of SABR receive the following benefits:
- ✓ Annual Friends of SABR Commemorative Lapel Pin
- ✓ Recognition in This Week in SABR, SABR.org, and the SABR Annual Report
- ✓ Access to the SABR Annual Convention VIP donor event
- ✓ Invitations to exclusive Friends of SABR events

SABR On-Deck Circle - $10/month, $30/month, $50/month
Get in the SABR On-Deck Circle, and help SABR become the essential community for the world of baseball. Your support will build capacity around all things SABR, including publications, website content, podcast development, and community growth.

A monthly gift is deducted from your bank account or charged to a credit card until you tell us to stop. No more email, mail, or phone reminders.

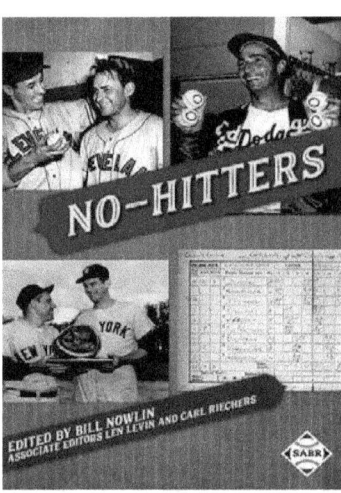

Join the SABR On-Deck Circle

Payment Info: _____Visa _____Mastercard

Name on Card: _____

Card #: _____

Exp. Date: _____ Security Code: _____

Signature: _____

○ $10/month

○ $30/month

○ $50/month

○ Other amount _____

Go to sabr.org/donate to make your gift online

New Books from SABR

Part of the mission of the Society for American Baseball Research has always been to disseminate member research. In addition to the *Baseball Research Journal*, SABR publishes books that include player biographies, historical game recaps, and statistical analysis. All SABR books are available in print and ebook formats. SABR members can access the entire SABR Digital Library for free and purchase print copies at significant member discounts of 40 to 50% off cover price.

JEFF BAGWELL IN CONNECTICUT:
A Consistent Lad in the Land of Steady Habits
This volume of articles, interviews, and essays by members of the Connecticut chapter of SABR chronicles the life and career of Connecticut's favorite baseball son, Hall-of-Famer Jeff Bagwell, with special attention on his high school and college years.
Edited by Karl Cicitto, Bill Nowlin, & Len Levin
$19.95 paperback (ISBN 978-1-943816-97-2)
$9.99 ebook (ISBN 978-1-943816-96-5)
7"x10", 246 pages, 45 photos

1995 CLEVELAND INDIANS:
The Sleeping Giant Awakens
After almost 40 years of sub-.500 baseball, the Sleeping Giant woke in 1995, the first season the Indians spent in their new home of Jacob's Field. The biographies of all the players, coaches, and broadcasters from that year are here, sprinkled with personal perspectives, as well as game stories from key matchups during the 1995 season, information about Jacob's Field, and other essays.
Edited by Joseph Wancho
$19.95 paperback (ISBN 978-1-943816-95-8)
$9.99 ebook (ISBN 978-1-943816-94-1)
8.5"X11", 410 pages, 76 photos

TIME FOR EXPANSION BASEBALL
The LA Angels and "new" Washington Senators ushered in MLB's 1960 expansion, followed in 1961 by the Houston Colt .45s and New York Mets. By 1998, 10 additional teams had launched: the Kansas City Royals, Seattle Pilots, Toronto Blue Jays, and Tampa Bay Devil Rays in the AL, and the Montreal Expos, San Diego Padres, Colorado Rockies, Florida Marlins, and Arizona Diamondbacks in the NL. *Time for Expansion Baseball* tells each team's origin and includes biographies of key players.
Edited by Maxwell Kates and Bill Nowlin
$24.95 paperback (ISBN 978-1-933599-89-7)
$9.99 ebook (ISBN 978-1-933599-88-0)
8.5"X11", 430 pages, 150 photos

Base Ball's 19th Century "Winter" Meetings 1857-1900
A look at the business meetings of base ball's earliest days (not all of which were in the winter). As John Thorn writes in his Foreword, "This monumental volume traces the development of the game from its birth as an organized institution to its very near suicide at the dawn of the next century."
Edited by Jeremy K. Hodges and Bill Nowlin
$29.95 paperback (ISBN 978-1-943816-91-0)
$9.99 ebook (ISBN978-1-943816-90-3)
8.5"x11", 390 pages, 50 photos

MET-ROSPECTIVES:
A Collection of the Greatest Games in New York Mets History
This book's 57 game stories—coinciding with the number of Mets years through 2018—are strictly for the eternal optimist. They include the team's very first victory in April 1962 at Forbes Field, Tom Seaver's "Imperfect Game" in July '69, the unforgettable Game Sixes in October '86, the "Grand Slam Single" in the 1999 NLCS, and concludes with the extra-innings heroics in September 2016 at Citi Field that helped ensure a wild-card berth.
edited by Brian Wright and Bill Nowlin
$14.95 paperback (ISBN 978-1-943816-87-3)
$9.99 ebook (ISBN 978-1-943816-86-6)
8.5"X11", 148 pages, 44 photos

CINCINNATI'S CROSLEY FIELD:
A Gem in the Queen City
This book evokes memories of Crosley Field through detailed summaries of more than 85 historic and monumental games played there, and 10 insightful feature essays about the history of the ballpark. Former Reds players Johnny Edwards and Art Shamsky share their memories of the park in introductions.
Edited by Gregory H. Wolf
$19.95 paperback (ISBN 978-1-943816-75-0)
$9.99 ebook (ISBN 978-1-943816-74-3)
8.5"X11", 320 pages, 43 photos

MOMENTS OF JOY AND HEARTBREAK:
66 Significant Episodes in the History of the Pittsburgh Pirates
In this book we relive no-hitters, World Series-winning homers, and the last tripleheader ever played in major-league baseball. Famous Pirates like Honus Wagner and Roberto Clemente—and infamous ones like Dock Ellis—make their appearances, as well as recent stars like Andrew McCutcheon.
Edited by Jorge Iber and Bill Nowlin
$19.95 paperback (ISBN 978-1-943816-73-6)
$9.99 ebook (ISBN 978-1-943816-72-9)
8.5"X11", 208 pages, 36 photos

FROM SPRING TRAINING TO SCREEN TEST:
Baseball Players Turned Actors
SABR's book of baseball's "matinee stars," a selection of those who crossed the lines between professional sports and popular entertainment. Included are the famous (Gene Autry, Joe DiMaggio, Jim Thorpe, Bernie Williams) and the forgotten (Al Gettel, Lou Stringer, Wally Hebert, Wally Hood), essays on baseball in TV shows and Coca-Cola commercials, and Jim Bouton's casting as "Jim Barton" in the *Ball Four* TV series.
Edited by Rob Edelman and Bill Nowlin
$19.95 paperback (ISBN 978-1-943816-71-2)
$9.99 ebook (ISBN 978-1-943816-70-5)
8.5"X11", 410 pages, 89 photos

To learn more about how to receive these publications for free or at member discount
as a member of SABR, visit the website: sabr.org/join

www.ingramcontent.com/pod-product-compliance
Lightning Source LLC
Chambersburg PA
CBHW081152070526
44583CB00021B/2807